Lecture Notes in Computer Science 2201

Edited by G. Goos, J. Hartmanis and J. van Leeuwen

T0216424

Springer

Berlin
Heidelberg
New York
Barcelona
Hong Kong
London
Milan
Paris
Tokyo

Gregory D. Abowd   Barry Brumitt
Steven Shafer (Eds.)

Ubicomp 2001:
Ubiquitous Computing

International Conference
Atlanta Georgia, USA, September 30 - October 2, 2001
Proceedings

 Springer

Series Editors

Gerhard Goos, Karlsruhe University, Germany
Juris Hartmanis, Cornell University, NY, USA
Jan van Leeuwen, Utrecht University, The Netherlands

Volume Editors

Gregory D. Abowd
Georgia Tech, College of Computing and GVU Center
801 Atlantic Drive, Atlanta, GA 30332-0280, USA
E-mail: abowd@cc.gatech.edu

Barry Brumitt
Steven Shafer
Microsoft Corp.
One Microsoft Way, Redmond, WA 98052, USA
E-mail: {barry,stevensh}@microsoft.com

Cataloging-in-Publication Data applied for

Die Deutsche Bibliothek - CIP-Einheitsaufnahme

Ubiquitous computing : international conference ; proceedings /
Ubicomp 2001, Atlanta, Georgia, USA, September 30 - October 2, 2001.
Gregory D. Abowd ... (ed.). - Berlin ; Heidelberg ; New York ; Barcelona ;
Hong Kong ; London ; Milan ; Paris ; Tokyo : Springer, 2001
    (Lecture notes in computer science ; Vol. 2201)
    ISBN 3-540-42614-0

CR Subject Classification (1998): C.2, C.3, D.2, D.4, H.4, H.5, K.4

ISSN 0302-9743
ISBN 3-540-42614-0 Springer-Verlag Berlin Heidelberg New York

Springer-Verlag Berlin Heidelberg New York
a member of BertelsmannSpringer Science+Business Media GmbH

http://www.springer.de

© Springer-Verlag Berlin Heidelberg 2001
Printed in Germany

Typesetting: Camera-ready by author, data conversion by DATeX Gerd Blumenstein
Printed on acid-free paper   SPIN 10840664   06/3142   5 4 3 2 1 0

Preface

Ten years ago, Mark Weiser's seminal article, "The Computer of the 21st Century," was published by Scientific American. In that widely cited article, Mark described some of the early results of the Ubiquitous Computing Project that he lead at Xerox PARC. This article and the initial work at PARC has inspired a large community of researchers to explore the vision of "ubicomp". The variety of research backgrounds represented by researchers in ubicomp is both a blessing and a curse. It is a blessing because good solutions to any of the significant problems in our world require a multitude of perspectives. That Mark's initial vision has inspired scientists with technical, design, and social expertise increases the likelihood that as a community we will be able to build a new future of interaction that goes beyond the desktop and positively impacts our everyday lives. The curse for the research community over the past decade has been that it has been hard to find the correct intellectual home for the dissemination of research results. It is the intent of the Ubicomp 2001 conference to begin the trajectory towards creating a premier research forum for work in ubiquitous computing.

The Ubicomp conference grew out of a series of symposia hosted in Europe on the theme of Handheld and Ubiquitous Computing (HUC '99 and HUC 2K). The change in name reflects the desire to be inclusive of all research activities related to ubicomp, from technology-centered work on sensing, embedded and distributed systems, wireless and ad hoc networking, and software engineering, to more human-centered research on applications design, development and evaluation and understanding of the social implications of pervasive technologies. Though there are forums for work in each of these separate areas, we hope to incorporate into this conference high quality research that pushes not only a single research perspective but also attempts to move us closer to the vision of Weiser, a world in which increased penetration of computational infrastructure serves to enhance our everyday interactions with the environment and other humans rather than invade and degrade that experience.

The 14 full papers in this volume were selected from 90 submissions to Ubicomp 2001. The 15 technical notes are also found in this volume: 10 were drawn from 70 technical note submissions, while 5 were adapted from full paper submissions. These papers cover a wide technical range, including work in novel input/output devices, location awareness, group applications, and software infrastructure. This breadth illustrates the complexity implicit in the field of ubiquitous computing.

The Ubicomp 2001 conference was organized in collaboration with Georgia Tech, in Atlanta, Georgia, where the event was held, and in cooperation with professional society sponsors ACM SIGCHI, SIGMOBILE, and SIGSOFT. It was supported by a number of commercial sponsors, including Accenture, FXPAL, Hewlett-Packard, Intel, IBM, Microsoft, and Phillips. We would like to thank these organizations for their interest in and support of the event.

We would also like to thank the numerous reviewers who offered invaluable comments on the many full papers submitted to this conference. Additionally, we would like to thank the reviewers for their quick evaluation of the technical notes; many more submissions were received than expected, representing a heavy load for these reviewers. Finally, thanks also go to Jonathan Simon (Microsoft Research), who provided his Conference Management Toolkit (http://cmt.research.microsoft.com), a web-based system for managing the complex distributed paper review process.

July 2001

Gregory Abowd
Barry Brumitt
Steven Shafer

Conference Organization

Supporting Societies

Association for Computing Machinery (ACM) with the special interest groups:
SIGCHI (Computer-Human Interaction)
SIGMOBILE (Mobile Computing)
SIGSOFT (Software Engineering)

Sponsors

Accenture , FXPAL , Hewlett-Packard, Intel, IBM, Phillips and Microsoft Research

Conference Chair

Gregory Abowd Georgia Tech (USA)

Organizers

Program Chair	Steve Shafer	Microsoft Research (USA)
Program Co-chair	Barry Brumitt	Microsoft Research (USA)
Publicity	Albrecht Schmidt	University Karlsruhe (Germany)
Workshops and	Anind Dey,	Georgia Tech. (USA)
Technical Notes	Joe McCarthy	Accenture (USA)
Student Volunteers	Khai Truong	Georgia Tech. (USA)
Local Administration	Joan Morton	GVU Center, Georgia Tech. (USA)
Webmaster	Jason Brotherton	Georgia Tech. (USA)

Program Committee

Steve Shafer (chair)	Microsoft Corp. (USA)
Barry Brumitt (co-chair)	Microsoft Corp. (USA)
Aaron Bobick	Georgia Tech. (USA)
Jim Crowley	INRIA Grenoble (France)
Nigel Davies	Lancaster University (UK)
Armando Fox	Stanford University (USA)
Masaaki Fukumoto	NTT DoCoMo Multimedia Labs (Japan)
Dai Guo-Zhong	Chinese Academy of Science (China)
Xu GuangYou	TsingHua University. (China)
Sumi Helal	University of Florida (USA)

Lars Erik Holmquist	Interactive Institute (Sweden)
Tim Kindberg	Hewlett-Packard Corp. (USA)
Wendy Mackay	INRIA Paris (France)
Beth Mynatt	Georgia Tech. (USA)
Chandra Narayanaswami	IBM Research (USA)
Paddy Nixon	University of Strathclyde (UK) & NMRC (IE)
Brian Noble	University of Michigan (USA)
Jun Rekimoto	SONY CSL (Japan)
Chris Schmandt	MIT Media Lab (USA)
Norbert Streitz	GMD-IPSI Darmstadt (Germany)
Yoichi Takebayashi	Toshiba Corp. (Japan)

List of Reviewers

John Barton, HP Labs (USA)
James Begole, Sun Microsystems Labs (USA)
Michael Beigl, TecO, University of Karlsruhe (Germany)
Mark Billinghurst, University of Washington (USA)
Staffan Björk, PLAY Research Group, Interactive Institute (Sweden)
Aaron Bobick, Georgia Tech. (USA)
Gary Boone, Accenture Technology Labs (USA)
Richard Borovoy, MIT Media Lab (USA)
Gaetano Borriello, University of Washington / Intel Research (USA)
Jason Brotherton, Georgia Institute of Technology (USA)
Barry Brown, University of Glasgow (UK)
Barry Brumitt, Microsoft Research (USA)
JJ Cadiz, Microsoft Research (USA)
Roy Campbell, University of Illinois, Urbana-Champaign (USA)
Deborah Caswell, HP (USA)
Keith Cheverst, Lancaster University, (UK)
Michael Coen, MIT AI Lab (USA)
Phil Cohen, Oregon Graduate Institute (USA)
Jeremy Cooperstock, McGill University (Canada)
Jim Crowley, INRIA Grenoble (France)
Rupert Curwen, AT&T Laboratories Cambridge (UK)
Nigel Davies, Lancaster University (UK)
Maria Ebling, IBM T. J. Watson Research Center (USA)
Christos Efstratiou, Lancaster University (UK)
Deborah Estrin, University of California, Los Angeles (USA)
Jennica Falk, Media Lab Europe (Ireland)
Andrew Fano, Accenture Technology Labs (USA)
Jeff Farr, BT Labs (UK)
Armando Fox, Stanford University (USA)
Masaaki Fukumoto, NTT DoCoMo Multimedia Labs (Japan)
Dai Guo-Zhong, Chinese Academy of Science (China)
Xu GuangYou, TsingHua University. (China)

Lars Hallnäs, PLAY Research Group, Interactive Institute (Sweden)
Steve Harris, Microsoft Research (USA)
Beverly Harrison, IBM Almaden Research Center (USA)
Sumi Helal, University of Florida (USA)
Steve Hodges, AT&T Laboratories Cambridge (UK)
Lars Erik Holmquist, Interactive Institute (Sweden)
Jussi Holopainen, Nokia Research (Finland)
Jason Hong, University of California, Berkeley (USA)
Eric Horvitz, Microsoft Research (USA)
Elaine Huang, Georgia Institute of Technology (USA)
David Ingram, AT&T Laboratories Cambridge (UK)
Brad Johanson, Stanford University (USA)
Emre Kiciman, Stanford University (USA)
Tim Kindberg, Hewlett-Packard Corp. (USA)
Rob Kooper, Georgia Institute of Technology (USA)
Gerd Kortuem, University of Oregon (USA)
Robin Kravets, University of Illinois, Urbana-Champaign (USA)
Brian Lee, Stanford University (USA)
Peter Ljungstrand, PLAY Research Group, Interactive Institute (Sweden)
Johan Lundin, Viktoria Institute (Sweden)
Kent Lyons, Georgia Institute of Technology (USA)
Wendy Mackay, INRIA Paris (France)
Blair MacIntyre, Georgia Institute of Technology (USA)
Petros Maniatis, IBM Research (USA)
David McGee, Pacific Northwest National Laboratory (USA)
Laurence Melloul, Stanford University (USA)
Brian Meyers, Microsoft Research (USA)
David Morse, Open University (UK)
Beth Mynatt, Georgia Tech. (USA)
Kristine Nagel, Georgia Institute of Technology (USA)
Chandra Narayanaswami, IBM Research (USA)
Les Nelson, FX Palo Alto Laboratory (USA)
Paddy Nixon, University of Strathclyde (UK) & NMRC (IE)
Brian Noble, University of Michigan (USA)
Urban Nuldén, Viktoria Institute (Sweden)
Elin Pedersen, Cisco Systems (USA)
Per Persson, Sweedish Institude of Computer Science (Sweden)
Shankar Ponnekanti, Stanford University (USA)
Mandayam Raghunath, IBM Research (USA)
Cliff Randell, University of Bristol (UK)
Johan Redström, PLAY Research Group, Interactive Institute (Sweden)
Jun Rekimoto, SONY CSL (Japan)
George Robertson, Microsoft Research (USA)
Tom Rodden, University of Nottingham (UK)
Nicolas Roussel, University of Fribourg (Switzerland)

Mema Roussopoulos, Stanford University (USA)
Daniel Salber, IBM T. J. Watson Research Center (USA)
Eric Saund, Xerox PARC (USA)
Bill Schilit, FX Palo Alto Laboratory (USA)
Chris Schmandt, MIT Media Lab (USA)
Mirjana Spasojevic, HP Labs (USA)
Pete Steggles, AT&T Laboratories Cambridge (UK)
Phil Stenton, HP Labs Bristol (UK)
Norbert Streitz, GMD-IPSI Darmstadt (Germany)
Yoichi Takebayashi , Toshiba Corp. (Japan)
John Tang, Sun Microsystems Labs (USA)
Khai Truong, Georgia Institute of Technology (USA)
Joe Tullio, Georgia Institute of Technology (USA)
Dadong Wan, Accenture Technology Labs (USA)
Andy Wilson, Microsoft Research (USA)
Billibon Yoshimi, IBM T. J. Watson Research Center (USA)

Table of Contents

Applications for Groups

Panel Discussion

Applications and Design Spaces

Research Challenges and Novel Input

Output

Assembling the Planetary Computer

Larry Smarr

Director, California Institute for Telecommunications and Information Technology
University of California, San Diego, San Diego, CA
lsmarr@ucsd.edu

Abstract. After twenty years, the "S-curve" of building out the wired internet with hundreds of millions of PCs as its end points is flattening out, with corresponding lowering of the growth rates of the major suppliers of that global infrastructure. At the same time, several new "S-curves" are reaching their steep slope as ubiquitous computing begins to sweep the planet. Leading this will be a vast expansion in heterogeneous end-points to a new wireless internet, moving IP throughout the physical world. Billions of internet connected cell phones, embedded processors, hand held devices, sensors, and actuators will lead to radical new applications in biomedicine, transportation, environmental monitoring, and interpersonal communication and collaboration. The combination of wireless LANs, the third generation of cellular phones, satellites, and the increasing use of the FCC unlicensed wireless band will cover the world with connectivity. The resulting vast increase in data streams, augmented by the advent of ass market broadband to homes and businesses, will drive the backbone of the internet to a pure optical lambda-switched network of tremendous capacity. Finally, peer-to-peer computing and storage will increasingly provide a vast untapped capability to power this emergent planetary computer.

G. D. Abowd, B. Brumitt, S. A. N. Shafer (Eds.): Ubicomp 2001, LNCS 2201, p. 1, 2001.
© Springer-Verlag Berlin Heidelberg 2001

GeoNotes: Social and Navigational Aspects of Location-Based Information Systems

Fredrik Espinoza, Per Persson, Anna Sandin, Hanna Nyström,
Elenor Cacciatore, and Markus Bylund

HUMLE Lab, Swedish Institute of Computer Science (SICS)
Box 1263, 164 29 Kista, Sweden
{espinoza,perp,sandin,hannan,elenor,bylund}@sics.se

Abstract. Location-based information systems allow the user to access information in relation to the user's position in geographical space. This paper outlines navigational and social aspects of such systems. It is argued that location-based systems must allow users to participate as content providers in order to achieve a social and dynamic information space. Moreover, as these systems allow commercial and private users to annotate space with information on a mass-scale, information filtering techniques will become essential in order to prevent information overload and user disturbance. We present a number of content-based and social filtering techniques to support this. We discuss implications for implementation and we describe a system (GeoNotes), which takes some of these aspects into account.

1 Introduction

Some location-based systems are centered on the notion of positioning people in relation to each other (e.g., [12]). Location-based information systems, on the other hand, position information. The basic idea is to connect pieces of digital information to a specific latitude-longitude coordinate via some mobile device, thereby 'attaching' them to a specific place in space. Later, users, again via some mobile client, can access that information. In this way, users will get the impression that the digital information is actually attached to a place in a way similar to post-its, graffiti and public signs and posters.

Quite a few systems have been working with this basic concept over the last five years within the fields of augmented reality, wearables and ubiquitous computing [8; 3;1;16;20;7,18,4]. Some have used goggles as access medium [21]. Most, however, work with handheld devices, that may not provide the same stunning and spectacular visual effects, but still preserve the basic functionality.

It is our intention not to repeat the results of these projects, but rather to discuss the communicatory, social and navigational implications of the mass usage of a location-based information system of this kind. We believe that the space of location-based information needs to be free for all users – not only professional content providers.

G. D. Abowd, B. Brumitt, S. A. N. Shafer (Eds.): Ubicomp 2001, LNCS 2201, pp. 2-17, 2001.

Moreover, once we allow for mass-annotations, this will impose serious design challenges in terms of navigation and filtering. In the same way as the World Wide Web user eventually needed a wide range of navigation support (e.g. search engines, collaborative filters, news-groups, link lists, index views, navigation bars, and "web-tips" in the press), so will users of location-based information systems.

First we discuss the communicatory and social functions of 'traditional location-based information systems', such as post-its, graffiti and posters. In the light of this, we then analyze some features and social shortcomings of digital location-based information systems, and present a more social emphasis for location-based information systems. Next, we address the design implications/requirements for such a social location-based information system in relation to the user's interaction with and experience of the system. Finally, we present an implementation – the GeoNotes system – that tries to address these design challenges.

Thus, the purpose of the paper is twofold. On a theoretical level, it seeks to analyze the social aspects of location-based information systems, and propose design solutions to support those aspects (both on a user-oriented and a technical level). On the other hand, we also present a system that goes some steps in the direction of the design we suggest.

2   Social Functions of Post-Its, Graffiti and Posters

Although location-based information systems need not slavishly replicate the features of paper post-it notes, graffiti, signs and posters, such technologies may provide design inspirations for their digital counterpart. In particular, their communicatory and social functions may provide insights.

Although they do not adhere to all surfaces, post-it notes stick to almost everything in an indoor environment. Other than primitive sketches, multimedia content is not possible. However, they are dispensable, cheap and easily accessible. Since creator and reader share the same spatial context, the message can rely on short deictic expressions such as 'Make 10 copies of *this*!' without loss of understanding. Such referencing can be quite exact since the note can be placed on rather small objects (e.g., pieces of paper, computer screens, mugs). Post-its are mostly used between peers and colleagues who know each other's habits, preferences, sense of humor and personality quite well. By exploiting and alluding to this shared context, messages need not be that long to contain much valuable information. Moreover, post-its need no greetings or wrapping up phrases as e-mails do.

At work, post-its are used to coordinate and plan tasks in order to make work more efficient. Reminding oneself and others is a central communicatory function of post-its. In domestic environments they can have additional expressive and social bonding functions (e.g., 'Good morning! I love you very much!'). Such communication may be less 'serious' and task oriented, but may in fact constitute the most common usage of post-it technology.

While post-its are oftentimes directed to individuals and peers, graffiti - which can be both textual and graphical in nature - is mostly anonymous and intended for a mass-audience ('Stop the deforestation! Stop eating at McDonalds!'). Because of this, graffiti is annotating public rather than domestic places, for instance public restrooms, walls, buildings, and public transportation. Often it has a strong expressive function in terms of emotional reactions, social and ethnic identity, politics, prejudices, humor, and sex. Because of its subversive character, graffiti is particularly prohibited in places with strong commercial interests. Although most graffiti stands on its own, sometimes it spurs remarks and counterarguments from readers (cf. public note boards).

Signs and posters in public space are also oriented to a mass-audience. Most of them are commercial and attempt to stimulate consumption, whereas some are more informative in nature. Posters may be private, for instance 'This car for sale' or 'Apartment for rent in this area'. Note boards are information hubs where signs and posters cluster. People will make use of note boards to find and place information. Note boards are often situated in places where people pass through, e.g. entrances/exists of buildings and stores, bus stops, and waiting rooms.

3   A More Social Location-Based Information System?

For several reasons, digital location-based information systems within ubiquitous computing and context aware-applications have been focused on developing the technological aspects of attaching and accessing location-based information. While analog annotation technologies uphold key social and communicatory functions, these have often been overlooked in digital location-based information systems.

For instance, with few exceptions, the information in those systems has been created by professional content providers, such as art institutions, museums, tourist organizations, and business interests [8,3,1,16,20]. Relying on professional content providers, these systems run the risk of making the information formal, official and impersonal. Although some users are great fans of museums and art galleries, these domains are not part of the fabric of everyday life, and they do not involve friends, families, (potential) acquaintances or other interpersonal relationships. Moreover, professionally created information often tends to be 'serious' and 'utility oriented' in ways in which post-its, graffiti and posters are not. The social, expressive, and subversive functions of analog annotation technologies tend to be overlooked.

Another problem with professional content is that information space easily becomes static. With large information spaces, maintaining and updating information is expensive and time consuming when relying on a few content providers. Since many users (and many information seeking situations) insist on information freshness, such an approach will eventually become untenable.

An alternative to this is to let information space free, allowing it to grow, expand and develop with users. Instead of making location-based information systems a vertical (one way) channel for information, by allowing and encouraging 'ordinary' users to provide, update, remove and comment information, the information space will become more of a horizontal communication medium between users. In this scenario, all users can leave traces in the system (and in the geography) for others to see, which will create a social awareness [10]. The information space overlaying physical space will become more social, reflecting the lives, concerns and social reality of the users in that space, rather than reflecting the views of some organization or authority. The physical space may become dotted with islands or places of rich concentrations of GeoNotes, places that exhibit meaning and character as a function of the contents and the usage of the GeoNotes in that physical space (analogously to the difference between space and place as described in [11], although in this case the space is the real physical space and the place is defined implicitly in the parallel digital space. See the discussion below about place labels).

Again, the analogy with the World Wide Web becomes relevant. It is precisely because no single authority controls the information that it has become such a success. Of course, the Web contains valuable 'professional' information, but it also allows *all* users to easily participate in creating, shaping and inhabiting the digital information space.

Some location-based information systems do allow users to create their own annotations or comments on the professional content, but few encourage it and make it the central aspect of the system. Marmasse & Schmandt's [18] GPS enabled ComMotion system and Rekimoto's [21] goggle system focus on user's annotations, but these are mainly directed to oneself as reminders and documents. The social aspect is still lacking.

A system allowing any user to act as content provider will encounter new design challenges. If we allow users to annotate digital space *en masse* and without restrictions, we may achieve a socially rich environment, but information space will become cluttered with unstructured information. How will users be able to find relevant and timely information in a system that has no central information designer? How can the system (or user) know what annotations are important for a user when she is in a position which contains 5000 annotations? If we allow annotations to be 'pushed' to the user's mobile device, how can we allow the user to regulate the tradeoff between curiosity about the spatial annotations and the disturbance? How can we impose a structure on the information space, and what will this structure be like?

No location-based information system has addressed these navigational issues. The Graffiti system [4], based on Wave LAN positioning and laptop computers as access terminals, enables users to annotate a university campus with virtual notes directed to friends and fellow students, but it provides little support for navigation.

The question is how to balance the trade-off between creating an open and social information space while still enabling people to find relevant information in that space. Below, we propose a number of techniques for navigational support for such a system. The underlying presumption in most of these techniques is that navigating digital or real-world information spaces is social in character. Computer Supported Collaborative Work (CSCW), collaborative filtering [15] and social navigation [19, 9] all emphasize that information seeking is not a single user activity, but often involves other people.

Navigation and work in digital information spaces may be enhanced by giving people access to the traces of other users or groups of users, who in some respect share similar interests with the navigator. Recommendation systems suggest books, movies and recipes, not by analyzing the content of the user profile and the content of the information item, but rather matching users' usage history in the system: 'people who bought the same books that you bought, also bought this one!' Clustering users into groups may be based on explicit voting as in *Movielens[1]* or can be generated by

---

[1] http://movielens.umn.edu/

machine learning techniques from the actions performed in the system [22]. Encouraging social awareness [10] and direct and indirect communication is a key objective for these researchers, not only because it supports work, but also because it enriches the experience of the system. For many user groups (e.g. young people) this can be seen as an end in itself.

In conclusion, our proposal for a location-based information system is social in two respects. On the one hand we allow all users to participate in creating the information space. On the other, we support navigation by collecting and aggregating users' usage of the system, and distribute this data to other users in some refined form.

3.1   Interaction Requirements

What are the implications for design of a more open and social location-based information system? In this section we discuss one design proposal in relation to interaction and user experience of the system. Some aspects of this proposal we implemented in our GeoNote system – which we will refer to throughout - whereas others are still awaiting implementation this year.

In relation to interaction, we identified three major design problems which all relate to navigation in one way or the other.

- How can the system allow users to annotate geographical places by posting virtual notes on a mass-scale via their mobile devices? Specifically, the creator's and reader's understanding of the place/position of the annotation becomes crucial.
- What modes of accessing annotations are required in the system? How can we allow the user to browse, search or get a sense of the information at a given place?
- How can filtering of information support users in finding relevant location-based annotations in this mass-scale information space?
- Posting Notes. Posting an annotation – or a virtual *note* - should be easy and quick. Still the note should contain valuable information. Besides the information itself, which could be in textual or multimedia format, the sender needs to specify four components (see Fig. 1):
- A title. In the GeoNotes system the title will appear as a header in the list of notes in a particular place (see below and **Fig. 2**). In this way the user can get a sense of the content of the note by reading the title.
- The recipient to whom the note is directed. Although most notes will be open to any other user, the system must allow users to restrict access to the note, not only for privacy reasons, but also to support navigation. GeoNotes allows the user to configure lists of friends, which can be chosen as recipient. Alternatively, GeoNotes can be directed to individual friends or 'to oneself'.
- The signature of the creator is an important regulator of privacy. In some cases the identity and contact information to the creator is essential (e.g. for advertisements). In others, as with digital graffiti, the identity of the creator needs to be recognized but not identified (e.g. 'Kilroy'). In GeoNotes, any signature can

be used when posting a note (e.g., 'SkateGirl', 'www.hem.passagen.se/anna', or 'Anna 070-633 15 07').

- A place label of the creator's own choice. This 'tag' christens the place or object in which the note is intended to be posted. If the precision of the latitude-longitude position coordinates is bad, either for the creator or for reader, such a label may help to focus the exact place for a note. By labeling the note, other users will be able to ascertain the correct placing without relying on the exact position. Such a semantic mechanism may be essential to understand the content of the note, and what it refers to in the spatial surroundings (e.g. deictic words such as *this* and *here*).

  But even when the position precision is good, place labels can be a valuable way of describing or discussing some aspect of a place. Even though the coordinates may be exactly the same, two users' understanding of a place may differ. In fact, *place* refers less to objective coordinates, and more to a mental construct in the mind of the beholder. People may have very different understandings of the same place depending on preferences, personality, cultural dispositions, situation or goal. A label is a good way for the creator to indicate the intended aspect of any given place.

The matter of the place labels warrants special attention. We choose to use the labels approach in contrast to a stricter a priori approach such as [14]. Their location scopes are predefined tree-like structures that describe the real world as locations within locations. For example, 'Engineering' is a building within 'South Area', which in turn is an area within 'Campus'. When mapping a service or some other digital entity to the real world, one chooses the most appropriate location in such a structure. The system associates the entity with the specified location and to all of its 'super-locations', i.e. locations of which the specified location is a part. Thus, in our example, a GeoNote placed at 'Engineering' would also be found in 'South Area' and 'Campus'.

This method of organizing the world makes it possible to place entities completely unambiguously. However, it has some weaknesses: the structure must be designed in advance; it is based on an administrator's conception of the appropriate places (this is similar to [4] and [16]; it is coarse; it is static.

The labels approach is superior on all counts: the structure is not preset but evolves during usage; the places are defined by users in response to the needs of the moment; the precision can be arbitrarily fine grained depending on what labels are defined; the structure is dynamic.

However, to make full use of the place labels approach one must implement *label sharing*. Label sharing means that labels for a given place are stored in the system and may be reused by other users. When a user creates a note, other notes in the vicinity (of that position) are scanned for their place labels. This list of other users' labels is made available as a list of choices of possible place labels. If the list is extensive, one may choose to sort the labels according to popularity. The creator may choose a label in the list or create a label of his or her own if none of them is appropriate.

Label sharing allows users to get a sense of how other users appreciate and interpret a given place, thus creating an awareness about the social connotations of a place (again emphasizing the indirect social aspect of information space). How such traces of others influence the creator's behavior and annotation activities is an interesting research problem that will have to be addressed in user studies. Another effect of label sharing is that valuable and efficient labels will be recycled more, whereas inefficient or extremely personal labels will be reused less. In this way, useful and popular place labels will continue to thrive in the system, similar to the ways in which vocabulary, expressions and grammar of natural language develops and transforms by its usage.

A label sharing system may be bootstrapped with predefined labels such as the places defined in previously mentioned systems or labels taken from the yellow pages or tourist databases.

The current version of GeoNotes implements posting of notes with title, recipient, signature and labels. It does not yet support label sharing.

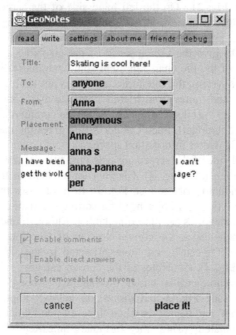

Fig. 1. Choosing a signature while posting a GeoNote

Accessing Notes: Pull and Push and In-Between. Users will want to access other people's notes in different ways, depending on preferences, situation and information need. In a retrieval mode, the user actively searches for or 'pulls' information, for instance by word-based search engines similar to the ones present on the World Wide Web today. In contrast to traditional web searches, location-based information systems may allow users to search for notes in confined geographical areas. Through some sort of map interface the user can indicate the area of interest and then execute the search. This is an interesting way in which searches can be constrained, but exactly how such searches differ from web-based ones and how they will be exploited by users are yet to be determined.

Of course, users will also be able to search for notes in the place/surroundings at which they are at the moment. If standing on the actual place, sharing the spatial context of the note creator may enable the information seeker to exploit this context in formulating more exact search queries. GeoNotes does not yet implement word-based search queries.

In a mixed push/pull access mode, the user is browsing the information space of notes but has no focused or well-defined information need. In contrast to active search, this mode of navigation is more *explorative* in nature, 'checking out' objects and information that *might* be of interest - cf. Benyon & Höök's [2] distinction between *way finding* and *exploration*. The information seeker may, for instance, not be able to formulate her information needs in words, or she wants to learn more about a specific subject. In GeoNotes this mode of navigation is supported through the 'read' interface (see **Fig. 2**). On the left hand side of the screen is a pie chart that provides an at-a-glance overview of all GeoNotes at the current position (within a certain radius). The size of the circle could be relative to the total number of GeoNotes in order to give the user a sense of the GeoNote activity of the current position. The slices of the pie chart represent some automatically detected aspect of the GeoNotes. In our system, the categories are 'notes not visible (directed to others)', 'notes from anyone' and 'notes from friends', but one may consider other categories here, for instance sender oriented (private/commercial/governmental or regional/national/international). Such categorization gives the user a scent and flavor of the surrounding GeoNotes information space.

On the right hand side of the screen are listed the titles of the individual GeoNotes for the current position (see **Fig. 2**). Clicking on an item in the list brings up the content of the individual GeoNote (see **Fig. 3**). In most cases the list will consist of quite a few notes, and there will be a need for sorting mechanisms, defining the order in which GeoNotes categories are placed in the list. Although one could imagine other valuable sorting mechanisms, the current version of GeoNotes implements sorting notes by 'popularity', 'recent', and 'notes directed to me'. By clicking the icons below the list (see **Fig. 4**), GeoNotes of the chosen category will appear first in the list. Popularity measurement is based on reading, 'saving' and 'ignoring' any individual GeoNote (see **Fig. 3** and discussion below). Popularity of a GeoNote increases when 'saved' and decreases when 'ignored', and the total popularity weight of a note is calculated using the formula: timesRead + (2*timesSaved) - (2*timesIgnored). One could also imagine that the default ranking of notes in the list would be based on the filter mechanisms (discussed below).

In order to support 'on-the-move' navigation, GeoNotes will have the circle and list automatically transform as the user moves through space. While walking or riding a bus the circle will continuously re-segment and change size, representing the changing 'landscape' of GeoNotes. If the user finds something interesting, she can click on the circle at any time to freeze the transformation in order to explore GeoNotes at that place (even though the user continues to move away from it).

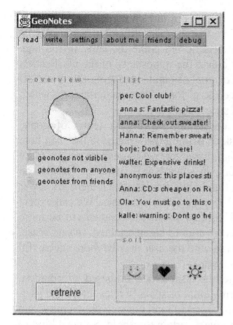

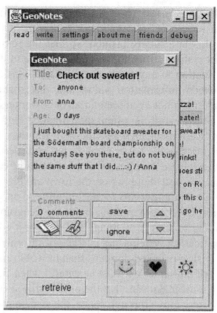

Fig. 2. The pie-chart circle provides an 'at-a-glance' overview of the immediate GeoNote information space. On the right hand side of the screen is the list of the titles of individual GeoNotes

Fig. 3. Clicking in the list brings up the individual GeoNote

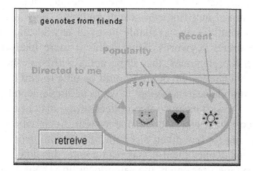

Fig. 4. The current GeoNotes application supports sorting by notes directed to me, most popular notes first, and the most recent notes first

The third way in which users will want to access notes is through notification. In a 'push' navigation mode, users will keep the mobile device in their pocket and when there is a high-ranking note in the vicinity, the device will signal and the individual note will pop up on the device. Most of the notes in a mass-scale annotation system will, however, not be relevant for the user in any given location. Many notes will for sure be commercial and non-commercial spam. The success of such a system fundamentally depends on its ability to filter out irrelevant notes. It is to those techniques we now turn.

Filtering notes. Notification systems alert, warn, remind or recommend users to consider some information or take some action. Successful notification systems must do this in a timely fashion, so that the reminders do not come too early or too late. Successful notification systems manage to evaluate the importance of the notification in relation to any given user, situation, task or goal at hand. Managing this trade-off between information value and disturbance is a formidable undertaking, which sometimes not even secretaries or coworkers succeed in [13].

Since work is often task-oriented and constantly shifting in terms of goals, notifications in such a setting will run the risk of being a disturbance rather than help (cf. Microsoft's paper clip). In a mobile setting, however, we can expect people to be more leisure oriented. On the metro, in bars, in schoolyards, with the family, on vacation and shopping on the town are places and situations in which there are fewer things that a user *has to* pay attention to and there are fewer deadlines. We can expect users to be more curious about the geographical and social environment, to be more willing to learn new things and to have a greater urge to be entertained. In one sense, notification systems and pushing of information onto the user may be more successful in leisure-oriented domains than in work related ones.

All the same, we must be careful when filtering pushed location-based information. We must make sure that the note is still informational or socially relevant for the user. As users move through space, the system must sort and rank notes in the vicinity, and only push those notes to the user that reach above a certain threshold. So what kind of filters may be efficient in this domain? Preferably, the filters should be based on both *content* and *usage*.

Content-based filters filter notes based on the user's interest and the content of the notes. In one such filtering technique, the user expresses his or her interest with a set of keywords of his or her own choice. Here one can imagine more or less sophisticated combinatorial and Boolean search methods. As a user moves through space, the system constantly scans available notes at any location and rates higher notes that match the user's keywords. This makes it more likely (or even certain, depending on the user's preferences) that some notes will be pushed to the user. As the interests of the user changes, he or she should be able to add or delete keywords. In GeoNotes, such a 'mobile search engine' is yet to be implemented.

In addition to this, the system may also collect *usage* data about how users read, click, save, choose, comment etc. notes in the system. Such actions can in different degrees be seen as voting for any given piece of information, which can then be used to rank notes. For instance, once the user has read a note, this note should probably be ranked lower next time the user enters the same location. The user must also be able to ignore the note, or even ignore the sender, which means that the note/any note from the sender will not be pushed to the user again (see **Fig. 3**). This function will be useful in situations with spam-GeoNotes, but probably requires that the GeoNote service stands fairly commercially independent. On the other hand, there should be mechanisms by which a user wants to 'save' valuable and reusable notes. Such a note will be given a high ranking next time the user is at the same location.

Usage based filters will become most forceful, however, when usage data is aggregated and matched with *other* users. Assuming that navigation is social, such data may be valuable in creating *social* filters, similar to those of collaborative filtering and social navigation. Simple cases of this are 'notes most recently put', 'notes most read' or 'notes most saved/commented'. Such filters or sorting mechanisms may be valuable in situations where freshness and popularity of the information is important.

In these cases, other users are anonymous and without identity, which may make the filters somewhat weak. The usefulness of following the traces of other people's behavior may be related to what *kind* of people that have left those traces. Trails may lead astray and the navigator wants to make sure that the person(s) who produced a trail was on the right track (in relation to my present information need). Thus, in order for collaborative filtering to work well, we may need to know the identity or some property (interest, hobbies, goals, age, nationality etc) of the other users in the system. At the same time, the system should be able to extract those aspects automatically without any major user overhead.

One simple way of doing so is to use the friends in the friends list as a basis for ranking notes. 'Notes put/read/rejected or commented on by friends/a particular friend' are forceful filters since users will know the tastes and preferences of their peers and acquaintances. The navigator can position his or her own preferences in relation to theirs. The ways in which experts, authorities and celebrities have put/read/rejected and commented upon notes may also have relevance for a user. Moreover, occasionally rather basic aspects of other people might be valuable. When abroad, shared national identity may be a quite valuable feature. When making a tourist trip to Teheran, for instance, I might want to know about all notes posted by fellow Swedes (i.e. users that have registered the GeoNote service in Sweden).

If we allow the system to keep track of posting, reading, picking, rejecting and commenting on notes for each user, then we will also be able to automatically cluster unknown users in 'interest groups' and then base the ranking on this. This is the core feature of collaborative filtering techniques and recommendation systems [15, 22]. The system, of course, does not 'know' the content of such interest groups, only that the users in the cluster have behaved in similar ways in the system. If someone in a user's cluster has put or read any notes in the vicinity that the user has not read, then this note would be ranked higher and potentially be pushed to the user. The ranking is thus based on automatic 'matching' of the usage history of users.

In a system that logs usage, it will also be possible to see all notes that were created by a specific friend, group of people or cluster of users (e.g. 'show me all notes Peter posted when he was traveling in Thailand last year'). One could also imagine a time slider, showing note-creating activities within any given geographical area over a period of time. Such a tool could be valuable for sociologists and historians in describing events and societal transformations.

Since the current version of GeoNote does not yet support logging of individual users' actions, only general and basic social filters are possible, for instance notes 'most read' and 'recently put'.

Setting filter preferences may be the responsibility of the system, or may be left up to the user, depending on type of user. Users' navigational modes may shift abruptly. In some situations the user will accept frequent note suggestions from the system; at other times, users will not want to be disturbed, or disturbed only when there is something really important (a top ranking note). Thus there should be an activity slider, which determines the general push activity of the system, independent of the content and usage-based filters. This is yet to be implemented in GeoNotes.

4   Implementation

Above, we described the interaction requirements for a real world annotation service with social filtering. We will now focus on our implementation of GeoNotes.

4.2   Requirements

The implementation of the GeoNotes service aims to meet a number of implementation requirements. These stem partly from the interaction requirements described above and partly from implementation constraints.

- The service must be able to store and retrieve data such as content, author, location, etc. about notes. Most of this data must be accessible and updateable by all users. Thus, the implementation should consist of at least two main parts: a client part that can execute locally on an end-user's mobile device and a server part that provides common functionality between all clients. The main reason for this is that the notes themselves and the meta-data about usage of the notes have to be available centrally to all users. Another reason relates to the fact that GeoNotes is a mobile service and as such it is subject to network connections of varying quality, and even complete loss of network connectivity. However, it is desirable to maintain some level of functionality when using the service off-line. The user might for example want to browse stored notes or edit user preferences. In cases of low bandwidth connections, the separation between client and server helps maintain a high level of quality of service since local functionality on the mobile device minimizes network traffic.
- User privacy must be maintained. Firstly, users should be able to remain anonymous while posting notes. The anonymous type of posting should complement posting under an alias and posting with a real name. Secondly, the set of personal data regarding which notes have been posted, which notes have been read, where the user posted notes, etc, must be protected from other users. Thirdly, it should be possible to address notes to specific persons or to the user group at large. This makes it possible to post notes that only certain users have access to.

We implemented GeoNotes in four parts as shown in the diagram in **Fig. 5**.

4.3   Client

The Java-based client contains functionality that is specific to individual users. Such functionality includes authoring, reading, and sorting of notes. Personal service data (user name and personal information) and user client settings (aliases, lists of friends, etc.) are also stored with the client.

The client also provides a device dependent user interface to the functionality of the GeoNotes service. Only one such user interface has been implemented so far (a Java Swing based GUI), but the client is designed to allow for the implementation of other interfaces as well (e.g. based on HTML or WML). The Swing based user interface allows users to post notes, retrieve notes, and to manage user settings. We have also provided a simple debug panel that is useful for simulating the user's position if positioning technologies are unavailable.

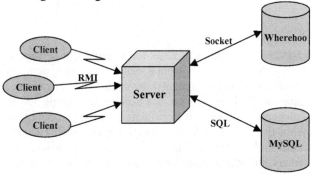

Fig. 5. The GeoNotes System Architecture. Clients connect to the server using RMI. The server uses a socket connection to store content data about notes in the Wherehoo database and SQL commands to store meta data about the usage of notes in the MySQL database

The client implementation does not assume a particular positioning technology, but relies on the assumption that latitude/longitude coordinates of its user are pushed to the client. The client can use any source of positioning information such as GPS or GSM if a plug-in Java class that represents it is installed. During the development of the service we built such a plug-in for a context simulator tool called QuakeSim [6]. QuakeSim is a graphical 3D tool that simulates real world space and outputs context information about actions that take place in the simulation. For GeoNotes, we used QuakeSim to simulate the movement and position of users in a 3D model of a well-known area on Södermalm in Stockholm.

The implementation of the client allows the use of many different underlying protocols for communication between client and server. This is desirable because the client is intended for use on various mobile platforms that provide varying support for communication protocols. However, so far the use of RMI has been sufficient. Choosing to use RMI was straight forward because of its relative ease of use. Alternative protocols include custom use of HTTP or method invocation using CORBA or SOAP.

We implemented the client as an sView service component [5]. The Java-based sView system is a platform for user access to electronic services. It is based on the concept of a service briefcase in which the user places and runs his or her services. The briefcase is able to move around the network to better service the user.

The usage of sView brings several advantages. Firstly, an sView service component is inherently mobile and persistent. Secondly, sView automatically packages functionality and data during migration or storage of the service component. Without sView, we would have had to implement all this functionality separately. In particular, persistence of personal user data and user client data is an important feature that is cumbersome to handle separately. Using sView, we can almost entirely leave such details to the underlying system.

We have also implemented a version of the client that runs as a standalone Java application. This version however, lacks the mobility and persistence features described above.

4.4   Server

The base server handles transactions of notes for all clients. It performs requests from clients to insert notes, to retrieve notes from a location, and to update a single note.

It stores the actual note data (its contents), be it text, audio, or video, as an entry in the Wherehoo database [24]. Wherehoo is a service for storing location dependent data in a client independent manner. It stores data coupled to a field that describes the physical location of the data as a latitude/longitude position. To retrieve data, one specifies the location and a radius and the service returns all entries in that area.

The server enters individual GeoNotes into Wherehoo by sending an insert command with the note content data and the position as parameters. It retrieves GeoNotes by sending a request command with the position and the radius as parameters.

The server stores meta information about the usage of the note, such as the number of times it has been read, when it was last read, and so on, as data in the MySQL database. When a note is posted the server creates an entry in the MySQL database and the resulting note ID is then used to tag the note content data when it is inserted into Wherehoo.

By storing the content data in Wherehoo separately from the GeoNotes service specific meta data in the MySQL database, client types other than GeoNotes clients are able to access the content data. However, special care has to be taken to ensure that private notes are not publicly available. We currently have made no provisions for this but it is straightforward to add an extension to the server to use encryption on note data before inserting it into Wherehoo.

5   Conclusions

Mobility seems to set completely new constraints on information technology usage. Things that users would not want to do, not dare to do, or have no time to do at their stationary work terminals, people will want to do with their mobile devices when in bars, cafés, on public transportation, or school breaks. GeoNotes creates a social awareness that encourages play, expressiveness and personal identity formation. Such aspects tend to be central for large user groups, e.g. teenagers [17, 23].

The GeoNotes system tries to bridge quite disparate areas of research within the Human-Computer Interaction community. It tries to blur the boundary between physical and digital space (ubiquitous computing, augmented reality), and at the same time strives to socially enhance digital space (CSCW, collaborative filtering, social navigation). In combination, it seeks to socially enhance physical space by letting users leave virtual conscious and non-conscious traces *that are tied to specific geographical positions*. When these traces are available to other users, we will be able to enhance and enrich the social awareness that already exists in physical space. Users will be able to observe, create, and participate in large-scale social patterns in geographical space. The societal and sociological implications of such an information space in terms of public discourse, democracy, urban planning and public places, are yet to be determined.

Acknowledgments

Jarmo Laaksolahti, Peter Lönnqvist, Fredrik Olsson & Martin Svensson took part in the initial GeoNotes brainstorming sessions. Kia Höök and Jussi Karlgren provided valuable inspiration and critique. Jim Youll helped with the Wherehoo related aspects of the server.

References

1. Abowd, G, Atkeson, C., Hong, J., Long, S., Kooper. R. & Pinkerton, M. (1997) Cyberguide: A mobile context-aware tour guide, *Wireless Networks*, 3 (1997), 421-433.
2. Benyon, D. & Höök. K. (1997) Navigation in information spaces: supporting the individual, In *INTERACT'97*, Sydney: Chapman & Hall.
3. Broadbent, J., and Marti, P. (1997) Location Aware Mobile Interactive Guides: usability issues, in *Proceedings of the Fourth International Conference on Hypermedia* and Interactivity in Museums (ICHIM97).
4. Burrell, J. & Gay, G. (2001) Collectively Defining Context in a Mobile, Networked Computing Environment, in Extended Abstracts, CHI'01, ACM Press.
5. Bylund, M., (2001) "sView – Personal Service Interaction", Ph.Lic. thesis, Computing Science Department, Uppsala University, Sweden.
6. Bylund, M. & Espinoza, F., (2001) "Using Quake III Arena to Simulate Sensors and Actuators when Evaluating and Testing Mobile Services", In Extended Abstracts, CHI 2001 Conference on Human Factors in Computing Systems, March31-April 5, 241-243.
7. Caswell, D. & Debaty, P. (2000) Creating Web Representations for Places, *Proceedings of HUC 2000*, Bristol, England, pp. 114-26.
8. Cheverst, K., Davies, N., Mitchell, K., Friday, A. and Efstratiou, C. (2000) Developing a context-aware electronic tourist guide: some issues and experiences; *Proceedings of the CHI'00*, ACM Press, 17 – 24.
9. Dieberger, A., Dourish, P., Höök, K., Resnick, P., and Wexelblat, A. (2000) Social Navigation: Techniques for building more usable systems, in *Interactions*, November-December issue, ACM, 2000
10. Dourish, P. & Bellotti, V. (1992) Awareness and coordination in shared workspaces. *Proceedings of CSCW'92*.
11. Harrison, S. and Dourish, P. (1996). Re-Place-ing Space: The Roles of Place and Space in Collaborative Systems. Proceedings of the Conference on Computer-Supported Cooperative Work (CSCW '96), New York, NY, pp. 67-76.

12. Holmquist, L.-E., Falk, J. and Wigström J. (1999) Supporting Group Collaboration with Inter-Personal Awareness Devices, Journal of Personal Technologies, Special Issue on Hand-Held CSCW, Springer Verlag, 1999.
13. Hudson, S. & Smith, I. (1996) Techniques for Addressing Fundamental Privacy and Disruption Tradeoffs in Awareness Support Systems, in *Proceedings of CSCW'96*, 248-57.
14. José, R., & Davies, N., (1999) Scalable and Flexible Location-Based Services for Ubiquitous Information Access, In *Handheld and Ubiquitous Computing, First International Symposiu*m, Karlsruhe, Germany, September 1999.
15. Konstan, J.A., Miller, B.N., Maltz, D., Herlocker, J.L., Gordon, L.R., Riedl, J. (1997) GroupLens: Applying collaborative filtering to Usenet news, *Communications of the ACM* 40 (3), 77-87.
16. Leonhardi, A., Kubach, U., Rothermel, K., Fritz, A. (1999) Virtual Information Towers - A Metaphor for Intuitive, Location-Aware Information Access in a Mobile Environment, *Proceedings of the Third International Symposium on Wearable Computers (ISWC'99)*, San Fransisco, CA, USA, IEEE Press, 1999.
17. Ling, R. (1999) "We release them little by little": maturation and gender identity as seen in the use of mobile telephony, *Telenor* R&D report 5/99, Norway.
18. Marmasse, N., & Schmandt, C. (2000) Location-Aware Information Delivery with ComMotion, *Proceedings of HUC 2000*, Bristol, England, pp. 157-171.
19. Munro, A., Höök, K. & Benyon, D. (eds.) (1999) *Social Navigation in Information Space*, London: Springer.
20. Pascoe, J. (1997) The Stick-e Note Architecture: Extending the Interface Beyond the User, in *Proceedings of IUI'97*, 261-64.
21. Rekimoto, J., Ayatsuka, Y., (1998) Augment-able Reality: Situated Communication through Physical and Digital Spaces. In *Proceedings of the 2nd International Symposium on Wearable Computers*, Oct 19-21, 1998, Pittsburgh, Pennsylvania, USA.
22. Svensson, M., Höök, K., Laaksolahti, J. & Waern, A. (2001) Social Navigation of Food Recipes, *Proceedings of CHI'01*, ACM Press, 341-48.
23. Weilenmann, A. (2000) Negotiating Use: Making Sense of Mobile Technology, *The Journal of Personal Technologie*s, no. 4, Springer Verlag.
24. Youll, J. & Krikorian, R. (2000) Wherehoo Server: An interactive location service for software agents and intelligent systems, Workshop on Infrastructure for Smart Devices - How to Make Ubiquity an Actuality, *The Second International Symposium on Handheld and Ubiquitous Computing*, Bristol (UK), September 27, 2000.

A Probabilistic Room Location Service for Wireless Networked Environments

Paul Castro[1], Patrick Chiu[2], Ted Kremenek[1], and Richard Muntz[1]

[1]UCLA, Department of Computer Science, Los Angeles, CA, 90095, USA
{castrop,kremenek,muntz}@cs.ucla.edu
[2]FX Palo Alto Laboratory, 3400 Hillview Ave, Bldg 4, Palo Alto, CA 94304, USA
chiu@pal.xerox.com

Abstract. The popularity of wireless networks has increased in recent years and is becoming a common addition to LANs. In this paper we investigate a novel use for a wireless network based on the IEEE 802.11 standard: inferring the location of a wireless client from signal quality measures. Similar work has been limited to prototype systems that rely on nearest-neighbor techniques to infer location. In this paper, we describe Nibble, a Wi-Fi location service that uses Bayesian networks to infer the location of a device. We explain the general theory behind the system and how to use the system, along with describing our experiences at a university campus building and at a research lab. We also discuss how probabilistic modeling can be applied to a diverse range of applications that use sensor data.

1 Introduction

One approach to ubiquitous computing is enabling applications and devices to detect and make use of changing environmental conditions. Such systems are also called *context-aware*, and important aspects of context include location, nearby people, and accessible resources (e.g. see [7], [15], [18]). In this paper, we address the problem of inferring the room location of a device such as a laptop or PDA in a wireless networked environment. Such environments are becoming more prevalent due to the popularity of wireless local area network products based on the IEEE 802.11 standard (Wi-Fi). These products offer good bandwidth and affordability for office buildings, university campuses, and homes.

Location-aware applications that have been explored or proposed include tour guides [1], interaction with or control of nearby computers, displays, and printers [18], and electronic Post-it notes associated with a location [3]. Like most existing location based systems, these require special hardware to detect the location of the device running the application. For example, one method to do location sensing is to employ an infrared transceiver system, as [18]. Another way to obtain location information is with commercially available GPS, which only works outdoors. By following the device until it enters a building, it can locate the nearest building in a research park or campus.

G. D. Abowd, B. Brumitt, S. A. N. Shafer (Eds.): Ubicomp 2001, LNCS 2201, pp. 18-34, 2001.
© Springer-Verlag Berlin Heidelberg 2001

Providing a location service that requires no extra hardware would make it easier to build location-aware application systems and enable more people to use them. In a Wi-Fi environment, it is possible to use software to infer the location of a wireless networked device by analyzing the signal strength or signal-noise-ratio of the wireless access points with respect to that device. By using software to infer location, no additional hardware needs to be attached to a laptop or PDA beyond a wireless network PC card.

Some techniques that may be applied to inferring location are multilateration, nearest neighbor, and Bayesian networks. For example, in multilateration, an object can infer its location by calculating its range from beacons with known locations using some type of signal measure like radio frequency (RF) or ultrasound. This works fine in environments of uniform density, but the walls and other structural as well as non-structural matter inside a building makes calculating ranges from signal measures difficult. In a sense, the space is warped. A nearest neighbor approach that compares signal samples in a table of values can work, but lacks a well-defined model for combining data from multiple sources. Our choice is to apply Bayesian networks, which can "learn" the room locations of a building, and its modular structure provides flexibility when the access points are added/removed or spatially reconfigured. A further advantage is that other contextual information such as the likelihood that the owner of the device will inhabit a particular location can be easily incorporated into the Bayesian network model.

Another important consideration is that the wireless signals undulate, which is caused by people walking around and other changes in the ambient space. This "noise" is handled by a Bayesian network, which assigns probabilities to locations.

The UCLA Multimedia Systems Lab has devised and implemented the Multi-use Sensor Environment (MUSE), a middleware architecture for sensor smart spaces employing Bayesian networks [4]. A location service for Wi-Fi networked environments was prototyped on top of this architecture, and a stand-alone version of this location service called *Nibble* was built. Nibble has been installed for evaluation at Boelter Hall, a university campus building at UCLA, and more recently at an industrial research lab, FXPAL. In this paper, we will describe how this location service works (section 2), our experiences with this system (section 3), and we will discuss ways of extending the MUSE sensor model, which is inherently simple because of the structure of the Bayesian networks, to compose component-based location services (section 4). Finally, we discuss plans for future work (section 5).

2   Location Service System

The IEEE 802.11 Wi-Fi wireless network infrastructure consists of many wireless clients and several access points that act as bridges between the wireless network and the local LAN. Clients primarily use, or "associate," with the access point that provides them with the strongest RSSI (received signal strength). As a clients roams, it periodically does a site survey of signal quality measures to determine the best access point with which to associate. As reported in [2] and [16], it is possible to infer the location of a client from these signal measures. Past approaches have been limited to nearest neighbor or error-minimization techniques to infer location from signal strengths. In this section we describe a modular probabilistic approach for inferring location that uses Bayesian networks. Through probabilistic modeling we can create a robust location service with a general, quantifiable measure of performance, easily incorporate additional data such as movement histories of users, as well as provide a flexible means to compose a location service out of heterogeneous components.

2.1 System Overview

Nibble is a stand-alone version of a Wi-Fi location service that is derived from an indoor location service prototyped within the MUSE pervasive sensor infrastructure [4]. Nibble relies on a *fusion service* to infer the location of a laptop from signal strength measures between itself and access points in the environment. A fusion service has two components: 1) an evidential reasoning model that aggregates and interprets (i.e. fuses) information from sensors and 2) a resource optimization model for minimizing the "cost" of gathering data.   Sensor data is characterized probabilistically and inputted into the fusion service. The output of the fusion service is a probability distribution over a random variable that represents some context data. This process is necessary since sensor information, such as Wi-Fi signal quality measures, is fundamentally noisy, subject to intermittent availability, and typically too-low level to be immediately useful to an application.

Bayesian Network Framework for Inferring Location

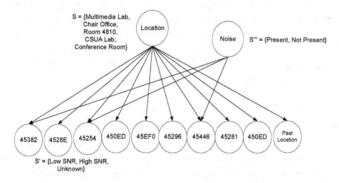

Fig. 1. Example Bayesian network for inferring location in a Wi-Fi network

In Nibble, the interpretive part of a fusion service is a Bayesian network (also called *belief network* or *causality network*). A Bayesian network is a graphical representation of a joint probability distribution that explicitly declares dependency relationships between random variables in the distribution [12].   Because these relationships are declared, a joint probability distribution can be constructed modularly thus making computation on this distribution feasible. In our view, the modular structure of Bayesian networks also eases the construction of component-based systems where the outputs of one fusion service can be used as an input to another.

Figure 1 shows a simple Bayesian network we can use to infer location from the Wi-Fi infrastructure. The network is a rooted tree with directed arcs going from the root to several terminal nodes. These arcs signify a dependency relationship between the root node and the terminal nodes. The root node is the "query" variable that describes $p(L)$, the *a priori* distribution over a set of locations $L=\{v_1,...,v_i\}$. The terminal nodes in the network represent "observable" variables that describe $p(E|L)$, the marginal conditional probability that you observe values $E=\{e_1...,e_n\}$ from a sensor given that you are in location v in L. Given this network, we can get sensor readings $R=\{e_1,...,e_m\}$, for sensors 1 thru m, and calculate $p(L|R)$, the *a posterior* probability distribution over L, the probability that we are in any location v_i given R. In general, any node in the network can be a query variable. For example, we could ask $p(s_1=e_1|\ L=v_3\ ,s_2=e_3)$, the probability that sensor s_1 will read e_1 given we are in location v_3 and sensor s_2 reads e_3. The figure also includes a noise node that could affect the outcome of several sensors.

In the Bayesian network for determining location, values for L and E are quantized into discrete values. Nibble can theoretically distinguish n^s different locations in a Wi-Fi network where n is the number of output values from a sensor and s is the number of access points. However, the topology and construction of the building, as well as various noise effects, influence the actual number of locations Nibble can distinguish. For Boelter Hall, $n=4$ and $s=10$ and for FXPAL, $n=4$ and $s=4$.

Nibble has been used to calculate the probability that a laptop is in one of 14 adjacent locations 10-15 feet apart in an area covering two floors in Boelter Hall, a large building on the UCLA campus. In the current implementation of our system, $E=\{$High, Medium, Low, None$\}$, where None=[0], Low=(0,16), Medium=(16,30), High=(30,70) representing the ranges of signal-to-noise ratios (SNR) at each quantized level as measured between a laptop with a wireless card and an access point. These quantizations are based on early experiments at UCLA. Future implementations could have quantizations that are more sensitive to the exponential attenuation characteristics of the RSSI. It may be beneficial to have more levels with smaller ranges for quantizations at the higher end of the scale.

Training the Bayesian Network

To infer location using the Bayesian network in Figure 1, it is necessary to provide values for the *a priori* distribution $p(L)$ and the marginal distribution $p(E|L)$ for each access point. While it is possible to construct an analytical model to get the marginals, empirical measurements seem to work best [2]. For one of our sites, we took samples of SNRs for 14 locations over several days. We sampled twice a day in the mid-morning and early evening. However, we observed that Nibble could correctly infer location with even just a few samples at each location.

Calibration can be tedious. Nibble does not require that all locations be declared *a priori*. Instead, L can be built incrementally. Locations can be added and deleted at anytime. Sampling occurs when a location is initially recorded and "re-sampling" can be done at anytime. Re-sampling allows the user to adjust the marginal distributions for an access point if there is a change that invalidates the current calibration, e.g. a change in the configuration of access points.

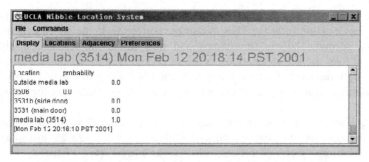

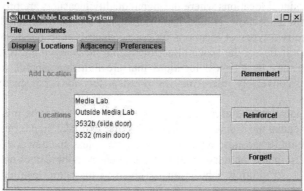

Fig. 2. Main Display of Nibble (top) and display for recording, calibrating, and deleting locations (bottom)

The default distribution for p(L) is uniform. However, certain people are more likely to be in some locations rather than others. Profiles of people's preferences for locations can easily be incorporated into the Bayesian framework by changing the *a priori* distribution p(L). Although not part of the current implementation, Nibble could create a profile automatically by recording the frequency a client is at a certain location and updating the distribution over time. This same process could also be used to detect adjacency relationships between locations and used to more accurately pinpoint the location of a user. For example, it may be physically impossible for a transition to occur between locations v_1 to v_2. Nibble models this similar to a Hidden Markov model where an additional node in the Bayesian network records the transition probabilities for all locations. Currently, these adjacency relationships are recorded manually.

2.2 Using Nibble

Nibble is implemented using Java JDK 1.3 and currently works with Lucent Orinoco Wi-Fi cards running under MS Windows (see Appendix). The basic Nibble package includes a GUI that allows users to build and calibrate a location service as well as display and log the results of the fusion service. There is also a simple API that programmers can use to interface their applications to Nibble and make them location-aware (see Appendix).

Figure 2 shows the main display screen in the Nibble GUI while it is running. Nibble infers location from the SNR measures received from the Wi-Fi network card every two seconds. Nibble timestamps and then prints the resulting probability distribution over the set of locations in the large text area at the bottom half of the screen. The most likely location value is printed at the top of the text box. In the figure, Nibble is tracking 5 locations and the most likely location is the "media lab (3514)."

Adding a location can be accomplished at the "Locations" screen. It is useful to think of locations in two ways when using Nibble. First, there are distinguishable physical locations such as offices, closets, hallways, etc. Second, there are distinguishable signal locations where the signal quality measures are probabilistically consistent within a location. Nibble identifies signal locations rather than physical locations. These two types of locations do not necessarily map one-to-one but since physical characteristics of the space affect the signal measures there is a correlation. However, there may be physical locations that are indistinguishable from a signal perspective and conversely, there may be physical locations that encompass many signal locations.

To record a location, the user should go to that location and type in a name for it. When the user clicks the "remember" button Nibble will take signal quality samples at 1 per second for 10 seconds. When sampling is complete, the new location is added to the location list and is included in all future inferences. Nibble does not enforce any naming schemes so multiple labels can be given to the same location or multiple locations can have the same name. The latter is useful when there are many signal locations for one physical location. The former is useful if you want to add attributes to location labels such as "Media lab (evening)" and "Media lab (morning)." This assumes that the signal measures are different in the morning and evening.

If Nibble is unable to infer a location, it will display "???" as the most likely location. This usually occurs for locations that are "under-sampled" (or not calibrated at all). When a location is under-sampled, the initial 10 samples for a single location are not sufficient and the calculated marginal conditional probabilities are incorrect. Users can remedy this by "reinforcing" a location by selecting a location value in the location list and clicking the "reinforce" button. Reinforcing is the same as sampling except new samples are added to modify the current marginals.

Reinforcement of locations may be insufficient to rectify incorrect location inferences particularly if there is a drastic change in the placement or configuration of access points. In this case, users can elect to delete locations from the location list using the "forget" button and build a new location model. Though not part of the current implementation, it is also possible to eliminate an access point from the model (e.g. if it moves). Locations can then be re-sampled and this will put the access point back in the model but with new marginals.

Nibble is mainly designed to be a component in a larger location-aware application. As such, Nibble has several interfaces that are available to application designers. For example, Figure 3 shows a simple graphing application that uses the Nibble API to get its location and display the probability distribution as a histogram. From the API, the application can start, stop, and read location data from Nibble. Nibble can also write a log file that applications can parse to get location data.

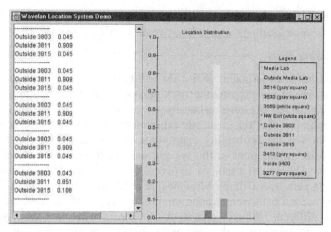

Fig. 3. Simple application that uses the Nibble API to display its current location as a histogram

3   Experiences with Location Service

We have used Nibble at two research sites. The first site is a large engineering building on the campus of UCLA. The second site is an industrial research lab in Palo Alto, CA. Both sites differed in terms of their relative sizes, density of access points, and noise sources. For example, the campus building has a high density of access points to accommodate a very dynamic signal environment with many people moving throughout the building at all times of the day. The industrial research lab had a relatively low density of access points with far fewer people in the building.

In this section we describe our experiences using Nibble in each of these facilities. Preliminary experiments were conducted on the campus to measure the accuracy of Nibble's location inferencing as well as its stability in the face of noise. Resource optimization was also considered. Exploratory usage tests were conducted at the industrial site and we report on the performance of Nibble in its support of a novel location-aware application.

3.1 Boelter Hall at UCLA

Boelter Hall is one of three engineering buildings on the UCLA campus. The hall is a large, 8-story building, which houses 4 engineering departments, the engineering library, and many classrooms. The building is square shaped, and in the center is an open-sky courtyard. During the daytime there are hundreds of students in Boelter Hall attending lectures and labs, and in-between classes the halls are filled with people. The Department of Computer Science is located on the third and fourth floors of Boelter Hall. Within the department there are 14 Wi-Fi access points that provide infrastructure support for many laptops.

The construction of the building causes severe attenuation of RF signal strength so a high density of access points is necessary. The current configuration allows connectivity to the wireless network in almost all locations in the department and even the courtyard. However, the density of access points varies in different parts of the building so some locations always have weak signals.

Hallway Tracking Tests

We conducted initial experiments to test the ability of Nibble to distinguish between different locations of a laptop as the user moves through the building at walking speeds. We conducted the tests primarily in the hallways of the building where connectivity was fair. To aid us in our experiments we implemented a distribution display that showed the probability distribution over locations as a histogram. We recorded 12 adjacent locations in the system and tested two different paths through these locations. There were a total of 10 access points that could be detected in these paths. The first path was a simple straight-line path from one end of the hallway to another. The second path went around the circumference of the building. This path went through different hallways and went from areas where the density of access points was high to areas where the density was lower. Part of the path also crossed an outdoor walkway.

We calibrated the system over a few days. For each location we took about 50 to 100 samples. In some locations we took fewer samples because we did not have access to the location after hours. Areas with weaker connectivity also prevented us from taking as many samples since our original implementation required connectivity to the MUSE infrastructure [4]. This is not an issue with the current implementation of Nibble.

We measured the performance of the system by tabulating the correct, incorrect, and "don't know" readings. Correct readings corresponded to when the most likely inferred location was the actual location as observed by the user. Incorrect readings corresponded to when the most likely location was not the actual location. "Don't know" readings occurred if Nibble could not infer any location; this primarily happened in locations where we could not take enough samples. We defined an accuracy metric as the #correct readings/(#readings − #don't knows).

We experienced very good performance overall. Nibble achieved an accuracy of around 97% for the two different paths. The total number of "don't know" readings accounted for about 15% of all the readings. However, these readings mostly occurred for the same parts in the building indicating either an under-sampled condition for those locations or a noisy space. For example, one of these spaces was near large metal fan ducts on an outdoor balcony.

The location service updates its inferred location every three seconds. As we changed our actual locations, the service sometimes took several inference cycles to update the most likely location to the correct one. This is most likely due to our sampling method where we concentrated mostly on the "center" of a physical space. We would generally have to come close to the center of the space for the location service to register the correct location. Later, we altered our sampling method to include samples from the boundaries (as perceived by the user) of the space. This generally produced more consistent results.

Several locations we recorded in the hallways of Boelter Hall could confuse the system. This is due to generally weak connectivity (all signal measures look similar) and noise. However, the system performed well in localizing our position in the hallway to several adjacent locations with one of those locations being correct. Even without adjacency information in the Bayesian network, the location service inferred we were in a location close to our actual location.

3.2 Research Lab at FXPAL

The FX Palo Alto Laboratory (FXPAL) resides on the second floor of a building that is rectangular in shape and measures 224 by 96 feet. There are about 40 offices, three small clusters of cubicles, and several conference rooms (see Figure 4). The FXPAL Wi-Fi environment consists of 4 WaveLAN access points and a number of wireless laptops. There are also 3 iPAQ Wi-Fi access points and wireless iPAQ PDAs; these have not yet been integrated with a location service.

Room Location Visualizer

We designed a room location visualizer and integrated it with the location data streamed out by Nibble. This visualizer is based on a blueprint of the building. The probabilities are quantized into 5 intervals: (0.0, 0.2], (0.2, 0.4], ..., (0.8, 1.0]. Rooms are show in different shading levels according to their probability (see Figure 5). A subset of the rooms is targeted for each device, and the targeted rooms are shaded in light gray. Restricting to a subset of rooms increases the accuracy of the location service because this leaves fewer rooms in close proximity. Nibble updates the location probabilities every two seconds.

Accuracy

We tested the Nibble location service by having one of the FXPAL researchers carry a laptop whenever he went to a meeting or to work in another room other than his own office. There are 9 room locations that are frequented by Patrick: 3 conference rooms, 2 collaborators' offices (cubicles), his own office, his manager's office, a lounge, and a patio outside the building near a coffee area.

We found Nibble always able to distinguish between the 3 conference rooms. The probabilities usually fell in (0.6, 0.8] and (0.8, 1.0]. One factor is that the conference rooms are not adjacent to each other.   The nearest two are diagonally across a hallway. Another factor is that conference rooms are larger than offices and cubicles.

Sometimes Nibble was confused between adjacent offices (dimensions are 8 x 14 feet).   The probabilities usually fell in the range (0.4, 0.6]. Nibble is able to distinguish offices that are separated by another office, with probabilities in (0.8, 1.0]. In our evaluation, this level of accuracy was sufficient, because the researcher did work on his laptop in his office and not his neighbor's.

Cubicle clusters tested the limits of Nibble. Nibble was able to locate a cluster, but not able to distinguish between the cubicles within a cluster. A cubicle's dimension is about 6 x 8 feet, with 2 to 4 cubicles per cluster. The clusters are dispersed far from each other on the building floor. Like the uncertainty caused by adjacent offices, accuracy can be improved for cubicles in the same cluster if we know which cubicle in that cluster a user and his laptop are more likely to frequent.

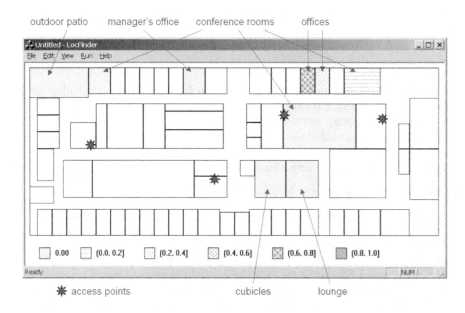

Fig. 4. Room location visualizer with floor plan of FXPAL

A Room-Aware Application at FXPAL

An application at FXPAL that makes use of room location is a multimedia meeting minutes system called *LiteMinutes* [5]. The main conference room at FXPAL is equipped for multimedia meeting capture with digital video, presentation slide images, and notes [6]. See Figure 5. Occasionally, video of meetings is recorded in other conference rooms, and we are considering plans to capture teleconferences between FXPAL and Fuji Xerox in Japan.

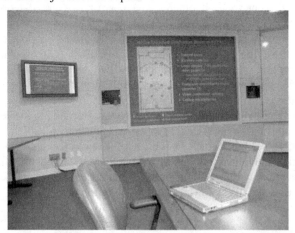

Fig. 5. Note taking on a laptop with the LiteMinutes application in a conference room equipped for multimedia meeting capture

In the LiteMinutes system, plain text notes are taken on wireless laptops running the LiteMinutes note-taking applet inside a Web browser. Each character in these notes is timestamped. These notes are sent to the LiteMinutes server that processes and reformats the notes into an HTML hypermedia document (See figure 6). The notes are parsed into note items by looking for line breaks in the original text notes, and for each note item links are generated by associating the time of the note item to the time of the recorded multimedia streams. Media recorded includes video and presentation slide images.

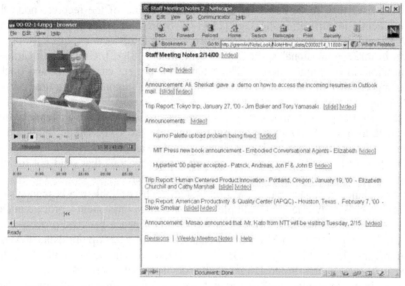

Fig. 6. Playing back of recorded video of a meeting from LiteMinutes notes

Since the laptop is mobile and the meeting capture can take place in different rooms, it is necessary to specify which room the laptop is used to take notes in so that they can be associated to the correct set of multimedia streams recorded in that room. The LiteMinutes system is designed to deal with this situation by recording a stream of contextual metadata, which handles location as a type of context. The LiteMinutes server uses the contextual metadata stream to generate links from the laptop notes that contain room and time information to the multimedia streams that were captured at a specified room and time.

4   Toward an Infrastructure for Wi-Fi Room-Aware Applications

Nibble is derived from a location service implemented within MUSE, an infrastructure designed to support a wide-range of sensor-based services. In this section we discuss how the fusion service model can be utilized to construct component-based location services that potentially offer better performance and more flexibility for application designers.

4.1 Categorizing Location Systems

Researchers have been interested in indoor locations systems for at least the past decade. Systems generally fall into two categories: 1) *tracking systems* that provide location information from a central infrastructure and 2) distributed *beacon systems* that allow a client to infer location from beacons they see in the environment.

In the first case, the location system depends on identification messages from tracked objects that get processed in an infrastructure specific way to infer the location of the client. For example, the Xerox ParcTab and Active Badge system can localize a user to a room based on the physical location of the receiver node that detects client's identification message [18][17]. More precise location systems such as BATS and 3D-iD use arrays of RF sensors capable of locating specially tagged objects in three-dimensional space within centimeters [8][13]. User identification is also possible in tracking systems. The SmartFloor project can identify and track a user using Hidden Markov models based on "footfall" signatures acquired from a floor equipped with load sensors [11].

In the second case, the environment provides beacons from which a client can infer its current location. Early examples of this include the CyberGuide that used IR beacons as proximity sensors [1]. A more recent example is the Cricket location system from M.I.T. [14] that uses RF and ultrasonic beacons that send out location identification strings that can be detected by a mobile user.

At first glance, a Wi-Fi –based location system such as Nibble is a beacon system. This is not necessarily true. For example, it is possible to implement a process at each access point that collects all SNR data from clients. Then a backend process could infer the location of any Wi-Fi client by considering all access point data. RADAR was implemented in this way [2]. One consequence of this implementation is that devices can easily know the location of other devices in the network. Privacy in this case is an important concern. The current "beacon" implementation of Nibble allows the device to be "invisible" as long as it just monitors the network and does not transmit any network packets.

4.2 Component-Based Location Systems

The fusion service model used in Nibble is not limited to a Wi-Fi indoor location system. Other location systems are compatible with probabilistic formulations. For example, Cricket beacons use radio frequency (RF) and ultrasonic signals to broadcast a string to nearby clients that identifies the current spatial location of the client. Since multiple beacons can be heard, the client assumes that the beacon that it is closest to identifies the correct location. One useful assumption is that the beacons are only placed near entranceways or partitions between spaces; this ensures that the closest (and hence correct) beacon can be identified with a high probability.

A fusion service utilizing Cricket beacons does not require exact placement of beacons though the trade-off is the need to calibrate the Bayesian network to get the marginals. For Cricket, the beacon values can be quantized as $E=\{$Heard and Closest, Heard, Not Heard$\}$, and the fusion service would calculate the P $(L|R)$, the probability that it is in some location in L given that it observes $R=\{E_1,...,E_m\}$ from the Cricket beacons. This potentially increases the resolution of Cricket from s locations to 3^s

locations since the original system requires one beacon per location. Given the limited range of the beacons, however, at anytime you will see less than s beacons at a location.

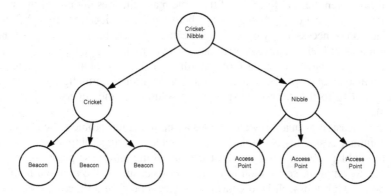

Fig. 7. Composing two location services

One distinct advantage of the fusion service approach is the ability to compose services together. Composability is a major reason MUSE adopts a general model of data aggregation and interpretation. For example, Figure 7 shows a possible Bayesian network that combines Cricket and Nibble into a new Cricket-Nibble fusion service that utilizes both. The Cricket-Nibble service can be used by applications in place of just Nibble or Cricket since the output is still a probability distribution over locations, and the resource optimizations possible in Nibble can be applied to Cricket-Nibble.

Composability is a step towards providing different degrees of privacy for a user of a location system. For example, a user may allow less privileged users access to coarse location information (e.g. the building level) about her and allow a restricted set of users higher resolution data (e.g. the room level). To set up this partition the infrastructure allows different permissions on accessing each fusion service where some users can only get "low quality" information while other users get "high quality" information.

Characterizing Information Quality

In many physical sensor systems, power or communication bandwidth is highly constrained [10]. Having a quantifiable measure of quality for a fusion service allows applications the ability to choose between fusion services based on a unified measure of expected performance for a given "cost." For example, there may be two different fusion services capable of inferring location but one service may consume a lot of power or bandwidth and be 90% accurate while another is only 75% accurate but consumes far less resources.

We define the term "Quality-of-Information" (QoI) to characterize the performance of a fusion service in terms of: 1) accuracy of the inference as measured by an outside observer and 2) the level of confidence it has in its measure [4]. For example, a uniform distribution over all possible locations is an undesirable result. The best result would be an "impulse" for a single value v in L and p(v)=1.0. We capture this intuition using the information theoretic concept of entropy, which we approximate by the probability of the most likely outcome of the query variable. Intuitively, a fusion service that infers a most likely location with p=90% is better than a service that infers a most likely location with p=50%. Note that there is a difference between the "confidence" of the system and the "resolution" of the system. A location service that can only distinguish between 2 large locations (e.g. 2 floors in a building) is not necessarily worse than a location service that can distinguish many small locations. If both are always 90% sure of their inferences and are 90% accurate, then we say they have the same QoI regardless of their resolution differences. Of course, someone may prefer higher resolution location information but QoI is a measure relative to the desired or specified resolution of the "query variable" (e.g. location).

Given a measure of quality, we can pose an optimization problem: achieve a high QoI at minimal cost. This is similar to the "trouble-shooting" optimization problem in [9]. In Nibble, we assume a unit cost for consulting an access point and now we would like to get accurate location information by consulting the minimal number of access points. Our approach is to consult one access point at a time until we reach a user specified level of QoI or we run out of access points. We consult access points that contain the "most information" about location before we consult access points with "less information." To measure the amount of information we can potentially get from consulting an access point we use a heuristic based on an off-line sensitivity analysis of the Bayesian network [4]. Note that this resource optimization approach can be generalized to all fusion services.

Optimizing QoI for a Wi-Fi Location Service

To test our ideas we used an enhanced version of the location service where the client can specify a desired level of quality for the inferred location information. The fusion service would attempt to achieve this quality but consult the minimal number of access points. For example, the client could specify a quality setting Y=0.9 which means that the most likely location should have a probability of 0.9. The location service will consult access points (ordered by our heuristic) one at a time until it achieves this quality setting.

Figure 8 shows the effect on accuracy and cost for quality settings of Y={0.1,0.5,0.9,ALL} where ALL means consult all access points. For a quality setting of Y=ALL, the location service was 97% accurate but it was the most expensive since it consulted all access points for each inference. For a quality setting of Y=0.9, the location service was 96% accurate but it was considerable less expensive because it only consulted around three access points for each inference. For the other settings, the location service was about 50% accurate.

5   Conclusions and Future Work

In this paper we described our experiences using Nibble, a probabilistic location service for a Wi-Fi networked environment. We explained the MUSE sensor fusion model and how it is possible to build component-based fusion services to infer location. We are currently implementing an enhanced version of Nibble that infers location using a heterogeneous set of sensors. The UCLA Multimedia Systems

Laboratory has constructed a small, inexpensive sensor board that can communicate with a PC through a standard serial port. The sensor board is capable of measuring temperature, humidity, orientation, and acceleration. The inclusion of this sensor data can improve the overall performance and resolution of Nibble. As an example, oftentimes when a user enters a room they will place their laptop in a specific location. If two locations are nearly indistinguishable from Wi-Fi measurements but the laptop is placed at each location with different orientations, we can use the digital compass to get the laptop location. This is also useful if we need to discriminate locations within a single physical space. Similarly, temperature and humidity can be used to distinguish colder and warmer environments (e.g. a machine room versus an office). The more general problem of "grafting" together services in an automated fashion is a topic of research we plan to investigate.

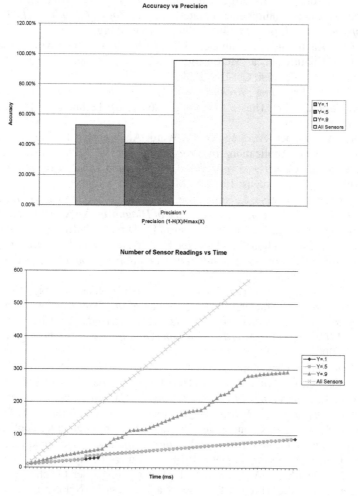

Fig. 8. Accuracy vs. QoI (left) and Cost vs. QoI

References

1. Abowd, G., Atkeson, C., Hong, J., Long, S., Kooper, R., and Pinkerton, M. Cyberguide: A mobile context-aware tour guide. *ACM Wireless Networks,* 3 (1997), pp. 421-4333.
2. Bahl, P., Padmananbhan, V. RADAR: An In-Building RF-based User Location and Tracking System. In *Proceedings of IEEE INFOCOM 2000*, Tel-Aviv, Israel, March 2000. IEEE Computer Society Press.
3. Brown, P. J. The stick-e document: a framework for creating context-aware applications. In *Proceedings of Electronic Publishing '96*, pp. 259-272.
4. Castro, P. and Muntz, R. Managing context for smart spaces, IEEE Personal Communications, vol.7, no. 5, October 2000.
5. Chiu, P., Boreczky, J., Girgensohn, A., Kimber, D. LiteMinutes: An Internet-based system for multimedia minutes. *Proceedings of Tenth World Wide Web Conference (2001,* pp. 140-149. See http://www10.org.
6. Chiu, P., Kapuskar, A., Reitmeier, S., and Wilcox, L. Room with a Rear View: Meeting Capture in a Multimedia Conference Room. *IEEE Multimedia Magazine*, vol. 7, no. 4, Oct-Dec 2000, pp. 48-54.
7. Dey, A. *Providing Architectural Support for Building Context-Aware Applications*. PhD Thesis. Georgia Institute of Technology, Department of Computer Science.
8. Harter, A., Hopper, A., Steggles, P., Ward, A., Webster, P. The Anatomy of a Context-Aware Application. In *Proceedings of the Fifth Annual ACM/IEEE International Conference on Mobile Computing and Networking*, Seattle, Washington, USA, August 1999. ACM Press.
9. Heckerman, D., Breese, J., Rommelse, K. "Troubleshooting Under Uncertainty," *DX-94-5th Int'l. Workshop on Principles of Diagnosis*, AAAI, 1994, pp. 121-130.
10. Intanagonwiwat, C., Govindan, R., Estrin, D., Directed Diffusion: A Scalable and Robust Communication Paradigm for Sensor Networks. In *Proceedings of the Sixth Annual International Conference on Mobile Computing and Networks*, Boston, MA, August 2000. ACM Press.
11. Orr, R., Abowd, G. The Smart Floor: A Mechanism for Natural User Identification and Tracking. In *Proceedings of the 2000 Conference on Human Factors in Computing Systems)*, The Hague, Netherlands, April 1-6, 2000.
12. Pearl, J. *CAUSALITY: Models, Reasoning, and Inference*, Cambridge University Press, 2000.
13. PinPoint, http://www.pinpointco.com
14. Priyantha, N., Chakraborty, A., Balakrishnan, H. The Cricket Location Support System. In *Proceedings of the Sixth Annual ACM International Conference on Mobile Computing and Networking*, Boston, MA, August 2000. ACM Press.
15. Schilit, B., Adams, N., and Want, R. Context-aware computing applications. In *Proceedings of the Workshop on Mobile Computing Systems and Applications*, Santa Cruz, CA, December 1994. IEEE Computer Society.
16. Small, J., Smailagic, A., Siewiorek, D. Determining User Location For Context Aware Computing Through the Use of a Wireless LAN Infrastructure. Project Aura report. htttp://www.cs.cmu.edu/~aura/docdir/small00.pdf

17. Want, R., Hopper, A., Falcao, V., Gibbons, J. The Active Badge Location System. *ACM Transactions on Information Systems*, 10(1):91-102, January 1992.
18. Want, R., Schilit, B., Adams, N., Gold, R., Petersen, K., Goldberg, D., Ellis, J., Weiser, M. The ParcTab Ubiquitous Computing Experiment. Technical Report CSL-95-1, Xerox Palo Alto Research Center, March 1995. Also appears In *Mobile Computing*, H. F. Korth and T. Imielinski, eds., Kluwer Academic Press, 1996.

Appendix: Getting Nibble

Nibble is available for download and experimentation at http://mmsl.cs.ucla.edu/Nibble. Applications can interface to Nibble though a simple API. The API is not designed to support the construction of models; this should be done through the GUI. Instead, the API allows users to activate and de-activate Nibble as well as access the results of its location inferencing. Figure A shows a Java code snippet that applications can use to access location data from Nibble.

```
Nibble nibble = new Nibble();
nibble.on();

/** wait a bit for Nibble to cycle*/

mywaithere(5000); // application defined (wait 5 seconds)

/** .. then get the data */

String location = nibble.getLocationName();
String distribution = nibble.getDistribution();

nibble.off();
```

Fig. A. Java programming example to access location data in Nibble

Location Information Managment

Hani Naguib and George Coulouris

Laboratory for Communications Engineering, Cambridge University
{han21,gfc22}@cam.ac.uk
http://www-lce.eng.cam.ac.uk/qosdream/

Abstract. We describe an approach to the management of location events deriving from a variety of sensors and sensor technologies. The approach uses a region-based spatial algorithm to integrate low-level location information, producing events that approximate closely to the needs of application programs. Preliminary experience indicates that the approach yields a very worthwhile reduction in the event traffic that must be handled by applications.

1   Introduction

A wide range of location sensing technologies already exist, and more are under development [WR00]. Some, such as the Active Badge system [HH94], provide information about the presence of a user in a region or a room. Other location technologies, such as the Active Bat system [HHSW+99] are much more precise, providing information that is accurate to a few centimetres. All location technologies generate sensor events in response to changes in the locations of locatable objects. The rate at which they are generated is high, especially for high precision location technologies. Only a fraction of the sensor events are of interest to any specific application. The multiplicity of this location information determines the need for a management system. A mechanism is required that will enable applications to see those events that are relevant to its responsibility while filtering out those that are not. Furthermore a uniform way of making this information available in a location-technology independent fashion is needed because of the increasingly varied technologies available. Compounding this requirement will be the usage of various location-technologies together.

In this short paper we outline our approach to meeting these requirements. Section 2 describes our Location Service which tackles these issues. Section 3 details some of our experimental results. We conclude in section 4.

2   Architecture

The research into location information management presented in this paper is part of the QoSDREAM project [QDream01]. QoSDREAM is looking into providing a

G. D. Abowd, B. Brumitt, S. A. N. Shafer (Eds.): Ubicomp 2001, LNCS 2201, pp. 35-41, 2001.
© Springer-Verlag Berlin Heidelberg 2001

middleware platform for developing distributed multimedia applications. Of relevance to this paper is its approach to handling context information and how this information is made available to the rest of the system.

Figure 1 shows the major constituents of the QoSDREAM architecture. It consists of four major parts. At the lowest level we have the **Location Service** It is in charge of gathering location information from specific location-technologies and presenting it to the rest of the system in a location-technology independent fashion. The Location Service's functionality also include managing and filtering the potentially large amount of location information that can be generated. This information is made available to the rest of the system and applications through an **Event Messaging System**. The Event Messaging System distributes events to interested parties and provides a number of filtering services. **The Distributed Multimedia Service** [MNCK99] (not presented in this paper) allows applications to construct and manage, distributed multimedia components. The Distributed Object Database Management Service provides a means of sharing system wide properties such as information about known physical objects. The information held by the database is largely 'static' (i.e. it is not modified very often), although some location-specific data may also be stored with it.

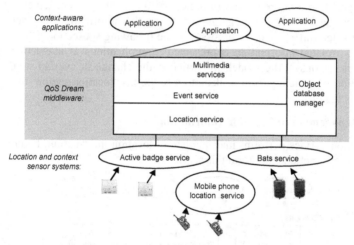

Fig. 1 Overview of QoSDREAM's Architecture

2.1   Location Information

Our Location Service provides location-dependent information. The Location Service is a collection of objects that retrieve location information from existing location sensors and make this information available to QoSDREAM applications. The type of location information available is highly dependent on the location-technologies being used. QoSDREAM's Location Service interprets this information and presents it in a location-technology independent format. This is achieved by representing location information in terms of regions and the interactions between regions.

2.1.1   Modelling Location Information

Within QoSDREAM, applications are presented with a simplified model of the real physical world. This model contains the following abstractions:

- **Locators**, which represent objects whose location can be determined by a given location-technology. Active badges and Bats are examples of Locators.
- **Locatables**, these represent objects whose locations need to be tracked. Examples include people and equipment. Locatables must have at least one associated locator, so that their location can be inferred from its locator.
- **Locatable Regions**. Each locatable will in general have one or more regions. These regions define various location specific characteristics of Locatables. For instance in the case of a person, they may include in addition to the person's location, their visual and audible fields.

The main reason for using regions as a way of presenting location information is the varying degree of precision of location technologies. Active Badges will only place a badge within a room, Active Bats provide more fine-grained information. Expressing location information as regions allows the incorporation of a wide range of location technologies. Furthermore the use of regions also aids in the management of location information particularly with regards to filtering this information in order to reduce location-related traffic. This is discussed in the following subsection.

Location related information is presented to applications as interactions between the various regions in the model. In particular the change in overlap status between regions (For example a person walks into a room, his 'location region' overlaps with the room's region).

2.1.2   Management of Location Information

Our Location Service performs management of location information. Figure 2 depicts the various abstractions that form this service.

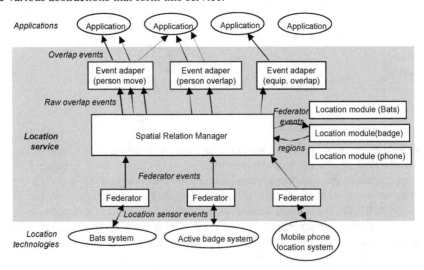

Fig. 2 Location Service Architecture

At the lowest level we have **Federator** objects, these interface with specific location technologies and can detect location information. In our lab we have an 'Active Badge Federator' which is capable of interpreting the data being generated by the Active Badge System. The information gathered by Federators is exported through light-weight events called **Federator Events**. These contain generic information such as the type and id of the federator as well as federator-specific data.

These events can be monitored by applications that require very detailed location information. In general applications are only interested in specific location-related information and so can use other types of events (described below) to receive only events that it is interested in. Federator events are also sent to our **Spatial Relations Manager** (SRM). The SRM's task is to convert information gathered by Federators into overlapping events between the regions in our world model. Before the SRM can reason about the regions and their interactions, **Location Modules** translate Federator events into regions. For example a Location Module for an Active Badge System, would generate a location region for the given locator in the Badge Federator Event. The shape of this region would be the same as that of the room where the locator was detected. This can be derived from the sensorID field in the Federator Event.

Location Modules are Federator-type-specific, and can be loaded from the database by the SRM. The SRM uses the federatorType field of Federator Events to determine the required Location Module.

Once the SRM has obtained updated regions from Location Modules it analyses them looking for changes in overlaps between regions. If those are found then the SRM produces what we call **Raw Overlap Events**. These contain the type of overlap between two regions as well as their previous relationship.

Applications can register to receive these events, but again these events are too general for most applications and cannot be filtered. Instead application register to receive specialised overlap events produced by **EventAdaptors**. These types of events can be filtered and relate to higher level abstractions, such as people and equipment.

EventAdaptors are objects that receive Raw Overlap Events generated by the SRM and can filter and transform these into events that are of interest to applications. The events generated by EventAdaptors are called **OverlapEvents**, and are transmitted by QoSDREAM's Message Service. New EventAdaptors can be easily created and dynamically incorporated into QoSDREAM. By default we provide three types of EventAdaptors:

- **PersonMovement Adaptor**: This generates overlap events when a person's location region overlaps with a geographical location. This event contains a personID and a LocationID fields.
- **PersonOverlap Adapter**: This generates overlap events when a person's location region overlaps with that of another. This event contains a person1ID and person2ID fields.
- **EquipementOverlap Adapter**: This generates overlap events when a person's location region overlaps with that of an equipment. This event contains a personID as well as a equipmentID fields.

Applications are free to choose what events they wish to receive. They can further filter OverlapEvents on the value of the fields in the event. For example, an application interested in the arrival at work of person George can register to receive PersonMovement events whose personID field equals George's id.

To aid with the scalability the representation of the physical world is divided into zones. These zones can be used by the SRM to cut down on the number of regions it must analyse when looking for overlap events. Zoning also allows for a federation of SRMs to be set-up, each of which is responsible for specific zones (as long as those don't overlap). For instance floors in a building might each be handled by a separate SRM.

2.2   Event Messaging Service

The QoSDREAM framework provides an event abstraction that enables applications to register for events by event type. Further selection is performed by event filters which the application can instantiate. Options for event queuing, communication, fault tolerance, event persistence, reliability and security will be offered in a future version of the DREAM framework. The event handling abstraction outlined here is compatible with most general-purpose event handling systems including Corba Events [CDK01], Elvin [ASBB+99, FMK+99] and Herald [BBMS98, Spi00].

QoSDREAM uses events primarily for delivery of contextual information to applications. The messaging service allows application objects to send and receive events and is also used by the Location Service to deliver events generated by EventAdaptors.

The Messaging Service facilitates the management of location information in a number of ways. It allows clients to request the delivery of events without having to know anything about the sources of these events. Similarly event sources do not require any knowledge about their clients. The messaging service also allows applications to specify filters on the events that are sent to it. This coupled with the location service greatly reduces location-related traffic. Without the location service and messaging service, applications would need to monitor all location information generated by the various underlying location technologies.

The Messaging Service is itself independent of the event delivery system used to transfer events from event sources to event clients. Our current implementation of the Messaging Service uses an implementation of the Cambridge Event Architecture called Herald [SPI00] as the event delivery system. Other event delivery systems can be easily added to our Messaging Service by the implementation of a single interface.

3   Experience

We have developed a pilot application for members of our laboratory to use as a communications aid, allowing them to locate one another, establish and participate in audio/visual conferences. It exploits location information provided by the Active Badge System deployed in the laboratory. Table 1 gives an indication of the typical location-specific traffic found in our lab. This traffic was measured over a five minute interval and at the time there were six members of the lab wearing badges.

The ActiveLab application registers interest only in PersonMovement events (in order to update its display). Thus in this application, the QoSDREAM location architecture reduces the event traffic that the application process is required to handle by a factor of approximately 17.

Table 1. Typical location related traffic

Badge Events (Federator Events)	671

These are the events generated by the ActiveBadge Federator. They are generated whenever a badge is picked up by a sensor. Many of the rooms in the lab have more than one sensor and therefore a badge may be picked up by more than one sensor. Most of these events are as a result of a person's badge being detected, since equipment badges emit their signal less often, than badges worn by people.

Raw Overlap Events	204

These are the events generated by the SRM.

PersonMovement Events	12

These events are generated by the PersonMovement Adaptor in response to people moving in and out of rooms.

PersonOverlap Events	40

These are generated by the PersonOverlap Adaptor. In this example those were caused by people moving into rooms where other people were present.

EquipmentOverlap Events	48

These are generated by the EquipmentOverlap Adaptor. Those were caused by people moving into different rooms and their region overlapping with those of the equipment in the new room.

4   Conclusion

We have described an approach to the management of location events derived from a variety of sources and technologies to support the construction of context-aware multimedia applications. Location events are integrated through the generation of overlap events that are constructed by geometric analysis according to the requirements of applications, reducing the incoming event traffic to proportions that are manageable by applications.

For a more comprehensive description of our research including the distributed multimedia framework where the ideas presented in this paper originate please visit our web site at http://www-lce.eng.cam.ac.uk/qosdream

References

[ASBB+99]   David Arnold, Bill Segall, Julian Boot, Andy Bond, Melfyn Lloyd, Simon Kaplan, "Discourse with Disposable Computers: How and why you will talk to your tomatoes", Usenix Workshop on Embedded Systems (ES99), Cambrdige Mass, March 1999. http://www.usenix.org/publications/library/proceedings/es99/full_papers/arnol/arnold_html/

[BBMS98]   J. Bates, J. Bacon, K. Moody and M. D. Spiteri, "Using Events for the Scalable Federation of Heterogeneous Components", Proc. ACM SIGOPS EW'98, Sintra, Portugal, Sep 1998.

[CDK01]   G. Coulouris, J. Dollimore and T. Kinberg, Distributed Systems: Concepts and Design, Edition 3, Addison-Wesley 2001.

[FMK+99]   G. Fitzpatrick, T. Mansfield, S. Kaplan, D. Arnold, T. Phelps, and B. Segall, "Instrumenting and augmenting the workaday world with a generic notification service called Elvin", Proc. ECSCW'99, Copenhagen, Denmark, Sep 1999

[HH94]   A. Harter and A. Hopper, A Distributed Location System for the Active Office. IEEE Network, Vol. 8, No. 1, January 1994.

[HHSW+99]   A. Harter, A. Hopper, P. Steggles, A. Ward and P.Webster, The Anatomy of a Context-Aware Application. In Proceedings of the 5th Annual ACM/IEEE International Conference on Mobile Computing and Networking (Mobicom'99), Seattle, Washington, USA, August 15 - 20 1999 1999. ftp://ftp.uk.research.att.com/pub/docs/att/tr.1999.7.pdf

[Mit00]   R. S. Mitchell, Dynamic Configuration of Distributed Multimedia Components. Ph.D. Thesis, University of London, August 2000. http://www-lce.eng.cam.ac.uk/qosdream/publications/

[MNCK99]   Scott Mitchell, Hani Naguib, George Coulouris and Tim Kindberg, A QoS Support Framework for Dynamically Reconfigurable Multimedia Applications. In Lea Kutvonen, Hartmut König and Martti Tienari (eds), Distributed Applications and Interoperable Systems II, pp 17-30. Kluwer Academic Publishers, Boston, 1999. Also in Proc. DAIS 99. http://www-lce.eng.cam.ac.uk/QoSDREAM/publications/

[MSBC00]   Scott Mitchell, Mark D. Spiteri, John Bates and George Coulouris, "Context-Aware Multimedia Computing in the Intelligent Hospital", In Proc. SIGOPS EW2000, the Ninth ACM SIGOPS European Workshop, Kolding, Denmark, September 2000. http://www-lce.eng.cam.ac.uk/QoSDREAM/publications/

[QDream01] QoSDREAM's project web page. http://www- lce.eng.cam.ac.uk/qosdream/

[Spi00]   M. D. Spiteri, An Architecture for the Notification, Storage and Retrieval of Events, Ph.D. Thesis, University of Cambridge, Jan 2000. http://www-lce.eng.cam.ac.uk/QoSDREAM/publications/

[WR00]   R. Want, D. M. Russell. "Ubiquitous Electronic Tagging". Distributed Systems Online, IEEE 2000. http://www.computer.org/dsonline/articles/ds2wan.htm.

Low Cost Indoor Positioning System*

Cliff Randell and Henk Muller

Department of Computer Science, University of Bristol, UK

Abstract. This report describes a low cost indoor position sensing system utilising a combination of radio frequency and ultrasonics. Using a single rf transmitter and four ceiling mounted ultrasonic transmitters it provides coverage in a typical room in an area greater than 8m by 8m. As well as finding position within a room, it uses data encoded into the rf signal to determine the relevant web server for a building, and which floor and room the user is in. It is intended to be used primarily by wearable/mobile computers, though it has also been extended for use as a tracking system.

1 Introduction and Background

There are three technologies commonly used for indoor location systems - ultrasonics, infrared and rf. These can be supplemented by inertial systems which are generally used for prediction. Infrared systems tend to rely on the user taking explicit actions to identify their presence [1] [2]; and rf-systems require sophisticated (and often cumbersome) aerials [3] [4] - ultrasonics offer a low cost solution which can operate without any user interaction. The disadvantages of an ultrasonic system are loss of signal due to obstruction; false signals due to reflections; and interference from high frequency sounds such as keys jangling, rustling paper etc. These disadvantages can be minimised and systems produced by commercial suppliers such as Intersense [5] and AT&T [6] [7] have successfully implemented ultrasonic positioning with impressive results. These commercial systems are too expensive for use by the average researcher - typically costing over U.S.$15,000. The Cricket Location-Support System developed by researchers at M.I.T. [8] provides low cost position estimation designed to achieve portion-of-a-room granularity using a network of beacons. We describe a simple system which can be implemented for around U.S.$150 and gives results providing accuracies of 10-25cm.

It is intended that this design is used to complement external positioning using GPS and hence provide results which have similar characteristics. For example, a typical GPS application will detect position in a 1km x 1km city centre to within 15m. We aim to be able to detect position in a 10m x 10m room to within 15cm. This system does not provide the accuracies achieved by commercial systems, nor does it provide continuous resolution between cells, nevertheless this simple design is suitable for many research applications.

---

* Funding for this work is received from the U.K. Engineering and Physical Sciences Research Council, Grant No. 15986

G. D. Abowd, B. Brumitt, S. A. N. Shafer (Eds.): Ubicomp 2001, LNCS 2201, pp. 42–48, 2001.

2 Design

To determine position in a 3D space using trilateration we require three distance measurements. In this system we use a rf signal - or 'ping' - as a synchronising pulse followed by four precisely timed ultrasonic signals - or 'chirps'. This arrangment allows the 'times-of-flight' between the four separately located transmitting transucers and the receiver to be determined. These times-of-flight are converted to distances by factoring them with the speed of sound. We use four to increase the range of the system and to compensate for occasions when one signal is lost - it also simplifies the geometric calculations.

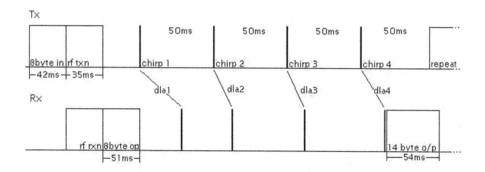

Fig. 1. Timing diagram (not to scale)

The ping, containing an eight byte coded packet broadcast by a 418MHz FM short range transmitter, ensures that the receiver is synchronised to the transmitter. The packet consists of an identifier byte, an IP address, floor and room number bytes and a spare byte which can be dynamically assignable to assist with two way communication e.g. for a tracking system which requires each new user entering the room to register with the system. The maximum range of the ping is 100m, though this can be reduced to enable separate systems to operate in adjacent rooms.

The chirps consist of 48 cycles - 1.2ms - of 40kHz generated by a PIC microcontroller and are transmitted sequentially at 50ms intervals as shown in Figure 1. We use 48 cycles as 1ms of signal is relatively easy to identify using simple test equipment. Theoretically it should be possible to reduce this to 3 cycles. Open face piezo transducers manufactured by Polaroid [9] have been selected to give optimum results. These devices provide the widest possible transmission angle combined with high output(tx)/high sensitivity(rx).

The four ultrasonic transmitters are mounted, facing vertically downwards, on the ceiling of the room to be covered. They are placed at the corners of a square and connected to the transmitter module which contains the ultrasonic drivers, the microcontroller and rf transmitter. In our 4.2m x 6.5m test room we have obtained satisfactory results using 2m, 3m, and 4m square configurations with a ceiling height of 3.2m.

The receiver uses a matching rf receiver, decoder and PIC microcontroller. A dual operational amplifier is used to provide additional control over how the incoming ultrasonic signal is processed. These components are mounted in a small module which is either attached to a palmtop or handheld computer with a graphic display, or, in the case of a wearable, placed on the shoulder of the user. A rechargeable PP3 9v battery can provide sufficient power for a full day's operation. A feature of this design is the potential for an unlimited number of receivers to operate in the area covered.

We experimented with various ultrasonic receiver configurations and signal processing techniques including envelope detection, bandpass filters and various gain settings. We concluded that a single transducer with a simple high gain amplifier with high pass filtering is sufficient. Experiments with multiple receiving transducers to provide omnidirectional reception were prone to picking up reflections; envelope detection introduced both delay and uncertainty; and bandpass filters were unnecessary as the sensing device is highly resonant.

The PIC is programmed to measure the number of 100us delay units occuring between transmission and reception of each chirp. These delay units correspond to 3.4cm, giving an optimum resolution of 2.4cm at one and a half metres below the centre of the transmitter square. The delay units are combined with the eight bytes from the pinger and passed to a RS232 output.

Extensions to the basic design include using additional transducers for greater coverage - a six transducer system has been successfully tested with transducers placed 7m above the floor giving coverage over an area of 10m by 18m. Larger configurations are feasible with the penalty of a slower response. An electronic compass has also been successfully integrated to provide heading as well as position data and work is underway to include an accelerometer for tilt sensing. A tracking system is under test using a 802.11 wireless network to send the analysed data via the internet to remote locations (see Figure 3).

3   Results and Data Analysis

3.1   Results

The resulting raw data is illustrated as a histogram in Figure 2. This shows 100 error readings obtained when the receiver was placed at x=0, y=0, and 2m below the ceiling. The maximum error is 10cm - this is an optimal result with accuracy degrading to around 25cm around the perimeter of the test room.

As we are detecting the first cycle of each chirp, and are not interested in the envelope of the signal, reflections are not relevant - except when the direct signal is blocked. This can be a problem when the user is close to, and facing, a wall resulting in the apparent position being on the other side of the wall. Obstruction of the chirps is the main cause of failure of the system. While only three of the four chirps are required, and this situation frequently arises when the

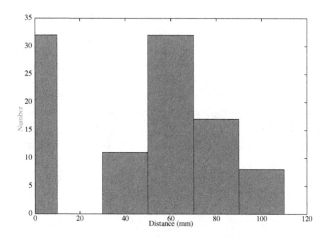

Fig. 2. Errors at x=0,y=0

user is directly between a transmitter and receiver, the problem only becomes serious when a number of people crowd around the receiver. The system is also affected by high level environmental ultrasonic noise, however in practice these sounds are usually short lived.

3.2   Data Analysis

Post processing of the time-of-flight data is carried out in the host computer - in our experiments we have employed Windows CE based devices (H-P Jornada palmtops and handhelds). This configuration enables the use of simple algorithms, as well as trilateration, to resolve the precise position of the user from the raw data. The primary techniques which have been found to be effective are:-

- **Best Signal Selection** - Initially, where more than three good signals were received, the results were averaged. This retained the poorest quality signal but made use of all the data available. An improved result was obtained by selecting the three shortest time-of-flight paths and using these for the position calculation.

- **Non-Incident Angle Compensation** - The most accurate results are obtained when the transmitting and receiving transducers are incident. A formula has been derived by experiment to compensate for non-incident reception.

- **Threshold Filtering** - the cursor indicating current position on a graphic display suffered from jitter. This effect was eliminated by the introduction of a threshold over which a change in x or y position had to exceed.

- **Speed Limit** - occasional spurious readings which indicate large changes in position can be identified and filtered by imposing a 'speed limit'. This is in two stages. The first stage simply limits movements to a maximum of 1 m/s. The second stage rejects any reading which indicates a movement exceeding 2 m/s.

- **2D Estimation** - where only two paths can be measured it is still possible to calculate a x,y position if the z co-ordinate (height) is estimated e.g. at waist level. In this case there are two possible x,y solutions, however only one of these solutions will apply in locations where there are only two received signals. Use of this algorithm extends the area covered to well beyond the area directly beneath the ultrasonic transducers.

- **Averaging** - The final readings used for the application interface takes the average of the current reading and the previous reading. This is effective in reducing errors and provides a smoother trajectory when moving across a room. The disadvantage is the inherent delay in this approach. This delay is less than 500ms and was considered acceptable.

The value of these algorithms varied according to the application. For example, if the speed limit was set at a low value e.g. 0.5m/s, feedback to the user using a graphic map display was considered to suffer from unacceptable lag. On the other hand the smoothing effect of a low speed limit for a remote viewer was found to make the tracking more acceptable.

4   Applications

Our first application has been designed to test and demonstrate the potential of the system. We have previously built a tourist application for use outdoors [10]. This application automatically renders web pages on a palmtop display when a visitor reaches a place of interest whose co-ordinates match the current position as determined by a GPS receiver. To test our indoor location system we are using an equivalent application which provides web pages related to objects in a room e.g. a computer terminal has a web page which gives it's name, associated administrator, printer and IP address. In practice this worked well enabling users to seek out and discover hidden information in the test room.

User tests were also carried out during a workshop linking a 'real' room with a Reactor (a CAVE like device [11]) in which a model of the room was projected. The user in the room was tracked using the receiver attached to a handheld device - see Figure 3 - and appeared as an avatar in the Reactor. The participants successfully explored the room - in reality and in the model - relating to the relative positions of each other and the objects in the room. Satisfaction with the x/y tracking was reported, however users in the Reactor commented on the avatar 'jumping' as a result of instability in the z axis data.

Further systems are being installed as part of other projects associated with the Equator EPSRC Project [12]. These projects aim to uncover and support the possible relationships between the physical and digital worlds. They include installations in a domestic setting to investigate models of spatial awareness and service discovery; in a 10m by 30m atrium to facilitate the discovery of hidden

Fig. 3. The prototype receiver in use with a handheld computer

worlds, and also to enable interaction with virtual performers; and for a user in a museum to provide a shared experience to a remote companion.

5 Conclusion

We have designed and built an effective indoor positioning system using a minimal infrastructure and readily available components. This system is relatively simple to install, requires no calibration after the initial installation, and has a low price tag. Sample applications have been tested with subjective results comparable to those obtained using GPS in an outdoor setting. The system can easily be adapted to provide extended coverage, and it's performance is suitable for facilitating many different virtual and augmented reality research projects.

References

1. R. Want and A. Hopper. The active badge location system. In *ACM Transactions on Information Systems*, pages 91–102, January 1992. 42
2. H-p cooltown home page. http://www.cooltown.com/. 42
3. F. Raab, E. Blood, T. Steiner, and T. Jones. Magnetic position and orientation tracking system. In *IEEE Transactions on Aerospace and Electronic Systems*, volume AES-15 no.5, pages 709–718, September 1979. 42
4. Polhemus home page. http://www.polhemus.com/. 42
5. Intersense home page. http://www.isense.com/. 42
6. A. Ward, A. Jones, and A. Hopper. A new location technique for the active office. In *IEEE Personal Communications Magazine*, volume 4 no.5, pages 42–47, October 1997. 42

7. A. Harter, A. Hopper, P. Steggles, A. Ward, and P. Webster. The anatomy of a context-aware application. In *Proceedings of the Fifth Annual ACM/IEEE International Conference on Mobile Computing and Networking*, pages 59–68, August 1999. 42

8. N. Priyantha, A. Chakraborty, and H. Balakrishnan. The cricket location-support system. In *6th ACM/IEEE International Conference on Mobile Computing and Networking.*, August 2000. 42

9. Polaroid home page. http://www.polaroid-oem.com/. 43

10. C. Randell. Design and construction of wearable computers. In *IEE Seminar - Wearable Computing*, pages 8/1–4. The Institution of Electrical Engineers, November 2000. 46

11. C. Cruz-Neira, D. Sandin, and T. DeFanti. Virtual reality: The design and implementation of the cave. In *Proceedings of SIGGRAPH 93 Computer Graphics Conference*, pages 135–142, August 1993. 46

12. Equator home page. http://www.equator.ac.uk/. 46

Making Everyday Life Easier
Using Dense Sensor Networks

W. Steven Conner[1], Lakshman Krishnamurthy[1], and Roy Want[2]

[1] Intel Architecture Labs, Intel Corporation,
Hillsboro, OR
{w.steven.conner,lakshman.krishnamurthy}@intel.com
[2] Intel Research, Intel Corporation,
Santa Clara, CA
roy.want@intel.com

Abstract. Advances in hardware are enabling the creation of small, inexpensive devices and sensors. Hundreds or thousands of these devices can be connected using low-power multi-hop wireless networks. These networks foster a new class of ubiquitous computing applications called proactive computing. In proactive applications, computing occurs in the background without requiring human interaction; humans participate to access information or to modify control policies. This paper provides an overview of the application of a large wireless network of sensors to solve everyday problems in the workplace. It describes the implementation of one application that allows people in the workplace to easily find empty conference rooms (e.g., for impromptu meetings). Drawing on this experience, we identify technical challenges and possible directions for building dense networks of sensors that enable proactive computing.

1   Introduction

The current generation of interactive devices and networks fosters a class of interactive ubiquitous computing applications [7]. These applications deliver information or provide services such as email, appointments, stock quotes, or multimedia to devices such as PDAs, cellular phones, and portable computers. Human participation in the compute-loop dominates these applications. Another class of ubiquitous-computing applications has been termed proactive computing [4]. In this class, computing occurs without human interaction; data is pre-processed and available on demand. Many of these applications connect users with the real world using networked sensors.

Today millions of sensors are deployed throughout the world. These include climate-monitoring sensors, safety and security devices, and traffic monitoring sensors that detect vehicles at intersections. In most cases, sensors are local to a specific application and access to sensor output is only available at that location. While these sensors serve many useful purposes for the individuals who rely on them,

G. D. Abowd, B. Brumitt, S. A. N. Shafer (Eds.): Ubicomp 2001, LNCS 2201, pp. 49-55, 2001.

many new applications emerge if these devices are made available through remote access and can be controlled through the network. These applications make everyday tasks easier and enhance our ability to examine and optimize the environments in which we live and work

Our research project in Intel Architecture Labs is investigating the network protocols and architectures required to realize ubiquitous access to sensor networks. To drive the investigation of the sensor network research space, we have identified a number of compelling applications in the Intel facilities, which we consider to be typical of many office environments. These applications are built using networks of low-cost, low-powered radios that are well-suited for connecting large numbers of sensors in an office environment.   This paper describes these ubiquitous sensor network applications and implementation and provides an overview of the challenges that need to be solved to realize the widespread deployment of the underlying sensor network.

2   Ubiquitous Sensor Network Applications Making Everyday Life Easier

Figure 1(a) illustrates several sensor network applications that make life easier in an office building, ranging from alleviating congestion in popular facilities to monitoring and maintaining environmental conditions.   In large buildings, it is difficult to maintain uniform environmental conditions across entire floors.   On occasion people may complain about the ambient temperature in cubicles or conference rooms. For example, people near windows may feel too warm due to direct sun, while others in the interior of the building may complain that it is too cold. Deployment of a wireless network of inexpensive temperature sensors provides us with a system that can support temperature-sensing applications and services in such an environment, to benefit people in the building as well as assist in maintenance.

It is also a common problem for people to encounter congestion and long lines in day-to-day use of facilities such as cafeterias, conference rooms, exercise rooms, vending rooms, and restrooms. Mostly, this is not due to the lack of facilities in a building; instead it results from a non-optimal usage pattern. For example, when one vending/microwave room is full of people, another down the hall may be empty. Motion detectors and sensors in doorways can be deployed to monitor and count the number of people occupying various facilities. By networking these devices and making their real-time output available in a pervasive fashion, people can quickly identify available resources, saving valuable time and eliminating frustration. On the other hand, such a network may also be used for identifying locations with large collections of people, implying that something interesting may be happening in that area.

The following is a description of the implementation of one particular sensor network application that enables people to quickly find empty conference rooms.

2.1   Implementation of a Sensor Network Application to Help People Find Empty Conference Rooms

In modern office complexes such as Intel, closed-wall offices have been replaced with high-density cubicles to inspire an atmosphere of open collaboration and accessibility among people in the building. However, the lack of private offices generates a problem when people wish to have impromptu meetings. Buildings are equipped with conference rooms, but these rooms may be reserved days or weeks in advance and it is often not possible to reserve a room with little or no notice. However, meetings commonly do not last the entire reservation time, thus it is common for people to wander around a building in search of an empty room for an impromptu meeting. We have built a system that provides people access to room usage status and allows them to find empty rooms from handhelds and PCs.

Many conference rooms are equipped with motion detectors that turn off the lights in an empty room. In most cases these motion sensors are hard-wired to the light switch in the same room and are not accessible from outside. In one building at Intel, we have networked motion detectors together using multi-hop network protocols implemented on a collection of inexpensive, low-power wireless radio nodes [1,2]. Each node has a transmission range of approximately 20 to 30 feet, and our initial prototype uses controlled multi-hop flooding to enable communication and the sharing of room occupancy status throughout the building. The topology of this prototype sensor network is shown in Figure 1 (b).

In this network, a gateway node receives sensor data which is aggregated and stored on a server to provide status information to desktop users over the web. Figure 1 (a) shows a sample screen shot from a web application that provides people with live occupancy information for rooms in a particular building floor. By referring to this webpage before leaving their desks to search for conference rooms, people are able to save time by walking directly to rooms that are reported empty.

We have connected PDAs directly to the sensor network, allowing mobile users to obtain usage information from the nearby conference rooms themselves. Due to the multi-hop nature of the network, contextual location information can be presented to mobile users, without the need for GPS, simply by querying only those sensors within a few radio hops of their location. Figure 2 (b) illustrates a PDA application showing the occupancy status of nearby conference rooms.

In addition to providing live occupancy data, motion detector data may also be compiled across days or weeks for future analysis. Figure 2 (c) illustrates an application to compare actual detected room usage statistics to reservation data from the online conference room reservation system. Such data provides the opportunity to automatically identify individuals who consistently reserve rooms without canceling reservations for rescheduled meetings. Moreover, collected usage data can be analyzed by facility analysts to understand usage patterns in a typical office building. Building planners can use this information to plan the design of buildings by providing statistics on the typical usage pattern of conference rooms.

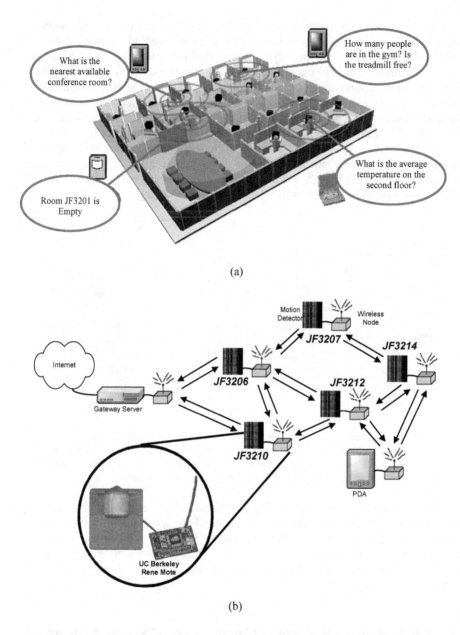

(a)

(b)

Figure 1. Example sensor networks.   (a) Applications to make life easier in a typical large office environment. (b) Multi-hop wireless topology of a sensor network to help people find empty conference rooms. This sensor network is comprised of motion detectors interfaced to UC Berkeley Rene Motes (http://tinyos.millennium.berkeley.edu).   At the time of writing our network consists of 36 motes; we are in the process of creating a network with 150 motes

It is worth noting that several other systems have previously been developed for locating people in an office environment, such as the Active Badge [5] and Active Bat [6] location systems. While these systems have different goals, they could be adapted to enable similar facility usage-monitoring applications. A primary difference between our multi-hop approach and the Active Badge system is the infrastructure cost and deployment effort. The Active Badge sensors were connected by a wired network, resulting in a very high labor cost for deployment of an active badge system in a typical industrial setting. Wireless sensors are far better suited to retrofitting existing buildings. Another difference is that by using simple inexpensive sensors to monitor the office environment, instead of identification tags, our system maintains the anonymity of people in the building, reducing the privacy concerns of individuals who do not wish to be tracked as they move through a building.

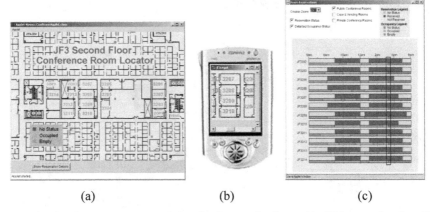

(a)   (b)   (c)

Figure 2. Conference room status monitoring applications. (a) Webpage showing live conference room occupancy status for rooms in the second floor of the JF3 building. (b) PDA application showing status of rooms in the vicinity of the mobile user. (c) Occupancy history application comparing actual usage data to conference room reservations

By adding inexpensive networking capabilities to pre-existing motion detectors that are designed for a particular application, a whole new range of applications are enabled that enhance the day-to-day lives of people in the building and provide the opportunity for optimization of facility usage. Our work uses these applications to explore the challenges in networking sensors and enabling ubiquitous access to information obtained from them.

3   Challenges for Widespread Deployment of Sensor Networks

The prototype implementation and deployment of the conference room occupancy monitoring sensor network demonstrates the power of communication to greatly increase the utility of simple sensor devices. Our objective when building this application was to develop a hands-on understanding of the real-world challenges related to deploying dense sensor networks. In this section, we provide an overview of the challenges in this space and the direction we are taking to solve them.

As we increase the size of our motion detector network toward a total of 150 nodes, it has become clear that we want to avoid the tedious requirements of optimally placing each individual node and configuring each node with topology and routing information. Based on this experience, dense sensor networks must have the ability to self-organize. As long as enough nodes are deployed to enable redundant communication paths, the network should be able to automatically configure routes and reconfigure itself when nodes fail or are added to the network. Such self-organization will significantly lighten the burden on administrators and increase the rate of deployment of compelling new applications.

Another challenge we encountered is that it is not always feasible to constrain sensors to be located near power outlets, even in buildings where these outlets are relatively abundant. For example, motion detectors are best positioned high on a corner wall to have a clear view of an entire room. Running new wires to sensors is expensive and time consuming, thus they must be able to run using batteries or scavenge their energy from the environment. In our motion detector network, the seemingly simple job of replacing batteries at every node also turns out to be very tedious. Under these circumstances energy is an expensive commodity, requiring network architecture and protocol solutions to conserve energy, maximize the lifetime of the network, and work in a resource-constrained environment.

While controlled flooding provided a convenient communication solution for the initial prototype of the conference room network, this technique does not scale well and is inefficient in the use of energy and bandwidth. Efficient data acquisition mechanisms [3] must be implemented to allow data to be gathered. To minimize communication in an effort to preserve energy, application-specific processing may be implemented within the network to aggregate and compress data as it is being routed toward a consumer node. In the conference room application, data was proactively acquired at a gateway server, aggregated, and made available to people and services over the Internet. This is the first step toward realizing the ubiquitous computing vision of data available anywhere at anytime. Protocols must also support mobile local consumers within the sensor field, who generally benefit from location-context support. As demonstrated in the conference room application, radio connectivity is one method that can be used to obtain information relevant to mobile user locations.

4   Conclusion

On a closing note, it is important to note the importance of maintaining the privacy of people who live or work in environments monitored by sensor networks. This particularly becomes a problem, for example, when networks and applications are able to track individuals as they move through a building. However, a number of interesting applications exist, such as those described in this paper, that provide useful information about the conditions and use of a building environment without gaining knowledge about the individuals who are in that environment.

The wide deployment of dense collections of networked sensors has the potential to greatly impact our everyday lives by making mundane tasks easier and enhancing our ability to examine and optimize the environments we inhabit. Just as modern computing systems are analyzed and optimized by instrumenting them with code to track their performance, inexpensive sensor networks provide the opportunity to instrument the real world around us. The conference room occupancy monitoring sensor network deployed at Intel has provided the opportunity to demonstrate the benefits of sensor networks in the everyday lives of people in a large office building. At the same time, this prototype network has served as a learning tool to investigate the challenges involved in progressing this technology to the point where it can be widely adopted.

We would like to acknowledge David Culler and Jason Hill at UC Berkeley as well as Marc Davis, Steven Fordyce, and Jasmeet Chhabra for their assistance in building the UC Berkeley motes used to implement the conference room monitoring sensor network.

References

1. UC Berkeley Mote and TinyOS. http://tinyos.millennium.berkeley.edu.
2. Hill, J., Szewczyk, R., Woo, A., Hollar, S., Culler, D., Pister, K. "System Architecture Directions for Networked Sensors". U.C. Berkeley, submitted for publication April 2000.
3. Intanagonwiwat, C., Govindan, R., Estrin, D., "Directed Diffusion: A Scalable and Robust Communication Paradigm for Sensor Networks". *ACM MOBICOM,* 2000.
4. Tennenhouse, D. "Proactive Computing", *Communications of the ACM,* May 2000, Vol.43, No 5.
5. Want, R., Hopper, A., Falcao, V., Gibbons, J. "The Active Badge Location System." *ACM Transactions on Information Systems,* Vol. 10, No. 1, January 1992, pp 91-102.
6. Ward, A., Jones, A., Hopper, A. "A New Location Technique for the Active Office." *IEEE Personal Communications,* Vol. 4, No. 5, October 1997, pp. 42-47.
7. Weiser, M. "The Computer for the 21st Century", *Scientific American,* September 1991 Vol. 265 No. 3, pp94-104.

ICrafter: A Service Framework for Ubiquitous Computing Environments

Shankar R. Ponnekanti, Brian Lee, Armando Fox,
Pat Hanrahan, and Terry Winograd

Stanford University

Abstract. In this paper, we propose ICrafter, a framework for services and their user interfaces in a class of ubiquitous computing environments. The chief objective of ICrafter is to let users flexibly interact with the services in their environment using a variety of modalities and input devices. We extend existing service frameworks in three ways. First, to offload services and user input devices, ICrafter provides infrastructure support for UI selection, generation, and adaptation. Second, ICrafter allows UIs to be associated with service patterns for on-the-fly aggregation of services. Finally, ICrafter facilitates the design of service UIs that are portable but still reflect the context of the local environment. In addition, we also focus on the system properties such as incremental deployability and robustness that are critical for ubiquitous computing environments. We describe the goals and architecture of ICrafter, a prototype implementation that validates its design, and the key lessons learnt from our experiences.

1 Introduction

In this paper, we propose ICrafter: a service framework for a class of ubiquitous computing environments known as *interactive workspaces* [6]. An interactive workspace is a physically co-located, technology-rich space consisting of interconnected computers (desktops, laptops, handhelds, etc), utility devices (scanners, printers, etc) and I/O devices (large wall-mounted and table-top displays, microphones, speakers, etc), where people gather (with their own laptops, handhelds, etc) to do naturally collaborative activities such as design reviews, brainstorming, etc. Example interactive workspaces include conference/meeting rooms and lecture halls.

The main objective of ICrafter is to allow users of interactive workspaces to flexibly interact with the *services* in the workspace. By *service*, we refer to a device (such as a light, projector, or a scanner) or an application (such as a web browser or Microsoft PowerPoint running on a large display) that provides useful functions to end-users. Users interact with the services using a variety of access/input devices (such as laptops, handhelds, etc). We use the term *appliance* to refer to such an access/input device. (In other words, service UIs run on appliances.) ICrafter is a framework that allows developers to deploy services and to create user interfaces to these services for various user appliances.

G. D. Abowd, B. Brumitt, S. A. N. Shafer (Eds.): Ubicomp 2001, LNCS 2201, pp. 56–75, 2001.

The design goals of ICrafter stem from our experiences with users in *iRoom*, a prototype interactive workspace at Stanford, which serves as the experimental testbed for our research. Many of these goals arise from fundamental character-istics of ubiquitous computing environments, such as heterogeneity, presence of legacy components, and incremental evolution. We have implemented a proto-type of the ICrafter framework in iRoom and have developed several services (and their UIs) using the framework.

Recent years have seen a spate of interest in service and UI frameworks for ubiquitous computing environments. Several industry and research projects have proposed various frameworks such as Jini [9], UPnP [17], Hodes et al. [10,11], and Roman et al. [12]. ICrafter extends the existing work in three important ways:

1. ICrafter places intelligence in the infrastructure to select, generate, and/or adapt service UIs. This helps offload services and appliances and has several advantages such as extensibility, and better handling of legacy services and resource-limited appliances.
2. ICrafter provides a novel scheme for "on-the-fly" aggregation of services.
3. ICrafter facilitates creation of UIs that are portable across workspaces but still reflect the context of the current workspace.

The rest of the paper presents the goals, architecture, and implementation of ICrafter. We also present several examples that illustrate its use and the lessons we have learned from our experiences.

2   Design Goals

The objectives of the ICrafter framework may be separated into three over-arching goals: *adaptability, deployability,* and *aggregation.* We believe that the first two goals are not specific to this framework alone but are central to ubiqui-tous computing in general, because heterogeneity, legacy components, and incre-mental evolution are the norm rather than the exception in these environments.

2.1   Adaptability

Interactive workspaces are characterized by heterogeneity at both the appliance-level and the workspace-level. (The workspaces themselves maybe widely dif-ferent depending on their physical geometries and which sets of devices they contain.) Thus, the framework should facilitate adaptation to these two types of heterogeneity.

Appliance adaptation. The framework should not only support several modal-ities (e.g. a gesture-based UI or a voice-based UI), but also different appliances with the same modality (e.g. a handheld computer vs. a pen-and-tablet form factor computer vs. the screen of a user's laptop). Also, appliances can vary widely in resources.

Workspace adaptation. The framework should allow the generated UIs to include *contextual information relevant to that workspace*, which helps the user identify the association between the UI elements and the environment. This association may be established by human readable descriptions (e.g., a projector control interface that says "projector for middle screen"), layout of interface elements (e.g., a light interface that positions widgets to indicate the actual physical positions of corresponding lights in that space), or by some other means. The challenge is to facilitate the design of UIs that can be reused across workspaces. It is impractical to hand-design UIs for common services at each installation for every appliance.

2.2 Deployability

For the framework to be easily deployable and evolvable, it must satisfy the following requirements.

Flexibility in language/ OS/ UI toolkit support. The system should not force the use of particular programming languages, UI languages, or operating systems, since it is unlikely that a single programming language and/or UI language will work for all devices in the near future. Also, supporting off-the-shelf UI renderers such as web browsers is essential.

Spectrum of UIs. It is impractical to manually design UIs for all services for each appliance, especially considering the incremental evolution inherent in this environment. When a new service is added, ideally it should be accessible without the necessity of having to manually design UIs for every appliance. Similarly, adding a new appliance must not force writing UIs for that appliance for all existing services. Thus, support for (possibly partial) automatic UI generation is desirable. On the other hand, because effective UI design is an art, the framework should allow the presentation of custom-designed UIs. The framework should therefore support a spectrum of UIs ranging from fully hand-designed custom UIs to automatically generated UIs.

Robustness. A complex system with many components must handle partial failures gracefully for deployment to be practical. Partial failures may be software-related (a service fails, or some component of the UI-generating infrastructure fails) or hardware-related (a physical device fails or stops responding).

2.3 Aggregation

The framework must facilitate the creation of user interfaces for combinations of services. Users often need to control several services simultaneously to perform a task, such as a presentation or a meeting; for example, during a slide presentation, it is convenient to aggregate the lighting controls with the slide show controls (start the slide show, etc.)

To the best of our knowledge, all existing frameworks attach UIs to individual services, which makes it difficult to control groups of services. Of course, an ad-hoc UI can be generated by just naively grouping together all the individual service UIs, but there is more to controlling a group of services than simply controlling each one separately. For example, suppose that a user wishing to take a picture from a camera and print it requests the UI for the camera and the printer. If an ad-hoc union of the camera UI and printer UI were returned, the user would still have to request the camera to take a picture, save it in a temporary location, upload the saved picture to the printer, and request for printing.

Ideally, a UI for the camera-printer combination should "recognize" that the two can be composed in a useful manner (that is, the output of the camera can be sent to the printer) and allow the user to do this as easily as possible. Of course, all existing frameworks allow creating a new specific printer-camera service, which in turn accesses the printer and the camera. However, creating services for every combination of services is impractical (the number of combinations explodes combinatorially). Thus, another goal of ICrafter is service aggregation without necessarily requiring the creation of composite services.

3   Architecture

In this section, we present the ICrafter architecture and explain how it achieves the goals enumerated in the previous section. In the ICrafter framework, user appliances request UIs for services from an infrastructure-centric component called the *interface manager (IM)* as shown in figure 1. When the IM receives a request for UI for one or more services, it first selects one or more *generators* based on the requesting appliance and the service(s) for which the UI was requested. (A generator is a software entity that can generate a UI for one or more services for a particular appliance). Next, the IM "executes" the generators and returns the generated UI to the requesting appliance. To generate the UIs, generators need access to information about the services, appliance, and the workspace context. This information is provided as follows:

- Services beacon [1] their presence, and the beacons include the *service descriptions* (information about the service, such as the operations supported by the service).
- When an appliance requests a UI from the IM, it supplies an *appliance description* that provides information about the appliance (such as number of pixels).

---

[1] A beacon is a periodic announcement to a broadcast medium which any other entity on the medium can "listen" to.

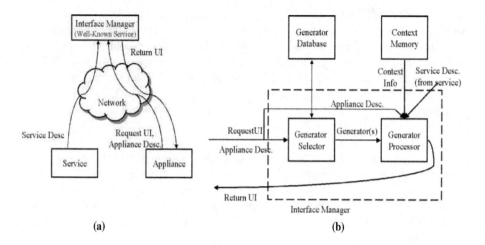

Fig. 1. ICrafter Architecture. Appliances request UIs from the Interface Manager while supplying an appliance description. The Interface Manager first selects appropriate UI generators based on the requesting appliance and the services for which the UI was requested. Next, it executes the generators with access to the service descriptions, appliance description, and the context to generate the UI

- Information about the workspace context is contained in a central datastore called the *context memory*.

Thus, when the generators are executed in the IM, they are provided access to the service descriptions, appliance description, and the context memory. Next, we explain how we address the design goals laid out in section 2 using the above framework.

3.1   Designing for Adaptability

Among existing approaches, the Hodes approach [10,11] best handles appliance heterogeneity. In this approach, if the service does not supply a predefined UI suitable for the appliance, the appliance-side generates a suitable UI for itself from the service description. However, if the appliance is resource-limited, there is a need for alternatives, such as appliance-side proxies. We apply ideas from previous research in related domains [7] to generalize this approach by allowing "intelligence" to exist in the IM (i.e., a third party other than the service or the appliance) to handle UI selection, generation, or adaptation. This lets the resource-rich, infrastructure-based IM select, adapt, or generate a suitable UI based on the requesting appliance.

We also rely on this level of indirection to handle workspace heterogeneity. We cleanly separate workspace context information from the UIs and store the workspace context information in the context memory. To avoid hard-coding workspace information in the UIs, we stipulate that UI generators (and not UIs) be hand-designed. The generators can access the workspace context information from the context memory and generate the actual UIs. Examples of workspace context information include physical locations and dimensions of various devices (such as lights and displays), descriptive information about the devices (e.g., "Display1" is the "front display", etc), and device relationship information (e.g., "projector2" projects onto display "screen1").

An alternative to a centralized context memory would be to allow each generator to read the workspace context information from its own configuration file. However, this approach requires keeping the configuration files for all generators for the same service synchronized. Furthermore, changes in multiple files may be required if the room geometry changes. These kinds of administration are simplified when such information is centralized. Other advantages of centralizing context are explained in [20].

3.2 Designing for Deployability

We accommodate incremental evolution by allowing for a range of generators, ranging from fully custom to fully generic. Fully generic generators are service-independent (but appliance-specific) and can generate a UI for any service for a particular appliance, and they enable rapid integration of new services and appliances. However, generators specific to a particular service class (such as InFocus projectors) can also be written and in the extreme case, they can also be written for a particular service instance. Since the generators are run in the infrastructure by default, they can be resource-intensive if necessary even if the resulting UIs may actually be simple.

Service descriptions in ICrafter contain only the service operations and their parameters. They do not contain machine names, port numbers, URLs, or UI elements unlike previous approaches [11,12,17]. This avoids the need for modifying the descriptions on a per-instance basis.

ICrafter is also designed to allow UIs for widely-deployed "legacy" renderers such as web browsers. Generic protocol gateways convert from the renderers' transport protocols (such as HTTP) to ICrafter protocols.

3.3 Designing for Aggregation

As mentioned in section 2, there is a need for creating UIs for combinations of services without necessarily having to create composite services for all combinations of services. Unlike existing frameworks, we allow UIs to be attached to groups of services rather than individual services. However, while useful, this only provides a partial solution, because this still requires creation of UIs (if not composite services) for every combination of services.

We propose a novel approach that exploits *service interfaces* to address this challenge. Here the term interface refers to programmatic interface (as in the interfaces defined by the keyword `interface` in Java), not user interface. It is general practice in object-oriented languages such as Java to have classes implement generic interfaces that represent particular behaviors. Similarly, services can also implement generic interfaces representing particular behaviors. Most devices (such as lights, projectors, etc) can implement a PowerSwitchInterface that contains the methods poweron and poweroff. Similarly, the printer can implement a DataConsumer interface while the camera can implement a DataProducer interface.[2] We then allow generators to be written for *patterns* of interfaces. For example, a generator can be written for a data consumer-data producer pattern. Such a generator can not only be used by camera-printer combination, but also by a scanner-display combination, a scanner-printer combination, etc.

When a user requests an interface for a camera and a printer, the IM searches for matching generators and finds the consumer-producer generator. Of course, the UI produced by this generator does not allow the user to perform operations specific to the camera or the printer (such as adjusting the zoom). However, these operations can be performed using the individual camera and printer UIs. Thus, the IM can (for example) return a simple aggregate of the producer-consumer UI, the printer UI, and the camera UI.

As another example, a simple generator can be written for one or more PowerSwitchInterface implementing services, that allows all these services to be powered on or off. Suppose the user requests a UI for all the lights in the room and a projector. The UI produced by PowerSwitchInterface generator can allow all the lights and 'the projector to be turned on with a single action.

4   Implementation

In this section, we describe the prototype implementation of ICrafter framework in the iRoom. The block diagram of the prototype is depicted in figure 2. The EventHeap [5] is a flexible event-based communication system used by all iRoom applications. The EventHeap is conceptually based on the tuplespace/blackboard model espoused by LINDA [1] and is currently implemented using IBM TSpaces [18]. Processes post events to the shared EventHeap and can subscribe to events matching a specified pattern. While the prototype ICrafter implementation uses the EventHeap, it can also be implemented using other communication abstractions such as RPC/RMI or message passing. Similar to the EventHeap, the context memory is also a generic workspace software component that is used by all iRoom applications (not just ICrafter). The context memory is implemented [20] as an XML-based lightweight datastore which allows storing and retrieving workspace context information using an XML-based query language. We do not discuss the implementation details of the EventHeap and the context memory any further in this paper.

---

[2] Of course, this assumes that the data types are inter-operable. However, such assumptions are not required by the mechanism itself, but by the service interfaces chosen here.

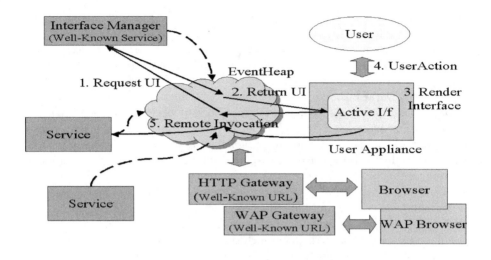

Fig. 2. ICrafter prototype implementation

As shown in figure 2, when a user requests a UI for one or more services (we explain how this process is bootstrapped later), the user appliance sends a request to the IM (step 1). The IM responds with the appropriate UI (step 2), which is rendered on the appliance by a renderer (step 3). The renderer itself is not part of ICrafter, and can be any native renderer, such as a web browser. User actions on the UI (step 4) result in remote invocations on the target services (step 5). Note that the remote invocations themselves are not mediated by the IM, so there is no slowdown in the user interaction with the UIs.

As seen by the application developers for the ICrafter framework, ICrafter is a set of specifications/APIs for developing workspace services and appropriate appliance UIs for them. Thus, to deploy a new service (such as a camera), an app developer needs to write a camera service using the ICrafter service APIs. Similarly, ICrafter provides specifications for an app developer to create UI generators. For example, to create a HTML UI for a service, the app developer needs to create a *HTML template* (which is explained below).

Before describing the implementation specifics, we first illustrate the end-user experience by presenting a walk-through for an example iRoom scenario.

4.1 Walk Through

A user walks into the iRoom with her laptop and starts the SUIML [3] interpreter. The SUIML interpreter is setup to first request the IM (which is a well-known service) for its own (i.e., the IM's) UI. The IM returns its UI which is shown in figure 3(a). The UI of the IM allows the user to select one or more services

---

[3] SUIML (Swing UI Markup Language) is a declarative markup language developed in iRoom for describing GUIs produced by the Java Swing toolkit.

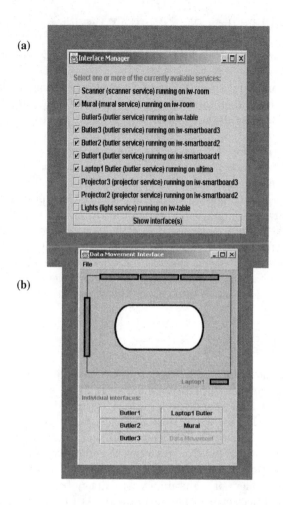

Fig. 3. Walk Through Example. The user first sees the IM's UI (part (a)), which allows her to choose one or more services. The returned UI is an aggregate of the UI for each service chosen and the data movement UI. The data movement UI (part (b)) is generated by the generator for "multiple consumers-multiple producers" pattern that has no specific knowledge of the services involved except that they implement the DataConsumer and DataProducer interfaces. The UI shows a top-down view of the room. (The white region is a table which is a fixed landmark in iRoom.) The dark grey rectangles identify the service locations (the three wall-mounted SmartBoards at the top, the mural on the left, and the laptop at the bottom). The user can drag and drop data from any of these services onto another. For example, dragging from the laptop to the middle SmartBoard results in the URL currently displayed on the laptop to be displayed on the middle SmartBoard. The user can also drag a URL from a browser on her laptop onto any of the consumer services. (As expected, dragging from the mural has no effect because it is only a consumer)

and request the UI for them. Note that the IM is just another service, and its UI is generated just as for any other service. That is, the IM locates a suitable SUIML generator for itself and executes it to produce the desired SUIML UI. While the UI shown here presents a list of services, a different generator could result in (for example) a spatial map of all available services. The user selects the instances of the *butler service* [4] running on her laptop and the three wall-mounted SmartBoards (all the SmartBoards are attached to Windows desktops) and the *mural service* [5].

The UI returned for this request is shown in figure 3(b). Apart from the individual service generators, the generator for the *multiple consumers-multiple producers* pattern also matches at the IM. Notice that the consumer-producer generator has *no* specific knowledge of the butler or the mural, but just uses the information that they implement the DataProducer and DataConsumer interfaces to generate a "data movement UI" that allows data to be moved between these services. This illustrates how aggregation works in ICrafter.

We now proceed to describe the internal workings of the ICrafter implementation in some detail. Throughout this description, we will refer to Figure 4 which shows a very simple example that illustrates the details of the interface generation process.

4.2   Service Descriptions

Our language for describing services is an XML-based language called SDL (Service Description Language). SDL is similar to ISL (Interface Specification Language) in Hodes et al. [11] and the UPnP [17] service descriptions. Figure 4(a) shows part of the SDL for the projector service. Just as ISL, it lists the operations supported by the service. However, unlike previous approaches, SDL does *not* contain addresses/ URLs. For services written in Java, SDL is generated automatically at runtime using Java reflection and included in the service beacons. This avoids the problem of maintaining consistency between services and their descriptions as services evolve. We also provide API calls to service developers that can *optionally* be used to refine the generated SDL.

4.3   Discovery and Remote Invocation

Discovery is handled by service beacons. Services beacon their presence by posting short-lived events to the EventHeap, and the IM (or any other entity including the appliances) can query the EventHeap for all (unexpired) beacon events

---

[4] The butler service can run on any Windows machine and provides two functions (among others). First, it allows a call event posted on the Event Heap to specify an arbitrary URL to be displayed in a browser running on its host machine. Second, when queried, it can return the URL currently displayed in the top-level browser window on its host machine. Thus, it implements both the DataConsumer and DataProducer interfaces.

[5] The mural service runs on a high-resolution display called the mural and displays data on the mural on-demand. Thus, it implements the DataConsumer interface.

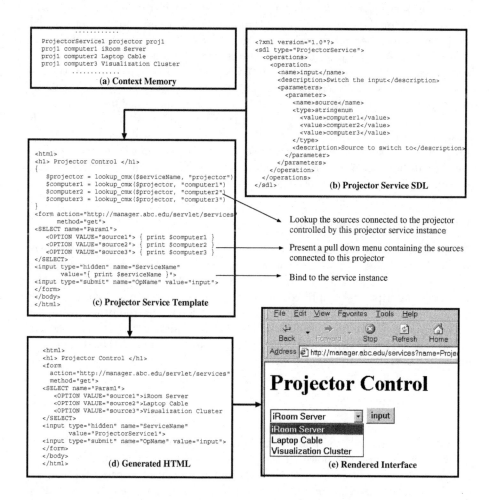

Fig. 4. Interface Generation Process. Part (b) shows portion of the projector service SDL with just one operation "input", which allows the source of the projector to be switched among any of the connected computers. Part (a) shows the information relevant to a projector service instance ("ProjectorService1") in the context memory. The projector service template shown in (c) can generate the UI for any projector service instance. It is passed the unique identifier of the projector service instance (whose UI is to be generated) through the variable serviceName. The template looks up the sources connected to the projector controlled by the projector service instance with the given name, and generates a UI that allows the user to select one of them. (The procedure *lookup_cmx* looks up a property in the context memory.) The HTML generated when the template is processed for the service instance "ProjectorService1", and the generated interface in the browser are shown in (d) and (e) respectively

to discover services.[6] Service beacons contain the service descriptions and also a unique name for the service instance that is used for remote invocations on the service instance. Because beacons are marked as short-lived, the EventHeap's event expiry mechanism eventually removes beacon events from failed services. Remote invocations are marshaled into call events and return events (if there is a return). The use of loosely-coupled, semi-persistent event-based infrastructure for communication instead of RMI/RPC (as in Jini and other frameworks) has led to increased robustness. First, certain transient failures of services are easily masked. (A service restarting after a transient failure can still pick up call events directed to it if they have not expired yet). Second, certain components such as the IM can be replicated for fail-over/efficiency such that any event directed to a replicated component is picked by exactly one of the replicas.

4.4   Appliance Descriptions

In our current implementation, we assume that every appliance supports one or more UI languages and we rely on the corresponding UI language interpreter (e.g., web browser for HTML) to render the UI and handle user actions. Thus, appliance descriptions simply consist of the set of UI languages supported by the appliance and optional (name, value) pairs describing the other attributes of the appliance. We have used four different UI languages in ICrafter so far: HTML, VoiceXML, MoDAL [19] (a markup language from IBM Almaden for PalmOS-based devices), and SUIML.

4.5   Generators

Most generators have been implemented using a *template system*. A template is UI markup in one of the supported UI languages with embedded Tcl or Python scripts. (An example template for the projector service is shown in Figure 4(b)). The embedded scripts may use a set of library routines to access the context memory, service description, etc. When a template is executed, the embedded scripts are executed and they are replaced by the output they produce. Custom templates can be written for a service and UI language or a generic service-independent template can be written for a given UI language.

4.6   Generator Database

The generator database lists the language (currently HTML, VoiceXML, MoDAL, or SUIML), platform (currently Tcl, Python, or Java), suitable text description, location, and the associated services/patterns for all the generators. Currently, simplified regular expression-like syntax is used for representing patterns. A generator can be associated with a service instance or a service interface (such as the PowerSwitchInterface) or any pattern of service instances

---

[6] Our current discovery scheme is relatively primitive and is an area of future work.

and interfaces. Example patterns include "*all* services that implement the Power-SwitchInterface" and "multiple services implementing DataConsumer and multiple services implementing DataConsumer". Generic generators are marked as service-independent, so that they can match any service. We have had relatively limited experience with pattern based matching for generators so far and we plan to explore it further in the near future.

4.7   Interface Manager

When the IM receives a request for UI for a single service, it first searches for a generator for that service instance, then for that service interface, and finally for the service-independent generator. For a UI request for multiple services, the generator selector first searches for generators for each service (according to the algorithm mentioned earlier). Second, the generator selector searches for all the generators that match any subset of the given set of services. Finally, the selector returns a simple aggregate of all the generators that matched in the first or the second step. In the execution stage, depending on whether the generator is a Tcl/Python template or a Java class, an appropriate processor is chosen to execute it. The execution produces code in a UI language supported by the appliance. (For example, figure 4(c) shows the HTML produced by the execution of the template in (b)).

5   Examples

We present more example service UIs written for ICrafter in this section that highlight various aspects of the system. Our experience so far indicates that template-based UIs are easy to write, because no code needs to be written by the UI developer apart from the simple embedded Tcl/Python scripts. Since our infrastructure provides generic back-end code (such as the HTTP gateway) for converting user actions in any supported UI language to remote invocation events, the UI developer need not write any backend code (such as servlets/CGI for HTML etc). For example, no back-end code was written by the UI developer for the projector service UI shown in figure 4.

Appliance adaptation. Figure 5 shows a simplified illustration of the butler UI for a PalmOS-based device. It offers the same functionality as the SUIML laptop UI for the same service (not shown here but similar to figure 3(b)) but is less convenient because of lack of drag-and-drop in PalmOS. Creating this UI involved only writing the MoDAL markup with the simple embedded Tcl statements for accessing the context memory. The IM automatically picks a suitable UI based on the requesting appliance.

Workspace adaptation. Figure 6 shows the light control SUIML UIs for two different workspaces. Note that the UIs are very different but are *generated by the same template* accessing different context memories. Equipment locations

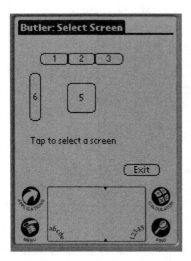 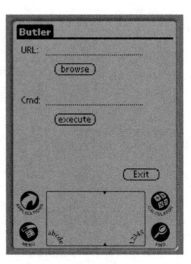

Fig. 5. Global butler control UI using MoDAL on a PalmOS device is shown above. This UI allows users to remotely display a URL on any screen in iRoom using their PalmOS device. Once the user selects a screen using the iRoom top-down view in the left form, the form on the right appears, which prompts the user to enter a URL

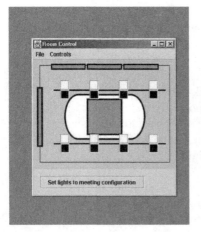 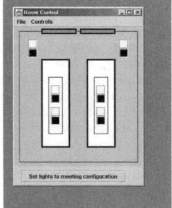

Fig. 6. Light control UIs for iRoom (left), which has a table, five displays, and eight lights on ceiling tracks, and another workspace (right), which has two tables, two displays, four overhead lights, and two corner lamps. The user turns a light on using the yellow button corresponding to the light, and turns a light off using the black button. The UIs show top-down views of the workspaces generated from the information in the respective context memories

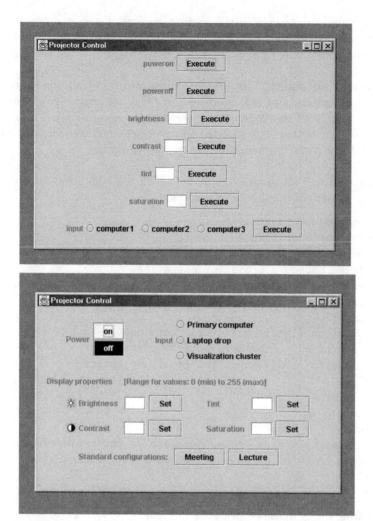

Fig. 7. Automatic and Custom Generation of UIs. The automatically generated SUIML UI (left) was generated solely based on the SDL using only knowledge of the operations, and the types of each parameter. Though not aesthetically pleasing, it is functional. The custom-designed SUIML UI (right) is superior in two respects. First, it is functionally more convenient. It has descriptive names for projector input sources (such as iRoom server, laptop cable, etc), and has commands for commonly-used settings (standard configuration buttons for meetings and lectures). Second, it is aesthetically pleasing, by using intuitive colors for power switches, easily-recognizable icons where appropriate, and logical grouping of commands by type (power, input, display)

and dimensions are detailed in the context memory; hence, the generated UIs reflect the context without user intervention or changes to code. This illustrates the ability to reuse templates while still creating UIs tailored to the workspace.

Custom and automatic UIs. Figure 7 illustrates the tradeoffs between UIs generated by custom and generic templates. The automatically generated UI doesn't require a UI developer, while the custom designed UI is functionally and aesthetically better. Note that the UI developer could use the automatically generated UI as a starting point for the custom UI design.

Voice Interface. Part of an example VoiceXML UI (simplified for illustrative purposes) written for ICrafter is shown below.

```
<form id="projectorcontrol">
  <field name="operation">
    <prompt>
      Please choose a projector operation.
      Available functions are turn on, turn off, switch input.
    </prompt>
    <grammar>
      [turn] on [[the] projector] "turn on"
      | [turn] off [[the] projector]"turn off"
      | (switch | set) input [of [the] projector]
                                    "switch the input of"
    </grammar>
  </field>
  <filled>
    You chose to <value expr="operation"/> the projector.
    <submit next="http://server:8080/servlet/voiceservices"/>
  </filled>
</form>
```

The resulting dialog is shown below:

```
COMPUTER: Please choose a projector operation. Available functions
are turn on, turn off, switch input.
USER (into microphone): Turn on.
COMPUTER: You chose to turn on the projector.
```

Though we can automatically generate UIs for some interaction styles, it is extremely difficult to model speech interactions (e.g., phraseology, for both humans and computers) in a generic fashion, short of full natural language processing. The above UI was thus hand-written by a UI designer, who customized it based on the projector service descriptions and her knowledge of speech interactions. Even though they are hand-designed, it is still easier to create these UIs using the ICrafter template framework since no back-end code needs be written and the Python/Tcl helper routines that provide access to context memory, service and appliance descriptions simplify appliance and workspace adaptation.

6   Related Work

We concur with other researchers' identification of many of our design goals, although we sometimes use different terminology. For example, PIMA [3], Portolano [2], and Borriello et al. [4] also identify many of our design goals as challenges to be addressed by researchers in ubiquitous computing.

Much work has gone into discovery [15,16,17]. We have not used existing discovery schemes since the simple mechanism based on EventHeap beacons has proven sufficient for us so far, given our smaller scale.

Recent work on generic UI modeling languages is orthogonal to our work. UIML [8] is an appliance-independent XML UI language, which uses style sheets to map the appliance-independent interface description to markup languages or programming languages. Eisenstein et al. [13] present model-based techniques for designing UIs in a platform-independent manner that also adapt to certain types of context . If widely deployed and available, such generic UI languages can be used in ICrafter for writing templates thus simplifying adaptation. We have leveraged some of the recent work in the design of context-aware applications in general and architectures for storing context information [21,20] to achieve workspace-adaptation in ICrafter. Projects such as EasyLiving [22] and iLand [23] are also investigating software architectures for technology-rich spaces, but they do not explicitly focus on service and UI frameworks.

Among related research and industry efforts, ICrafter is most closely related to Jini [9], UPnP [17], Hodes et al. [10,11] and Roman et al. [12]. The Jini ServiceUI [14] project allows Java UI code to be registered as a service attribute with the lookup service. Clients are responsible for selecting one of the registered UIs based on which toolkits (such as Swing) the UI code needs. In UPnP (which is a generalization of controlling devices via embedded Web servers), service descriptions include control and presentation URLs which can be accessed by the client using a HTTP-based protocol. In the document-based approach of Hodes et al., service advertisements include a URL where the service documents can be downloaded from. The service documents contain the machine addresses and URLs to download UI code from. If there is no suitable UI, the client can automatically generate its own UI from the service document. Roman et al. propose a "device-independent" representation of services that attempts to capture both service functionality and UI, but the UI elements they use are GUI-centric. As mentioned earlier, ICrafter extends all these four approaches in three significant directions: infrastructure support for UI generation/selection/adaptation, aggregation, and workspace adaptation. In addition, some of these existing approaches allow only certain programming languages and UI languages/ modalities to be used, some others restrict the clients to be web browsers, while yet others do not support web browsers at all.

7   Lessons and Conclusions

We identified the goals for a service framework for interactive workspaces and designed a framework that is compatible with these goals. Although the framework was specifically designed for interactive workspaces, many of the ideas carry over to service frameworks for many other ubiquitous computing environments also. Our framework makes three contributions: infrastructure support for UI selection/adaptation/generation, associating generators with service patterns for on-the-fly aggregation, and workspace adaptation. In addition, our design gives utmost importance to system properties such as incremental deployability, support for legacy components, and robustness which are critically important for ubiquitous computing environments. To validate the design, we implemented a prototype in our experimental workspace, the iRoom, and built several services and appliance UIs for them.

In conclusion, we attempt to abstract away the domain-specific details and examine in retrospect the key design techniques that were used in ICrafter to address the challenges that arise in ubiquitous computing environments. While these techniques are not new, we believe they will serve as useful reminders for ubiquitous computing researchers.

- ICrafter often leverages a "level of indirection" for dealing with heterogeneity. Whenever two sets of variable entities need to inter-operate with one another, a level of indirection is useful. For example, the key for the inter-operation of services and appliances in ICrafter is the existence of intelligence in a resource-rich third party to select and execute appropriate generator(s) from among a range of generators. Similarly, to deal with the inter-operation of UIs and workspaces, we introduce the context memory.
- To accommodate incremental evolution, we follow the guideline: "Provide a reasonable default but allow for fine tuning". For example, default UIs are automatically generated by the generic generators, but custom generators can always be written if desired.
- The use of loosely-coupled, semi-persistent event-based infrastructure for communication instead of RMI/RPC has led to increased robustness. As explained in section 4.3, certain transient failures are easily masked and some components can be easily replicated for fail-over/efficiency.

Acknowledgements

We are grateful to Brad Johanson, Susan Shepard, Emre Kiciman, Caesar Sengupta, Meenakshy Chakravorthy, Kathleen Liston, Kathy Richardson, George Candea and Petros Maniatis for their help with this work. We also thank the anonymous reviewers whose comments helped improve this paper. This work was supported in part by the US Department of Energy, Contract B504665.

References

1. David Gelernter. Generative communication in linda. *ACM Transactions on Programming Languages and Systems*, 7(1):80–112, January 1985. 62
2. M. Esler, J. Hightower, T. Anderson, and G. Borriello. Next Century Challenges: Data-Centric Networking for Invisible Computing. The Portolano Project at the University of Washington. In *Proceedings of the Fifth ACM/IEEE International Conference on Mobile Networking and Computing*, pages 256-262, August 1999. 72
3. Guruduth Banavar, James Beck, Eugene Gluzberg, Jonathan Munson, Jeremy Sussman, and Deborra Zukowski. Challenges: An Application Model for Pervasive Computing. In *Proceedings of the sixth annual international conference on Mobile computing and networking*, pages 266-274, August 2000. 72
4. Gaetano Borriello and Roy Want. Embedded Computation Meets the World Wide Web. In *Communications of the ACM*, 43(5):59-66, May 2000. 72
5. Brad Johanson and Armando Fox. The EventHeap: A Coordination Infrastructure for Interactive Workspaces. 2001. *Unpublished draft.* http://graphics.stanford.edu/~bjohanso/papers/ubicomp2001/eheap_ubicomp.pdf 62
6. Stanford Interactive Workspaces Project. http://graphics.stanford.edu/~iwork/ 56
7. Armando Fox, Steven D. Gribble, Yatin Chawathe and Eric A. Brewer. Adapting to Network and Client Variation Using Active Proxies: Lessons and Perspectives. IEEE Personal Communications (invited submission), August 1998. 60
8. Marc Abrams, Constantinos Phanouriou, Alan L. Batongbacal, Stephen M. Williams, Jonathan E. Shuster. UIML: An Appliance-Independent XML User Interface Language. *Eighth International World Wide Web Conference.* May 1999. 72
9. Jim Waldo. The Jini Architecture for Network-centric Computing. *Communications of the ACM*, pages 76-82, July 1999. 57, 72
10. T. D. Hodes, R. H. Katz, E. Servan-Schreiber, L. A. Rowe. Composable Ad-hoc Mobile Services for Universal Interaction. *Proceedings of The Third ACM/IEEE International Conference on Mobile Computing (MobiCom '97)*, pages 1-12. September 1997. 57, 60, 72
11. Todd D. Hodes and Randy H. Katz. A Document-based Framework for Internet Application Control. *2nd USENIX Symposium on Internet Technologies and Systems*, pages 59-70. October 1999. 57, 60, 61, 65, 72
12. Manuel Roman, James Beck, and Alain Gefflaut. A Device-Independent Representation for Services. *Third IEEE Workshop on Mobile Computing Systems and Applications*, pages 73-82. December 2000. 57, 61, 72
13. Jacob Eisenstein, Jean Vanderdoncki, and Angel Puerta. Adapting to Mobile Contexts with User-Interface Modeling. *Third IEEE Workshop on Mobile Computing Systems and Applications*, pages 83-92. December 2000. 72
14. The Jini ServiceUI Project. http://www.artima.com/jini/serviceui/ 72
15. S. Czerwinski, B. Zhao, T. Hodes, A. Joseph, and R. Katz. An architecture for a secure service discovery service. In *Proceedings of the Fifth Annual ACM/IEEE International Conference on Mobile Computing and Networking*, pages 24-35, August 1999. 72
16. J. Veizades, E. Guttman, C. Perkins, and S.Kaplan. *Service Location Protocol*, June 1997. RFC 2165. http://www.ietf.org/rfc/rfc2165.txt 72

17. Universal Plug and Play. http://www.upnp.org/. 57, 61, 65, 72
18. P. Wyckoff, S. McLaughry, T. Lehman, and D. Ford. TSpaces. *IBM Systems Journal*, 37(3):454–474, 1998. 6 62
19. MoDAL (Mobile Document Application Language).
    http://www.almaden.ibm.com/cs/TSpaces/MoDAL/ 67
20. Terry Winograd. Architectures for Context. *Human-Computer Interaction, 16.* 2001. 61, 62, 72
21. A. K. Dey, D. Salber, and G. D. Abowd. A conceptual framework and a toolkit for supporting the rapid prototyping of context-aware applications. *Human-Computer Interaction, 16.* 2001. 72
22. B. Brumitt, B. Meyers, J. Krumm, A. Kern, and S. Shafer, EasyLiving: Technologies for Intelligent Environments, *Handheld and Ubiquitous Computing 2000 (HUC2K)*, September 2000. 72
23. Norbert Streitz, Jorg Geibler, and Torsten Holmer. Cooperative Buildings - Integrating Information, Organization, and Architecture. *First International Workshop on Cooperative Buildings (CoBuild 98)*, pages 4-21, February 1998. 72

Using JIT Compilation and Configurable Runtime Systems for Efficient Deployment of Java Programs on Ubiquitous Devices

Radu Teodorescu and Raju Pandey

Parallel and Distributed Computing Laboratory
Computer Science Department
University of California, Davis
{teodores,pandey}@cs.ucdavis.edu

Abstract. As the proliferation of ubiquitous devices moves computation away from the conventional desktop computer boundaries, distributed systems design is being exposed to new challenges. A distributed system supporting a ubiquitous computing application must deal with a wider spectrum of hardware architectures featuring structural and functional differences, and resources limitations. Due to its architecture independent infrastructure and object-oriented programming model, the Java programming environment can support flexible solutions for addressing the diversity among these devices. Unfortunately, Java solutions are often associated with high costs in terms of resource consumption, which limits the range of devices that can benefit from this approach. In this paper, we present an architecture that deals with the cost and complexity of running Java programs by partitioning the process of Java program execution between system nodes and remote devices. The system nodes prepare a Java application for execution on a remote device by generating device-specific native code and application-specific runtime system on the fly. The resulting infrastructure provides the flexibility of a high-level programming model and the architecture independence specific to Java. At the same time the amount of resources consumed by an application on the targeted device are comparable to that of a native implementation.

1 Introduction

As a result of the proliferation of computation into the physical world, ubiquitous computing [1] has become an important research topic. The goal of ubiquitous computing is to bridge cyberspace and physical space. The Internet provides a uniform mechanism for accessing and manipulating information stored on conventional computer systems. Until recently, the Internet was accessible to common users primarily through desktop computers. Now several devices (including cell phones, PDAs and messaging devices) provide users some access to the Internet.

G. D. Abowd, B. Brumitt, S. A. N. Shafer (Eds.): Ubicomp 2001, LNCS 2201, pp. 76-95, 2001.

Ubiquitous computing research envisions extending this accessibility to all ubiquitous devices in a uniform and transparent manner. Thus, in the future an Internet user could check in real-time the weather conditions provided by a network of intelligent sensors distributed worldwide and connected to the Internet; the processors embedded in a car would be enabled to send a notification when the car needs an oil change; or one could check from his workplace whether all the dangerous electrical appliances are turned off at their home. However, in order realize this vision, a software infrastructure must exist that integrates ubiquitous devices into a general distributed system framework, and allow one to interact with and manipulate them in a transparent manner.

Ubiquitous computing systems introduce a new class of hardware devices that may no longer be compatible with the traditional desktop model. Thus, in addition to the traditional problems raised by a distributed system, system designers must take the following characteristics of ubiquitous devices into account:

- **Functional heterogeneity**. In traditional systems the interoperability problem primarily relates to the differences in specific implementation choices (for instance, differences in instruction set, operating system and data representation). In the ubiquitous computing environment, on the other hand, since the nodes implement different computational behaviors, they introduce a new type of heterogeneity, which we call *functional heterogeneity*. Thus, a software infrastructure must not only deal with *how* a node provides certain functionality but *whether or not* it provides a specific functionality.
- **Resource limitations**. Ubiquitous computing devices also have limited computing capabilities due to the concerns about power, size and price. Thus, the footprint of a traditional operating system or language runtime system may be too large for these devices.

Thus, software infrastructure solutions must implement a more complex interoperability problem, while meeting stricter resource limitations. Overcoming the heterogeneity problem requires considerable computation overhead even in traditional distributed systems. Since functional heterogeneity includes the traditional heterogeneity problems and adds new ones, it is expected that the mediation overhead would accordingly be higher. On the other hand, the resource limitations restrict the amount of computation that can be dedicated to solving the heterogeneity problem. Traditional middleware solutions (such as MPI, CORBA, and RM) typically have heavyweight implementations. Each device integrated in such a system must be able to support a substantial runtime system overhead. This limits [28] the approach to only small number of devices[30,31,32].

The primary goal of our research is to make integration of ubiquitous devices within an overall distributed system framework as transparent as possible. This means that end users should be able to continue to use high level programming languages and tools for developing distributed programs. Further, their ability to deploy distributed programs on these devices should not be constrained by the resource limitations of the devices. In this paper, we present an infrastructure, called *JUCE* (*Java for Ubiquitous Computing Environments,* that addresses these concerns. JUCE supports the Java programming environment for developing distributed programs. It addresses the functional heterogeneity problem by transparently translating Java program components into device-specific programs, and migrating them to the devices. JUCE addresses the resource limitations constraints by dynamically constructing an execution environment that is customized to include only those runtime services needed for an execution of an application on a ubiquitous device.

The JUCE architecture restructures the traditional JVM by introducing two new concepts: **Remote Just-In-Time compiler (R-JIT)** and **Configurable Runtime System (C-RTS)**. R-JIT exploits the fact that much of the overhead associated with Java byte-code processing (for instance, code verification or just in time compiling) can be relocated to a remote host from the device executing the code. Thus, the code targeting an embedded device is compiled just in time on a remote host and migrated to the device in the native code format. This means that a resource-limited device can efficiently execute a Java application while a more powerful node supports the actual Java-specific overhead. The C-RTS has a modular structure that allows JUCE to adapt its configuration according to the resources availability and application requirements. Thus, in JUCE, the different RTS modules are loaded as required by the application. In the traditional approach the Java VM is entirely loaded before starting the execution of the application.. This way a device running a Java application has to deal only with the overhead produced by the RTS services currently required by the application.

We have implemented the JUCE infrastructure and a Linux-based application that emulates ubiquitous devices. We have run several experiments that analyze the overall behavior of the JUCE infrastructure. The experiments show that the infrastructure provides the flexibility of a high-level programming language. At the same time the resource consumed by an application on a targeted device is comparable to that of a native implementation. Further, the resources required by runtime services can be scaled up or down dynamically according to the needs of applications.

This paper is organized as follows: In Section 2 we describe the JUCE architecture in detail. In Section 3, we present quantitative and qualitative analysis of the architecture. Section 4 presents a brief survey of the related work. Finally, we conclude with a brief summary and a description of the future work in Section 5.

2   System Architecture

We now describe the JUCE system architecture. First we provide an overall view of the architecture. We then describe a configurable runtime system that spans across hosts and embedded devices.

2.1 Overview

The goal of this research is to integrate physically distributed embedded devices within a distributed computing framework that includes general-purpose hosts. Thus, we assume a generic distributed system architecture that includes conventional hosts, including desktop computers and server machines, and ubiquitous mobile and embedded devices. We also assume that the hosts and the devices can communicate with each other through various network infrastructures. JUCE exploits the additional processing power available at general-purpose hosts to compensate for the limitations of embedded devices.

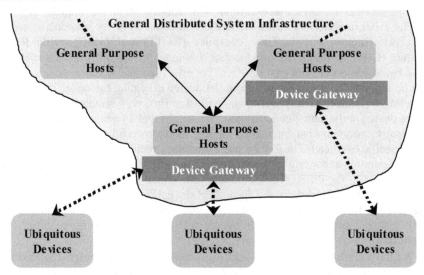

Fig. 1. Distributed System Architecture with Gateways

The JUCE programming environment aims to hide the heterogeneity among the general purpose systems and embedded devices by a single distributed programming model, based on Java and MAGE [9]. Users write programs in Java and use high-level Java-based APIs for accessing services provided by specific devices. As these programs are run, the JUCE runtime environment manages the execution of programs on hosts and devices. As shown in Figure 1, the JUCE runtime environment is divided into two kinds of computational hosts: hosts that run the JVM (called *JUCE gateways*), and *embedded devices*[1]. A JUCE gateway adapts application and runtime system code (represented as Java byte code) for specific devices. It first intercepts Java byte code intended for an embedded device. It then arranges for generation of code for the specific device. It also determines a runtime system configuration that is needed for an execution of the code. It then migrates both the runtime system and the application code to the specific device. During the execution of the program on the remote device, the JUCE runtime environment also interacts with the device and sends necessary supporting runtime routines and program objects. It is also the gateway's role to capture any abnormal behavior at the device and formulate it in terms of Java exceptions. The embedded devices implement a small runtime environment that evolves to adapt to the runtime requirements of a program.

Next we describe the JUCE gateway and the runtime in detail.

---

[1]We use the term embedded device to refer to hosts that cannot run a full JVM due to resource constraints

2.2 JUCE Gateway Implementation

We now look at the details of the JUCE gateway. There are two components of the JUCE infrastructure: **Remote Just-in Time** (R-JIT) compiler and **Configurable Runtime System** (C-RTS). The R-JIT compiler translates application Java byte code into device-specific native code. The resulting native code application can be executed directly on the embedded device. The C-RTS provides high level services for the native code (such as dynamic linking, virtual method invocation, memory allocation, exception handling and synchronization).

2.3 Remote JIT Compiler

The RJIT compiler converts Java byte-code into native code, which is transmitted to the embedded device. The RJIT compiler performs the required code verification to guarantee that the generated code preserves Java safety and security properties. We have implemented the remote JIT compiler by modifying the Open JIT compiler [9]. The OpenJIT compiler is a reflective JIT compiler. It provides a clean separation between the Java front end and the back-end target machine. The JIT compiler can be easily extended to a new device by implementing a corresponding back-end. The R-JIT compiler is extensible as well in that a gateway can be transparently extended to control a new class of embedded devices by dynamically downloading a new backend. The JUCE infrastructure can also be similarly extended dynamically over newly discovered devices.

2.4 The Configurable Runtime System (C-RTS)

The C-RTS supports a set of libraries that implement several services for the compiled code. For scalability purposes, the C-RTS has a component-based structure. Each component corresponds to a specific runtime service provided by the Java Virtual Machine. The C-RTS is partitioned between a gateway and an embedded device. This partitioning is dynamic, and depends on the nature of the device, resource availability, frequency of usage and efficiency. Heavyweight RTS components that are seldom required are placed on the gateway machine, whereas frequently utilized RTS components are placed on the embedded device. The partitioning of the virtual machine between the gateway and device varies according to the application requirements and underlying device configuration. The JUCE architecture divides the overall C-RTS components into three separate modules: **micro-kernel, Gateway Resident RTS (GR-RTS)**, and **Device Resident RTS (DR-RTS)**. The goal of this partitioning is to reduce the amount of processing done at the embedded device task by pushing the resource-expensive computation on the gateway. The division is based on the observation that a large portion of the Java RTS functionality (such as class initialization or dynamic linking) is used sparingly during a program execution (for instance only for class initialization). We described each module in detail below:

The primary component of the C-RTS is a **micro-kernel**. The micro kernel forms the basis for dynamically bootstrapping the rest of the runtime system. A device, thus, must be able to host a micro-kernel in order to be part of the overall distributed runtime infrastructure. The micro-kernel (μK) implements the ability to connect with a gateway through a communication medium, download a block of code from the gateway, execute the downloaded code locally, and return the result back to the gateway. Note that while code mobility has been traditionally handled as a high level feature, it is a fundamental element in the JUCE architecture.

The micro-kernel supports a limited subset of Java. This subset includes primitive data types (such as **int, char** and **float**)[2], control flow constructs (such as **if, while** and **for**) and *static native* methods. In the absence of a real Java VM, the micro-kernel only supports the execution of a single static method. It does not support nested method invocations or structured data types.

The programming model supported by the micro-kernel is used as the starting point for implementing the actual runtime system. From the micro-kernel perspective, the rest of the C-RTS is just another migrating application that needs to be executed. Thus, whenever the micro-kernel programming model is not expressive enough for an application, the required components of the rest of the C-RTS are migrated to the embedded device in order to provide the required mediation layer.

GR-RTS stores the *constant pool table* associated with a Java program. The Java runtime system uses the constant pool for dynamic runtime linking. The table contains a set of symbolic references that are resolved during program execution. As the Java interpreter comes across an unresolved symbol, it uses the dynamic class loader to map the symbol to a specific program entity. It then replaces all occurrences of that symbol with its direct reference. Accordingly, the application running on the embedded device generates a remote invocation on the gateway the first time it comes across a symbol. The gateway resolves the symbol for the device, and downloads the native code on the device. The device can then continue to execute the method. Thus, after each symbol has been resolved at least once, a program can run autonomously on the embedded device without requiring any additional information from the gateway.

DR-RTS manages class information and the code required by the embedded device. Unlike the traditional Java approach, where code migration is done at the class level, JUCE uses methods as the basic code migration unit. This allows the gateway to export only those methods that are currently required, thereby reducing the memory usage on the embedded device. Clearly, there is a tradeoff between memory space and how long it takes to download different components. The gateway can provide a balance between the two through the knowledge of the resource availability on a remote device.

In order to further minimize the overhead on the embedded device, the Device-resident RTS is split into a Dynamic-RTS (D-RTS) and a Static-RTS (S-RTS). The Static-RTS represents the code that is permanently loaded on the embedded device while the Dynamic-RTS is written in Java and is loaded from the gateway during execution according to application needs. Thus, each component of the DR-RTS is divided into a dynamic component and a static component. A resource-thrifty design

---

[2] The number of supported primitive types reflects the types supported by the underlying hardware while the rest of the Java types are implemented on top of them by the RTS components. For instance, the OpenJIT X86 implementation invokes JVM for operations with **double types.**

of the local RTS components places all the implementation logic in the dynamic side such that the static side code is reduced to a minimum set of low-level primitives (for instance, direct memory access, direct access to communication I/O ports, and interrupts handlers).

S-RTS mediates between the D-RTS and the device. The JIT compiled application, running on the device, makes calls to a standard set of runtime routines. These routines correspond to the services performed by a JVM (such as method resolution and invocation, memory allocation and exception handling). A typical lightweight S-RTS implementation redirects these calls to the corresponding D-RTS component.

The concrete implementation of the S-RTS varies according to the underlying architecture. The set of primitives provided by the S-RTS also differs between different devices down to the extreme cases in which no primitives are implemented. Of course, the availability of the high-level features provided by the D-RTS is limited by the set of primitives present on each machine. For instance, if the S-RTS does not provide mechanisms for saving and restoring context information associated with an execution, it will be difficult for the D-RTS to implement multithreading support. Thus, the resources available on a device inherently limit the complexity of an application that can be executed on the device.

In order to maximize the range of applications that can be executed on an underlying device, the S-RTS must support suitable programming features for machine deployment and must be lightweight at the same time. Because a solution to the S-RTS design problem is particular to each type of device, the JUCE architecture does not impose a standard design. However, we believe that a static RTS should provide several services: The first is the ability to provide a memory model for storage and access. A simple approach is to use Java byte arrays to model memory. The S-RTS should also provide access to the underlying device registers, which can be used to control low level runtime structures (such as system stack). Since applications must communicate with the gateway, the S-RTS also needs to provide control over I/O ports for communication with the gateway. In addition these low level primitives, our implementation of S-RTS includes several high level services, including support for method retrieval from a gateway, method invocation, and code patching to allow an application to change the method code to point to the actual symbol's value after symbol resolution.

Note that many of the primitives can be written in Java using the low level primitives. For instance, *method invocation* can be expressed as a sequence of register operations. However, such an implementation tends to be considerably more inefficient than a corresponding native one. Further, given the frequent usage of these methods, the native approach seems more appealing. Also, since these services are likely to be required by most applications, there is no real benefit in having them implemented as dynamic components.

The **Dynamic Runtime System (D-RTS)** consists of a set of components corresponding to the various services provided by the RTS (such as object creation, method invocation, symbols resolution and exception handling). Each dynamic component is written in Java and is loaded on the embedded device through the R-JIT compiler in the same way as other application components. The implementation of a dynamic component is defined by establishing an *implementation hierarchy* among the components. Thus, each component implementation can utilize the RTS services provided by the D-RTS components at a lower level. The implementation of the components at the lowest level of the hierarchy deals only with abstractions implemented by the S-RTS and micro kernel. The higher-level components provide increasingly more complex features such as the notion of objects, object creation, exception handling, garbage collection and synchronization. Figure 2 shows the dependencies among several RTS components. The *method invocation* component is used to retrieve a specific method from the gateway and execute it locally. The *symbol resolution* function performs the conversion between symbolic references used in the compiled code and real references. *Virtual method invocation* component first identifies the actual method that needs to be invoked (using the *symbol resolution* service) and then invokes it using the *method invocation* service. Creation of an object takes place in two steps: first the RTS allocates memory for the object. It then invokes the constructor. The allocation may require *symbol resolution* in order to find information about the class such as object size. The second step is handled implicitly as a virtual method invocation.

The Java classes implementing the dynamic components are stored in a *Dynamic Runtime System Repository* either locally or on a remote machine, and can be accessed by the gateway. This architecture allows us to efficiently upgrade RTS components. In addition, the approach allows alternate implementations of the components for different devices. For instance, we can implement device-specific memory allocators and garbage collectors that exploit the properties of the underlying device to provide a more robust, flexible and efficient implementation

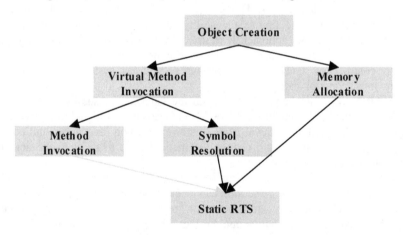

Fig. 2. Partitioning of Dynamic RTS

2.5 Device API

While the JUCE gateway and the C-RTS provide general purpose Java support, a device also exports an API that enables applications to access device-specific services. The JUCE device API implementation follows the same design principles as the Device-resident RTS. It is split into two: a low level static (Native) API hardcoded for the device, and a dynamic API written in Java that can be loaded on demand. Figure 3 summarizes the overall JUCE architecture:

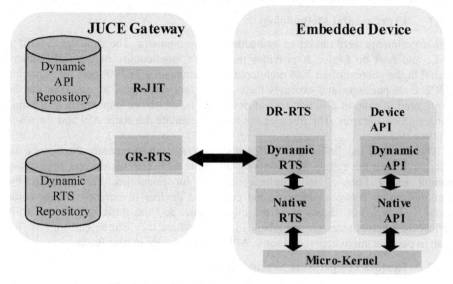

Fig. 3. Overall architecture of JUCE infrastructure

3   Analysis

In this section, we analyze the characteristics of the JUCE architecture. We first experimentally evaluate how the JUCE architecture can dynamically configure both applications and the runtime components in order to meet the resource limitations of an embedded device. We then examine the security implications of the proposed architecture. Finally we discuss the autonomy of devices with respect to JUCE gateways.

3.1 Experimental Analysis

The central goal of the JUCE architecture is to facilitate each application to dynamically choose the right balance between the supported features and resources requirements. This means that an application should incur runtime system overhead for only those features that it uses. Also, it should be able to adapt its behavior according to runtime resources availability.

In this section, we describe three experiments that highlight the tradeoffs among resources availability, performance and features at three different levels. We have used memory as the primary resource benchmark and the basis for adaptation in the experiments. In the first experiment, we have implemented an application that requires very little resources, and can be implemented by the micro-kernel directly. The second experiment outlines the way in which specific components of the runtime services are incrementally migrated to a remote device based on application needs and the cost of each individual service. The final experiment highlights how an application can dynamically partition itself between a gateway and a remote device in response to resource constraints at a device.

3.1.1   Experimental Methodology

The experiments were run on an embedded device emulator. The emulator is written in C, and runs on Linux. It provides the default functionality of the JUCE micro kernel in the context of an X86 architecture. It listens on a TCP/IP port for incoming JUCE code packages and executes them as they are received. The emulator can be configured to support different sets of device APIs, which are implemented as Linux dynamic link libraries. The libraries are used to emulate the static API and the static runtime system.

The emulator has limitations in that it cannot be used to measure the size of the micro-kernel or the system implementing the static API. The micro-kerne uses heavy weight Linux libraries for implementing its functionalities. For instance, the communication between gateways and embedded devices is currently implemented using TCP/IP. Thus, the sizes of the micro-kernel and the static API do not truly reflect their actual sizes on an embedded device where they can be customized. We plan to port the micro kernel and static API to a real device in near future.

3.1.2   Remote Temperature Sensing Device

In this experiment, we simulate an application running on a device with extremely limited resources, and analyze the minimal set of runtime services required for such applications.

We consider an embedded device that represents an intelligent thermometer. This device represents a base deployment scenario. The thermometer implements the JUCE micro-kernel. It also provides a native API that includes three methods: `network_read` to read from the network, `network_write` to write to the network, and `temperature_read` to read the temperature. The remote thermometer executes a program that continuously reads the temperature and sends the average value to the gateway device every 1000 cycles. Also the device sends an alarm if the temperature goes above a threshold.

The size of the code generated by the R-JIT compiler is 204 bytes. Since the application uses only primitive data types and only invokes static native methods, it does not require any runtime support beside what is already provided by the micro-kernel. Given that the application data consists of three local variables and a function argument, the entire application consumes a total of about 220 bytes.

Note that the micro kernel only supports primitive data types and static methods. The programmer, thus, has access to a non object-oriented subset of Java. This limits the kind of applications that can be easily written and targeted for such devices. However, the programming model may be sufficient for devices that support extremely limited amount of resources. Note that the JUCE approach represents a step ahead from the traditional approaches, which typically involves implementing these applications in assembly language. If the embedded device application is part of a larger distributed application, it is easier for the developer to deal with the same programming language instead of having separate modules written in different languages.

3.1.3   Controlling Device Grids

In the second experiment, we outline the behavior of the dynamic runtime system and the usability of the available runtime services. The experiments show how each service affects the cost of application deployment.

The experiment simulates a grid of devices that monitor the integrity of a building structure. The devices are distributed over the surface of the structure. There are three kinds of devices: temperature sensors, vibration sensors and monitors. The temperature and vibration sensors monitor the current sensor readings and send periodic updates to the gateway. They also exchange the readings between them. Each such device notifies the closest *monitor* device when abnormal conditions are detected. Monitors primarily sense the behavior of the overall surface and react when the combination of temperatures and vibration levels crosses a certain acceptable level. The devices are equipped with low power communication antennas that allow them to communicate with their direct neighbors. For the sake of simplicity, the devices are placed in one-dimensional space (See Figure 4.).

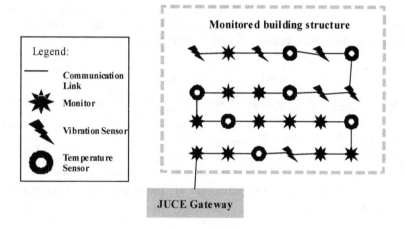

Fig. 4. Sensor Grid

The experiment involves using the gateway to control the grid of devices. The devices in the grid have limited resources. In addition, they provide a limited set of primitives that can be used to build applications. There is no predefined distribution of the devices. Thus, a device does not have any local information about distribution of the rest of devices. To overcome this problem, the device broadcasts a request identifying the type of the device it wants to interact with. The request is propagated until it reaches the closest requested device. The available device handles the request and sends information back to the requesting device. The devices, thus, implement a tunneling protocol to communicate with each other and with the gateway.

Each device runs a JUCE micro-kernel. A JUCE gateway communicates with the nearest device on the grid. Below we describe the behavior of the application:

- **Application propagation**: The application is first propagated from the gateway to the nearest device. The devices then use the tunneling protocol to migrate the application to all of the devices in the grid.
- **Message routing**: Each node continuously reads incoming messages and routes them according to an internal protocol..
- **Application adaptation**: The application uses polymorphism for implementing both generic and device specific behavior. The application uses a device API to detect the type of the device on top of which it is currently running. It then creates a device handler, which implements device specific behavior of the application.

In our simulation, we ran the application until each device has retrieved the code it requires. We then measured the size of the code executed on each device. Table 1 shows the code sizes for the devices. The total size of the code on each device is around 5KB, which is one order of magnitude less than a comparable application on a complete Java system. The devices customize their application code environment by downloading code specific to their needs. JUCE achieves this small footprint by loading only required methods of the application and runtime system. Note that JUCE uses methods as a basis for name resolution unlike the standard JVM approach where it is done at the class level. We note that the size of D-RTS is comparable to the size of the application.can be viewed as an empirical indication that the infrastructure scales down according to the needs of specific applications.

Table 1. Application code size

Application code	Temperature Sensor	Vibration Sensor	Monitor
D-RTS	1.7 KB		
Device independent	2 Kbytes		
Device Specific	1.4 KB	1 KB	0.2 KB
Total	5.1 KB	4.7 KB	3.9 KB

In Table 2 we show the resource requirements of the components of the dynamic runtime system.

Table 2. Sizes of components of the Dynamic Runtime System

Function	Description	Memory Usage
rt_newarray	Provides support for primitive data type array allocation	133
rt_callstatic	Enables applications to make static method invocation. It intercepts programmer's calls, retrieves method from remote host and redirect the call to it.	263
rt_new	Handles object creation and constructor invocation	312
rt_callspecial	Invokes a static method referred by a symbolic reference	204

rt_getfield	Resolves symbolic reference to an object's field	132
rt_virtual	Resolves symbolic reference to a virtual method and retrieves method from virtual method table reference	332
rt_virtual_qu ick	Replaces rt_virtual once a symbolic reference to a method is resolved. (if method is available locally, it can complete without invoking the JUCE gateway.)	280

3.1.4   Dynamic Distribution Micro-Benchmark

In this experiment, we develop an application that performs optimally when the embedded device on which it executes has enough resources. The performance of the application degrades gracefully as less resources become available.

The application is a micro-benchmark designed to perform frequent invocations to the embedded device API. The application, thus, performs optimally if it is executed entirely on the embedded device. Due to memory constraints, the embedded device may not host the entire application. In these cases, the application has the capability to distribute itself between the gateway and the embedded device. Splitting the application, however, increases the network traffic, thereby decreasing the application's performance. By allowing the application to be reconfigured at runtime, the application can still improve its performance, as more memory becomes available and still function correctly under severe memory constraints.

The experiment analyzes the tradeoff between memory availability and application performances. For this purpose, we run the application with different memory availability and measure the traffic between the gateway and the device. To make the experiments more relevant for code migration effect analysis, we separate the memory allocated for code and data. Thus, the experiment can control directly the memory allocated for application code and eliminate the side effects produced by memory allocated for application data. The memory range used in the experiments spans between the minimum amount of memory required on the embedded device for the application to run and the entire application footprint.

Another parameter varied throughout the experiments is the problem size. Given the structure of the tested application, the number of times each method is invoked is proportional to the input size. This parameter directly affects the performance of the application. If each invocation is performed as RPC, the method invocation generates network traffic and slows the application down significantly. Thus, by changing the input size and memory, we can observe the tradeoff between resource availability and application performance. The results of the experiment are shown in Figure 5.

The graph in Figure 5 shows that beyond the memory size of 45KB, the network traffic is not affected by the problem size. This is because the entire application is executed on the embedded device. The rest of the graph show how the network traffic increases as the memory available on the embedded device reduces. The experiment highlights the ability of the JUCE infrastructure to manage dynamically the tradeoff between performance and resources availability. The general problem of dynamic application distribution is more complex and it goes beyond the scope of this paper.

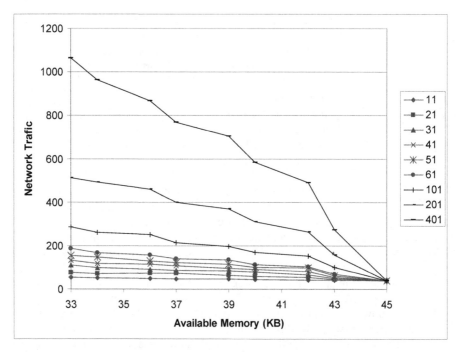

Fig. 5. Tradeoff between Memory and Application Performance

3.2 Security

The current architecture has several potential vulnerabilities. It assumes that devices can trust the gateways for enforcing all Java-specific security and safety constraints on application code. Further it assumes that the connection between the gateway and the device is secure. These assumptions follow the overall JUCE design principle of pushing many resource-intensive concerns into powerful nodes.

There are cases (especially for mobile devices) where a device can be placed in an environment for which the above assumptions do not hold. For instance, a PDA can be enabled to collaborate with devices in its proximity. In this environment, untrusted systems may be able to download malicious code to the remote device. A possible solution is to ensure that remote devices accept code that is authenticated by a trusted JUCE gateway. In this case, the PDA would have to find an appropriate JUCE gateway and request it to authenticate the downloaded code. Thus, the ability to enforce security depends on the ability to build a trust model effectively and cheaply between gateways and remote devices. We are currently examining ways in which this can be achieved.

3.3 Autonomy

In the proposed JUCE architecture, components of the application and runtime system are built incrementally and dynamically. This suggests that remote devices and gateways are closely coupled. For instance, as an application runs and comes across new symbols, the device resident runtime system must interact with the gateway to resolve names and download new services. This dependence on the remote gateway, however, tends to reduce as an application reaches a point where all symbolic references have been resolved and required services have been downloaded. The devices, thus, tend to become autonomous over time.

In certain cases, this level of dependence may not be sufficient. In these cases, the JUCE gateway can force the embedded device to upload a set of methods and resolve a set of symbols before starting the application. The components of this set can be determined as a result of application flow analysis or semi-automatically when the set returned by the flow analysis is not bounded or too large.

4   Related Work

There has been significant research on developing ways in which ubiquitous devices can be used to assist in everyday-life activities (such as office interaction [1, 2], note-taking and home activities [3, 10, 11, 12]).

In this section, we focus primarily on middleware techniques for integrating ubiquitous devices in an overall distributed system framework.

We can classify the different middleware solutions according to how they address and manage interoperability among traditional and ubiquitous devices. The different solutions, thus, approach the interoperability problem at different levels and from different perspectives: At the **application level,** the main focus is placed on providing high level application programming models (such as mobile agents) that can deal in a convenient way with new types of devices. Solutions that provide application level interoperability typically assume the existence of an underlying middleware (for instance, a JVM) that allows the applications to be executed in a platform independent manner. At the **middleware level**, on the other hand, solutions deal with one or more of code, data, and protocol interoperability. The notion of protocol interoperability can cover the entire range of communication protocols from physical layer up to application layer. Note that the protocol interoperability is different from code and data interoperability in that while the first two deal with mediation between computational nodes, the protocol interoperability deals with mediation among communication channels.

Next we describe the different solutions.

4.1 Java Micro Edition

Java 2 Platform Micro Edition (J2ME) provides a compact Java middleware for embedded devices. J2ME features a *configuration layer* that allows the developer to adapt the system to the resources constraints that are specific to a given class of devices. Also, it provides a *profile layer* that allows the developer to provide access to the functionality specific to each type of device. In the J2ME approach both *configuration* and *profile* layers are defined at device's design time and cannot be changed dynamically according to particular application needs. J2ME provides two versions representing different levels of features/resource requirements trade-off. The smaller JVM version – the KVM – still requires around 100KB for the base case scenario. The JUCE approach adds the possibility of scaling the system down for much smaller applications (on the order of 1KB). Also, while J2ME provides two distinct JVM choices, JUCE provides a continuous spectrum between a basic Java VM and a fully featured JVM.

4.2 Ninja Project

The Ninja project supports both application and protocol interoperability. It has developed techniques for integrating devices with limited computation capabilities into the Ninja Distributed System [5]. The devices, called motes, have limited computation and communication power. The devices are controlled by a micro operating system (TinyOS), and can be reprogrammed by downloading code into the devices. The Ninja system integrates these devices into the overall Ninja distributed system through an *Active Proxy* mechanism. An Active Proxy is aware of the protocols supported by each ubiquitous device and is responsible for bridging the gap between the protocols used in the rest of the system and the device. Active Proxy provides an extensible mechanism for adding different kinds of devices with differing protocols, thereby insulating the rest of the system from the differences in the devices. The Active Proxies, thus, implement an important design principle for developing ubiquitous computing systems: Instead of having all nodes support a fully featured system protocol, the responsibility can be placed in a small subset that then work as a gateway to the rest of the systems. The JUCE architecture applies the same principle in the area of code mediation.

The ideas proposed in the Ninja Project are similar to our approach. For instance, the TinyOS has functionalities similar to the one provided by the JUCE micro-kernel. Our work, however, adds the possibility of programming such a system in a high level language while still exploiting the advantages of native code execution. Also, there is a well-defined distinction between motes and regular Ninja nodes in the Ninja architecture. The JUCE architecture, on the other hand, opens up the possibility of utilizing any intermediate architecture scaling between extremely simple nodes up to fully featured ones.

4.3 PATH Project

The PATH project [27] addresses the problem of data level interoperability in the ubiquitous computing environments. The project is motivated by the fact that the proliferation of the new generation of computing devices would be associated with an explosion in the variety of data representation standards. Classic mediation solutions based on generally accepted standards or on conversion layers aware of a fixed set of formats fail to provide the flexibility and scalability required to deal with this continuously increasing number of data representations. PATH project proposes a compositional approach: the architecture consists of simple conversion modules capable of performing the conversion between two given data types. Every time two devices are required to exchange data, PATH infrastructure generates a chain of conversion modules that perform data conversion between the types supported by the two devices. Thus the PATH infrastructure can be extended dynamically to support a potentially unlimited number of data formats. From conceptual perspective, the JUCE project complements PATH project in that while PATH provides data interoperability, JUCE provides code interoperability.

4.4 Teco

The focus of the Teco research group at University of Karlsruhe is on improving the protocol interoperability between ubiquitous computing devices and traditional distributed systems. The research group has developed an open architecture for integrating a wide range of communication protocols [7] such as Inferno [16], JetSend [17], Jini [18], Salutation [19], Tspaces [20], and UpnP [21].The primary focus in this project is to provide an abstraction over several communication protocols.

The code mobility features of the JUCE infrastructure also provide protocol-level interoperability. For instance, such an infrastructure can be enabled to dynamically add support for new protocols by downloading a new protocol handler. Devices can, thus, support any protocol without having to store the corresponding protocol code locally.

4.5 F-Desktop and other Examples of Application Solutions for Ubiquitous Computing Infrastructure

F-Desktop [29] framework is an example of mobile agent technology applied in the area of ubiquitous computing environments. The project focuses on the fact that in a ubiquitous computing environment, the application components are bound to the user and are therefore mobile. The research primarily focuses on issues such as detecting user's location or providing quality of services as application migrates to different types of devices. The system assumes the existence of a platform independent middleware.

There has been other efforts [24,25,26] in building software infrastructure for integrating mobile devices within a distributed framework. The primary focus in most of these approaches has been on building distributed programming models. All of these approaches assume that the devices can run Java programs directly. Our focus, on the other hand, is more on providing services that enable one to run any Java program on any device.

5   Summary

We have presented a Java middleware solution that can scale to a wide range of device sizes. The middleware provides services for running Java programs on remote ubiquitous devices. It achieves this by first compiling an application using a Just-In-Time compiler on a general-purpose gateway. In order to support runtime services required by the compiled code, the gateway also builds a runtime system customized specifically to the needs of the applications. The gateway then sends the compiled native code to a remote device. The remote device executes the applications and downloads the components of the runtime system dynamically. The proposed solution is appealing for several reasons: it improves the performance of remote devices, and requires little resources on these devices. In addition, application programmers can continue to use Java's high-level abstractions and tools for developing applications for these devices.

Our current implementation focuses on the core features of the infrastructure. It does not provide full support for all Java applications. For instance, the current implementation does not support exception handling and multithreading. We are extending our implementation to provide a comprehensive set of functions. We are also looking at deploying the JUCE system within a real ubiquitous infrastructure in order to fully analyze its performance, scalability, and security characteristics.

Acknowledgement

The authors would like to thank the reviewers for their comments. This work is supported by NSF grant no. CCR-0082677.

References

1. Mark Weiser. Some Computer Science Issues in Ubiquitous Computing. *Communication of the ACM*, July 1993.
2. Roy Want, Bill Schilit, Norman Adams, Rich Gold, David Goldberg, Karin Petersen, John Ellis, Mark Weiser. An Overview of the ParcTab Ubiquitous Computing Experiment. *IEEE Personal Communications*, December 1995, Vol. 2 No.6, pp28-43.
3. Gregory D. Abowd and Elizabeth D. Mynatt. Charting Past, Present and Future Research in Ubiquitous Computing. *ACM Transactions on Computer-Human Interaction, Special issue on HCI in the new Millennium,* 7(1):29-58, March.
4. Steven D. Gribble, Matt Welsh, Rob von Behren, Eric A. Brewer, David Culler, N. Borisov, S. Czerwinski, R. Gummadi, J. Hill, A. Joseph, R. H. Katz, Z. M. Mao, S. Ross, and B. Zhao. The Ninja Architecture for Robust Internet-Scale Systems and Services.
5. Kari Kangas and Juha Röning. Using Mobile Code Interfaces to Control Ubiquitous Embedded Systems. *USENIX Workshop on Embedded Systems,* March 29-31, 1999.
6. Markus Lauff, Hans Werner Gellersen. Adaptation in a Ubiquitous Computing Management Architecture. *ACM Symposium on Applied Computing*, Como, Italy, March 2000.
7. Earl Barr, Raju Pandey, Michael Haungs. MAGE: A distributed Programming Model. In Proceedings of the International Conference of Distributed Computing Systems 2001.
8. Open JIT, www.openjit.org
9. G. D. Abowd. Classroom 2000: An experiment with the instrumentation of a living educational environment. *Pervasive Computing* Vol 38, No. 4.
10. Daniel Salber, Anind K. Dey, Rob J. Orr and Gregory D. Abowd. Designing for Ubiquitous Computing: A Case Study in Context Sensing. *GVU Technical*

Report GIT-GVU-99-29. Submitted to the 1999 Conference on Human Factors in Computing Systems (CHI '99), July 1999.

11. Essa I., Ubiquitous Sensing for Smart and Aware Environments: Technologies towards the building of an Aware Home. *Position Paper for the DARPA/NSF/NIST Workshop on Smart Environments*, July 1999.

12. A. Birrell and B. Nelson. Implementing remote procedure calls. *ACM Transaction on Computer Systems*, February 1984. 2(1).

13. James Stamos and Davis Gifford. Remote evaluation. In *ACM Transactions on Programming Languages and Systems*, October 1990. 12(4).

14. D. Chess, C. Harrison, and A. Kershenbaum. Mobile agents: Are they a good idea? *Technical report, IBM T.J. Watson Research Center*, 1995.

15. S. Dorward, R. Pike, D. L. Presotto, D. Ritchie, H. Trickey, and P. Winterbottom. The Inferno operating system. *Bell Labs Technical Journal*, 2(1):5-18, Winter 1997.

16. HP. JetSend Communications Technology Protocol Specification Version 1.5. *HP, White Paper*, 1999.

17. J. Waldo. Jini Architecture Overview. *Sun Microsystems, Inc., 901 San Antonio Road, Palo Alto, CA 94303*, 1998.
    http://www.javasoft.com/products/jini/index.html

18. Salutation Consortium. Salutation Architecture: Overview, *White Paper*, 1998.

19. P. Wyckoff, S. McLaughry, T. Lehman, and D. Ford. TSpaces. *IBM Systems Journal*, 37(3):454-474, 1998. 6.

20. Christensson, Bengt and Larsson, Olof, "*Universal Plug and Play Connects Smart Devices*," WinHEC 99, 1999.
    http://www.axis.com/products/documentation/**UPnP**.doc

21. Sun Microsystems, Java 2 Platform Micro Edition (J2ME) Technology for Creating Mobile Devices, *White Paper*, May 19, 2000.

22. Sheng Liang, Gilad Bracha, Dynamic Class Loading in the Java Virtual Machine, *OOPSLA '98*, 1998.

23. E. Kovacs, K. Rohrle, and M. Reich, Integrating Mobile Agents into Mobile Middleware, *Proc. Mobile Agents Int'l Workshop*, Springer-Verlag, Berlin, 1998, pp 124-135.

24. D. Kotz et al. "Agents TCL: Targeting the Needs of Mobile Computers, *Internet Computing*, July/Aug 1997, pp. 58-67.

25. S. Lipperts and A. Park, An agent-Based Middleware: A Solution for Terminal and User Mobility, *Computer Networks*, Sept 1999, pp 2053-2062.

26. Emre Kiciman, Armando Fox: Using Dynamic Mediation to Integrate COTS Entities in a Ubiquitous Computing Environment, *The Second International Symposium on Handheld and Ubiquitous Computing (huc2k)* Bristol, 25-27 September, 2000.

27. Barry Brumitt, Brian Meyers, John Krumm, Amanda Kern and Steven Shafer: EasyLiving: Technologies for Intelligent Environments, *The Second International Symposium on Handheld and Ubiquitous Computing (huc2k)* Bristol, 25-27 September, 2000

28. Kazunori Takashio, Gakuya Soeda, and Hideyuki Tokuda: A Mobile Agent Framework for Follow-Me Applications in Ubiquitous Computing Environment,

The 21st International Conference on Distributed Computing Systems (ICDCS-21) April 16-19, 2001. Phoenix (Mesa), Arizona, USA

29. MPI http://www.mpi-forum.org
30. David Curtis: Java, RMI and CORBA, White paper, *Object Management Group*
31. Calvin Austin and Monica Pawlan, JNI Technology, Advanced Programming for the Java[TM] Platform Chapter 5.

Software Infrastructure for Ubiquitous Computing Environments: Supporting Synchronous Collaboration with Heterogeneous Devices

Peter Tandler[1]

GMD – German National Research Center for Information Technology,
IPSI – Integrated Publication and Information Systems Institute,
AMBIENTE – Workspaces of the Future,
Dolivostr. 15, D-64293 Darmstadt, Germany
Peter.Tandler@darmstadt.gmd.de

Abstract. In ubiquitous computing environments, multiple users work with a wide range of different devices. In many cases, users interact and collaborate using multiple heterogeneous devices at the same time. The configuration of the devices should be able to change frequently due to a highly dynamic, flexible and mobile nature of new work practices. This produces new requirements for the architecture of an appropriate software infrastructure. In this paper, an architecture designed to meet these requirements is proposed. To test its applicability, this architecture was used as the basis for the implementation of BEACH, the software infrastructure of i-LAND (the ubiquitous computing environment at GMD-IPSI). It provides the functionality for synchronous cooperation and interaction with roomware components, i.e. room elements with integrated information technology. In conclusion, our experiences with the current implementation are presented.

1 Introduction

Ubiquitous computing environments offer a wide range of devices coming in many different sizes and shapes [45]. In situations where tight collaboration is necessary, users must be able to work synchronously with information shared among all these devices. Due to the heterogeneous nature of ubiquitous computing devices, their software infrastructure must provide a user interface taking advantage of their different properties. At the same time, it must enable tight collaboration of users working with different devices or sharing the same device.

We developed a software architecture that offers both flexibility and extensibility for different devices that are part of such ubiquitous computing environments. We used this architecture to create a software system called "BEACH", the Basic Environment for Active Collaboration with Hypermedia. BEACH provides the software

---

[1] Peter Tandler, until his marriage in the summer of 2000, was known as Peter Seitz.

G. D. Abowd, B. Brumitt, S. A. N. Shafer (Eds.): Ubicomp 2001, LNCS 2201, pp. 96-115, 2001.
© Springer-Verlag Berlin Heidelberg 2001

infrastructure for environments supporting synchronous collaboration with many different devices. It offers a user interface that fits also to the needs of devices that have no mouse or keyboard, and which require new forms of human-computer and team-computer interaction. To allow synchronous collaboration BEACH builds on shared documents accessible via multiple interaction devices concurrently.

In the following section, requirements for the software infrastructure of a ubiquitous computing environment to support synchronous collaboration are discussed, also pointing to related work. Based on these requirements, the proposed architecture has been designed, which is presented next. Some example settings taken from our implementation of the architecture are used to show how it can be used. The paper closes with an overview of our experiences and ideas for future work.

2   Requirements for the Software Infrastructure

The software infrastructure of a ubiquitous computing environment with multiple heterogeneous devices has additional requirements compared to collaborative software running on distributed standard PCs. This section explains these requirements organized in five categories:

A. interaction with devices using different forms of interaction (section 2.1)
B. collaboration of users supported by a wide range of devices (section 2.2)
C. integration of devices in the environment (section 2.3)
D. support for different tasks (section 2.4)
E. hardware configuration (section 2.5)

To give a concrete description of requirements, among others, the example of roomware components (i.e. room elements with integrated information technology [38]) is used. The roomware components mentioned here have been developed in the context of the i-LAND project [36]. Similar environments are described in [1, 9]. The meeting context is used when application scenarios are given.

2.1 Interaction with Devices

In a ubiquitous computing environment, a variety of different interaction devices is available. Compared to a "traditional" desktop PC equipped with screen, mouse, and keyboard, these devices come in many different forms and support different styles of interaction, with the aim of providing "natural interfaces" [2].

Requirement A-1: Different Forms of Interaction. It is important for the software infrastructure to be open for different styles of interaction and extensible for future developments [24, p. 15 f]. As current operating systems and platforms only offer direct support for "traditional" interaction techniques and devices, a software infrastructure for a ubiquitous computing environment must allow the *integration of other device drivers* [3, p. 82].

Different interaction styles like pen, speech, or gestures, require the introduction of *new interaction models*. E.g. pen input cannot be dispatched to one single point at a display but might affect a wide area on the screen, while speech or gestures require different processing levels. Here, higher levels influence the recognition steps made on lower levels, always being aware of possible ambiguity [17].

For each of these types of input, *abstractions* must be defined that can be easily mapped to the invocation of functionality [3, p. 81]. For mouse, keyboard, and pen input, events are a useful abstraction, but for other types of input, other concepts might be adequate [24, p. 24]. Other interaction techniques like hardware buttons (often found in PDAs) offer a very similar functionality compared to software button widgets. Therefore the same interaction model should be usable, but it must be possible that some kind of "button-pressed" events can be triggered directly by the device driver and flexibly mapped to software functions.

Requirement A-2: Adapted Visualization. Due to the different form-factors of interaction devices in a ubiquitous computing environment, displays appear in a broad range of different sizes and with different orientations. For differently sized devices different scaling factors, a different representation, or a different selection of objects must be used. This could take into account, whether the user needs an overview of the whole document, or just a part of the document is being edited. The more the devices differ, the harder it becomes to use a similar interface for all devices [3, p. 81; 24, p. 16], as other interface metaphors and concepts then become appropriate.

Another problem arises at an interactive table [36]: the orientation of the output does not necessarily have a common top-bottom/left-right for all users working at an InteracTable, as different users can look at the surface from different positions. At a traditional paper-based table, the users would simply rotate a sheet of paper to show it to someone else. At an interactive table, the same should be possible. In addition, the user should be able to keep a view of this object oriented towards her so that they can both look at the object with the preferred orientation.

Requirement A-3: Non-Visual Output. In analogy to the different input techniques (req. A-1), other output devices besides visual displays can be found in a ubiquitous computing environment. This can range from audio-based output [20] to ambient displays [13, 25].

While for different visualizations a common interface can be provided at a rather low level describing the visual appearance, another approach has to be taken here. One idea is the separation of the models for the *abstract* and the *physical* UI [44]. Depending on the used output device it might be possible to generate the physical user interface automatically from generic elements [24, p. 13]. In general, it is important, that all different interaction models use a common interface to the underlying functionality.

2.2 Collaboration of Users Supported by Devices

One characteristic property of a ubiquitous computing environment is the presence of many collaborating and communicating users and devices.

Requirement B-1: Multiple-Device Interaction. In a ubiquitous computing environment, a user usually has access to more than one computer. Within a meeting, a user might leave an interactive chair and walk up to a large public presentation surface to give a presentation. Here, the software must be able to detect and quickly change the assignment of the current user at these devices to give the user access to private information, for instance to the prepared material for the presentation.

The continuation of this scenario brings up a different case of multiple-device interaction: the user giving the presentation might have access to another device in parallel to the public display. To view her private annotations in addition to her slides, she uses e.g. an electronic lectern. Here, she uses several devices simultaneously with the same information displayed on both devices — but within a *different context* which influences the resulting view (different size, different level of detail, private annotations). This relates to the adapted visualization (req. **A-2**) where the context is defined by the *used devices* in contrast to the *usage of the device*.

Many examples where a PDA-like device (personal digital assistant) is used concurrently with a digital whiteboard, a table, or PC are given in literature [9, 22, 27, 28]. The PDA is used to have access to additional information or functionality without wasting space on the main display. On public displays, the PDA can be used for private information [11] or for functionality only relevant for its user. In these cases, both devices show different information and offer a different functionality.

Requirement B-2: Collaboration with Different Devices. The situation becomes even more complicated in the case of multiple users working together. Here, standard methods of shared editing cannot be used. E.g. WYSIWIS ("What-You-See-Is-What-I-See" [34]) would require that all collaborating users have coupled workspaces of exactly the same size in pixels, which is not possible if the devices cover a display size from very small to very large.

Fig. 1. The CommChair allows interacting remotely with documents displayed on the DynaWall. In addition, a private workspace can be accessed

Instead, the software must allow even tightly coupled components to use different view properties, but ensure that the users get a representation that fits to the current working mode. A user in a "CommChair" working on a shared workspace together with a user at a "DynaWall" (fig. 1) will need both an overview representation of the whole workspace content and a second, zoomed view to work with. If the CommChair is located directly in front of the DynaWall so that the user can see the overview there, the overview representation displayed at the CommChair can be shrunk much more, as it is only needed for navigation.

Requirement B-3: Multiple-User Devices. Some devices like interactive tables or walls offer another challenge for the software: several people can use one device together and interact simultaneously with a single device. This is often called Single Display Groupware (SDG) [7, 22, 35].

In addition to SDG, multiple users at one display can collaborate with multiple users at other displays. This leads to a n:m relation between collaborating users and devices.

Software running on this device must therefore be able to receive events from several input-streams, to recognize input from different users, and to track several concurrent event sequences. Examples for event sequences are the drawing of a stroke or the dragging of a window [12].

Beside these technical issues, the user interface should be designed to allow the interaction of multiple users without interference.

2.3 Integration of Devices in the Environment

Another important area of requirements arises from the integration of devices and software within the working environment or working context.

Requirement C-1: Context Awareness. Software being aware of its context can act depending on the state of the surrounding environment. Common examples of context are the current location of devices and specific users [2, p. 35ff], but also the kind of device a software application is actually running. Besides the physical environment, other contextual information like the current task or project could influence the behavior of the software, as far as it is available to the software.

The software infrastructure must therefore maintain a representation of the current context. To be able to update this representation, an interface to sensors collecting context information (distributed all over the environment) is needed. If context changes are detected, mechanisms must exist to inform the application. Similar to what was described for different input devices, the data collected by the sensors will normally need preprocessing in order to generate information on a layer of abstraction useful for the application [29].

Requirement C-2: Physical Interaction. Since the configuration of physical objects in a meeting room strongly depends on the current work mode of a team, changes made to "real" objects can be used to trigger actions of the software. It is especially useful to reflect adaptations made by users to the setting of devices, due to changes of the current collaboration mode.

There are cases where a state change of the software is essential to maintain the consistency of the "real" and the "virtual" parts of the world ("augmented reality"). For example, "ConnecTables" are small interactive tables that can be assembled quickly to yield a larger homogeneous interactive area if desired [40, 43]. This is useful to support flexible splitting into and re-joining of subgroups. Here, the software must be capable of *dynamic changes* to the size and format of the currently available visual interaction area, and it is necessary to reflect these possibilities in the conceptual design of the user interface.

2.4 Support for Different Tasks

An interview study that we carried out found that creative teams have several recurring tasks [39]. Consequently, the software should offer dedicated help for a selected set of such tasks, which should be extensible to meet future needs [18].

Requirement D-1: Generic Functionality. Many functions are common to a wide range of application scenarios. This functionality should be reusable.

Requirement D-2: Tailorable Functionality. Important examples for typical group tasks that should be supported are creative sessions, presentations, meeting moderation, and project or task management. To be able to provide tailored support, a module concept should be available that is capable of extending the generic functionality. Of course, this should be possible without the need to change existing code and without interference to other modules.

Requirement D-3: Capture and Access Information. Another recurring task is that of gaining access to previously generated information. Within a context-aware ubiquitous computing environment, a lot of information can be captured automatically in addition to what is generated manually [1, 2]. For both capturing and accessing this information, dedicated support is needed.

2.5 Hardware Configuration

The restrictions of currently available hardware also place some requirements on the software.

Requirement E-1: Multiple-Computer Devices. What a user perceives as one *device* might actually consist of many individual hardware components. Some roomware components (e.g. the DynaWall, see fig. 1) are composed from several segments, each run by a separate PC. Due to the limitations of the available hardware (currently, each SMART Board [33] can only recognize a single pen position at any one time) this configuration allows each segment to receive pen input by one user each, thereby supporting many users simultaneously. To give the user the impression of a homogeneous interaction area, the segments must therefore be coupled via software. This enables multiple users to collaborate on the same visual interaction area in spite of the limitations of hardware or physical space.

Requirement E-2: Dynamic Configuration. During a meeting it often happens that several independent problems are identified that have to be solved in parallel. In such situations, a team usually divides into a set of subgroups, each trying to solve one of these problems. After a defined amount of time, the team forms a plenary again and all solutions are presented. This scenario shows that different kinds of collaboration modes must be supported within a ubiquitous computing environment, each demanding a different configuration of available devices. The dynamics of a meeting must therefore be reflected in the design of the software, which should be flexible enough to give a team the necessary freedom to work efficiently.

3   Architecture of the Software Infrastructure

With respect to the requirements described in the previous section, an architecture has been developed that offers the flexibility necessary for supporting heterogeneous devices and ensures the extensibility for future devices. This section first gives an overview of the different layers and models before discussing the layers and their duties in more detail.

3.1 Architecture Overview

In order to provide reusable components on the one hand and hooks for adaptations for different devices on the other, the architecture is organized in four horizontal layers defining different levels of abstractions. Orthogonal to these layers, the architecture is structured by five models separating basic concerns within each layer (fig. 2).

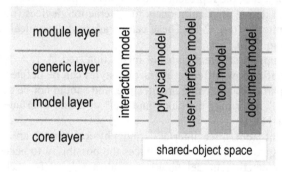

Fig. 2. The software architecture is horizontally organized in four layers defining different levels of abstractions and vertically by five models separating basic concerns. Crucial for synchronous collaboration is a shared-object space provided by the core layer enabling distributed access to objects

Levels of Abstraction. As mentioned, the proposed architecture is organized in four layers defining different levels of abstractions. The *module layer* (section 3.4) is most specific containing modules that provide tailored functionality for distinct tasks (req. D-2). It can be used to extend the functionality defined by the *generic layer* (section 3.3), which contains generic components that provide the basic functionality necessary in most teamwork and meeting situations (req. D-1).

While the two top layers consist of components perceivable by the user, the two lower layers are introduced to structure the application and ensure extensibility. The *model layer* (section 3.2) specifies the basic structure for the two top layers by defining interfaces for documents, tools, user interface, the physical environment, and interaction styles as the common abstractions for all devices (req. **A-1**, **A-3**, **B-2**, **C-2**). Thus, it can be seen as the implementation of the five basic concerns that are separated by the architecture (see below).

The *core layer* (section 3.5) offers a specialized infrastructure making the implementation of the higher layers easier (req. **A-2**, **B-3**, **D-2**). Most important, it provides *shared objects* that are crucial to allow distributed access from multiple computers (req. **E-1**, **B-1**).

Basic Models. To ensure a clear separation of concerns, models for document, tools, user interface, interaction, and physical environment are distinguished (fig. 2). While the interfaces and abstract classes used to implement these basic models are defined by the model layer, parts of the core layer can also be structured according to these concepts.

The *document model* defines the base classes and functionality of all objects that can be part of a document (req. D-1).

The *tool model* describes the elements that are directly attached to the user interface, providing additional functionality to the documents. In addition, the tool controls the possible work modes like the degree of coupling.

The *user interface model* is needed to define an alternative user interface concept suitable for different devices (req. A-1). Furthermore, multiple-computer devices (req. E-1) require that the user interface elements are part of the shared-object space. This enables user interface elements to be distributed among several computers.

The *physical model* is the representation of relevant parts of the "real" world. The two top layers can define physical models for interaction devices (req. A-1) or other objects to be monitored (req. C-1). These can be adapted dynamically if sensors recognize changes (req. E-2).

To be able to support different styles of interaction (req. A-1, A-3, C-2), the *interaction model* specifies how different interaction styles can be defined. The term used here describes a part of the software architecture, and should not be confused with the "interaction model" describing the "look and feel" of a user interface at a conceptual level as defined in [4].

While document, tool, user interface, and physical model are implemented as shared objects to give several users or devices the possibility to access these objects simultaneously, interaction model objects are always local to each machine. This allows each client to adapt the interaction style according to its local context, especially its physical environment and interaction capabilities (see examples in section 4). To connect the interaction model objects to the other models, the architecture uses the constraint mechanism described below.

A more extensive discussion of these models is given in [42].

3.2 Model Layer: Basic Separation of Concerns

The aim of the model layer is to provide an implementation of the basic models to be used as the basis for the implementation of the higher layers. This is important to ensure extensibility and interoperability of both generic components and modules.

For example, the interaction model defined by this layer could specify to use the *model-view-controller* (MVC) concept [14] to separate the handling of input and output. In this case, the model layer would contain not only the base classes for views and controller, but also the code necessary to create, update etc. the views and to dispatch events to specific controllers. For visual-based interaction, BEACH uses an adapted version of the model-view-controller concept (see section 3.5).

Similarly, the document model separates the *domain model* (sometimes also called "business domain objects" or just "model objects") and the *application model* [15, 41]. Domain models represent entities of the domain world. Application models are used to describe all application aspects such as presentation and manipulation of domain objects. For, e.g., a "text" object, the domain model includes the string describing the text and text attributes like font or size. The application model adds the editing state for text, like cursor position or selection. The shared editing state gives the ability to provide awareness, e.g. to display cursors of other users [31]. In addition, it specifies the degree of coupling between different users, i.e., which parts of the editing state are shared by all users and which allow private values. The workspace application model allows for instance different rotation of the workspace for two users working at an interactive table (see req. A-2), while all other properties are tightly coupled.

3.3 Generic Layer: Generic Collaboration Support

One important goal of every software system is to provide generic components that are useful in many different situations and for different tasks (req. D-1). To illustrate the generic components layer, some examples taken from BEACH are presented, which are further elaborated in section 4.

The basis for *documents* created with BEACH is a hypermedia data model. The generic document elements include hand-written input (scribbles), texts, images, and links as basic objects constituting information and workspaces to structure information (the equivalent of a page).

The *tools* currently realized by the generic layer of BEACH are toolbars and document browsers. Document browsers have a special role in defining the connection between the user interface and the document, i.e. specifying which part of the document is shown where, also offering possibilities of navigating in the document to a different workspace.

The main elements of the *user interface* of BEACH are segments and overlays [26]: the complete visual interaction area of a roomware component can be partitioned into "segments", which define the space available for a tool, e.g. a document browser. In addition, "overlays" reside in front of the segments in the background and can be positioned freely and are used in a similar way to the windows of most popular operating systems. They also contain a tool, but they would normally be used for toolbars and other smaller tools that have to be at hand for the user all the time.

One important part of the representation of the *physical environment* is the configuration of roomware components. A "station" refers to computers running a BEACH client. To be able to combine several stations to a composite roomware component (req. E-1, C-1) the current setting is available as shared objects, as shown in figure 3. A roomware component consists of one or more stations. Each station can have a display. The displays of all stations belonging to a roomware component are combined to a display area, which represents the complete interaction area of the roomware component, e.g. the complete area of a DynaWall (see fig. 1).

If displays are added to or removed from the display area, the views showing it will immediately adjust the size of the available area (req. **E-2**) due to the dependencies between the physical model and the views.

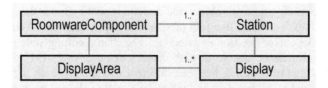

Fig. 3. The display area combines all displays of its roomware component's stations to one homogeneous interaction area

To provide an adequate *interaction* with roomware components, the traditional mouse-based interaction has been extended with support for gestures written with a pen (req. A-1), support for audio output is currently being implemented [20]. To generate the gesture events needed to handle pen input, each stroke that is drawn is sent to a gesture recognizer to check whether it is similar to one of the set of supported gesture shapes. In this case, a gesture event is generated and dispatched. In contrast to mouse events, which refer to a specific point, a gesture event is associated with a stroke — which could cross the bounds of multiple view objects. Therefore, a dispatcher for gesture events has been implemented that is capable of selecting the right view's controller.

3.4 Module Layer: Tailored Support for Tasks

The generic elements that are provided by BEACH are useful in many different situations. For some tasks it is of help if specific support is given (req. **D-2**). Therefore, the proposed architecture has a module layer, which allows modules to add further model elements and to extend the functionality of existing components. By providing hooks already in the core layer to add new toolbars and services, modules can be plugged into BEACH without having to change existing code.

At present, only one BEACH module is available. It provides support for creative teams to collect ideas during brainstorming sessions. Ideas generated between sessions can be collected using a PDA and transferred to a public roomware component (e.g. a DynaWall) in the next meeting [16] (similar to [11]).

3.5 Core Layer: Specialized Infrastructure

The aim of the core layer is to provide functionality that will make the development of the higher levels more convenient. This includes

- synchronous access to distributed objects,
- automatic update and dependency detection,
- multi-user event handling,
- view transformations,
- device and sensor management, and
- module and services interface.

Here, we will focus on the first four items, as these are of main interest within the scope of this paper.

Shared-Object Space. In order to provide computer support for synchronous collaboration a platform for the distributed access to shared objects is needed (requirements B-1, B-2, C-1, and E-1). This section does not discuss the properties of different groupware frameworks and toolkits; it rather highlights the important features of the software infrastructure of a ubiquitous computing environment.

BEACH uses a replicated model, as some roomware components are connected via a wireless network with a rather low bandwidth of currently 10 Mbps shared by all connected clients (fig. 4). After an initial replication, only incremental changes to the shared objects have to be transmitted, thus reducing necessary communication. A server synchronizes all replicates of shared objects and ensures persistency. To minimize the coordination overhead, objects are grouped in "clusters" being the atomic elements for replication.

Transactions are used to guarantee consistency in spite of concurrent changes to objects. As a ubiquitous computing environment is highly interactive, it is important to ensure a fast response of the user interface. Avoiding delays waiting for the server's commit, optimistic transactions offer a significant speedup whenever conflicting actions are unlikely or harmless.

Automatic Update and Dependency Detection. As changes to shared objects can be initiated by an arbitrary computer for a variety of reasons, it is very important that mechanisms are provided to trigger updates automatically when the state of shared objects changes (req. C-2, E-2).

Therefore, a declarative description of views (or other kinds of output objects) is used. The dependencies between views and attributes of shared objects are automatically detected and re-computation is triggered whenever these attributes are changed [30]. When, e.g., the attribute 'color' of a workspace is set to 'blue' while a view for this workspace is open somewhere, this view will be repainted, regardless who changed this value on which device. This is very similar to the constraints used in systems like Amulet [23], but works also for a distributed setting.

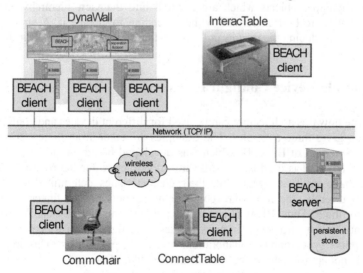

Fig. 4. BEACH clients running on different roomware component are synchronised by a server

Multi-user Event Handling. For multiple-user devices (req. B-3), it is necessary to provide an interface to hardware that is capable of handling multiple users at the same time using the same device. Multiple device drivers can send events, tagged with an identification of the originator, to BEACH. As an alternative to the standard mouse button-up or -down events, these can also be events like pen-up, pen-moved, or pen-down (req. A-1).

To support an adapted user interface for roomware components equipped with a pen, the events generated by the device drivers can first be assembled to higher level events. As it is very intuitive to draw strokes with a pen instead of just clicking on a document, pen events can be combined to strokes. For these strokes, gesture events can be generated depending on the shape drawn with the pen (like tap, line, circle [10]).

As different kinds of events need different strategies for dispatching, the event can choose an appropriate dispatching strategy. For example, key-pressed events are received by the controller having the keyboard focus, button-down or pen-down events are dispatched to all views at the mouse or pen position. Mouse-moved events are directly discarded — as they only have an effect after a button- (or pen-) down event.

To track several concurrent event sequences, the concept of "trackers" has been extended. A tracker is an object receiving events directly, without using the view hierarchy for dispatching. This is the same mechanism as is used by Myers' multi-user interactors [21]. BEACH is capable of handling several trackers at the same time by keeping a mapping of input device IDs to the different trackers, which will get all events from this device.

View Transformations. As views should be displayable in different orientations and sizes (req. A-2, B-2), depending on the current context, the core model replaces the standard "graphics context" (which handles the drawing) by an adapted version that supports transformations. A transformation is an object that responds to messages for transforming points and graphic primitives like images. These transformations are applied by wrapper objects which are inserted into the view hierarchy and which "wrap" the view to be transformed without needing to change it. A similar idea is followed by introducing the *portals* in Pad++ [5] or the *internal cameras* in Jazz [6].

4   Example Device Configurations

To illustrate how this architecture can be used for different devices and configurations this section gives three examples. The examples are taken from the experience with the implementation of BEACH, which was developed based on the proposed architecture. As BEACH is used as the software infrastructure for the roomware components we have built at GMD-IPSI, their characteristics determined the focus of BEACH. Currently, the roomware components support pen or finger as the main medium for input. Thus, BEACH emphasizes direct visual interaction. All roomware components have a permanent (in parts wireless, see fig. 4) network connection aiming to support synchronous collaboration, and no "slow" CPUs. This implies that BEACH is not appropriate for very small devices like PDAs and for devices not having a permanent connection to the network.

The examples show elements of the generic layer only, as this layer defines the concrete classes used to implement generic support for roomware components. First, the DynaWall is an example for a multiple-computer device (req. **E-1**). Second, the collaboration between a large public and a smaller private device (req. **B-2**) is shown in the case of a DynaWall in conjunction with a CommChair. And third, the Interac-Table is used to demonstrate a device that can be used by multiple users at the same time, but with different viewing preferences (req. **A-2**, **B-3**). These examples focus on the four shared models, leaving the interaction model aside. Another configuration showing the relationship of the shared models to the interaction model using the example of ConnecTables is presented in [43].

4.1 Combining Multiple Computers to One Interaction Device

As mentioned before, the DynaWall (fig. 1) consists of three computers (multiple-computer device, req. **E-1**), each with an attached SMART Board [33]. Therefore, the physical model defines the roomware component "DynaWall" (DWRWC in fig. 5) to consist of three stations (DWStation1 to DWStation3) with their displays combined to one large display area. While the three SMART Boards in our lab are mounted to one wall (fig. 1), the software allows changing this setting dynamically (req. **C-2**, **E-2**), e.g., when the boards are mobile and equipped with sensors (similar to the ConnecT-able [43]).

If the display area is not divided into several segments (DWSegment1), it can be used to display one large workspace (DWWorkspace1) within one document browser (DWDocBrowser1). As mentioned above, the application model (DWWorkspaceApp1) is used to define the editing state and functionality for the workspace.

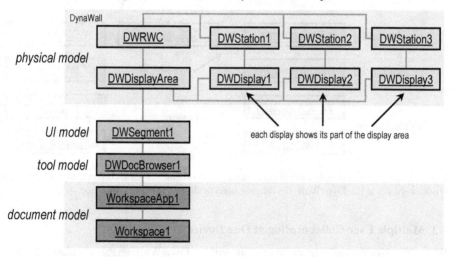

Fig. 5. The representation for a DynaWall consisting of three computers, which are combined to form a homogeneous display area. This allows the complete area to be used to show one large workspace

4.2 Tight Collaboration Using Two Different Devices

When a CommChair connects to the DynaWall specified in the previous example, it is interesting to see, on the one hand, how the tight collaboration between CommChair and DynaWall is implemented (req. **B-2**). On the other hand, it shows how the CommChair's display area is separated into two segments for public and private workspaces.

The display area, which consists of only one display in the case of a CommChair (CCRWC in fig. 6), is split into two segments (CCSegment1 and CCSegment2). While one segment is used to show a document browser (CCDocBrowser2) for the private workspace (Workspace2), the other connects to the document browser shown at the DynaWall (DWDocBrowser1). This enables very tight collaboration, as using a shared browser results in coupled navigation. As always the same application model is used, all editing state is also shared between the DynaWall and the CommChair, which allows providing awareness information [31].

As the size of the segments at the DynaWall and the CommChair differs, the inter-action model (not shown in figure 6) has to provide an appropriate mechanism to display the public workspace at the CommChair. Well know techniques are scrolling and/or zooming.

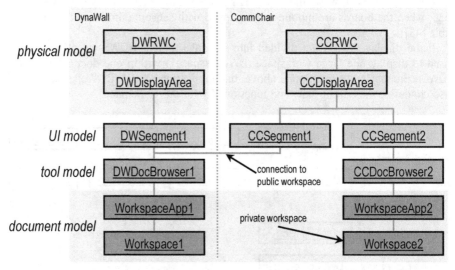

Fig. 6. The CommChair splits its display area into two segments. One connects to the document browser shown at the DynaWall, the other is used to show a private workspace

4.3 Multiple User Collaborating at One Device

While the CommChair in combination with a DynaWall enables collaboration of users with different devices, the InteracTable aims at supporting several users at the same device (req. **B-3**). As mentioned, it is necessary that horizontal displays require different orientation for users with different orientation towards the display (req. **A-2**).

To realize this, we used an approach where each user can open an overlay that can be freely moved around the display area, similar to a window (e.g. ITOverlay1 and

ITOverlay2 in fig. 7). Each overlay gets an own document browser and workspace application model, but connected to the same workspace. In this case, the interaction model will open two views showing the same workspace. This allows each user to rotate her/his workspace to the preferred direction, as the rotation is specified by the workspace application model.

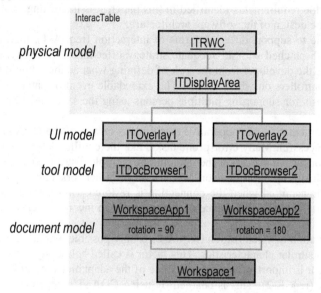

Fig. 7. Two user working at an InteracTable with the same workspace. By using separate browsers with separate application models, each user can look at the workspace with the preferred orientation

5   Current State and Experiences

The implementation of BEACH based on the proposed architecture shows that it helps to provide the functionality needed as the software infrastructure of the currently existing roomware components. BEACH is implemented using VisualWorks Smalltalk [8]. As shared-object space the COAST framework [30, 32] (developed at GMD-IPSI) has been chosen.[2] The former version of this framework was used in the DOLPHIN system [37].

Our experiences with the current version of BEACH are quite promising. We used the prototype at the international computer fair CeBIT at Hannover, Germany, in March 1999 to give interactive presentations using a DynaWall and a CommChair and for exploration by visitors. Since May 2000 there has been an installation of a roomware environment with a specialized version of BEACH at the German Occupational Safety and Health Exhibition in Dortmund (DASA). It is open to the public and visitors can experience "future work situations" for themselves. For our own work in

---

[2] COAST is now available as open source from http://www.opencoast.org.

the AMBIENTE team, we use BEACH both for internal and external presentations and for discussions and design meetings.

5.1 Conclusions

Concerning the requirements identified in this paper, it is interesting to see how they influenced the design of the software architecture.

To be able to support different forms of interaction (req. **A-1**), high-level events that can be dispatched with an adequate strategy offer much flexibility. However, it does not free the developer from the task of defining what actions should be triggered by which controllers on which events. The extendable event dispatching mechanism is a good basis for supporting multiple persons using the same devices concurrently (req. **B-3**).

The implementation of cooperative applications on top of the COAST framework was very successful. Many error-prone tasks, like the conflict detection and handling caused by concurrent actions or the updating of multiple distributed views are carried out automatically by the framework. In case of brief network failures, queued trans-actions are transmitted when the connection is restored. However, if multiple other users continue working, the chance of rollbacks due to inconsistencies increases over time.

The adaptation of visualization (req. **A-2**) is only possible within a certain range of devices with similar characteristics. This factor is called "plasticity" of the user inter-face in [44]. It is important to note that some of the adaptations might have to change dynamically (req. **E-2**). This is enabled by using COAST's dependency mechanism for generating the visualization.

The shared object space provided by COAST together with a consequent separa-tion and of application and domain models is the key to allow multi-device interaction (req. **B-1**) and composite roomware components (req. **E-1**). Since all models are im-plemented as shared objects stored on a server, clients can easily be restarted after crashes and resume exactly where they stopped.

Combining the shared object space and the dependency mechanism allows the modeling of dynamic changes of collaboration using different devices (req. **B-2**). For the integration of contextual information provided by sensors (req. **C-1**), this is also a flexible platform, as sensors need not be attached to the local machine, but can be connected to an arbitrary computer. Since the sensors are part of the shared-object space, their state can be monitored by any client, thus allowing state changes to trig-ger actions.

The possibility to include modules with added functionality in BEACH offers the specialization needed for certain tasks (req. **D-2**).

5.2 Future Work

Currently, we are developing new BEACH modules, e.g. for navigation and access to created information, and for integration of audio output. Other issues are the integra-tion of mobile devices that are not always connected to the server and devices with restrictions on CPU and memory like PDAs. One approach to realize the connection to PDAs is to provide an interface to shared-event-based system as described in [9].

While asynchronous work is possible as long as different groups work on non-overlapping parts of the shared-object space, this is not feasible in practice. For asynchronous, unconnected collaboration, it is essential to deal with inconsistencies. One solution could be the automatic creation of different versions for all objects changed while not connected.

The latest information about BEACH can be found at http://www.darmstadt.gmd.de/ambiente/activities/beach.html.

Acknowledgements

The author would like to thank all the colleagues and students of the AMBIENTE division at GMD-IPSI for helpful discussions and for the support with the time consuming implementation work. He especially thanks Norbert Streitz, Jörg Finger, Richard Stenzel, Thorsten Prante, and Carsten Magerkurth who helped to improve this paper.

References

1. Abowd, G. D., et al. (1996). Teaching and learning as multimedia authoring: the classroom 2000 project. In *Proceedings of the ACM Conference on Multimedia (Multimedia '96)*, pp. 187–198.
2. Abowd, G. D., Mynatt, E. D. (2000). Charting Past, Present, and Future Research in Ubiquitous Computing. *ACM Transactions on Computer-Human Interaction*, Vol. 7, No. 1, March 2000, pp. 29–58.
3. Abowd, G. D. (1999). Software Engineering Issues for Ubiquitous Computing. In *Proceedings of the 21st international conference on Software engineering (ICSE'99)*. ACM Press, pp. 75–84.
4. Beaudouin-Lafon, M. (2000). Instrumental Interaction: An interaction model for designing post-WIMP user interfaces. In *Proceedings of the ACM Conference on Human Factors in Computing Systems* (CHI'00), ACM Press, New York, NY, pp. 446–453.
5. Bederson, B. B., et al. (1996). Pad++: A Zoomable Graphical Sketchpad for Exploring Alternate Interface Physics. *Journal of Visual Languages and Computing*, 7, pp. 3–31.
6. Bederson, B. B., Meyer, J., Good, L. (2000). Jazz: An Extensible Zoomable user Interface Graphics Toolkit in Java. In *Proceedings of User Interface and Software Technology (UIST 2000)*, ACM Press.
7. Bier, E., Freeman, S. (1991). MMM: A user interface architecture for shared editors on a single screen. In *ACM SIGGRAPH Symposium on User Interface Software and Technology, Proceedings UIST'91*, pp. 79–86.
8. Cincom Homepage. (2001) http://www.cincom.com
9. Fox, A., Johanson, B., Hanrahan, P., Winograd, T. (2000). Integrating Information Appliances into an Interactive Workspace, *IEEE CG&A*, May/June 2000, pp. 54–65.

10. Geißler, J. (1995). Gedrics: The next generation of icons. In *Proceedings of the 5th International Conference on Human-Computer Interaction (INTERACT'95)*, Lillehammer, Norway, pp. 73–78.

11. Greenberg, S., Boyle, M. and LaBerge, J. (1999). PDAs and Shared Public Displays: Making Personal Information Public, and Public Information Personal. *Personal Technologies*, Vol.3, No.1, pp. 54–64, March. Elsevier.

12. Hourcade, J. P., & Bederson, B. B. (1999). Architecture and Implementation of a Java Package for Multiple Input Devices (MID). Tech. Report HCIL-99-08, CS-TR-4018, UMIACS-TR-99-26, Computer Science Department, University of Maryland, College Park, MD.

13. Ishii, H., Ullmer, B. (1997). Tangible bits: towards seamless interfaces between people. bits and atoms. In *Proceedings of the ACM Conference on Human Factors in Computing Systems (CHI'97)*, ACM Press, New York, NY, pp. 234–241.

14. Krasner, G. E., Pope, S. T. (1988). A Cookbook for Using the Model-View-Controller User Interface Paradigm in Smalltalk. *Journal of Object Oriented Programming.* 1(3), pp. 26–49.

15. Luo, P., Szekely, P., Neches, R. (1993). Management of interface design in humanoid. In *Proceedings of the ACM Conference on Human factors in computing systems (CHI'93)*, pp. 107–114.

16. Magerkurth, M., Prante, T. (2001). „Metaplan" für die Westentasche: Mobile Computerunterstützung für Kreativitätssitzungen. In *Proceedings of Mensch & Computer 2001*. Bad Honnef (Bonn), Germany, pp. 163–171.

17. Mankoff, J., Hudson, S., and Abowd G. (2000). Providing integrated toolkit-level support for ambiguity in recognition-based interfaces. In *Proceedings of the ACM Conference on Human Factors in Computing Systems (CHI'00)*, ACM Press, New York, NY, pp. 368–375.

18. Moran, T., van Melle, W. (1998). Tailorable Domain Objects as Meeting Tools for an Electronic Whiteboard. In *Proceedings of the ACM 1998 Conference on Computer Supported Cooperative Work (CSCW'98)*, ACM Press, pp. 295—304.

19. Müller-Tomfelde, C., Reischl, W. (1998). Communication Chairs: Examples of Mobile Roomware Components. CHI '98 Summary. Suite on Late-Breaking Results: "The Real and the Virtual: Integrating Architectural and Information Spaces".

20. Müller-Tomfelde, C., Steiner, S. (2001). Audio Enhanced Collaboration at an Electronic White Board. To appear in *Proceedings of the 7th International Conference on Auditory Display (ICAD'01)*, Espoo, Finland.

21. Myers, B. A. (1999). An Implementation Architecture to Support Single-Display Groupware. Technical Report CMU-CS-99-139, CMU-HCII-99-101, Human Computer Interaction Institute, School of Computing Science, Carnegie Mellon University, Pittsburgh, PA 15213-3891, May 1999, http://www.cs.cmu.edu/~bam.

22. Myers, B. A. et al. (1998). Collaboration using multiple PDAs connected to a PC. In *Proceedings of the ACM 1998 Conference on Computer Supported Cooperative Work (CSCW'98)*, ACM Press, pp. 285–294.

23. Myers, B. A., et al. (1997). The Amulet Environment: New Models for Effective User Interface Software Development. *IEEE Transactions on Software Engineering,* 23(6), pp. 347–365.

24. Myers, B. A., Hudson S. E., and Pausch R. (2000). Past, Present, and Future of User Interface Software Tools. *ACM Transactions on Computer-Human Interaction*, Vol. 7, No. 1, March 2000, pp. 3–28.

25. Mynatt, E. D. et al. (1998). Designing Audio Aura. In *Proceedings of the ACM Conference on Human Factors in Computing Systems (CHI'98)*, ACM Press, New York, NY, pp. 566–573.

26. Prante, T. (1999). A new pen-centric user interface to support creative teamwork in roomware environments (in German). Diploma thesis, GMD-IPSI, Darmstadt Technical University, Department of Computer Science.

27. Rekimoto, J. (1998). A Multiple Device Approach for Supporting Whiteboard-based Interactions. In *Proceedings of the ACM Conference on Human Factors in Computing Systems (CHI'98)*, ACM Press, New York, NY, pp. 344–351.

28. Rekimoto, J. (1998). Multiple-Computer User Interfaces: A cooperative environment consisting of multiple digital devices. In Streitz, N., Konomi, S., Burkhardt, H. (Eds.), *Cooperative Buildings – Integrating Information, Organization and Architecture. First International Workshop on Cooperative Buildings (Co-Build'98)*, Darmstadt, Germany, February 1998. Lecture Notes in Computer Science 1370. Springer: Heidelberg, pp. 33–40.

29. Salber, D., Dey, A. K., and Abowd, G. D. (1999). The Context Toolkit: Aiding the Development of Context-Enabled Applications. In *Proceedings of the ACM Conference on Human Factors in Computing Systems (CHI'99)*, ACM Press, New York, NY, pp. 434–441.

30. Schuckmann, C., Kirchner, L., Schümmer, J., Haake, J. M. (1996). Designing object-oriented synchronous groupware with COAST. In *Proceedings of the ACM 1996 Conference on Computer Supported Cooperative Work (CSCW'96)*, ACM Press, pp. 30–38.

31. Schuckmann, C., Schümmer, J., Seitz, P. (1999). Modeling Collaboration using Shared Objects. In *Proceedings of International ACM SIGGROUP Conference on Supporting Group Work*, November 14-17, 1999, Phoenix, Arizona, USA, pp. 189–198.

32. Schümmer, J., Schümmer, T., Schuckmann, C. (2000). COAST – Ein Anwendungsframework für synchrone Groupware. Presented at net.objectdays 2000, Erfurt, Germany.

33. SMART Technologies Homepage. (2001). http://www.smarttech.com

34. Stefik, M., Bobrow, D. G., Foster, G., Lanning, S., Tatar, D. (1987). WYSIWIS revised: early experiences with multiuser interfaces. *ACM Transactions on Information Systems*. 2(5), pp. 147–167.

35. Stewart, J., Bederson, B. B., Druin, A. (1999). Single Display Groupware: A Model for Co-Present Collaboration. In *Proceedings of Human Factors in Computing Systems (CHI'99)*, ACM Press, New York, NY, pp. 286–293.

36. Streitz, N. et al. (1999). i-LAND: An interactive landscape for creativity and innovation. In *Proceedings of the ACM Conference on Human Factors in Computing Systems (CHI'99)*, Pittsburgh, Pennsylvania, USA, May 15-20, 1999, pp. 120-127.

37. Streitz, N., Geißler, J., Haake, J., and Hol, J. (1994). DOLPHIN: Integrated meeting support across LiveBoards, local and desktop environments. In *Proceedings of CSCW '94*, ACM Press, pp. 345–358.

38. Streitz, N., Geißler, J., Holmer, T. (1998). Roomware for Cooperative Buildings: Integrated Design of Architectural Spaces and Information Spaces. In Streitz, N. et al. (Eds.), *Cooperative Buildings – Integrating Information, Organization and Architecture. First International Workshop on Cooperative Buildings (Co-Build'98)*, Darmstadt, Germany, February 1998. Lecture Notes in Computer Science 1370. Springer: Heidelberg, pp. 4–21.

39. Streitz, N., Rexroth, P., Holmer, T. (1998). Anforderungen an interaktive Kooperationslandschaften für kreatives Arbeiten und erste Realisierungen. In *Tagungsband der D-CSCW'98*. B.G.Teubner, Stuttgart, Leipzig, pp. 237–250.

40. Streitz, N., Tandler, P., Müller-Tomfelde, C., Konomi, S. (2001). Roomware: Towards the Next Generation of Human-Computer Interaction based on an Integrated Design of Real and Virtual Worlds. In J. A. Carroll (Ed.): *Human-Computer Interaction in the New Millenium,* Addison Wesley, pp. 551–576.

41. Szekely, P., Luo, P., Neches, R. (1992). Facilitating the exploration of interface design alternatives the HUMANOID model of interface design. In *Proceedings of the ACM Conference on Human factors in computing systems (CHI'92)*, pp. 507–515.

42. Tandler, P. (2001). Modeling groupware supporting synchronous collaboration with heterogeneous single- and multi-user devices. To appear in *Proceedings of CRIWG'01*, Sep. 6–8, Darmstadt, IEEE CS Press.
    http://www.darmstadt.gmd.de/ambiente/publications.html

43. Tandler, P. et al. (2001). ConnecTables: dynamic coupling of displays for the flexible creation of shared workspaces. To appear in *Proceedings of User Interface and Software Technology (UIST 2001)*, Nov. 11–14, Orlando, ACM Press.
    http://www.darmstadt.gmd.de/
    ambiente/publications.html

44. Thevenin, D., Coutaz, J. (1999). Plasticity of User Interfaces: Framework and Research Agenda. In *Proceedings of Human-Computer Interaction – INTERACT'99*, pp. 110–117.

45. Weiser, M. (1993). Some computer science issues in ubiquitous computing. *Communications of the ACM,* 36 (7), pp. 75–84.

Smart-Its Friends:
A Technique for Users to Easily Establish Connections between Smart Artefacts

Lars Erik Holmquist[1], Friedemann Mattern[2], Bernt Schiele[3], Petteri Alahuhta[4],
Michael Beigl[5] and Hans-W. Gellersen[6]

[1]PLAY Research Studio, Interactive Institute, Gothenburg, Sweden
leha@interactiveinstitute.se
[2]ETH Zurich, Distributed Systems Group, Zurich, Switzerland
mattern@inf.ethz.ch
[3]ETH Zurich, Perceptual Computing and Computer Vision Group,
Zurich, Switzerland
schiele@inf.ethz.ch
[4]VTT Electronics, Oulu, Finland
petteri.alahuhta@vtt.fi
[5]TecO, University of Karlsruhe, Germany
michael@teco.edu
[6]Lancaster University, Department of Computing, Lancaster, UK
hwg@comp.lancs.ac.uk

Abstract. Ubiquitous computing is associated with a vision of everything being connected to everything. However, for successful applications to emerge, it will not be the quantity but the quality and usefulness of connections that will matter. Our concern is how qualitative relations and more selective connections can be established between smart artefacts, and how users can retain control over artefact interconnection. We propose *context proximity* for selective artefact communication, using the context of artefacts for matchmaking. We further suggest to empower users with simple but effective means to impose the same context on a number of artefacts. To prove our point we have implemented *Smart-Its Friends*, small embedded devices that become connected when a user holds them together and shakes them.

1 Introduction

The drive toward ubiquitous computing gives rise to smart artefacts, which are objects of our everyday lives augmented with information technology. These artefacts will retain their original use and appearance while computing is expected to provide added value in the background. In particular, added value is expected to arise from meaningful interconnection of smart artefacts. Advances in wireless networking will in principle enable large numbers of artefacts to be interconnected, but how can more

G. D. Abowd, B. Brumitt, S. A. N. Shafer (Eds.): Ubicomp 2001, LNCS 2201, pp. 116-122, 2001.
© Springer-Verlag Berlin Heidelberg 2001

specific relationships be established across such networks? And how can users retain control over information exchange among artefacts? In this technical note we propose to base artefact relationships on the artefacts' context, and describe a very easy-to-use technique for users to explicitly establish artefact connections.

The work we describe was conducted at the early stages of the Smart-Its project on technologies for computer-augmentation of everyday artefacts, inspired by previous work in the Mediacup project [1]. One of the project objectives is to develop a range of small, embedded devices as platforms for augmentation and interconnection of artefacts. These devices, *Smart-Its*, in general integrate sensing, processing and communication with variations in perceptual and computational capability. Sensors and perception techniques are integrated to facilitate autonomous awareness of an artefact's context, independent of infrastructure. Wireless communication is added to facilitate the sharing of such context among artefacts. In our earlier work we have explored applications enabled by artefact-based context acquisition and sharing [3]. The research focus in this project is on collective behaviour of Smart-Its-enabled artefacts, such as collective perception of the environment.

One area of investigation is correlation of context across artefacts as foundation for collective functionality. In a sense, such correlation can be used for matchmaking among artefacts, enabling artefacts to discover others with the same or similar context. Hence, the idea is to have connections established based on *context proximity*, which we will discuss further in section 2. As we will point out in that discussion, context may well be created by explicit user action, and context proximity may thus be exploited in direct manipulation interfaces. In section 3 we describe a prototype implementation of such an interface, the *Smart-Its Friends*. With this interface technique, a user can establish a connection between two smart artefacts by simply holding them together and shaking them.

2   Context Proximity as a Paradigm for Connecting Artefacts

The traditional approach to connect computational entities over a network is to select them by means of a unique address. In mobile computing environments, new paradigms have emerged to support more spontaneous connection of computing nodes that do not require a priori knowledge of each other. In such a setting, connections are dynamically established based on discovery of all devices within sending range.

Another paradigm that emerges with ubiquitous computing is proximity-based communication, to support connection of temporarily co-located artefacts [6]. The required proximity is often defined by the network technology, for instance infrared, and may be the basis for specific techniques to connect artefacts explicitly, for example *point-and-shoot*. Spatial proximity may also be handled for connections at a higher level of abstraction, for instance for situated communication in which spatial locations are used to relay messages [7]. Spatial proximity can be further generalized to a notion of context proximity. The stick-e-notes system may serve as an example for the use of context proximity, using space and time to establish context-dependent information flow [2].

Context proximity as a paradigm for connecting artefacts is of particular interest in our project, as artefacts enabled with Smart-Its have built-in context awareness. Context in Smart-Its generally refers to information about the system environment obtained through sensors. Context comprises raw sensor data, generic percepts extracted from sensors, and artefact- or application-specific information resulting from further abstraction. Hence, Smart-Its are near to each other in terms of context proximity when they experience similar situations or conditions. We envision two general ways of exploiting such context proximity for connection of artefacts: *implicit connection* and *explicit connection*.

Implicit connection based on context proximity means that artefacts will be automatically connected if their individual contexts are within certain proximity, depending on a suitable distance metric. For example, artefacts or devices worn by a person will experience similar context (e.g. same movement patterns) which could be used to establish a private body network that is not easily fooled to provide information access to other devices that may be detected near-by.

Context proximity can be used for explicit user-controlled connection of artefacts, if user actions are employed as context. For example, a user may perform the same gesture on different artefacts, imposing on them the same kind of context. We have explored this interface concept further in a prototype implementation of *Smart-Its Friends*.

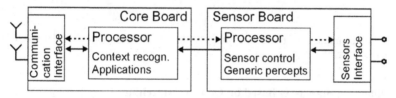

Figure 1. Smart-Its Device Architecture

3   Smart-Its Friends

The Smart-Its devices are based on a modular design with two boards, separating the sensor unit from the core unit. The main components and the data and control flow on the device are illustrated in figure 1. Acquisition of data is allocated on the sensor unit, with a dedicated processor for sensor control and extraction of generic features. Overall device control, application-specific processing, and communication with other Smart-Its is allocated on the core unit. Application-specific processing might for example be computation of artefact-specific context or any other further abstraction from sensor data. The communication interface may support different kinds of network. Generally we assume that all Smart-Its communicate over a shared wireless medium, but some Smart-Its may support additional networks to implement gateways.

The Smart-Its device prototypes that were implemented to explore the Friends concept is shown in figure 2. The two boards have a size of about 4 x 5 cm, and are mounted on top of each other. The device uses PIC micro-controllers on both boards. The sensor unit is further equipped with a two-axis accelerometer. Another sensor, a simple ball switch, is integrated on the core board and directly connected to an interrupt on the core processor. This enables the device to go into an energy preserving mode when no movement occurs, and to wake up instantly on movement. The core board is further equipped with an RFM interface for wireless communication. The communication is based on detection of Smart-Its within sending range. All Smart-Its use RFM as shared broadcast medium, based on a simple carrier sense collision avoidance protocol (CS/CA).

Fig. 2. Prototype implementation of the Smart-Its device for validation of the Friends technique (scale in centimeters)

3.1 Connecting Smart-Its Based on Context-Matching

When the Smart-It device is awake, its accelerometer is read with a hard sampling rate of 1 MHz, but only in intervals of short duration at a much lower soft sampling rate to minimise energy consumption. The movement data captured per interval is passed from the sensor unit to the core processor. The data together with the Smart-Its ID is then broadcast over the shared medium to all other Smart-Its in listening range. A Smart-It that receives movement data from another device compares the data to its own most recent movement pattern. If the difference is below a specified threshold then it accepts the other Smart-It as Friend and establishes a dedicated connection. It is up to specific applications, how such a connection will then be used.

The connection may physically break when the Smart-Its move out of each others sending range. However, as soon as they are close enough again they would still recognise each other as friend and re-establish the connection. However, depending on the application, it may also make sense that some friends' connections are given up over time or when the context changes in certain ways.

3.2 Shaking Artefacts to Impose a Connection: An Invisible User Interface

The behaviour built into Smart-Its Friends as described above provides users with a very easy-to-use interface to impose friendship on Smart-Its (or artefacts augmented with Smart-Its). Users can now simply take two devices they wish to connect and move them together, for instance holding them in the hand, briefly waving or shaking. This imposes the same movement pattern on the devices. In all likelihood, this pattern will be different from that measured at the same time in other Smart-Its in the vicinity, ruling out unintended connection. This interface technique is particularly easy to use, as it does not matter what kind of movement is carried out: it only matters that it is imposed simultaneously on all devices that are to be connected. It is also different from simply having the objects touch, since it requires an additional user action, which should help making unintentional connections less likely.

3.3 Application of Smart-Its Friends

For our proof-of-concept we have built a simple awareness application for Smart-Its Friends. As soon as a device becomes connected, the application will notify the user with a brief beep. This notification also occurs after a "friend" has been temporarily out of range and hence disconnected. In this way, two Smart-Its-augmented objects can be connected and will then notify the users when they venture within a certain range, acting as a sort of support for "proximity awareness".

This kind of awareness support is similar to that provided by colleague or group awareness devices such as the Hummingbird [4]. In fact, the Smart-Its Friends technique might be used as an interface for Hummingbird-like devices. People arriving together at a crowded party who want to maintain mutual awareness over the evening, would briefly put their augmented awareness devices together and give them a shake. The devices can then notify the users whenever they are close to each other, creating a sense of awareness similar to that of on-line applications such as ICQ.

Another similar application for Smart-Its Friends could be a child monitor: By taking two Smart-Its enhanced objects, e.g. two brooches than can be worn by child and parent, and shaking them together, a connection would be established. Whenever the child strays out of reach, the parent will get a notification. In a different kind of application domain, one can further imagine to use Smart-Its Friends to connect personal objects. For example, a user may connect their credit card to other personal items such as a car key or pen knife. A smart credit card would then only function if a friend was around, rendering the card useless if it is lost or stolen.

4   Discussion

The Smart-Its Friends technique has obvious application potential for dynamically creating a logical proximity relation and communication channels between artefacts, without having to worry about underlying protocols. In the extension, the method can also be used for other types of end-user programming of smart artefacts. From a user interface perspective the programming and customisation of ubiquitous computing artefacts is often problematic, especially for artefacts where there are no explicit input or output devices. Therefore, it is important to find ways to customise and program artefacts using other natural activities – gestures, sounds, etc. – something that the Smart-Its Friends mechanism achieves.

A natural extension of the concept would be to introduce "modifier objects" that can change the behaviour of other artefacts. By holding a Smart-It augmented object together with a modifier and shaking them, the artefact's behaviour could be changed to that specified by the modifier. One example of such a modifier would be a "magic stick" with an easy-to-use slider that would allow to parameterise the distance a child wearing a Smart-It is allowed to be away from the parent's Smart-It before an alarm is raised. Another example would be a simple ear-shaped object that might tell another Smart-It to start paying attention to data from its audio sensors – in other words, to start listening – whereas an eye-shaped object might turn on the Smart-It's visual perception. In the child monitor example above, this might mean that the two Smart-Its open an audio channel between each other, so that the parent can hear sounds from the child. This would make it useful for also monitoring the activities of smaller children and babies, where aural information is more likely to be important than movement.

It should be pointed out that "modifier objects" do not really add any functionality that could not be accessed by other means, for instance by adding specialised buttons. Instead they are intended to make interaction simple and more intuitive by acting like physical representations or "tokens" for different functions, much like icons on the computer desktop call up different programs [5]. We believe that making different functions physically manifested in this way can be a way to achieve the invisible or "disappearing" computer interface, thus giving end-users easier access to complicated functionality in ubiquitous computing applications.

Acknowledgements

The Smart-Its project is funded in part by the Commission of the European Union (contract IST-2000-25428), and by the Swiss Federal Office for Education and Science (BBW 00.0281). More information on the project is available at http://www.smart-its.org.

References

1. Beigl, M., Gellersen, H.-W. and Schmidt, A. MediaCups: Experience with Design and Use of Computer-Augmented Everyday Objects. *Computer Networks*, Vol. 35, No. 4, Special Issue on Pervasive Computing, Elsevier, March 2001, pp. 401-409.
2. Brown, P.J., The stick-e Document: a Framework for Creating Context-aware Applications. *Electronic Publishing '96*, pp. 259-272, 1996.
3. Gellersen, H.-W., Schmidt, A., Beigl, M. Adding Some Smartness to Devices and Everyday Things. *Proceedings of IEEE Workshop on Mobile Computing Systems and Applications 2000 (WMCSA '00),* Dec. 2000, Monterey, USA, IEEE Press.
4. Holmquist, L.E., Falk J. and Wigström, J. Supporting Group Collaboration with Inter-Personal Awareness Devices. *Personal Technologies*, Vol. 3, Nos. 1&2, pp. 13-21, 1999.

5. Holmquist, L.E., Redström J. and Ljungstrand, P. Token-Based Access to Digital Information. *Proceedings of First International Symposium on Handheld and Ubiquitous Computing (HUC '99),* Karlsruhe, Germany, Springer-Verlag, pp. 234-245, 1999.
6. Hupfeld, F. and Beigl, M. Spatially Aware Local Communication in the RAUM System. *Proceedings of Workshop on Interactive Distributed Multimedia Systems (IDMS 2000),* Enschede, The Netherlands, October 17-20, 2000, pp. 285-296.
7. Rekimoto, J., Ayatsuka, Y., Hayashi, K. Augmentable Reality: Situated Communication through Digital and Physical Spaces. *Proceedings of IEEE 2nd International Symposium on Wearable Computers (ISWC '98),* pp. 68-75, 1998.

Integrating Meeting Capture
within a Collaborative Team Environment

Heather Richter[1], Gregory D. Abowd[1], Werner Geyer[2], Ludwin Fuchs[3],
Shahrokh Daijavad[2], and Steven Poltrock[3]

[1]Georgia Institute of Technology, Graphics, Visualization, & Usability Center
801 Atlantic Drive, Atlanta, GA 30332, USA
{hrichter,abowd}@cc.gatech.edu
[2]IBM T.J. Watson Research Center
30 Saw Mill River Road, Hawthorne, NY 10532, USA
{Werner.Geyer,shahrokh}@us.ibm.com
[3]Boeing Mathematics & Computing Technology
PO Box 3707, Seattle, WA 98124, USA
{Ludwin.Fuchs,Steven.Poltrock}@boeing.com

Abstract. Meeting capture has been a common subject of research in
the ubiquitous computing community for the past decade. However,
the majority of the research has focused on technologies to support the
capture but not enough on the motivation for accessing the captured
record and the impact on everyday work practices based on extended
authentic use of a working capture and access system. Our long-term
research agenda is to build capture services for distributed workgroups
that provide appropriate motivation and further understand how access
of captured meetings impacts work practices. To do this, we have
developed a testbed for meeting capture as part of a larger distributed
work system called TeamSpace. In this paper, we discuss the
requirements for meeting capture within TeamSpace, describe the initial
prototype developed, and report on initial usage.

1   Introduction

Many work practices consist of repeated discussions among teams of people: status is
discussed, decisions are made, alternatives are considered, and details are explained.
A large amount of this rich, often informal, information that is generated during these
discussions often does not get recorded in formal documentation. Yet this information
is later useful for providing additional context, details, and decisions surrounding a
project. Ubiquitous computing has as one theme the capture, integration, and access
of everyday activities, in order to provide a multimedia record of those activities for
later perusal [3]. By applying automated capture and access technologies to work
discussions, specifically meetings, large amounts of informal project information may
be recorded and preserved for later use.

G. D. Abowd, B. Brumitt, S. A. N. Shafer (Eds.): Ubicomp 2001, LNCS 2201, pp. 123-138, 2001.
© Springer-Verlag Berlin Heidelberg 2001

In order to understand how to capture meetings, we must first understand how the captured information might be useful to project team members. Understanding these potential uses is difficult, however. Meetings vary greatly, differing in purpose, formality, and content across domains, organizations and teams. One person may participate in a variety of different kinds of meetings, each with different importance. People have difficulty envisioning how they would take advantage of captured information, and what information would be most useful to their work. Thus, understanding meeting capture will involve putting a system into real use in a variety of situations and domains and being able to adapt the capture services to the needs of a particular project group. Multiple meeting capture prototypes have been built over the past decade, yet little real-world evaluation of these systems has been done. Building a system that can be used in real situations over a long period of time has important design implications. The system must work and provide a valuable service all of the time so we can evaluate under the conditions of authentic experience. The system must be simple and easy to use while supporting many different users. The system will support general purpose meeting activities, but must be evolvable to support more specific activities as the need arises. Additionally, researchers must be able to study how the system is used.

To support a wide variety of meetings, we focus not on supporting specific content, but on general meeting structures and artifacts. To get a better idea of general meeting types and information, we interviewed several meeting facilitators at Boeing who work with teams to improve or enable different types of meetings. We learned that the meetings they deal with are very heterogeneous. Yet, most meetings do have common and simple artifacts, such as agendas, action items, issues, presentations, and minutes. The most important artifacts are often action items, which can serve as valuable minutes of a meeting. Additionally, there was no standard way to create and present most of these artifacts other than word processing software. Thus, users may not be opposed to using new tools if they add benefit.

We have previously argued that for captured information to provide value, it needs to be related to the rest of users' work and everyday tasks [14]. Meeting capture research has primarily focused on supporting and recording meetings. However, users perform many other meeting-related activities that tools can support, and should be able to move easily from meeting-related to other work activities. Additionally, streams of meeting information should become just another form of multimedia information that people will be creating, viewing and sharing. By integrating meeting capture within a larger collaborative work environment that encompasses more than just conducting a meeting, we not only better support the activities surrounding meetings, but also provide a more relevant view of captured information. This additional support will encourage more realistic use of captured information, encouraging users to integrate meeting capture and access as part of their everyday activities.

To that end, we are integrating meeting capture into a larger team environment called TeamSpace, which is being developed in a joint project between IBM Research, Boeing, and Georgia Tech. TeamSpace is a prototype team collaborative workspace for managing shared work processes and maintaining shared artifacts in distributed projects. The overriding goal of the system is to facilitate inter-company teams, which are becoming increasingly common in large projects, such as the development of aerospace systems. Integrating meeting capture into this environment introduces the following additional requirement that we support inter-company distributed meetings.

The goal of this paper is to describe the meeting system of TeamSpace that serves as the foundation for our longer term research agenda to evaluate capture and access in an authentic meeting environment. In Section 2 we discuss related work in automated capture and access. In Section 3 we further discuss the many meeting-related activities we seek to support and the benefits of integration with TeamSpace. In Section 4 we describe the implementation of the TeamSpace prototype. In Section 5 we discuss our experiences in usage thus far and the impact on the prototype. Finally, in Section 6, we conclude with a discussion of our future plans.

2   Related Work

Ubiquitous capture environments have been built in several domains over the past decade: education, personal note-taking, and meetings. In exploring the meeting domain, we are following an approach similar to the eClass project, known formerly as Classroom 2000 [1,2], which studied capture through evolving and evaluating the system through ongoing use in real classrooms. EClass is an education system focused on providing automated access to lecturers' slides and notes, augmented with audio and video. The system has been used to record over 2000 lectures at several universities, resulting in a deeper understanding of why capture works and how it is useful over short and long time periods.

One reason eClass was so successful is that it aided an already important task for students – studying. Motivation for reviewing meeting notes is less clear and more varied, and has been the subject of some study. Whitaker et al. [17] interviewed people on the problems of note-taking during meetings. They found many difficulties that capture could help overcome, such as the failure to note important facts, not enough time to write everything, reduced ability to participate, and the inadequacy of notes for later detailed understanding. Meeting capture could also be used to record information such as design and decision rationale and other informal project information that often disappears over time. Which reasons are most important and will drive the use of a capture system over the short and long term is unclear. We aim to discover this through creating a prototype general enough to enable those motivations to be discovered and then further supported through evolution of the prototype.

Similar to the education domain, systems such as AutoAuditorium [4] and eSeminar [15] record seminars consisting of a presenter with slides. Reviewing of this captured information is primarily for people who were not in attendance. He et al. [8,9] at Microsoft Research have studied the access of such recorded seminars, including access patterns and auto-summarization techniques. Other more general meeting capture systems, such as Notelook [5], Dolphin [16], and Filochat [17] have focused on augmenting presentations or hand-written notes with audio and video streams. Tivoli [12] augmented "domain objects" representing meeting content, with audio. The objects were text and gestures that could be created and manipulated on an electronic whiteboard. However, none of these systems has explored meeting-specific artifacts, such as agendas or action items, nor have they focused on integrating the captured information with other work activities. Additionally, researchers have done little evaluation of these systems in real work environments.

The exception to this is a study by Moran *et al.* [13] with Tivoli, which observed one user preparing reports based on captured meetings. They found that the user did not merely replay meetings, but "salvaged" information by extracting, organizing, and writing information based on multiple records. They further stated that "the development of effective practices of capturing and salvaging meetings must be done by interrelating them with other work practices." We aim to do this with TeamSpace and plan to evaluate the system with different teams in different environments. It is important to point out that the person salvaging with Tivoli had a real motivation, to write a summary report of a technical topic typically out of his range of expertise. Finding similar motivating aspects for captured meeting review is a challenge nobody has yet addressed. Exploring motivations for accessing captured meetings is the long-term research objective that that has driven building our system.

Several commercial distributed conferencing systems, such as NetMeeting [11] and Sametime [10], are beginning to add capture capabilities to conferencing. These systems allow users to conduct distributed meetings by sharing whiteboards, chat, video, and even applications. However, the capture currently involves recording system events and users can then replay the meeting like a movie. This simple form of capture and replay does not support any browsing or searching mechanisms, and thus will be inadequate to help users find pieces of information in even one meeting, let alone a large set of them.

3   Integrating with TeamSpace

The collaborative environment we are integrating with is TeamSpace [7]. TeamSpace is a prototype team collaborative workspace for managing shared work processes and maintaining shared artifacts in distributed projects. The goals of TeamSpace are to support inter-company collaboration through awareness, information sharing, communication, and coordination. TeamSpace aims to support both synchronous and asynchronous team activities, and to provide a seamless transition between the different work modes and tasks of team members. The classification of the work modes and activities we envision are shown in Figure 1. Team members work in different modes: individual, meeting, and social modes. Additionally, tasks can be work-related, meeting-related, and people-related. Meeting capture systems often focus on supporting some of the work-related activities in the meeting mode through recording notes, audio, and video of a meeting. However, meetings are part of many of the other activities and modes. Individuals asynchronously prepare for meetings, create agendas or presentations, invite participants, or schedule rooms. During a meeting, people greet and introduce each other, take notes, and give presentations; facilitators change the agenda or the flow of discussion. After a meeting, an individual may use the captured material to create minutes or write a report. A user may search through meetings for pieces of information, or people who made certain decisions. Thus, by making meeting capture and access part of a system that supports all of these different kinds of modes and tasks, we can potentially support more meeting-related activities and improve the transition between those activities, including those that are not captured and those that use captured information.

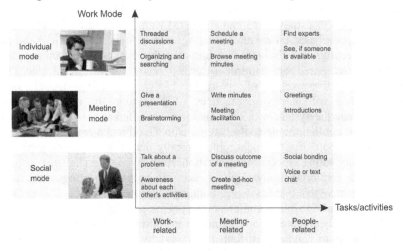

Fig. 1. Matrix of work modes and task

In addition to supporting more meeting-related activities, integrating into TeamSpace will potentially allow us to relate meetings with other team artifacts that are in the environment, such as project schedules, documents, or threaded discussions. Thus, meetings become just another artifact in a large repository of inter-related information. While the current object set in TeamSpace is limited to meeting-related items such as agenda, action items, presentations, meetings, and users, we will be able to add mechanisms for relating meetings with other kinds of artifacts as they are incorporated into TeamSpace.

4   TeamSpace Implementation

In the previous sections we have highlighted how the desire for real-world usage has led us to integrate our capture prototype within a larger work context. We will now demonstrate how we have implemented this prototype as part of TeamSpace. TeamSpace is implemented as a mostly web-based application. This allows it to be accessible from a large number of platforms with no installation. To add meeting capture to TeamSpace, we have added specific meeting-related objects based on the interviews highlighted in Section 1, namely, *Agenda, Action Item, Presentation, Meeting*, and *Person*. We have written additional software to conduct and capture distributed meetings, and replay and review meetings. We have attempted to design all of this software to provide general functionality, yet be flexible and evolvable so that more specific features can be added as we better understand its use by particular project teams. We have also focused on reliability and consistency of the software and interfaces as we want the system to be used and studied over a long period of time. Finally, we wanted to instrument the software to facilitate understanding of users' interactions.

The need to gain as much information for as many users as possible leads us to focus on public (as opposed to personal) meeting capture. While capturing personal meeting notes is certainly important, we would like to make the captured information available to as many people as possible, with as little effort in capturing as possible. One instrumented meeting room can be used by many people for multiple meetings. We also want to require as little instrumentation as possible to enable more locations for capture.

Meeting activities can be thought of in three phases: preparation before the meeting, conducting of the meeting, and later review of the meeting. Each of these phases mainly corresponds to one piece of the TeamSpace prototype implementation. In the following sections we will discuss each in turn. To better illustrate the features of each, we begin each discussion with a running scenario. We then continue the discussion with the user interface implementation, and then with architectural or other implementation issues.

4.1   Meeting Preparation: Main TeamSpace Interface

Bill, the team lead, prepares for a weekly status meeting planned the next day. He checks the meeting information in TeamSpace to make sure the rooms are scheduled and adds a few guest participants. He checks which action items generated discussion last week, and adds those to the meeting. Finally, he adds a small presentation he has prepared for the meeting. The participants are then automatically emailed a meeting invitation.

Meeting preparation is accomplished using the main TeamSpace interface. From this interface users can create, edit, and view any of the objects that TeamSpace supports, such as users, agendas, action items, and meetings. Figure 2 shows a screenshot of this interface. After logging in, users are taken to their starting page which highlights their current day's meetings and their open action items. Users can access additional information using the context tabs of *People*, *Meeting*, and *Task*. The *Meeting* tab provides both a calendar and list view of meetings. The list view is shown in Figure 2, and provides mechanisms to constrain and search the meeting list. Under *Task* a user can view her own action items or browse and search the entire team list. The lower half of the window is a document view for displaying and editing the details of each individual object. In Figure 2, this displays the details for the selected meeting.   For the preparation scenario above, Bill would go to the *Meeting* tab to create a new meeting, then enter in all of the information in the document view. Invited participants would then see that meeting on their calendar or meeting list when they logged into TeamSpace that day.

Besides the meeting environment, TeamSpace is intended to support other activities such as project management, document management, and team awareness and communication. In other words, this interface is meant to serve as the main portal for all team activities, including meeting capture and access. However, these capabilities are less mature, and have been left out of the current interface to provide a fully functional yet simplified view of the system. As TeamSpace evolves to include additional artifacts and activities, we will provide mechanisms to relate these to the current set of information.

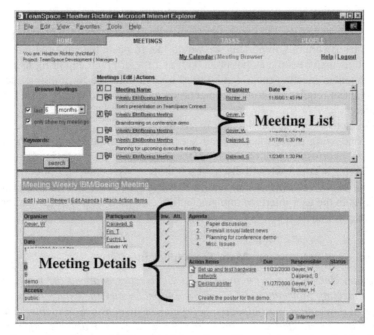

Fig. 2. Screenshot of the main TeamSpace interface. The user is viewing the details of one captured meeting. The top is the meeting list view, the bottom pane is the detailed view

4.2   Meeting Capture: MeetingClient

The day of the meeting, team members in Seattle gather in their conference room. Mary, the meeting facilitator arrives a few minutes early to log into TeamSpace and start the meeting. Meanwhile, team members in other locations enter the virtual meeting from their desktop browsers. After team members greet one another and chat for a few minutes, Mary opens the meeting agenda to start. She adds any new items proposed by the team. Pushing the agenda aside, she opens the action item list to get an update on each of the unfinished tasks. As each team member lists their progress, Mary updates the item list, marking off items, changing items, and adding new action items.

The next item on the agenda is a presentation by Bill about an interface problem just discovered between their component and another component. Bill opens the presentation and explains the problem. Working at her desktop in St. Louis, Sally circles a region on one of the components and notes some of the manufacturing constraints that influenced its design. Also from his desktop, Jim draws a sketch to explain the reason for these constraints.

The presentation spawns a brainstorming session for solutions. The team sketches their ideas on the whiteboard, with distributed team members drawing at their desktops.

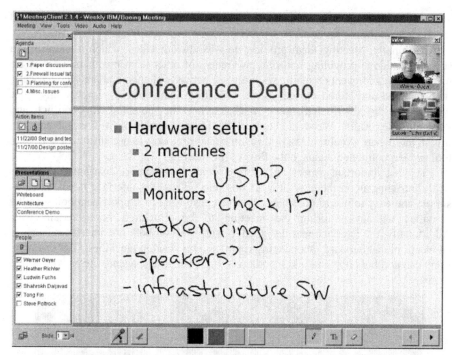

Fig. 3. Screenshot of MeetingClient. The user is viewing an annotated presentation. The overview bar on the left of the screen shows the agenda, action items, presentations, and participants

The meeting capture phase is supported through the MeetingClient interface, shown in Figure 3. MeetingClient is launched automatically on a client's machine from the main TeamSpace web interface when joining a meeting. This client provides viewing, editing, and annotating of agendas and action items, as well as viewing and annotating of PowerPoint presentations. Thus, MeetingClient records events such as joining and leaving a meeting; viewing, editing, and checking off agenda items; viewing, editing, and creating action items, and viewing and annotating presentations. Participants are not required to use or interact with any of these objects. However, the more objects they use, the more events that are recorded, and the more indices that will be created to help in review, as discussed next in Section 4.3.

The panel on the left of Figure 3 provides an overview and navigation of the meeting. The list of agenda items, action items, presentations and invited participants can be seen and individual items can be selected. The main view shows the selected presentation, or the agenda or action item editor. The toolbar at the bottom of the screen contains the pen and text tools. In the above scenario, Mary would begin the meeting by selecting "Agenda" in the overview panel. She would then edit and rearrange the agenda. Next, she would move to the action item view to go through the list of action items. Bill would then view his presentation, which everyone could annotate. Finally, Bill would create a blank presentation to function as a whiteboard for the brainstorming session.

Additionally, MeetingClient provides low-bandwidth video, which is viewed in a separate window, providing real-time awareness of other team members. All of the meeting data and events remain synchronized between clients, and are automatically time-stamped and stored on the server. MeetingClient does not impose any floor control on the distributed users, thus leaving the potential for conflict and unpredictable results. We wanted to keep the interface as simple as possible and will investigate where synchronization through social protocols is not sufficient and what tool support could help manage the flow of the meeting.

The most important aspect of MeetingClient is to support distributed meetings while intruding upon them as little as possible. Thus, the interface needs to be as simple and easy to use as possible. We have also tried to support common meeting activities without requiring the meeting to be structured in a certain way. Additionally, the interface was designed to work well on both pen interfaces, such as an electronic whiteboard in a meeting room, and on desktop machines. For example, users can add both text and ink annotations to presentations, agenda items, and action items.

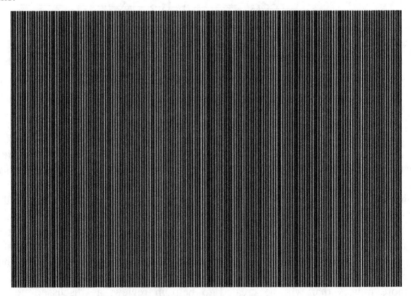

Fig. 4. The TeamSpace architecture

In addition to interface challenges, we faced other issues in implementing a capture system for inter-company distributed meetings, such as complicated communication and security. The current architecture of the TeamSpace system is shown in Figure 4. The TeamSpace server consists of servlets and Java Server Pages (JSP) that access and store the data. MeetingClient is a Java application that connects via our own protocol directly to the Conference Server, which is in charge of distributing messages to the clients. The Conference Listener is a passive client that stores a current version of the state so that it can update late-joining clients and store all the data permanently on the server. This solution enables the meeting clients to communicate through firewalls given that the server is located on the open Internet and the firewall allows outgoing TCP and HTTP traffic. It also supports and synchronizes any number of clients in one meeting. We further discuss security and communication issues of this architecture in Section 5. While we use our system to distribute video images, to guarantee audio quality of service we are not digitally transmitting and mixing audio. We expect participants to use a conference call that is then input to any one of the meeting clients so the audio can be recorded and digitized. The Conference Listener stores the audio, video, and event streams as raw data on the server's file system. All other information, such as action items and meeting descriptions, are stored in a database.

4.3   Meeting Access: MeetingViewer

During the meeting, the team was split between two different solutions to their problem and needed more discussion to make a decision. Pat and Jim meet later that day to further discuss one of the proposed solutions. During their meeting, which they also capture, they recall a contact Sally mentioned during the earlier meeting. They open up the meeting and browse through it by using a timeline that indicates the spots where Sally was talking. They easily find and replay the portion where Sally was sketching on the components and hear her mention her co-worker Dave. The group looks up Dave's contact information and gives him a call.

Chris had to leave the weekly status meeting early. Before he tackles his new tasks, he returns to the meeting records to listen to the portions he missed. He skims the meeting with a time slider by jumping from one agenda item to the next. Then he dives into Bill's presentation, using a thumbnail navigation, to replay the portion of the presentation where the group talked about the manufacturing constraints. Chris also listens to the comments Dave made to Pat and Jim during their conversation.

One year later, Bill is leading a team that runs into a similar component interface problem. He asks Harry, one of his team members, to look at the problem the old project had, and why they chose their solution. Harry reads the documentation, accesses the meeting records and replays pieces of various discussions, and prepares a presentation using some of the older material to present his findings.

After a meeting is completed, the meeting records are automatically available for retrieval. In this prototype we have focused on retrieving meeting details of one or several meetings. Users can select completed meetings in TeamSpace and launch a MeetingViewer applet to view and playback these meetings.

The MeetingViewer, shown in Figure 5, integrates all of the meeting information based on time. The viewer uses a two-scale timeline for navigating a set of selected meetings, providing random access playback. The timeline is painted with interesting events as both a visual summary of the meeting, and as an aid for navigation. Interesting events currently are people joining and leaving, agenda items being discussed, action items visited or created, and slides visited, but could include any envisioned events such as people speaking and keyword locations. Users can control which of these events they view and can use the events to find relevant portions within a meeting to playback. Playback of a meeting not only involves playing the audio and video, but also involves playback of all of the recorded events of a meeting such as slide visits or agenda item discussion.

The remainder of the meeting information is displayed on a series of tabbed panes for each of the objects related to the meeting, including descriptions and summaries of the meeting, agenda, presentations, action items, and video images. These panes are a very general approach for displaying a large amount of related information. However, to enable customized views, each pane can be opened in a separate window, moved and resized. In this way, users can view any subset of the information they wish at once. Additionally, as we add more objects to TeamSpace, we can easily add more meeting-related objects to this interface as another tabbed pane, such as documents that were reviewed or referenced during the meeting.

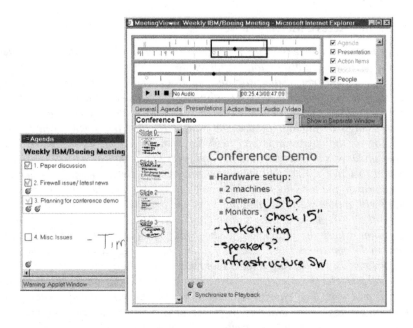

Fig. 5. Screenshot of MeetingViewer showing a single meeting. MeetingViewer can also be used to view multiple meetings

When reviewing meetings in the short term, users can potentially use any kind of context to find a piece of information – from a note, to when someone spoke, to what the general subject matter was. For this reason, we started with a very general review interface. We anticipate that as we learn more about the types of information users need for various tasks, we can design task-oriented views that are simpler and more integrated. While detailed context is appropriate to aid short-term browsing and search, longer-term searches, such as Harry's in the above scenario, will probably require different mechanisms that emphasize summaries. We would like to investigate additional visualizations to navigate and search a large set of meetings as our set of captured material grows.

4.4   Summary

While we have not implemented every feature our scenarios describe, we feel we have a reasonable prototype that successfully allows users to do a number of meeting-related activities. The capture system supports capturing both work-related artifacts, such as presentations, but also meeting-related artifacts, such as agendas. The main interface serves as the starting point for many of the individual mode activities, such as preparing for a meeting and reviewing meeting information. The various objects are inter-related and can be viewed in multiple ways, but the interface could still be improved to make this more explicit. For example, when the user is viewing an action item, she should be able to view where that item was discussed in a meeting and jump directly to replaying that meeting. Additionally, we would like to extend search to searching other meeting content, such as slide texts. Evaluation of the system will hopefully help prioritize the features that can provide the most benefit to users. Finally, as TeamSpace evolves to add additional objects and activities, we can provide mechanisms to relate these to meetings and also integrate them into the capture and access software without changing the structure of their interfaces.

5   Initial Experience

Our research team has been using TeamSpace to conduct and capture our distributed meetings for the past six months. We have successfully recorded over a dozen weekly meetings, as well as a distributed presentation for a yearly project review, and two 4-hour strategy sessions. Typically the meetings were held at three separate locations, both in meeting rooms and at desktop machines. The meeting environment has been useful for brainstorming and for discussing presentations. Team members have revisited several meetings to view the annotations we made, or review a missed meeting.

The first thing to examine is how TeamSpace has affected our meetings. Prior to the completion of the prototype, we did not make much use of an agenda, although team members would often privately note items to discuss prior to the meeting. These items are now publicly listed in the agenda, yet this has not been too important as most meetings only contain a few agenda items. However, the agenda was used extensively and much appreciated for the 4-hour strategy meetings. Additionally, we now create information to be shared during a meeting in PowerPoint®. As we did not have a standard way to share information previously, this has not been a problem, although we would certainly like ways to share information in other formats. Finally, we are experiencing an interesting phenomenon common to distributed collaborative systems – knowing what the other party is seeing. One frequently asks if others can see that he has joined or made an annotation. While this was often necessary when the prototype was not stable, we continue to ask these questions even now. We need to investigate how the system can give users these cues so that they do not have to interrupt the meeting to ensure that the system is still working.

Captured information has been most useful for team members who missed the meeting. We also find that we do have moderate needs to review information in our meetings. Note-taking prior to TeamSpace was sparse. Yet, the annotated slides have been useful to review brainstorming or edit a presentation. We do occasionally discuss an action item and review the list the following week to make sure we didn't forget to do anything. Thus, while a group such as ours does not do large amounts of meeting review, we do rely on the system to record our activities and find TeamSpace useful. One team member even likes to use TeamSpace to record other non-distributed meetings. Capture seems to add a comfort level of knowing that the meeting is being recorded even though we might not know if we will review it.

Our usage has highlighted several deficiencies in our interface designs, and has led to revisions of both the main interface and MeetingClient. In a meeting, navigation, particularly navigating between different pieces of information, such as an agenda item and a slide, was awkward. This navigation needs to be extremely simple, particularly for those using a pen on an electronic whiteboard. We will not learn much about capturing meeting artifacts if information such as agendas or action items is not captured because it is too difficult to use during a meeting. For example, we found that it would be useful for the agenda to be more easily viewed so that moving on to the next agenda item does not require multiple user actions. To address these difficulties, we added the overview panel to the capture client - the left hand panel in Figure 3. This enables a quick overview of meeting information and easy switching between viewing any items in more detail. The look of the main TeamSpace interface was simplified by adding multiple ways to view items, such as the calendar and list views for meetings. In this way, only relevant information for each user is shown and can be modified to reduce information overload.

We have also encountered other implementation problems in building such a distributed system. Enabling inter-company collaboration is more difficult than we expected [6]. Security is a major issue in any system, and is only compounded by cross-firewall communication. Security infrastructures are in place to inhibit the flow of information outside of the company, yet collaboration requires circumventing security mechanisms without violating their principles. We first attempted to use existing meeting conferencing software to handle communication and distribution. However, this did not work across companies and we eventually created our own communication protocols. While our current prototype can communicate through firewalls, the information is not secure enough for real use as the server resides on the open Internet. We are exploring alternative architectures to address security concerns. We are also continuing to investigate if existing conferencing software can meet our communication requirements so that we may take advantage of other existing features.

6   Conclusions and Future Directions

Our long-term research agenda is to discover the impact of automated meeting capture for distributed workgroups. While meeting capture has been a popular theme in the ubiquitous computing research community, there has been relatively little work reporting on the use of a capture system for an extended period of time by a distributed workgroup. There are several requirements that must be met by a research testbed intending to explore authentic meeting capture in this kind of setting, including evolvability of a general purpose meeting support system that is tailorable to the work practices of a specific team, the distribution of capture over several work sites, the integration of meeting capture within the larger electronic workgroup support system, and a reliable system that can be used over a long period of time to permit observation by a research team. To meet these requirements, we have built a meeting capture system as part of the TeamSpace project. In this paper, we described the features of this meeting capture system and demonstrated why it is an appropriate vehicle for further exploration in this domain.

While our experiences with TeamSpace have highlighted several technical and user interface issues, we need much more extensive usage to understand the impact of such a capture system. TeamSpace now provides us a research vehicle for gaining that experience. We will be deploying the current prototype to multiple teams in Boeing, IBM, and elsewhere. We have found that our implementation has made instrumenting the various pieces of software easy by using a servlet that will store log information that the software sends to it. We now need to understand the kinds of analysis we can do with this data.

As we better understand users' motivations for capturing and reviewing meetings, we can evolve TeamSpace to better support these motivations. There are already a myriad of features and capabilities we could add. We have not yet implemented a visualization for browsing a large set of meetings. We could integrate with other technologies, such as speaker identification or auto summarization, to make access more powerful. It is difficult to prioritize which of these features will provide the largest benefit to users, and thus help highlight important uses and motivations.

Designing and implementing a research prototype for real-world evaluation of meeting capture has been challenging. Our research goals led us to build a system that integrates the meeting capture into a larger team workspace, which we hope will encourage realistic and repeated usage. We have implemented a general solution that we feel can be used and evolved over time. We continue to face issues of any system that is deployed for real use, such as usability, security, and scaling. But building such a system becomes increasingly important in ubiquitous computing as we seek to understand its impact in people's everyday environments.

Acknowledgements

We would like to acknowledge the other members who have contributed to the TeamSpace project: Carolyn Brodie, Tong Fin, and Tom Frauenhofer at IBM T.J. Watson Research and Khai Truong at Georgia Tech. This work was partially supported by DARPA/ITO under the Information Technology Expeditions, Ubiquitous Computing, Quorum, and PCES programs, and by the National Science Foundation (grants 9703384, 9818305 and 0070345).

References

1. Abowd, G., Atkeson, C., Brotherton, J., Enqvist, P., and LeMon, J. "Investigating the capture, integration, and access problem of ubiquitous computing in an educational setting," in Proc. CHI 98, 1998.
2. Abowd, Gregory D. "Classroom 2000: An Experiment with the Instrumentation of a Living Educational Environment," *IBM Systems Journal*, Special issue on Pervasive Computing, **38**(4): 508-530, October 1999.
3. Abowd, Gregory D., Elizabeth D. Mynatt. "Charting Past, Present and Future Research in Ubiquitous Computing," in *ACM Transactions on Computer-Human Interaction*, Special issue on HCI in the new Millenium, 7(1): 29-58, March 2001.
4. AutoAuditorium Homepage: http://www.autoauditorium.com.
5. Chiu, P., Kapuskar, A., Reitmeier, S., and Wilcox, L. "Notelook: Taking Notes in Meetings with Digital Video and Ink," in Proceedings of ACM Multimedia'99, 1999.
6. Fuchs, Ludwin, Werner Geyer, Heather Richter, Steven Poltrock, Tom Frauenhofer, and Shahrokh Daijavad. "Enabling Inter-Company Team Collaboration," in Proceedings of the 10th International Workshop on Enabling Technologies: Infrastructure for Collaborative Enterprises (WetICE 2001), June 2001.
7. Geyer, Werner, Heather Richter, Ludwin Fuchs, Tom Frauenhofer, Shahrokh Daijavad, and Steven Poltrock. "A Team Environment Supporting Capture and Access of Virtual Meetings." In Proceedings of Conference on Supporting Group Work (Group 2001), September 2001.
8. He, L., Sanocki, E., Gupta, A., and Grudin, J. "Auto-Summarization of Audio-Video Presentations," in Proceedings of ACM Multimedia '99, 1999.
9. He, L., Sanocki, E., Gupta, A., and Grudin, J. "Comparing Presentation Summaries: Slides vs. Reading Vs. Listening," in Proceedings of CHI 2000, April 2000.
10. Lotus Sametime Homepage, "Real-Time Collaboration That's Fit for Business", URL: http://www.lotus.com/Sametime, November 2000.
11. Microsoft NetMeeting Homepage:
    http://www.microsoft.com/windows/netmeeting.
12. Minneman, S., Harrison, S., Janssen, B., Kurtenbach, G., Moran, T., Smith, I., and van Melle, B. "A Confederation of Tools for Capturing and Accessing Collaborative Activity," in Proceedings of ACM Multimedia '95, 1995.
13. Moran, T.P., Palen, L., Harrison, S., Chiu, P., Kimber, D., Minneman, S., vanMelle, W., and Zelweger, P. "'I'll Get That Off the Audio:' A Case Study of Salvaging Multimedia Meeting Records," in Proc CHI '97, Atlanta, GA, 1997.
14. Richter, Heather A., and Gregory D. Abowd. "Automating the capture of design knowledge: a preliminary study." Technical Report GVU-99-45, Georgia Institute of Technology. December 1999.
15. Steinmetz, Arnd, and Martin Kiezle. "The e-Seminar Lecture Recording and Distribution System," in Proceedings of SPIE (International Society for Optical Engineering) Vol. 4312, Multimedia Computing and Networking, San Jose, CA 2001.

16. Streitz, M. A., Geibler, J., Haake, J. M., and Hol, J. "DOLPHIN: Integrated Meeting Support across Local and Remote Desktop Environments and LiveBoards," in Proceedings of Computer Supported Collaborative Work Conference (CSCW '94), 1994.
17. Whittaker, Steve, Patrick Hyland, and Myrtle Wiley. "Filochat: Handwritten Notes Provide Access to Recorded Conversations," in Proceedings of CHI 1994, Boston, MA, 1994.

A Ubiquitous Service Environment
with Active Documents for
Teamwork Support

Patrik Werle, Fredrik Kilander, Martin Jonsson,
Peter Lönnqvist, and Carl Gustaf Jansson

The FUSE Research Group, KTH Center for Wireless Systems, KTH
DSV, Electrum 230, SE-164 40 Kista, Sweden
{werle,fk,martinj,peterl,calle}@dsv.su.se

Abstract. We present a ubiquitous service environment for teamwork, supported by Active Documents. The environment consists of a physically dressed conference room and a software architecture based on Java and Jini. At the application level, mobile agent technology provide Active Documents that utilize context information and distributed resources to support users. We also present a prototype and preliminary results from observations in a meeting scenario.

1 Introduction

This paper consists of three major parts. Each relates in its particular way to the issue of ubiquitous computing and an environment created for that purpose. The first part consists of a brief background followed by a conceptual description of the fuseONE environment. The second part details a prototype implementation, while the third part of the paper describes a pilot case study carried out in the realized prototype environment.

2 Background

A ubiquitous service environment, or USE, is a physical and logical space where users can collaborate supported by multiple services providing adequate computing and communication facilities. The physical space is dominated by the material manifestation of computing resources, such as computers, screens, keyboards, pointing devices, PDAs, sensors and so on.

The logical space is to a large extent shaped by the amount of communication available between the physical devices. None or very little communication tends to partition the logical space into cells which more or less equate the confines of a particular device. In this situation, each attempt to transfer data of effect an operation becomes hampered by the technicalities involved.

G. D. Abowd, B. Brumitt, S. A. N. Shafer (Eds.): Ubicomp 2001, LNCS 2201, pp. 139-155, 2001.

With extensive communication, the logical space is widened and unified, and works with the users to better reflect that what is physically close is also conceptually close. At the beautiful end of this dimension, the logical space extends beyond the physical confines of the real world and allows for communication and co-operation without drawing attention to the mechanics of each actual interchange.

However, the mere possibility to employ a dazzling range of far-reaching operations contains an inherent difficulty which grows with the number of added alternatives. Any broad expanse, be it the Gobi desert or a logical service space, needs to be navigated with knowledge and deliberation. A confusion created by too many options is just as hampering as too few.

The inescapable conclusion with respect to USEs is that a good USE should present its human participants with a well-prepared set of tools. The software in the USE should, as far as is practical, unobtrusively anticipate the needs and actions of its users and make the necessary facilities available. There are caveats lurking in this ambition, as many users exposed to animated paper-clips probably are ready to testify, but the pitfalls should in no way be regarded as a detriment, but as a challenge.

While the issue of communication and interoperability to some degree is negotiated with existing and new technologies, it leaves us at the level where we can establish many client-server interactions, but have a difficult time finding out which ones will be most beneficial in a given moment. As humans we want software and services to guide or choice, but how to guide the software? There is the problem of modalities, in which familiar content has to be presented on new devices with unexpected capabilities. There is the problem of choice and selection, in which there are several possible actions to take and each cannot be unambiguously evaluated. There is the problem of routing, addressing and access, in which the physical location of the intended recipient has to be ascertained. Software services have to deal with this distributed and heterogeneous hardware environment as well as with new ways of interaction. The challenge we have to tackle is how to design services that support users, and itself, in these kinds of hard- and software environments.

One important property of a USE is that it should not be limited to single users but work as a support for several people working together, thus making it an aid for collaborative work. Working together in modern organizations most often includes producing, consuming and modifying different kinds documents. Since most of the work processes are based on, or driven by, document flows it is critical for an organization that users and applications have access to documents [1] [2]. But the way documents are managed today seems to be a remnant of the times when users had continuous access to the organization's environment through established and working channels with only a few options to reach the systems. Once in this environment, they were connected. In a USE, where we are surrounded with a plenitude of communication tools and the possibilities to contact the organization's computer environment by using a collection of heterogeneous hard- and software which could be unpredictably disconnected, the instant access and instant feedback on our actions have been lost. It is all too easy to be in the wrong place with the wrong people at the wrong time carrying the wrong documents.

We have to handle issues related to the large volume of documents originating from different sources, such as email, faxes, groupware and different desktop applications and the problem that documents may exist in several places: as a word processor file on a personal computer, as an attachment or text-only version in an email, as a rendered copy in a fax etc. In addition, several instances of each format may be multiplied across the recipients' storage devices, in some cases truncated or converted to suit local software or user preferences. To further complicate the issue, presentation facilities in some devices may be inadequate for some properties of the document or the size of it is simply too expensive for a low-speed connection.

Another problem is that information, which other users would benefit from having access to, is either physically mobile in a mobile device or unavailable in a shutdown personal computer. Access to and use of documents are generally neither controlled nor automated. Just keeping track of what documents exist and to retrieve the latest version can be an overwhelming task, especially when considering mobile and remote users in a USE. The challenge is to make the right information available to the right people, at the right time, and at the right place.

3   fuseONE

At the department of Computer and Systems Sciences, KTH, we have dressed a small conference room with a few selected appointments, nowadays more often than not found in similar locations. The room, the equipment and the software used therein have been nicknamed 'fuseONE'.

The physical space of fuseONE contains a full bandwidth videoconference system, a SmartBoard [3] combined projection screen and pointing device, a cordless keyboard and mouse, a set of iButton identification devices [4], a VGA projector and a server computer. When there is a meeting in fuseONE, most participants bring along further equipment in the form of laptop computers with 11 Mbit IEEE 802.11 compliant wireless LAN transceivers.

The logical space of fuseONE consists of the department systems on the local area network, the Internet, standard application software and our own applications and middleware. Our ambition with fuseONE has not been to replace standard software like web browsers and word processors, but to ease their deployment for the participating users. As it turns out, many practical issues revolve around communication and how to navigate focus of attention.

A gathering in fuseONE usually follows a similar pattern: the participants gather with their laptops around the conference table and insert their iButtons in the receptors scattered on the tabletop. The laptops display representations of the other participant's, the fuseONE server computer and other software services. The projector and SmartBoard are activated and displays the desktop of the server computer with more of the fuseONE software.

As someone wants to display a document on the SmartBoard, a local drag and drop operation on the personal laptop transfers a copy of the document to the server computer where it is automatically launched. Interpersonal document exchange can be similarly arranged by dropping the document on the icon representing the receiver.

Depending on who is attending the meeting (as indicated by the iButtons present), an 'Active Document' may sense that a meeting is in progress and announce itself on one of the available displays. Files relevant to the group can be retrieved and saved by interacting with the Active Document (assuming one is present for the project or task). The Active Document serves as a roaming repository for the group's efforts and is constantly watchful for changes to its payload or congregations in which it should participate.

One of the important properties of fuseONE is that the services available in it, such as Active Documents, should respond and react to dynamic, ad-hoc behavior from its human users. For instance, there is no need specify anywhere that a meeting of a certain group is under way. This event is instead inferred by components in the environment from the people present and their activities.

Our system design embraces the idea of graceful degradation when faced with a point failure. Modular components, general interfaces and redundancy are long-proven means to that end. For example, if the context system is not responding, there are other ways to find a user's document launcher. We want to build a USE that is not inherently dependent on specific software (such as in [5]) or specific hardware (such as in [6] [7]). Compared to [8] our goal is to, as mentioned above, design a more decentralized system capable of providing ad-hoc services in a more dynamic, distributed and heterogeneous environment.

4   fuseONE Services

We strive for providing fuseONE with a lot of different kinds of services, from simple reactive services and user-interface services to proactive more complex services. We also embrace the use of standard application programs like the whole host of software from Microsoft and other vendors. It would be impossible otherwise, since we believe that users would not accept their absence. Therefore, we want to operate on the unit of standard files and applications, but let our services and software provide additional actions which enhance the use and availability of the standard tools. There are issues raised by this, as how to smoothly involve tasks such as concurrent editing, application sharing and so on, without being tied down into a specific vendor or operating system.

Below are some services we have developed described, some of them simple which main purpose is to be exploited by other services and other that have a more complex and advanced behavior (i.e. Active Documents).

4.1   USE Context-Sensitive Desktop

In the fuseONE environment, it is vital to have a visual handle on both human and machine participants as they appear in the logical space. This handle and the grips on it are provided by an application on the user's computer (commonly a laptop), intended to integrate with the native user interfaces.

The USE desktop presents a representation of the logical space and its participants, and familiar means of operation (click, drag and drop). To give someone a file from the local file system, simply drop the file icon on the receiver's icon. To wake up an Active Document, click on it. It should be emphasized that the desktop metaphor is convenient because it is familiar and works well when interacting with the native system, but it is by no means uncontested as the best one.

As the number of visible service grow, the desktop view soon becomes cluttered and additional measures must be taken to prevent confusion and aid navigation among the icons. One of these measures is to make the USE desktop sensitive to the current context and thereby adjust the view that meets the user. In fuseONE, this is accomplished by hiding those desktop items which are not relevant to the current context. The task of estimating relevance is performed by a context inference system.

4.2   Context Inference

The availability of services in fuseONE can be expressed as the sum of its parts, but that quickly becomes an unwholesome endeavor as the number of components grows. To navigate the logical space in terms of services available to the users and certain applications, a special subsystem called 'Context Shadow' [9] has been introduced. Context Shadow makes it possible for humans and software services to ask questions about a persons current context, and specifically what services that are relevant to that context. In the system, services and sensors are organized in meaningful collections, creating a searchable topology of context information.

In fuseONE, the context inference system silently monitors users and their activities and maps the services available to each user. Properties of services and users, such as their location, project membership etc. can be used to e.g. find services near the user or near other users within a shared project. For example, a document application launcher may be running as registered to a particular user, in which case it makes sense to present a document addressed to that user on that particular service. The Context Shadow system is able to provide answers to questions such as: *"Is there a document application launcher available in the same room as Martin?"*

Location information is provided by user actions and the attributes and presence of certain software services. User actions include the manipulation of iButtons which explicitly announces their location and the detection of screen savers on stationary computers.

Unlike e.g. [10], the aim with Context Shadow is mainly to offer context information for other services, and not directly to users. Context Shadow is also application independent, which is not the case with systems such as [11].

The USE desktop application subscribes to information from the context inference system to filter out from its display those resources which are not pertinent to the immediate situation. The Active Documents also exploit the context inference system by monitoring the contents of a location, like the fuseONE conference room, rather than collecting information from separate iButton terminals.

4.3   Document Application Launcher

In order to receive a document most computers participating in fuseONE run a small service which accepts a file and then presents it, using the application associated with the document type. Both users and other services like Active Documents could use the launcher. When it is operating, the user's personal environment is open to sudden disturbances, such as an application suddenly starting. We have found indications that ordinary social protocol cushions this when the parties are within talking range, as in the conference room setting. At larger distances, however, other modes of transfer, like email, appear to be preferred. A polite negotiation mechanism, like that of ICQ's document transfer [12] could easily be implemented but at the moment we have not done that.

4.4   Public Address Notifications

At the time of this writing, recent additions to fuseONE include a notification service in the form of a scrolling banner. A banner is displayed on the SmartBoard and user and other services can direct messages at it. The idea is that general announcements or a stream of updated background information which do not require immediate and disturbing notifications can be presented there. A small Active Document could for example use it to display its content.

In the spirit of the document application launcher, individual users are free to run their own notification services if they so desire.

4.5   Mobile Messenger Agent

The mobile messenger agent application is a small application which basically tries to hunt down the recipient and execute as close to it as possible. Originally envisioned as a kind of self-delivering information parcel, it was quickly realized that if wrapped correctly, the content of the messenger agent could be almost any program. The messenger agent thus has the ability to deliver secure content, extensive graphics or multimedia or any other form of messaging which requires local processing power or user interaction.

Our goal is also to make the Active Documents truly mobile and thereby provide them with the capability to execute near the users, e.g. for supporting disconnected operation.

In order to allow mobile code to move around a code execution server is needed. In fuseONE there is such a service which receives and runs objects. Given the security implications of such a service, it has not seen any general distribution so far, but it is obviously needed as part of the environment.

4.6   Active Documents

The notion of active documents has been used in several works. In [14] 'active document' refers to documents that perform activities as a result of users' manipulations on the documents, such as opening and scrolling. In [15] active documents react to changes in context information and accordingly adapt the information displayed. In [16] 'active document' denotes a new technique for modeling documents that includes physical, semantic, and functional properties. In the work presented in [17] 'active documents' is a document that has been enhanced with the ability to autonomously create 'adlets' that contain metadata and that will advertise the document to other documents.

The work presented in [18] is, like the one presented in this paper, based on the idea that the documents themselves are active. The documents support coordination functionality by using 'active properties'; they should be "situationally aware". The activity is distributed to the documents, but the approach is based on a shared infrastructure where documents are structured according to their properties.

Our idea of Active Documents takes off from the agent-programming paradigm [13], and turn documents into autonomous mobile agents and by that give them some useful qualities. A document should, for example, be *aware of its content* and the intention with it, and be *aware of the context it is operating in,* e.g. its receivers (who, why, preferences about formats, physical surroundings, etc.). The documents are active in the sense that they are autonomous (act independently), reactive (react on changes in the environment), and proactive (have their own goals and plans).

The goal is to make a document capable of making decisions on its own and capable of performing different actions through its lifecycle, thereby supporting users. One example of this is that a document could decide, depending on how important its role is, if it should summarize itself and move to the user's mobile phone, or if it should move to the user's desktop computer and there wait for the user. Agent technology has also other advantages for programming services that should operate in a USE [13].

5   Prototype

We have implemented a prototype that illustrates some of our ideas. The prototype's main components are: Tipple – the USE desktop, FileStarter – the document application launcher and Ad – the Active Document.

The need to cover different platforms and operating systems, as well as mobility, has guided us towards the use of Java. The Jini extension to Java, in combination with remote method invocation and remote launch, has given us the ability to deploy and update a developing body of distributed software without constant reinstallation on each participating computer. One particular rewarding feature of Jini is the discovery mechanism whereby clients can locate and employ services without prior knowledge of host names and port numbers.

5.1   Distributed Software Deployment

The very nature of having multiple instances of client and server processes running simultaneously and in concert on eight different hosts is no easy feat. One of the most irritating problems is that of distributing updated versions of the client software. Users may not feel confident enough to do the upgrade themselves or they may not be able to do it in time, with the risk of unnecessary system brittleness introduced by conflicting versions of software.

FuseONE software uses a main repository of deployed software, located on an http server. All that clients need to install are a small bootstrap loader (written in Java) which fetches the corresponding JAR file from the http server and executes it. In practice this process is condensed into small command scripts or desktop shortcuts.

The load taken off software maintenance with this scheme is very valuable, in that a new version of a program is installed in a single location and immediately available. There is a strong analogy to network file systems, except that the client computers do not have to mount any remote device, only know the URL to the http server, and the http server can (at least in theory) be on the other side of the planet.

Even so, the requirement to distribute the correct URL has been an obstacle at times. For example, our group successfully transported the fuseONE environment into another location some 700 kilometers away from our laboratory, using only laptops and a portable projector. This however, required that all participants mended their shortcuts and scripts to point to another http server, a procedure which took some time and effort.

Since one of the greatest benefits of Jini and Java is location independence (within the limits set up by multicast propagation outside the local area network), it appears natural to modify the bootstrap loader so that it can request the necessary and current invocation details from a Jini service in the network. With that achieved, the details of the distributed system installation ought to be completely transparent to the user.

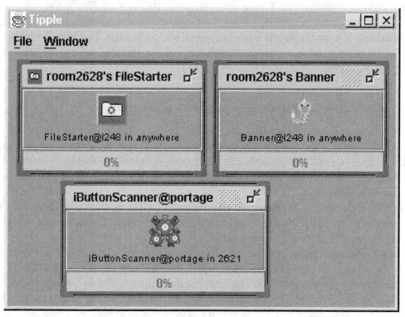

Fig. 1. The USE desktop prototype Tipple

5.2   Tipple – the USE Desktop

The prototype implementation of the USE desktop is called Tipple. Tipple is a graphical user interface that presents services for the user. A sample view is shown in figure 1. Which services that are appropriate for the current context will be received from Context Shadow [9], the context information infrastructure. The idea is that local resources, both stationary and resources on nearby computers should be presented.

Tipple makes it possible for the user to click on and drop different items on the icons that represent the services. What will happen depends on the actual service's implemented behavior. The range of services depends on the current context.

The Tipple is basically a Jini service browser. It monitors the local offerings of Jini services and attempts to display any service which has registered under the Jini attributes Name and Location. If the service also implements the attribute ServiceType, an icon is retrieved and placed together with the text on the desktop.

Icons for services which implement our *putfile* interface allow drag and drop of files from the surrounding system desktop. These are also expected to respond to a mouse-click on their icon.

The Tipple retrieves the name of the current user from the command-line or from the system. Using that name as a key, it attempts to contact the Context Shadow system. If successful, the user is given the option to enable a filtered view. When the filtered view is enabled, the Tipple compares the Jini service IDs it has discovered with a list of service IDs obtained from the Context Shadow system. The intersection of the two sets is kept displayed while the remainder is hidden. The idea is that the list from the Context Shadow system contains only those services which are relevant to the user in the current location.

5.3   FileStarter – the Document Application Launcher

The Filestarter is a Jini service that accepts an arbitrary remote file and launches it. It does this by storing the file in a temporary directory and then applying the native operating system's start command. On Microsoft Windows this usually works quite well. On other platforms additional programming is needed to select the most appropriate application.

When the document is finished, the temporary file is deleted. However, if a permanent copy is needed there is often ample opportunity of making one while the application is waiting for user interaction.

As the FileStarter came into use, we discovered that we sometimes wanted to send a web page, i.e. not the HTML code itself, but actually a URL. We found two different ways to accomplish this. The first involved the transfer of a small HTML file which simply used the META element to request a reload of the actual target URL. The second strategy (between Ms Windows systems) was to construct a local shortcut to the target URL and then simply drag and drop the shortcut to the recipient.

The FileStarter is being run both by fuseONE conference room server computer and by individual users. Since the FileStarter is displayed by the Tipple service browser, the FileStarter has become the de facto indicator of another user. Without any explicit intent in that direction, it has come to serve as a rudimentary user avatar in fuseONE's logical space.

5.4   Ad – the Active Document

Ad is a service that, for example, stores and presents content files. The files could be of any type (e.g. Word files) and it can use other services to present its content. Ad uses the context information provided by the Context Shadow system, for instance who the project members are and their location. When Ad recognizes that two persons, members of the same project as the document itself, are in the same meeting room, the document assumes that there is a meeting going on. It then enters the room (for the moment only virtually) and tries to find a public resource available that it can present itself on, for instance a projector. Information about appropriate resources is received from Context Shadow. When the document enters the room, it also becomes part of the service collection that Context Shadow informs Tipple to present.

When a user 'clicks' on Ad's icon in Tipple, the document gets information about who the user is and tries to find a FileStarter, suitable for that user, to present itself on. The document then dynamically creates a list of its content, i.e. the files it has stored (Word documents, URLs, memos etc.). The document sends this list to the FileStarter with a reference to the computer where the document currently is executing. The document then starts an http server that gives access to the files.

When a user drops a file on Ad's icon, the file will be added (or updated) to the project's information structure, held by the document, and thereby the file will be available to all other project members.

One of the main ideas is that a document by *actively participating* at the meetings should be able to support the other (human) participants. From the system's point of view, a document is actually modeled (as far as possible) as a human meeting participant.

6   Case Study

A pilot study was performed in order to see if the environment built by the research group would be empowering for the users and to determine whether the fuseONE environment performed well in a user situation, to give input on what should be further developed in the environment. The goal of the study was also to be a test-bed for further studies, giving input on what methodology to use for studying environments of this kind and how to design usability studies in wireless, ubiquitous and distributed work environments. We summarize this as two major goals:

1. To examine if our efforts in developing services for such environments are somewhat on the right track.
2. To unconditionally examine the effect of wireless technology on local collaboration. What are the benefits and what new problems arise?

To achieve a real need for teamwork we chose to use the planning of a course at Department of Computer and Systems Sciences (DSV) as the setting for the study. A number of meetings (5) were scheduled and the participants chosen were those who lecture at this course or in any other way are responsible for parts of it. The goal of the meetings was to plan the coming course together. This is the usual way courses are planned at this workplace and thus a natural situation to try to empower with new technologies.

We tried to evaluate how and if users are helped by the new technology in the fuseONE environment. We also wanted to look at the problems that might occur when using new artifacts and services in an environment like fuseONE. In our approach this emphasizes the need for an anthropological approach to the studying of the users in a natural setting.

Fig. 2. Study setting

6.1   Study Setting

Participating in this initial pilot study was the developer group themselves, with a few additions. Due to causes such as illness and other work the participatory frequency varied somewhat. The fewest number of participants was three and the highest seven. All participants were staff at DSV. Two were female and five male. All participants were to a very high degree familiar with computers although three were new to using laptop computers equipped with wireless local area network access in their daily work.

Each meeting was recorded to video and as some of the meeting participants were those performing the study, they also took notes. As this was a pilot study with the goal to give input on how to design further studies and enhance the system the results should be looked upon just as observations.

All participants in the study were equipped with a laptop computer with wireless access to the network. Most of the participants had already access to that equipment and had been using it regularly in their daily work for a longer period. Only two of the participants were new to the technology. Each participant was also equipped with a personal iButton, a small memory device associated with the user. When entering the room the user pressed the iButton into a reader, thus identifying him/herself to the room. This identification, together with each user's personal software, enabled the room to distribute its services to each user.

On each users laptop computer were installed a standard package of commercial software for text editing, Internet browsing, e-mail etc. Each computer was running the fuseONE software.

For the users to be able to collaborate locally and distributed the room was set up with the following software: The SmartBoard software and the same commercial software as on the users laptop computers. To enable collaboration the fuseONE system was used. At one meeting one of the participants worked remotely using Microsoft NetMeeting to be able to see and talk with the participants in the room. He also used the fuseONE environment software remotely (Fig. 2).

6.2   Breakdowns

There were some breakdown occasions observed:

- Specific information is not directly accessible from a person's laptop, e.g.: "Oh that document resides on my other computer, or maybe I have it on paper somewhere"
  "My calendar is not accessible through this computer"
- Searching for information. On several occasions the meetings halted while someone was trying to find a document on a hard drive, or trying to remember the address to a certain web page.
- The different computer screens in the room (personal and public) displays different content (or different versions of the same content):
  CJ looks at the shared screen, which shows an old copy of a schedule, PW looks at a newer version on his own laptop   .
  CJ: "...But this lecture about social navigation..."
  PW: "...There are two such lectures"
  CJ: "Hmm? ...Two?"

There were also some breakdowns related to the fuseONE software identified originating from unpredicted system behavior. The fuseONE tools failed to send information to another computer. This was a fairly common problem that clearly disturbed the work process. Often several minutes were spent on finding other ways to send the information.

6.3   Results

6.3.1   Useful Support

The ability to easily display personal information on a public display was commonly used, liked by the participants and seemed very useful. At some occasions a person would write something on his/her computer, not focusing on the meeting, then actively interrupting the meeting to use fuseONE software to display the document on the big screen. Another way this functionality was used was to provide information related to what someone in the meeting is currently talking about, e.g. a web page. This was often done without interrupting the person speaking.

Another interesting observation was that the observed meetings often continued from the point where the previous meeting ended. Support for this behavior was given by the ability to easily store and retrieve documents in preparation by using the Active Document software. Thus also more work was efficiently performed during the meetings, rather than the more common way of just using the meeting to set up goals and waypoints for the participants to be fulfilled until the next meeting. With the help from the new environment one participant could (and would) act as a note-taker or secretary, using the shared wireless keyboard to type on the SmartBoard screen. In this fashion all participants could cooperate on what should be appended to the document on the SmartBoard and use this as a shared focus of attention and at the same time use their own laptop computers to retrieve information relevant for the work in the room and add it to the shared focus (or each other) if needed. Participants could also, without losing focus on the work-process take care of personal work such as answering e-mail, take personal notes or other activities. The meeting room became an actual workspace while the participants still were able to stick to the meeting agenda.

6.3.2   Observations from a Distributed Scenario

At one of the meeting occasions we tried to extend the meeting to also include a person that was not present in the room. The person was present through the Microsoft NetMeeting videoconference application. The distributed participant was shown to the participants in fuseONE room on the same SmartBoard as mentioned above. The person not in the room could watch the group in the room through a small stationary camera turned to where the participants sat in the room. He could not follow if any of the participants went up to the SmartBoard to physically show anything on it or any other activities taking place outside the camera focus. The group used application-sharing software implemented in NetMeeting so that the remote person could see and manipulate the documents that were run on the shared screen in the meeting room. The person also had access to fuseONE software. The audio quality in this meeting was very poor. Since the remote person's picture sometimes was hidden behind different screens on the SmartBoard the issue of sound became even more important. Noted was also that the fact that the remote person could see the group as a whole was satisfying, although movement by participants in the room could not be followed. The known problem of gaze-direction by the remote person was observed (the remote person looked at his screen and not into the camera) but not much discussed since, as mentioned above, sound became a more interesting issue.

One important observation was the need for the distributed person to have access to the information being displayed on the big screen in the meeting room. It was also preferable to share the same view of a document over NetMeeting, than to have to equal copies of a document. This way you could point to certain parts of the document while talking about it, without confusing the remote part. It also gives opportunities to co-write a document.

6.3.3   General Observations

The support for sending information between each other during the meetings was not used to the extent we had expected. One factor that might have affected this behavior is that the service did not work reliably during the study, due to network problems.

A common situation was that the meeting chairperson has control over the big screen, i.e. that person used the keyboard and the mouse connected to the shared screen. The other participants were mainly giving oral suggestions of what should be written or in other ways manipulated on the shared screen. The other participants used fuseONE software to 'throw' documents to the screen, but in most of the observed occasions the meeting chairperson, acting as a moderator, took control of the document after it had arrived to the shared screen. In this setting the other participants have to ask for the mouse and keyboard to be able to manipulate the information on the shared screen. If it should be possible to use the laptops to interact with documents on the big screen this might change.

Over this series of meetings, most of the documents were created during the meetings, and not so much between meetings. Therefore the process of compiling information that was brought into the meetings was not examined in depth.

7   Discussion

We have investigated a ubiquitous service environment that integrates services and gives them and its human users the possibility to navigate and exploit resources by means of direct manipulation and by using context information. We have implemented a prototype with some services for a meeting scenario and a first case study has been performed. The fuseONE USE has, according to our early results, turned out to be useful.

The fuseONE environment in its current implementation seems to empower its users in several ways. The users are able to quickly and easily share information between each other and to provide a shared view of personal information. Also, more efficient and satisfying work can be done during a meeting situation. Participants can be remotely present and make full use of the fuseONE environment but there is a flagrant need for better tools for audio and video communication over computer networks for this to be really feasible and efficient. Breakdowns in the work-process occur, often due to that the environment does not support enough heterogeneous technological artifacts.

The fuseONE environment is in a constant process of development and already some of the technological causes of breakdowns have been taken care of. It has also been very rewarding to observe the emergence of unplanned utilitarian behavior among both users and software. For example, the FileStarter application in combination with the Tipple were invaluable during a workshop as they removed much of the cable switching which otherwise occurs between talks. On the same occasion, it was discovered that an Active Document could serve as a repository for the presentation files, giving some users the option to view the slides on their laptop computers.

It is important to take note of the fact that with a few steps towards a local collaborative computer environment we can see tendencies towards rather big changes in the work process of the users. The fact that the work *in* the room gets a higher weight and also is experienced as more fun when participants are technologically empowered through the fuseONE environment gives us the notion that we are on the right track in developing wireless, distributed and local tools for collaboration.

It is also notable that the fuseONE system has been, and continuously is, in almost daily use since the end of the abovementioned pilot study. The fuse group always uses it in their group work and meetings. The group members like the system and rely on it. It is most noticed when it due to some or other technicality is not working, a breakdown observation pointing at the fact that the systems level of transparency and "ubiquitousness" is high. It should thus be taken into account that the system functionality and HCI-aspects has not only been investigated during a specific study, but is continuously evaluated.

7.1   Future Work

Much work remains to be done. The fuseONE prototype, for instance will be dismounted and rebuilt in another location as fuseTWO. It stands to reason that the software will face a similar revision and extension. In particular we would like to incorporate support for security, add physical artifacts like PDAs and tangible interface prototypes, and extend the sensory apparatus by which the agents and inference mechanisms perceive the physical space of the service environment.

7.1.1   Security

There are of course a number of security issues involved when so many computer systems and programs are interacting as they do in fuseONE. For example, the ability to launch a program on another user's computer without prior warning or non-repudiation is not a comfortable concept. The traditional question of identification and authorization apply with full force and it is quite obvious that deployment on a larger scale requires a security layer to manage them.

A simple security scheme can be built around opaque tokens of certification. When a client is started it obtains such a token, using information required from a trusted facility. When the client makes demands on a remote service, the token is passed along with the request. The service inspects the token using the same or another trusted facility and is then able to reject or accept the client, as well as logging the client's identity. The server may of course also be required to surrender a token to the client, to prevent server spoofing. The exchange tokens themselves must be one-time tokens, to prevent playback attacks. They should of course also be tamper-proof.

The trusted facility is most likely a piece of library code (or classes in Java) which performs the necessary user authentication and compiles the opaque tokens handed between clients and servers.

Basic authentication is the foundation for a security system. With the identity of another party ascertained, it becomes necessary to establish what that other party is allowed to do. A computer system, such as for example a Windows NT system, enforces a set of privileges and user rights among the resources it controls. Sometimes these rights are extended to other systems in the vicinity with the use of authentication servers. There is yet no complete intuition of how to model the security of a distributed system with many artifacts, like the fuseONE environment. For example, how public should a public display service be? Should presentation on it be available to all users or only the group of users who currently benefit from it?

7.1.2   Beyond Laptops

The commercial range of small computing devices appears to expand each day. The promise of Bluetooth [19] has by now left most workers a trifle jaded of the hype although actual products recently have materialized. For many of the small and personal devices, like cell-phones and PDAs, there is no easy way to integrate them into the USE without special measures. Since many of them are not yet powerful enough to host a full Java virtual engine, one cannot continue to exploit Java's portability in that arena. Instead, native code must be produced, something which often takes too much time and requires both devotion and skill. Power requirements, communication speed and expensive access to the appropriate APIs also constitute limiting factors.

Still, what we would like to investigate further, is a set of lightweight devices which both physically and logically are available as public resources, but very quickly can be turned into personal interaction platforms. One practical example would be so called 'webpads', flat panel computers that lie scattered around the conference room, waiting to be picked up and used by anyone. In such a scenario, user identification must be smooth and transparent using electronic tags, fingerprint readers or some other convenient technology.

References

1.   Sprague, R. H. Jr.: Electronic Document Management: Challenges and Opportunities for Information System Managers. MIS Quarterly (March, 1995)
2.   Ranadivé, V.: Power of Now – How Winning Companies Sense and Respond to Change in Real Time. McGraw-Hill New York (1999)
3.   SmartBoard is a product of SMART Technologies Inc. <http://www.smarttech.com>
4.   iButton is a product of Dallas Semiconductor Corp. <http://www.ibutton.com>
5.   Roseman, M., Greenberg, S.: TeamRooms: network places for collaboration. Proceedings of the ACM 1996 conference on Computer supported cooperative work. (1996) 325-333
6.   Nunamaker, J. F., Dennis, A. R., Valacich, J. S., Vogel, D., George, J. F.: Electronic Meeting Systems to Support Group Work. Common. ACM 34, 7 (Jul. 1991) 40-61
7.   Stefik, M., Foster, G., Bobrow, D. G., Kahn, K., Lanning, S., Suchman, L.: Beyond the chalkboard: computer support for collaboration and problem solving in meetings. Commun. ACM 30, 1 (Jan. 1987) 32-47
8.   Fox, A., Johanson, B., Hanrahan, P.; Winograd, T.: Integrating information appliances into an interactive workspace. IEEE Computer Graphics and Applications, Vol. 20 Issue 3 (May-June 2000) 54 -65
9.   Gustafsson, H., Jonsson, M.; Collaborative Services Using Local and Personal Facts. Proceedings of the PCC Workshop, Lund, (November 1999)
10.   Caswell, D., Debaty, P.: Creating Web Representations for Places. Proceedings of the 2nd International Symposium on Handheld and Ubiquitous Computing (HUC2K) Bristol, UK, (September 25-27, 2000) 114-126

11. Dey, A.K., Understanding and Using Context, Personal and Ubiquitous Computing, Special issue on Situated Interaction and Ubiquitous Computing, 5(1), (2001)
12. ICQ is a product of ICQ Inc. <http://web.icq.com>
13. Jennings, N. R., Wooldridge, M.: Applications of Intelligent Agents. In Jennings, N. R., Wooldridge, M. (editors): Agent Technology: Foundations, Applications, and Markets. Springer-Verlag (1998)
14. Ahonen, H. et al: Intelligent Assembly of Structured Documents. Technical Report C-1996 40, University of Helsinki, Department of Computer Science (June 1996)
15. Voelker, G. M., Bershad, B. N.: Mobisaic: An Information System for a Mobile and Wireless Computing Environment. Workshop on Mobile Computing Systems and Applications (November 1994)
16. Sauvola, J., Kauniskangas, H.: Active multimedia documents. Proceedings of the Fifth International Conference on Document Analysis and Recognition 1999 (ICDAR '99). (1999) 21–24
17. Chang S.-K., Znati, T.: Adlet: an active document abstraction for multimedia information fusion. Transactions on Knowledge and Data Engineering, IEEE, Volume: 13 Issue: 1 , (Jan./Feb. 2001) 112–123
18. LaMarca, A., Edwards, K. Dourish, P., Lamping, J., Smith, I., Thornton, J.: Taking the Work out of Workflow: Mechanisms for Document-Centered Collaboration. Proceedings of the European Conf. Computer-Supported Cooperative Work ECSCW'99. (1999)
19. Bluetooth wireless technology <http://www.bluetooth.com/>

Digital Assistant for Supporting Conference Participants: An Attempt to Combine Mobile, Ubiquitous and Web Computing

Yasuyuki Sumi and Kenji Mase

ATR Media Integration & Communications Research Laboratories, Advanced
Telecommunications Research Institute International,
Seika-cho, Soraku-gun, Kyoto 619-0288, Japan
{sumi,mase}@mic.atr.co.jp
http://www.mic.atr.co.jp/~sumi

Abstract. This paper describes a project of providing digital assistants
to support participants in an academic conference. We provided participants at the conference with a personal assistant system with mobile
and ubiquitous computing technologies and facilitated communications
among the participants. We also made online services available via the
Web to encourage the participants to continue their relationships even
after the conference. In this paper, we show the system we provided for
the project and report the results.

1 Introduction

This paper describes a project of providing digital assistants to support participants in an academic conference, the 14th Annual Conference of the Japanese
Society for Artificial Intelligence (JSAI 2000, in short), which was held at the
International Conference Center of Waseda University from July 4th to 7th,
2000.

The aim of the project, called the JSAI 2001 Digital Assistant Project, was to
enhance communications among JSAI 2000 participants. The events of various
societies, such as annual conferences, give society members an attractive opportunity to experience new encounters and face-to-face knowledge exchanges, and
enable them to become informants as well as audience members. However, it is
unexpectedly difficult to efficiently exploit this opportunity within the period
of a conference: we tend to miss other participants having shared interests or
fail to attend noteworthy presentations. In addition, even if we could meet and
have good discussions with other participants at the site of a conference, these
relationships would likely terminate after the conference.

We provided JSAI 2000 participants with a personal assistant system with
mobile and ubiquitous computing technologies and facilitated communications
among the participants. We also made online services available via the Web to encourage the participants to continue their relationships even after the conference.
The services of the project covered from paper submission, online previewing via

G. D. Abowd, B. Brumitt, S. A. N. Shafer (Eds.): Ubicomp 2001, LNCS 2201, pp. 156–175, 2001.

the Web, personal assistance and information sharing support at the conference site, up to Web services after the conference.

In this paper, we show the system we provided for the project and report the results.

2   Digital Services for Society Events: Related Works

Digital services for society events are not rare. With the recent spread of e-mail and Web services, it has become common to use the Web to announce conferences, call for papers, submit papers, and review papers. Such digital data, however, has only been used by conference organizers to manage their conferences, not to facilitate information sharing among participants to the conferences.

Recently, a lot of research has been done on communityware, software that allows large decentralized groups of people to form communities, share preferences and knowledge, and perform social activities [1]. Considering that academic societies are knowledge-centered communities, the JSAI 2000 Digital Assistant Project was therefore an attempt to build a communityware system.

Related works have been done. Salomon et al. [2] provided CHI'89 participants with conference information, e.g., presentations, participants, and venues, by kiosk terminals located at the conference site. They also evaluated the usability of their services.

Dey et al. [3] prototyped a mobile assistant system for conference participants by using a position detection technology with RF tags. Their aim included the facilitation of information sharing among conference participants after a conference by using not only digitized papers but also presentation materials. Although their work is of interest to us, the actual workings of their system at conferences have not been reported.

There have been many works on building tour guidance systems for museum visitors and travelers (e.g., [4,5,6,7]). However, none of them have focused on the enhancement of information sharing among users.

Classroom 2000 [8] was an attempt to support the sharing of course materials and hand-taken notes by applying ubiquitous computing technologies in a living educational environment. The focus of this work was on the personalization of rich digital documents automatically captured at fully equipped classrooms. Our focus, in contrast, is the enhancement of communications among users by exploiting their nomadic experiences in a larger space, i.e., a conference site.

Meme Tag, an electronic name tag that is capable of exchanging short messages while facing other tags, and Community Mirror, a big screen that visualizes the spread of messages [9], are interesting efforts at facilitating interaction between people sharing interests at actual party locations. However, the exchanged information among users consists only of short messages, which are insufficient for communities.

The most related work to ours has been the ICMAS'96 Mobile Assistant Project [10]. They provided portable digital assistants with various services to assist conference participants. The users could use e-mail and online-news services. They were also able to use a service that supported the exchange of information related to the conference with the other the users. The characteristics of our project in comparison with theirs are that we combine mobile assistant services with services on kiosk terminals located at the conference site, and we integrate online services via the Web, which can be accessed before/after the conference, with services provided at the conference site.

3   Overview of the Project

3.1   Data Preparation

The conference was four days and had about 250 presentations (oral presentations and demos) and about 600 participants.

We prepared a Web server to receive paper submissions before the conference. Upon submission, the authors were automatically registered as users of the JSAI 2000 Digital Assistant Project and their IDs and passwords were created.

In order to provide a service enabling the browsing of conference data (papers and authors), we had to quantify these data and the user's intention (interests, preference) somehow. For this purpose, we used keyword vectors. At the time paper were submitted, we received all of the keywords freely attached to the papers: The amount was over 650, which was not useful for indexing the papers and the user's interests. Because of this, we prepared a thesaurus to absorb these keywords to 28 formal keywords.

The data treated by the project included not only the above static data, but also data dynamically captured and updated during/after the conference, such as a user's history of our system, preferences, and Internet resources (homepage URLs) employed by the user.

3.2   System Overview

We provided all participants with services at the conference site (called onsite services) and online services via the Web (called off-site services). The aim of the onsite services was to provide the users with information situated "now", "here", and "with who" in order to encourage them to share information with other conference participants while attending presentations and having face-to-face discussions. The aim of the off-site services was to remove tempo-spatial constraints from information services by using the Web.

Figure 1 illustrates the overview of our system. The system principally consisted of mobile devices (a portable guidance system called PalmGuide and infrared badges) carried by the users at the conference site and a Web-based online system.

PalmGuide is a portable guidance system for a conference participant. It is not constantly connected with the network, but has an infrared communication port so that it can access network resources by connecting with kiosk terminals located at the conference site.

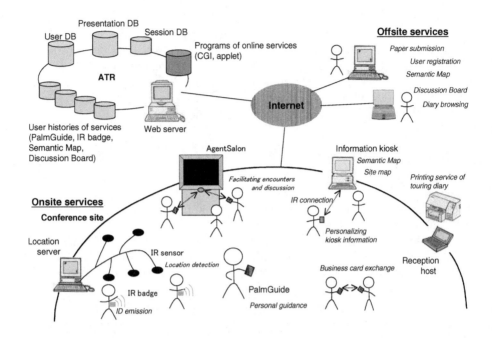

Fig. 1. System overview

The kiosk terminals (and AgentSalon, a kind of kiosk) were connected with the local-area network (LAN) at the conference site and accessed, via the Internet, the Web server located at ATR (our laboratory). The location server with several infrared sensors, to detect the IDs emitted by the infrared badges worn by the users, was also connected with the LAN. All of the collected data by the location server was utilized to show the current locations of the users on the site map, a service available on the kiosks.

The Web server, remotely located at ATR, accumulated the data collected at the conference site, such as the users' records using PalmGuide and infrared badge, and provided tailored service contents based on requests remotely sent from kiosks via CGI. The Web server also continuously provided off-site services for paper submission, user registration, and conference information viewing.

As described above, the system was the combination of various platforms and programming languages, i.e., the Web server with a Java applet and about forty CGI programs written in Perl, PalmGuide running on PalmOS devices, information kiosks and AgentSalon with JavaScript and Microsoft Agent [1] running on Web browsers and infrared communication components written in C++, and the location server programmed with Java.

---

[1] http://www.microsoft.com/msagent/

4   Services Provided

4.1   Portable Guidance System: PalmGuide

We provided the participants at the conference site with PalmGuide, a hand-held guidance system. PalmGuide runs on PalmOS PDAs (Personal Digital Assistants). We prepared fifty PalmOS devices (IBM WorkPads) for the PalmGuide system. Upon borrowing a device, a user selected an agent character from among eight characters we prepared beforehand. The character representation was intended to have the agent increase the believability, consistency, and transparency of services, by having the agent show up on PalmGuide as well as on the kiosk displays and AgentSalon when the user connected his/her PalmGuide to them.

Figure 2 shows example displays of PalmGuide. PalmGuide provided its user with the following four functions.

- Browsing of conference program (left of Figure 2): The user could hierarchically browse dates, sessions, individual presentations, and their abstracts and authors.
- Recommendation of presentations: Presentation recommendations for the next participation were calculated based on the current time and the user's ratings for the presentations he/she had earlier attended.
- Management of touring records: The user could check the presentations he/she had earlier attended (right of Figure 2). A dialogue box for the user to check a rating (1: not interesting, 2: average, 3: interesting) automatically popped-up when he/she checked the box besides the corresponding presentation title.

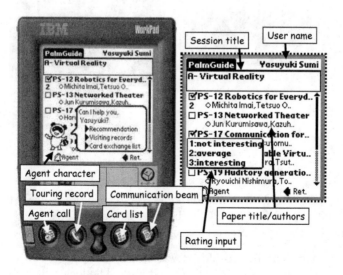

Fig. 2. Displays of PalmGuide

– Exchange of "virtual business cards": All PalmGuide users could exchange "virtual business cards" by turning their PDAs towards others.

4.2 Infrared Badge

We prepared infrared badges for location detection as wearable devices more casual than PalmGuide. Each badge was used as a name tag as well.

We used the EIRIS system by ELPAS (Figure 3)[2]. With this system, a badge emits a unique ID every four seconds and the nearest sensor detects it. All detected data is collected at the location server, which updates a table of the current location of every wearer. The table can be referenced by other machines on the LAN, and then the site map on the kiosks can show the wearers' current locations.

As can be seen in Figure 3, an EIRIS badge has a button on its back. Pushing the button emits a signal with its ID. We used this button as "marking button". That is, the badge user could mark an interesting presentation by pushing the button when attending the presentation. The data collected by the location server was used for creating the user's touring diary.

We installed the infrared sensors of the EIRIS system at three halls for oral sessions, at eight booths for poster demonstration sessions, and at AgentSalon.

Infrared badge worn by a user   A booth for poster presentation

Fig. 3. Infrared badge and sensor

4.3 Information Kiosk

We set four terminals as information kiosks. As can be seen in Figure 4, each kiosk terminal was a Windows PC with an LCD touch panel.

We provided the following services on the kiosk.

– The site map: The user could browse the titles and abstracts of ongoing presentations by touching the displayed map. The locations of badge users

---

[2] http://www.elpas.com/technology/

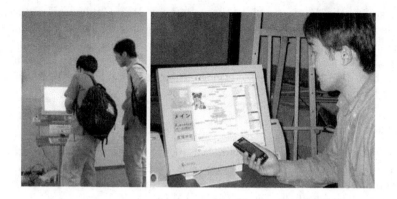

Fig. 4. Information kiosk located at the conference site

were also shown on the map, and so the viewer could immediately know the popularity levels of the current presentations (Figure 5).
- Semantic Map: The user could browse the semantic relationships between the presented papers, topic keywords, and participants.
- Since the kiosk was connected with the Internet, the user could access Internet resources from the site map and Semantic Map, such as other participants' Web pages.

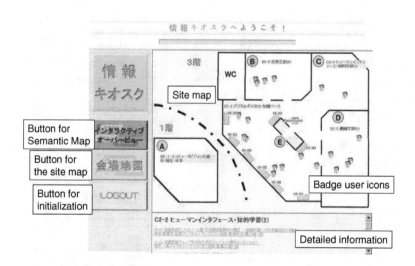

Fig. 5. Example display of an information kiosk

Although the kiosk could be used without PalmGuide, the services on the kiosk could be personalized by connecting PalmGuide. By connecting PalmGuide, the agent character on PalmGuide would migrate to the kiosk display and guide the user on how to use the kiosk. Semantic Map could also be personalized by filtering displayed information based on the user's touring history and preferences.

4.4 Semantic Map

We provided a system called Semantic Map [11], a visual interface for browsing conference information. Semantic Map is implemented by a Java applet so a user could seamlessly use it as a front-end interface of the kiosk services at the conference site and off-site services via the Web.

Semantic Map shows a graph consisting of presentation icons (rectangular icons), keyword icons (oval blue icons), and author icons (oval green icons). The user can select interesting keywords and/or participants from their lists on the right of the applet. By selecting them, the displayed icons are filtered: This shows the user's personal viewpoint.

On the graph, the icons of PalmGuide users (oval pink icons) are also displayed and linked with presentation icons according to the users' ratings: That is, if a user evaluates a presentation as "interesting", his/her icon is linked with the presentation icon.

There is a "Web Search" button at the bottom of the applet. Pushing the button opens a window showing a list of related Web pages searched by a search

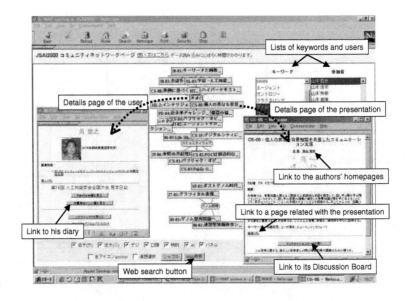

Fig. 6. Semantic Map interface

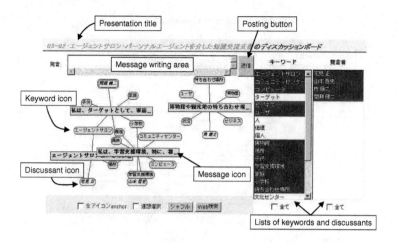

Fig. 7. Example display of Discussion Board

engine (currently, Google), using keywords currently selected on Semantic Map. This means that Semantic Map enhances the user's exploration not only within the community information collected by our servers but also among the open resources on the Web.

Double-clicking presentation icons and participant icons opens their pages, which include paper abstracts and links. Semantic Map functions as a portal of our other online services, such as our Discussion Board and touring diary services.

4.5   Discussion Board

To encourage deeper interactions between presenters and audience members without tempo-spatial restrictions, we provided Discussion Board, an online discussion system. Discussion Board was provided along individual presentations and was accessible from the details page of a presentation. We intend for it to be used as a way of sending questions about a paper before a conference so that its authors can improve the presentation of the paper at the conference, as well as discussing and reporting updated information after the conference.

Figure 7 shows an example display of Discussion Board. Although its interface is very similar to that of Semantic Map, Discussion Board visualizes relationships between posted messages and their writers. In the case of Discussion Board, displayed keywords are automatically extracted from posted messages by using a Japanese parser, called Chasen, developed by NAIST[3].

---

[3] http://cl.aist-nara.ac.jp/lab/nlt/chasen/

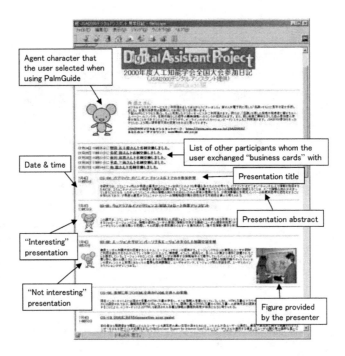

Fig. 8. Example of a touring diary

4.6   Touring Diary

By using PalmGuide and infrared badges, the electronic "footprints" of the individual users were accumulated in the Web server. We provided the users with automatically created touring diaries by using the data.

Figure 8 shows an example of a touring diary. The figure shows a list of other PalmGuide users whom the user has exchanged "virtual business cards" with and a list of the presentations he/she had attended. Since the diary was provided as a Web page, the user could use the diary as a portal for Web pages of presentations and people he/she had met at the conference.

4.7   AgentSalon

We set a big display at the conference site, called AgentSalon [12], as a chatting space for the participants. AgentSalon has a big display for use by two to five users simultaneously.

We intended for AgentSalon to facilitate new encounters and face-to-face discussions between conference participants by tempting them to chats by their personal agents, which maintained their personal interests and experiences. The personal agents would migrate from PalmGuide to AgentSalon by infrared connection.

The chatting by the agents was dynamically created according to the touring records of the users of the agents, i.e., presentations they had attended up to that point and the personal ratings they gave to them. When the users shared many presentations in their touring records, their agents mutually recommended the presentations not shared by them, and/or exchanged their users' opinions about the individual shared presentations. We expected that such chatting by agents would provide just-in-time topics and stimulate the users' discussions.

Figure 9 shows an example display of AgentSalon and its usage at the conference. Semantic Map was displayed behind the animations of the agents and showed the touring records of the current users. The users could touch the icons of Semantic Map and browse their detailed information.

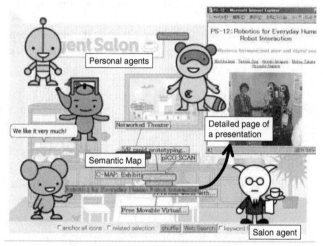

(1) Display of AgentSalon.

(2) AgentSalon being used by two users.

Fig. 9. AgentSalon

5 Results of Users' Data

In this section, we analyze our systems' users' data and describe the lessons we learned.

5.1 Distribution of User Types

The users of our systems were classified the types described below. Note that only identifiable users were classified.

- Registered users: All users registered for the project. This type contains users who automatically registered when they submitted a paper and users who signed-up themselves.
- PalmGuide users: Users who carried the PalmGuide device at the conference site.
- Badge users: Users who wore an infrared badge at the conference site.
- Off-site service users: Users who logged-in to our off-site services at least once.

The number of these groups naturally overlapped. Figure 10 shows the numbers and distribution of the groups' members. From the diagram, we can make the following observations.

- Over half of the users who used PalmGuide and/or the badge at the conference site logged-in to the off-site services.
- Of the 203 of off-site service users, 162 utilized only the off-site services.

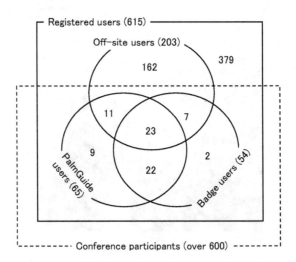

Fig. 10. Distribution of user types

- Over 60% of registered users did not use PalmGuide, badge, or off-site services. Most of them are assumed to be auto-registered participants who submitted papers, so they did not have enough motivation to use our systems. Note that there is no way to count the users who only used the kiosk service, so we cannot say how many users never used any service.
- There is much overlap between users of PalmGuide and the badge. We intended these two services to be used as alternatives, but most of the active users were interested in using both of them.

We prepared 50 PDAs to lend out for use with the PalmGuide system. Since most of them were used by one person during the entire conference, the total number of PalmGuide users was 65. Among them, five users used their own PalmOS devices. We expect that we will not have to prepare such PDA devices for lending out in the near future.

We prepared 100 infrared badges, but the number of its users was small. We expected that the effect of a site map would be displayed on the kiosks (Figure 5), depending on the number of worn badges; however, this effect was not achieved. Such badges should be distributed to all participants like name tags for effective usage; this would also make user registration easier. However, the EIRIS badge we used is too expensive to give to all participants. Considering how to use cheaper RF tags or IC cards for this purpose is a future work.

We registered 479 presenters as users of our system beforehand. In addition to these users, 136 people signed up for our services in the two-month period after we started our online service. Even now, the number of signed-up users continues to increase. As shown in Table 1, while the ratio of logins to our online service of the auto-registered users was only 18.16%, the ratio of signed-up users was over 85%. This seems reasonable considering that signed-up users are generally more highly motivated.

Table 1. Numbers of users who logged in to off-site services

	user (persons)	login (persons)	login ratio (%)
Auto-registered users	479	87	18.16
Signed-up users	136	116	85.29
Total	615	203	33.01

5.2   Utilization of Off-Site Services

Figure 11 shows the overall activities of our off-site services. The x-axis indicates the date and the y-axis indicates the numbers of user sign-ups and logins. Note that the login count before the conference is larger than during the conference; this indicates that online services provided by the Web offer great potential as "warming-up" activities among participants before social events.

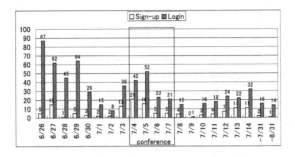

Fig. 11. User sign-up and login to our off-site services

Figure 12 shows the utilization of individual off-site services. Semantic Map was constantly accessed; which implies that it functioned as a browser for pre/post viewing conference information. Concerning Discussion Board, while it was launched more than a few times, its posting numbers were very low. We think the reason for this is that the posted messages could be read anonymously but those posting messages had to use their names. In the future, we need to find a way to motivate the users to join the discussions. Touring diaries were viewed after the conference, but not so much. Although we expected the touring diaries to be effective for continuously connecting users after the conference, the synergistic effect remained low among utilizations of PalmGuide (or the badge), the amount of information provided by users, and the touring diaries.

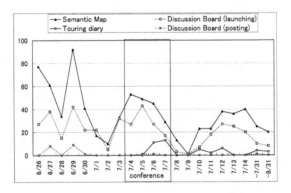

Fig. 12. Utilization of off-site services

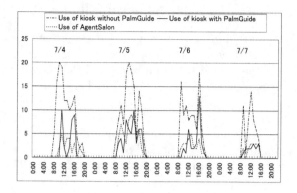

Fig. 13. Utilization of kiosks located at conference site

5.3   Utilization of Onsite Services

In order to analyze the utilization of services at the conference site, we tracked the daily utilization of the information kiosks, which was the most casual service. Figure 13 shows the access numbers of four kiosks (with and without PalmGuide) and one AgentSalon system. Kiosk use without PalmGuide was consistently most popular.

Figure 14 shows the utilization of individual services on the kiosks and AgentSalon. The access number of Semantic Map was significantly higher than the other services since it was launched as the default display. Interestingly, the access frequency of the touring diaries increased from the beginning to the latter part of the conference. This seems reasonable because the value of the diary increased with the utilization of PalmGuide and infrared badge.

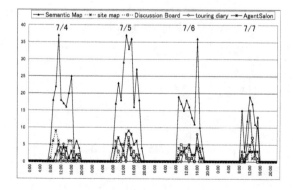

Fig. 14. Utilization of onsite services on kiosks

5.4   User Distribution of PalmGuide Utilization

Thus far, we have only discussed the aggregated results of all users. Now, we will discuss the trends of system utilization by individual users.

Figure 15 shows the user distribution of utilized PalmGuide functions. Concerning the numbers of kiosk access and card exchange, users who never used these services were the majority, and the user numbers nearly decreased with the increase in utilization numbers. On the other hand, the utilization of the presentation check function was completely different depending on the users. Over half of the PalmGuide users checked over 10 presentations for attendance histories, and there were 11 users who checked more than 30. This implies that

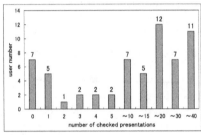

(1) Presentation checking

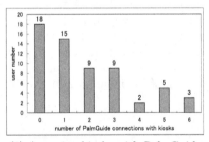

(2) Accessing kiosks with PalmGuide

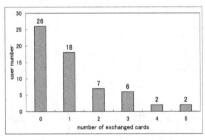

(3) "Virtual business card" exchange

Fig. 15. User distribution of PalmGuide utilization

PalmGuide was accepted by most users as a casual interface during conference attendance.

5.5   User Distribution of Off-Site Service Utilization

Figure 16 illustrates the utilization of our off-site services. Figure 16 (1) shows the user distribution of logins to the off-site services. While about half of the users logged in only once, some of the users logged in about 40 times over two months. The most utilized off-site service was Semantic Map for browsing conference information such as papers and presenters. Figure 16 (2) shows the utilization of Semantic Map. Most of the users launched Semantic Map a few times. Surprisingly, there were few users who launched it over 30 times for the two-month

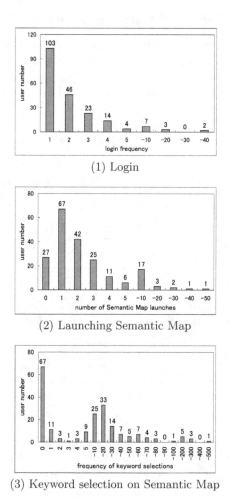

(1) Login

(2) Launching Semantic Map

(3) Keyword selection on Semantic Map

Fig. 16. User distribution of off-site service utilization

period. In order to more deeply understand this utilization of Semantic Map, let us look at the number of keyword selections on Semantic Map in Figure 16 (3). On Semantic Map, a user can select keywords to explore conference information. Therefore, the frequency of keyword selections can be regarded as the user's activity while using Semantic Map. In our case, since one third of all users never selected a keyword, we can assume that quite a few users launched Semantic Map without any aim. On the other hand, we can also see a gentle peak around 20 times, indicating that most of the users understood and actually used Semantic Map. Some very active users made keyword selections over 100 times. According to our records, the most active users used Semantic Map before the conference (for only eight days). This implies that Semantic Map functioned effectively as a way to preview the conference.

5.6   Correlations between Utilizations of Services

In a more detailed analysis, Table 2 shows the correlations between the utilizations of various services (PalmGuide functions and off-site services) by PalmGuide users. We assumed a positive correlation between two with a correlation factor of more than 0.4, which is bold-faced in the table.

Table 2. Correlations between utilizations of various services by PalmGuide users

	kiosk	record	card	login(1)	login(2)	login(3)	login(t)	over-view	discuss	diary
kiosk	1									
record	.2605	1								
card	.0926	.2716	1							
login(1)	-.1853	-.0520	-.0014	1						
login(2)	-.0410	.0868	.0030	-.0785	1					
login(3)	-.0102	.2878	-.0249	-.0359	-.0821	1				
login(t)	-.1914	.0493	-.0076	**.9388**	.1332	.2223	1			
overview	-.1920	.0576	-.0039	**.6668**	.3514	.1474	**.7669**	1		
discuss	.0532	.3783	.1080	.0296	.1075	.3567	.1521	.1215	1	
diary	.0502	.1928	.0062	-.0733	.3778	.0000	.0167	**.4245**	.3617	1

kiosk: kiosk access with PalmGuide, record: presentation check, card: card exchange,
login(1,2,3,t): off-site service login (before, during, after conference, total),
semmap: Semantic Map, discussion: Discussion Board, diary: touring diary

A very strong correlation appears between off-site service login before the conference and its total, which means most logins were done before the conference. Additionally, there was a positive correlation between Semantic Map utilization and off-site service login. Therefore, we can assume that such active users, who used PalmGuide at the conference site, were highly motivated by our service before the conference. A positive correlation also appears between diary browsing and Semantic Map utilization. This means that Semantic Map functioned as a portal of personal diaries and Internet resources related to the presentations and participants of the conference.

6   Subjective Evaluations

We asked onsite service users to fill out a questionnaire when they returned the PDAs and/or the badge. We received answers from 35 users.

Our questions asked whether the user has used individual functions on Palm-Guide, information kiosks, and AgentSalon, and if so, whether it was effective. At the same time, we also asked about off-site services for previewing the conference. The following is a summary of the results.

- All functions of PalmGuide except card exchanging were used (or noticed) by most of the PalmGuide users without the need for detailed instructions and their effectiveness was acknowledged.
- The migration of agent characters from PalmGuide to kiosks was easily understood and used with pleasure.
- Although some authors registered links to their personal Web pages for details pages of their papers, most users were not aware of these. The major reason was thought to be the fact that the number of linked pages was very small.
- We employed the same Semantic Map applet for the kiosk displays and the AgentSalon's background. In spite of this, the Semantic Map on AgentSalon was regarded as more effective. We believe that conference participants would prefer collaborative Web browsing with a big screen rather than single use with a kiosk terminal.

7   Conclusions

We reported the implementation and experimental results of a digital assistant system for conference participants. Our trial use showed that the system was still in an early stage because the provided services were not well matured and the participants were typically not used to such services. We believe that online services for pre/post conferences and onsite services for enriching face-to-face meetings at a conference site are mutually compensable and synergic. Therefore, it is important to continue such services so that they will eventually be firmly rooted in the conference operations of academic communities.

Acknowledgments

The JSAI 2000 Digital Assistant Project was a highly collaborative work. Valuable contributions to the systems described in this paper were made by Tetsushi Yamamoto, Tadashi Takumi, and Yasuhiro Tanaka. Keiko Nakao took part in the design and illustration of the agent characters. We would also like to thank the JSAI 2000 Program Committee for supporting our project. Finally, we would like to thank Ryohei Nakatsu for his continuous support. This work was supported in part by CREST of JST (Japan Science and Technology Corporation).

References

1. Toru Ishida, Toyoaki Nishida, and Fumio Hattori. Overview of community computing. In Toru Ishida, editor, *Community Computing: Collaboration over Global Information Networks*, chapter 1, pages 1–11. John Wiley & Sons, 1998. 157

2. Gitta B. Salomon. Designing casual-use hypertext: The CHI'89 InfoBooth. In *Proceedings of CHI'90*, pages 451–458. ACM, 1990. 157

3. Anind K. Dey, Daniel Salber, Gregory D. Abowd, and Masayasu Futakawa. The conference assistant: Combining context-awareness with wearable computing. In *The third International Symposium on Wearable Computers*, pages 21–28. IEEE, 1999. 157

4. Katashi Nagao and Jun Rekimoto. Agent augmented reality: A software agent meets the real world. In *ICMAS-96*, pages 228–235. AAAI Press, 1996. 157

5. Gregory D. Abowd, Christopher G. Atkeson, Jason Hong, Sue Long, Rob Kooper, and Mike Pinkerton. Cyberguide: A mobile context-aware tour guide. *Wireless Networks*, 3(5):421–433, 1997. 157

6. Steven Feiner, Blair MacIntyre, Tobias Höllerer, and Anthony Webster. A touring machine: Prototyping 3D mobile augmented reality systems for exploring the urban environment. In *The first International Symposium on Wearable Computers*, pages 74–81. IEEE, 1997. 157

7. Keith Cheverst, Nigel Davies, Keith Mitchell, Adrian Friday, and Christos Efstratiou. Developing a context-aware electronic tourist guide: Some issues and experiences. In *Proceedings of CHI 2000*, pages 17–24. ACM, 2000. 157

8. Gregory D. Abowd. Classroom 2000: An experiment with the instrumentation of a living educational environment. *IBM Systems Journal*, 38(4):508–530, 1999. 157

9. Richard Borovoy, Fred Martin, Sunil Vemuri, Mitchel Resnick, Brian Silverman, and Chris Hancock. Meme Tags and Community Mirrors: Moving from conferences to collaboration. In *Proceedings of CSCW'98*, pages 159–168. ACM, 1998. 157

10. Yoshiyasu Nishibe, Hiroaki Waki, Ichiro Morihara, Fumio Hattori, Toru Ishida, Toshikazu Nishimura, Hirofumi Yamaki, Takaaki Komura, Nobuyasu Itoh, Tadahiro Gotoh, Toyoaki Nishida, Hideaki Takeda, Atsushi Sawada, Harumi Maeda, Masao Kajihara, and Hidekazu Adachi. Mobile digital assistants for community support. *AI Magazine*, 19(2):31–49, 1998. 157

11. Yasuyuki Sumi and Kenji Mase. Communityware situated in real-world contexts: Knowledge media augmented by context-aware personal agents. In *Proceedings of the Fifth International Conference and Exhibition on the Practical Application of Intelligent Agents and Multi-Agent Technology (PAAM 2000)*, pages 311–326, 2000. 163

12. Yasuyuki Sumi and Kenji Mase. AgentSalon: Facilitating face-to-face knowledge exchange through conversations among personal agents. In *Proceedings of Agents 2001*, pages 393–400. ACM, 2001. 165

The Family Intercom: Developing a Context-Aware Audio Communication System

Kris Nagel, Cory D. Kidd, Thomas O'Connell, Anind Dey, and Gregory D. Abowd

College of Computing & GVU Center, Georgia Institute of Technology
Atlanta, GA 30332-0280 USA
{kris,coryk,thomas,anind,abowd}@cc.gatech.edu

Abstract. We are exploring different forms of intra- and inter-home audio communication. Though much technology exists to support this human-human communication, none of them make effective use of the context of the communication partners. We aim to augment a domestic environment with knowledge of the location and activities of its occupants. The Family Intercom provides a test bed to explore how this context supports a variety of lightweight communication opportunities between collocated and remote family members. It is particularly important that context about the status of the callee be communicated to the caller, so that the appropriate social protocol for continuing a conversation can be performed by the caller.

1   Introduction

Human-human communication is an essential part of our everyday lives. Advances in communication technology have enabled anytime-anywhere connection between people, but not always in the most socially acceptable fashion. In this paper, we focus on communication between family members, both collocated and distributed. While there are many tools enabling direct communication, there is little support for the appropriate social mediation of communication between persons with a trusting relationship, such as a family. In the Georgia Tech Aware Home Research Initiative [3], we are building and evaluating applications that exploit knowledge of the whereabouts and activities of members of a family. For human-human communication, we are interested in how awareness of location and activity can facilitate both intra- and inter-home communication. We want to provide a variety of lightweight interfaces that facilitate a human's ability to decide whether a proposed conversation should be initiated or not. Our intent with the Family Intercom project is to explore how context-aware communication can support family communication, but before we can embark on authentic evaluation we need to provide a flexible test bed to support our experimentation.

G. D. Abowd, B. Brumitt, S. A. N. Shafer (Eds.): Ubicomp 2001, LNCS 2201, pp. 176-183, 2001.

2   Understanding Home Communication

The most common technology to support intra-home communication is the intercom system. To reach a particular person, the intercom requires the caller to press a button for each station, until the recipient is located. Once this connection between two individuals is made, they may not roam from station to station without explicitly resetting the communication path. The caller has no knowledge of the recipient's location or availability for a call, and may disturb others while searching for the desired recipient. The push-button activation is not convenient when hands are occupied by tasks other than communication. Intercoms directly support place-to-place communication, rather than person-person connections desired at home.

Inter-home communication is commonly supported by telephony systems. Phone calls are most commonly activated by a push button interface, although some voice-activated systems are available. Cellular phone service has the advantage of connecting to a person, rather than a place, and to roam with the person. However, it does not provide the caller or recipient with situation awareness, such as location or whether this is a good time have a conversation. Calls. calm [7], Context-Call [9], and *live addressbook* [4] extend telephony to enable the caller and callee to interact and determine a desirable choice of time and communication media using context the participant explicitly supplies. Each relies in some measure upon the user remembering to provide desired context, or responding to a prompt. While some telephone systems provide a more person-oriented connection, there is single mode of call activation and a lack of situation awareness.

Providing hands-free call activation mechanisms and contextual-awareness would support more satisfying interpersonal communications. Context-aware desktop conferencing tools in the office, such as Portholes [2] and Montage [10], provide some situation awareness, but require explicit user interactions with technology not commonly found in the home. Thunderwire, a lightweight and always-on audio-only space [1], supports informal communication, but lacks adequate presence cues and has no private communications channel. In contrast, the context-aware Family Intercom we present in this paper requires less explicit activity on the part of its users to establish desirable communications. Information gathered automatically from the environment provides context for either automatic or human-mediation of communication at each end-point of the connection:

Where is the intended recipient located?

What is the recipient doing, and is it OK to interrupt the recipient at this time?

We explore a variety of interaction modes to initiate and terminate family communication within a richly sensored environment and distributed to a home with minimal context. The following two sections describe two prototypes supporting different communication scenarios. These prototypes are described in fuller detail elsewhere [6].

3   Exploring the Intra-home Intercom

The initial context-aware intercom prototype has been installed in the Aware Home, where our model of interaction is made hands-free by providing voice interaction. To better portray the communications patterns we hope to support with a context-aware Family Intercom, we describe a usage scenario in detail before presenting our prototype to support these capabilities.

3.1   Scenario: Having an Intra-home Conversation

From the kitchen, Mom sends Sally down to the basement to get some items from the pantry. Once Sally gets down to the pantry, she cannot find the items Mom sent her to retrieve. Sally wants to ask for some clarification from Mom, but Mom cannot hear even if Sally yells. So, Sally instructs the house intercom, "House, I want to talk to Mom." Meanwhile, Mom has set up a baby monitor connection to her younger son, Joey. She can hear Joey crying, so she departs to the family room to care for him. When the house recognizes the request from Sally down in the basement pantry, it then locates Mom is in the family room. The house knows that baby Joey is also in the family room, so tells Sally, "Mom is now in the family room with Joey. Do you still wish to speak with Mom?" Though Mom's attention will be divided, Sally still wants to speak with her, so she responds, "Yes." A two-way audio connection is established between Sally in the basement pantry and Mom in the living room. Sally asks Mom to help her determine which items to bring up to the kitchen. During the course of the conversation, Mom finishes with Joey and returns to the kitchen to see what else she needs Sally to bring up from the pantry. The conversation between Sally and Mom continues uninterrupted as both move about the house. As Sally finally returns to the kitchen where Mom is, the house determines that their remote conversation has ended and automatically terminates the audio connection between them.

3.2   Environmental Instrumentation and Software Design

The hardware design consists of an electronically configurable audio system containing:

- speakers mounted in the ceiling of each room throughout the house;
- personal wireless microphones worn while walking around the house;
- audio switch to support simultaneous point-to-point connections;
- positioning system providing room-level location.

We are interested in rapidly prototyping and easily evolving the context-aware features of the intercom application. The Context Toolkit [8] provides useful abstractions for organizing the functionality of the intercom software and incorporating sensed context (Figure 1). For example, the location widget automatically delivers position changes when individuals leave or enter rooms in the house. The Audio Switch service allows us to send commands to connect the microphone of one person to the speakers in some room to support roaming. Each of these components can be shared by any context-aware application.

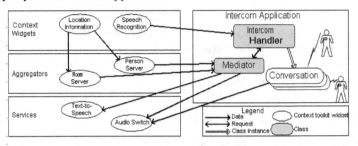

Fig. 1 Intercom Application Software Design

The intercom application itself supplies the appropriate context-aware functionality, and consists of three components, the Intercom Handler, the Mediator and Conversation widgets. The Intercom Handler subscribes to the Speech Recognition context widget, receiving only commands recognized as intercom requests. When an intercom request is received, the Person Aggregator of both the caller and recipient will be queried to figure out which rooms are involved in the connection. The Mediator component then determines whether the connection should be established. If the connection is approved, a Conversation context widget is created to manage the connection. The Conversation widget requests the Audio Switch service to make the appropriate one- or two-way audio connections. This widget also subscribes to the relevant Person aggregators of the caller and recipient to be informed when either changes rooms. If a room change is detected, the Audio Switch is instructed to alter the connection path to follow the caller and recipient. The intercom application can easily receive inputs commands from a GUI interface widget or location updates from an alternate positioning system, with no changes to the application's three components.

4   Exploring the Inter-home Intercom

The second context-aware prototype developed for the Family Intercom explores communication between homes. Communication is initiated from outside the Aware Home, where less context of the initiator is known.

4.1   Scenario: Inter-home Conversation

Kim notices the digital portrait of his mother on the end table and wonders how she is feeling today. The portrait is a portal providing communication to the pictured family member and context from their remote home. Kim touches the portrait to initiate a conversation. The portrait is replaced by a visualization of the conversation request, Figure 2(A). Kim's mother is at home and available to talk. In the mother's home, a background chime alerts her to the conversation request. Kim says, "Hi, Mother, this is Kim". "Oh, Kim, good to talk with you." The conversation continues until either party explicitly stops it, Kim by touching the stop sign on the display or mother via voice command.

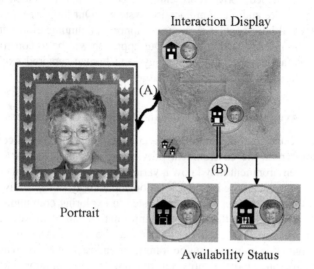

Fig. 2 (A) Touching portrait opens communication (B) Stylized House indicates available, not available, and wait a moment

4.2   Environmental Instrumentation and Software Design

The sensor rich site is the Aware Home, described above. The remote communication portal consists of:

- flat-screen monitor with a touch screen for input;
- microphone to capture the family speaking to the photo;
- speakers placed so the voice comes from the image of the remote person;
- RFID system providing identity of individuals near the portal.

We are interested in prototyping and evolving the initiation of inter-home communication where different amounts of context are available. In this prototype, the Digital Family Portrait, that displays a qualitative perception of activity for the remote family member [5], was augmented to provide an interactive communication portal to the Aware Home. The availability status of the callee is simulated as the sensing in the instrumented home does not yet provide the context required to mediate the communication requests. The Aware Home automatically delivers availability updates to the remote Family Intercom for mediating initiation of conversation. If the remote status is "do not disturb", then no connection is made and the initiator's display shows this status and that no connection is made. The initiating site uses identity of the caller to appropriately display status, respecting the callee's differing privacy concerns between the several remote family members.   The audio connection between homes is an Internet voice connection, established and maintained as a service at each end of the inter-home Family Intercom.

5   Building an Extensible Test Bed for Research

The prototypes described above represent only two points in a much larger design space of context-aware audio communication systems. Our long-term research goal is to better understand how context-awareness supports communication within a family or other small and informal workgroups. Our approach will be to construct an extensible test bed to facilitate deeper technology- and human-centered exploration. We briefly discuss some of the features of this larger design space.

5.1   Context Availability for Initiator and Recipient of a Conversation

A conversation occurs between an initiator and a recipient, and we are concerned with the level of awareness the environment provides to the intercom for each of these individuals. The environment may know a variety of contextual information about the initiator or recipient, including identity, location and activity of that individual and the people around that individual. We are interested in exploring communication scenarios when all or any subset of this contextual information can be made available to the communication system. For example, in our intra-home scenario, we are assuming that the same context is known about both initiator and recipient, whereas in the inter-home scenario we only have identity information for the initiator and much more context on the recipient. Being able to design interactions that support appropriate social protocols across spaces that provide differing amounts of context is an interesting challenge. Also, there are few reliable sensing technologies that provide activity and availability information as depicted in the inter-home scenario. Through use of simulated context widgets in the Context Toolkit, we can use Wizard of Oz techniques to explore context-aware audio communication in the absence of sophisticated sensing. In so doing, we can determine what kind of activity and availability sensing would be appropriate, thus providing a goal for computational perception research in the Aware Home.

5.2   Structure of Conversation Management

Our experience in designing and using the Context Toolkit shows that the appropriate separation of concerns can facilitate long-term evolution of a technology-driven research test bed. In considering support for audio communication, we see three distinct phases - the initiation of a conversation, the management of an on-going conversation, and the termination of the conversation. Each of these phases uses contextual information about the communication partners in different ways.

5.3   Variability of Interaction Styles

We also want to separate out the establishment of a communication path between two individuals from the physical interface that is used to manifest their communication. We showed the use of wireless microphones, which would ultimately be replaced by open-air microphones mounted on the walls or ceilings, in the intra-home intercom as an example of a hands-free and mobile interaction. The inter-home prototype through the Digital Family Portrait demonstrated how the communications interface might be integrated with other, stationary artifacts in a home. We are interested in exploring the use of handheld technologies, such as cellular telephones or PDAs as well. The important point here is that the context-aware communication service suggested by the Family Intercom should be separated from the physical devices used for the specific communication between individuals. Thus, the device used for communication can vary from conversation to conversation. It might even change in the middle of a conversation, for example, when the recipient places headphones over their ears to make a conversation carried out in their living room more private.

6   Conclusions and Future Work

We have motivated the need for context-aware audio communication in a home environment and presented our initial prototype exploration of this problem in the Family Intercom project that is part of the Aware Home Research Initiative. We have investigated both intra- and inter-home communications scenarios, suggesting how effective communication of initiator or recipient context can enable family members to engage in socially appropriate conversations. Our immediate research goal is to subject one or both prototypes to authentic use, so that we can learn what changes in mediation strategies and feedback are appropriate and which forms of context we need to more automatically incorporate into the Aware Home. A longer-term goal is to merge our existing prototypes into a single framework for exploring the rich space of family communication services. This test bed will allow research into a variety of interaction styles for communication beyond the simple hands-free and GUI examples shown in this paper. It will also allow us to examine representations of context, specifically those aspects of context dealing with human activity, that support the sophisticated forms of social mediation that appear to be important for managing conversations.

Acknowledgments

This work is supported by the Aware Home Research Initiative, an industrial consortium coordinated by the Future Computing Environments Group at Georgia Tech. We are particularly thankful for the collaboration by Motorola Labs which has influenced the directions we have taken on family communications. The Aware Home research is conducted in the Georgia Tech Broadband Institute Residential Laboratory under the direction of Nikil Jayant and Gregory Abowd. Dr. Abowd's research in ubiquitous computing is partially supported by DARPA/ITO under the Information Technology Expeditions, Ubiquitous Computing, Quorum, and PCES programs, and by the National Science Foundation (grants 9703384, 9818305 and 0070345).

References

1. Ackerman, Mark, Debby Hindus and Scott D. Mainwaring. (1997) Hanging on the 'Wire: A Field Study of an Audio-Only Media Space. *ACM Transactions on Computer-Human Interaction*, Vol. 4, No. 11, (March 1997) pp. 39-66.
2. Dourish, Paul and Sara Bly, (1992) Portholes: Supporting awareness in a distributed work group. In *Proceedings of CHI '92*, pp. 541-547.
3. Kidd, Cory D., Robert J. Orr, Gregory D. Abowd, Christopher G. Atkeson, Irfan A. Essa, Blair MacIntyre, Elizabeth Mynatt, Thad E. Starner and Wendy Newstetter. The Aware Home: A Living Laboratory for Ubiquitous Computing Research. In *Proceedings of the Second International Workshop on Cooperative Buildings – CoBuild '99*.
4. Milewshi, Allen E. and Thomas M. Smith. (2000) Providing Presence Cues to Telephone Users. In *Proceedings of CSCW 2000*, December 2-6, 2000, Philadelphia, PA, pp. 89-96.
5. Mynatt, Elizabeth D., Jim Rowan, Annie Jacobs, and Sarah Craighill. (2001) Digital Family Portraits: Supporting Peace of Mind for Extended Family Members. In *Proceedings of CHI 2001*, March 31-April 4, 2001, Seattle, WA, pp. 333-340.
6. Nagel, Kris, Cory D. Kidd, Thomas O'Connell, Anind Dey, & Gregory D. Abowd. (2001) The Family Intercom: Developing a Context-Aware Audio Communication System. Georgia Institute of Technology GVU Center Technical Report GIT-GVU-01-04.   http://www.cc.gatech.edu/gvu/reports/2001/index.html - 01-04.
7. Pedersen, Elin Ronby (2001). Calls.calm: Enabling Caller and Callee to Collaborate. In *Proceedings of CHI 2001*, March 31-April 4, Seattle, WA, pp. 235-236.
8. Salber, Daniel, Anind K. Dey and Gregory D. Abowd. (1999) The Context Toolkit: Aiding the Development of Context-Enabled Applications.   In *Proceedings of CHI '99*, pp. 434-441.
9. Schmidt, Albrecht, Antii Takaluoma and Jani Mäntyjärvi. (2000). Context-Aware Telephony over WAP. Springer-Verlag, London, Ltd., *Personal Technologies*, Vol 4, 4, pp. 225-229.
10. Tang, John C., Ellen A. Isaacs and Monica Rua. (1994) Supporting distributed groups with a Montage of lightweight interactions. In *Proceedings of CSCW '94*, pp. 23-34.

Ubiquitous Computing and The Disappearing Computer – Research Agendas, Issues, and Strategies

Norbert Streitz

GMD – German National Research Center for Information Technology
IPSI – Integrated Publication and Information Systems Institute
AMBIENTE – Workspaces of the Future
Dolivostr. 15, D-64293 Darmstadt, Germany
streitz@darmstadt.gmd.de

1   The Panel

Organizer and Moderator
Norbert Streitz (GMD-IPSI, Darmstadt, Germany)
Panelists
Tom Rodden (University of Nottingham, UK)
Dan Russell (IBM Almaden Research Center, San Jose, USA)
Jean Scholtz (DARPA-ITO and NIST, Arlington, USA)

2   Goal

The goal of this panel is twofold. The first objective is to present different research initiatives on the topics addressed by the UBICOMP 2001 conference, as they currently exist in Europe and in the US.

The second objective is to use these presentations to initiate a discussion on commonalities and differences in the respective research agendas. This discussion should address technical issues as well as the implications of this kind of research for the relationship between people and technology in the future. The panel will also try to identify opportunities for joint activities of the different programs in the future.

Examples of recent research programs are: "The Disappearing Computer" (DC) (www.disappearing-computer.net) launched and funded by the European Commission as a proactive initiative, the EQUATOR Interdisciplinary Research Challenge (IRC) (www.equator.ac.uk) funded by the Research Council in the UK, and the "Ubiquitous Computing" program (www.darpa.mil/ito/research/uc/index.html) funded by the Information Technology Office (ITO) of DARPA, and the Pervasive Computing program on Smart Spaces (www.nist.gov/smartspace) at the National Institute of Standards and Technology (NIST), both in the US. This will be complemented with the view from a research laboratory in industry, in this case on the Pervasive Computing activities at IBM.

G. D. Abowd, B. Brumitt, S. A. N. Shafer (Eds.): Ubicomp 2001, LNCS 2201, pp. 184-186, 2001.
© Springer-Verlag Berlin Heidelberg 2001

3   Structure and Topics

Due to the different goals of the panel, the panel will be divided into several parts. After an introduction by the moderator, there will be short presentations about the different research initiatives.

Tom Rodden is a professor of computer science at the University of Nottingham (http://www.cs.nott.ac.uk). As the coordinator of EQUATOR, Tom will present the goals and research agenda of this program.

Dan Russell is a senior research manager heading up the USER lab (User Sciences & Experience Research, http://www.almaden.ibm.com/cs/user.html) at IBM's Almaden Research Center in San Jose, California. Their focus is on people using technology and designing the user experience of Pervasive Computing. Dan's role is to contribute the industrial research lab perspective to the panel.

Jean Scholtz (http://www.darpa.mil/ito/personnel/jscholtz.html) is on leave from NIST and currently the program manager of the "Ubiquitous Computing" program at DARPA. She will report about the projects funded by DARPA as well as about the activities in this area at NIST.

Norbert Streitz is the manager of the research division "AMBIENTE – Workspaces of the Future" (www.darmstadt.gmd.de/ambiente) at GMD-IPSI, an institute of the German National Research Center for Information Technology. In his role as the chair of the Steering Group of the Disappearing Computer (DC) initiative, he will present the approach and an overview over the 16 projects of the DC initiative.

After the presentation of the initiatives, there will be a discussion where the audience will be involved at a very early stage. Examples of topics and issues are:

- Are there and if so for what reasons differences between the publicly funded research agendas and those funded by industry and/or carried out as part of industry cooperations?
- Are there differences between the projects in the US and in Europe and if so why?
- Where is the focus more on the basic technology and where more on the human-computer interaction issues and implications for the user?
- Being confronted with shorter and shorter R&D cycles, what are the implications for the topics of short term vs. medium range vs. long term, blue-sky research?
- Is it correct to assume that industry will focus more on form factors, do shorter-term user requirements for types of functionality needed by users, and be interested even more in vertical market research?
- What are technology requirements for a world where really ubiquitous computing can take place?
- How can one quickly devise a ubiquitous computing infrastructure if there does not exist one in the first place?
- What is the role of personal mobile devices in relationship to static and/ or embedded public devices?

- What are the implications of putting sensors everywhere allowing to monitor, capture, and record all kinds of interactions between people and devices and, of course, between different people?
- How can we retain and promise privacy in future "intelligent" environments?
- How can people who inhabit these environments continually make sense of the world within which they live and what are the main technical and conceptual architectures needed to promote this?
- Will ubiquitous smart artefacts produce "intelligent" behaviour and how will users interpret this?
- How can people interact with "invisible/ disappearing" computers/devices?
- How do people migrate from explicit interfaces/interactions to implicit interfaces/interaction?
- What are the basic models of interaction that promote coherence of individual as well as social experiences?
- What are the roles of physical architectural space and the affordances of real objects in relationship to the role of digital objects in virtual information spaces?
- Which are the domains that might be able to generate/ provide the "killer application" for ubiquitous computing?
- Can an evaluation program contribute to the development of ubiquitous computing?   If so, what type of evaluation efforts should be implemented?

4   Audience

The panel wants to address people coming from a wide range of disciplines and research areas, e.g., networking, sensing, infrastructure, information sciences, human-computer-interaction, augmented reality, CSCW, graphic and product design, ergonomics, psychology, sociology, and architecture.

The Conversational Role of Electronic Guidebooks

Allison Woodruff, Margaret H. Szymanski, Paul M. Aoki, and Amy Hurst*

Xerox Palo Alto Research Center
3333 Coyote Hill Road, Palo Alto, CA 94304, USA

Abstract. We describe an electronic guidebook prototype and report on a study of its use in a historic house. Visitors were given a choice of information delivery modes, and generally preferred audio played through speakers. In this delivery mode, visitors assigned the electronic guidebook a conversational role, e.g., it was granted turns in conversation, it introduced topics of conversation, and visitors responded to it verbally. We illustrate the integration of the guidebook into natural conversation by showing that discourse with the electronic guidebook followed the conversational structure of storytelling. We also demonstrate that visitors coordinated object choice and physical positioning to ensure that the electronic guidebooks played a role in their conversations. Because the visitors integrated the electronic guidebooks in their existing conversations with their companions, they achieved social interactions with each other that were more fulfilling than those that occur with other presentation methods such as traditional headphone audio tours.

1   Introduction

Visitors often go to cultural heritage locations, such as museums, with companions. Many seek what has sometimes been called a "learning-oriented" experience [8]. To facilitate learning, institutions typically present information through guidebooks and prerecorded audio guides as well as through labeled exhibits and docent-led tours. However, sharing the experience with companions is often a higher priority than learning, particularly for infrequent visitors [12]. Unfortunately, existing presentation methods interfere with the interaction among visitors. For example, visitors frequently complain that audio tours with headphones isolate them from their companions, and visitors have few opportunities to interact effectively with each other while docents "lecture" to them.

We are interested in identifying electronic guidebook designs that facilitate rather than hinder social interaction. To this end, we conducted a qualitative study of visitors using an electronic guidebook. We first constructed a prototype, designing it to provide a range of options for information presentation and sharing. In particular,

---

* Work performed during an internship from the College of Computing, Georgia Institute of Technology.

G. D. Abowd, B. Brumitt, S. A. N. Shafer (Eds.): Ubicomp 2001, LNCS 2201, pp. 187-208, 2001.
© Springer-Verlag Berlin Heidelberg 2001

we provided a mechanism for visitors to hear each other's audio selections. We then observed fourteen visitors using the guidebook in a self-guided tour of a historic house and conducted semi-structured interviews. Visitor actions were captured using audio recording, video recording, and device logging.

In this paper, we report an analysis of how different properties of the device helped visitors to interact with their companions while preserving their ability to engage in independent activity. A previous analysis focused on issues of attentional balance, drawing on content from the interviews supplemented by informal observations of visitor use of the guidebooks [27]. The work reported in this paper focuses on social interaction and is based on a detailed analysis of video taken while visitors used the electronic guidebooks.

This analysis demonstrates that visitors integrate the electronic guidebooks into their conversations, thereby achieving their goal of having a social experience with their companions. Specifically, visitors possess a strong desire to have conversations in which they share information and responses. A natural way for them to include information in conversation is to simply assign the information source (the electronic guidebook) a conversational role. When the guidebook plays a conversational role, the visitors are naturally positioned to have shared responses to its statements, which leads to gratifying social interactions. Further, directly incorporating the electronic guidebook in conversation is an elegant solution, since it does not require visitors to develop new skills for coordinating their interaction with the guidebook; they can simply use their existing conversational conventions.

In this paper, we show that visitors in our study assigned a conversational role to the electronic guidebook, e.g., the electronic guidebook was granted turns in the conversation, the electronic guidebook introduced topics of conversation, and visitors verbally responded to the electronic guidebook. To demonstrate this role, we show that discourse with the electronic guidebook followed the conversational structure that occurs in traditional human storytelling. We also present behavioral evidence that visitors made many efforts to listen to the same content at the same time so they could better incorporate the guidebook in conversation. For example, they chose to listen to audio through speakers so they could listen simultaneously, they negotiated about which descriptions to listen to, and they physically positioned themselves and their electronic guidebooks so they could be shared effectively.

Because the guidebook was assigned a conversational role, it enhanced social interaction between visitors. For example, visitors shared reactions to stories told by the electronic guidebook, e.g., they offered opinions or stories of their own. These shared reactions are key social interactions that do not occur with traditional presentation methods such as audio tours with headphones.

The transcription shown in Example 1 is helpful in understanding what we mean by "storytelling" and "reactions." (Table 1 summarizes the transcription notation used in all of our examples.) Two women, A and S, are interacting with each other and the guidebook. A looks at the view of the room shown in the guidebook and finds that same view in the physical room.[1] A announces this information to S so they will have a shared orientation. A then tells S which object she is about to select, thereby alerting S that a description is about to begin. Next A and S listen to the

---

[1] The design of the guidebook is discussed in the next section.

Example 1 The story of the deer head

A:	Okay, so here's over here, looking this way. (A takes step towards fireplace wall)
A:	We can see about the heh heh deer head. (A selects description of deer head)
A-PDA:	*This deer was shot by the Bourns' son-in-law at the Irish estate the* *Bourns purchased as a wedding gift for their daughter.*
S:	Oh...
A:	An Irish estate.
S:	Wouldn't you want that for a wedding gift?
A:	Eh hm.

Table 1 Summary of transcription notation

X: X-PDA:	Visitor X is speaking. *Visitor X's guidebook is speaking.*
(*n*)	A conversational pause of *n* seconds.
[Speech of first speaker [Speech of second speaker	Overlapping speech.

description of the object. Following this, they have a brief interaction about the contents of this description.

In the next section, we describe our guidebook prototype. We then describe our research methods. We next describe and analyze the visitors' behavior. We then focus in detail on the conversational structure of storytelling interactions, demonstrating that the electronic guidebook has a conversational role. We discuss these findings, and then review related work and conclude.

2   Prototype

In this section, we describe the electronic guidebook used in the study. The design rationale and many of the details discussed here have been reported elsewhere [3,4,27]. However, it is important to review these details because some of the observations reported in the analysis sections are best understood with our specific design in mind.

The electronic guidebook application runs on a Casio Cassiopeia™ E-105 personal digital assistant (PDA), a small device weighing 255g (9 oz.). Its display is a color touch-sensitive screen. A user generally holds the PDA in one hand and a stylus in the other hand, touching the stylus to the screen to interact with the device.

Fig. 1 Electronic guidebook prototype with outlines visible

Visitors obtain information about objects in their environment using a visual interface. The interface is akin to a set of Web browser imagemaps, but has many refinements [4] that simplify operation on a handheld device. Our prototype presents visitors with one of a collection of photographs. Each of these photographs was taken facing one wall of a room in a historic house. Visitors change the viewing perspective (i.e., display a different photograph) by pressing a button on the device. When visitors tap on an object in a photograph, the guidebook gives a description of that object, if one is available. Many, but not all, of the objects visible in a given photograph have descriptions. (These objects with associated descriptions are known as *targets*.) Because the historic house environment is complex, many different kinds of objects may be targets. Figure 1 shows a photograph with a number of targets, including a wood panel and a doorway. To help visitors identify targets, the guidebook displays outlines around each target, triggered when the user taps on the photograph but does not "hit" a target.

The visual selection design is motivated by the principles described in [3]. We learned through a combination of observation, informal interviews, and professional study [5] that system designs that seem plausible in a museum are not workable in a historic house. Most notably, location-aware systems that use sensors to select content automatically are not feasible in historic houses for a number of reasons (e.g., barriers often prevent visitors from approaching objects). Usability testing of the prototype by thirteen users, conducted prior to the study reported in this paper, confirmed that visual selection is a viable alternative that allows visitors to select objects that interest them quickly and easily.

The prototype gives visitors several choices with regard to the presentation of the descriptions. Visitors have the option of seeing a text description of an object or hearing an audio clip with identical content read by a female voice. Visitors can change the choice of textual or audio presentation at any time. Audio clips can be played at a low volume through speakers on the device or at a user-controlled volume through headphones.

The descriptions themselves are typically two or three sentences (40 words) long but do vary, with the audio duration ranging from 3 to 23 seconds. For example, the 20-second description of a portrait of the Duchess of Richmond and Lennox reads:

> "This 17th century portrait shows the Duchess of Richmond and Lennox, about whom Pepys said in his diary, 'Never had a woman more beauty nor less wit.' The portrait was done by Sir Peter Lely, who was the first of the great English portrait painters. Lely created the distinctive look of British portraiture, including the three-quarter pose and the emphasis on beautiful clothing."

3   Method

In this section, we describe the study participants, the procedure (including the setting) by which we collected the observational data, and the methods we used to analyze the data.

3.1   Participants

The study participants were members of the Xerox PARC community (not necessarily employees), accompanied by friends or relatives with whom they would normally attend a museum.   For example, a grandmother attended with her 7-year-old granddaughter and a husband attended with his wife. The visitors comprised a total of seven couples and ranged in age from 7 to over 60 years of age. Two of the couples were adult-child pairs; all other visitor pairs consisted only of adults. Eight of the visitors were female and six were male. Visitors were instructed to bring glasses if they used them for reading (to our knowledge one visitor who wore glasses forgot to bring them). One visitor used hearing aids. Even with them, he was still slightly hard of hearing. Many of the visitors were non-technical and/or had not previously used a PDA. Two of the visitors had used a previous version of our prototype. Most of the visitors had not previously visited the study site.   Half of the visitors described themselves as frequent museum visitors (visiting museums three or more times a year) and half described themselves as infrequent visitors (visiting museums fewer than three times a year).

3.2   Procedure

Participants were observed during a private visit to Filoli, a Georgian Revival house in Woodside, California.[2] Each visit consisted of three phases: a partial tour using a paper guidebook, a partial tour using the electronic guidebook, and an interview.

The visitors went through the first several rooms of the house with a paper guidebook, accompanied by a docent who was available to answer questions. In some cases the docent was one who worked at the house regularly, and in other cases the

---

[2] http://www.filoli.org/

Fig. 2 Observation of visitors using the guidebook

Fig. 3 Composite video of visitors and screens of their electronic guidebooks

docent was an escort from the research team (the research escort was always present, even when the regular docent was accompanying the visitors). During this phase, the visitors' comments and conversation were recorded using wireless microphones.

The visitors used the electronic guidebook in the next two rooms of the house. One of these rooms contained security barriers and the other did not. The visitors received brief instructions from the research escort in the use of the guidebook. They were then asked whether they would each like their own guidebook or if they would prefer to share. They were also offered headphones. They were told that they could change their decisions at any time and that the research escort could answer questions about the use of the device (this was rarely necessary). The visitors then toured the two rooms, referencing their electronic guidebooks as desired (the electronic guidebook contained a total of 42 descriptions of objects in the two rooms). The visitors' comments and conversation were recorded using wireless microphones, the visitors were videotaped by a camera placed in a corner of each room (Figure 2), the visitors were directly observed by the research escort, and the visitors' actions in the electronic guidebook were logged by the device for future reference.

After the visitors were finished in these two rooms, the research escort conducted a semi-structured interview to elicit visitors' reactions to their experience with the electronic guidebooks.[3]

No time limits were imposed on the visitors during any portion of the study. Visitors spent approximately 20-30 minutes using the electronic guidebooks in total and approximately 10-15 minutes in the interview. The entire procedure took approximately 75 minutes.

3.3   Analysis

The analysis reported in this paper primarily uses conversation analytic methods. A key goal of conversation analysis is to examine social interaction to reveal organized patterns or practices, under the fundamental assumption that interaction is structurally organized.

A conversation analytic research program involves analyzing a collection of interactive encounters that contain a specific practice that is visibly relevant for the participants producing it [23]. The analysis is twofold. First, each encounter is described in the detail of its moment-by-moment, turn-by-turn unfolding. Then these encounters are comparatively analyzed to reveal the practice's generalizable orderliness. The ultimate goal of a conversation analysis inquiry is to describe a practice in a way that is more general than the particulars of any one specific occurrence, yet specific enough to render "how to" instructions for the way it is accomplished.

In this study, our goal is to describe, in an empirical way, visitors' systematic practices as they use an electronic guidebook to tour a historic house with a companion. To identify these systematic practices, we examine in detail the data collected during selected visits. Specifically, we create a video that includes the audio and video recordings of the visitors, as well as video of the screens of each visitor's electronic guidebook (these screens are re-created based on the activity logs of the visitors' guidebooks). See Figure 3. The resulting data are transcribed and analyzed.

4   Patterns of Electronic Guidebook Use

In this section, we describe the usage patterns of the visitors. In general, the typical adult-adult visit consisted of two adults operating separate electronic guidebooks, playing audio through the speakers on these guidebooks, chatting with each other, and frequently looking at objects in the room. The typical adult-child visit consisted of the child operating an electronic guidebook, playing audio through the speakers on the guidebook while the adult watched and listened, the adult and child chatting with each other, and the adult and child frequently looking at objects in the room. However, there were some variations in these patterns, so in this section we discuss visitors'

---

[3] The results of these interviews (which indicate that visitor response to the prototype was generally very positive) are discussed at length in [27].

usage patterns in more detail. We begin by discussing visitors' preferences for separate versus shared electronic devices and for delivery mode. We then discuss visitor attention and visitor-visitor engagement.

4.1   Separate versus Shared Electronic Guidebooks

Each member of the five adult-adult pairs chose to use their own electronic guidebook. (One of these pairs began by sharing, but quickly decided that they would each like to use their own device.)

One adult-child pair shared a single electronic guidebook during the entire visit, with the child operating the device (playing audio descriptions through the speakers) and the adult looking on and making suggestions. The second adult-child pair began by using separate electronic guidebooks, but gradually evolved to the same shared model as the other adult-child pair. This evolution was initiated by the adult, who gradually stopped using his own electronic guidebook and began to listen to the audio from the child's electronic guidebook.

4.2   Delivery Mode

Four of the five adult-adult pairs predominantly used audio played through the speakers of the electronic guidebooks. These visitors would frequently stand right next to each other playing different audio clips through the speakers. Visitors had a high tolerance for these overlapping audio clips. (Members of one pair discussed the audio, one member asking the other if it was bothering them, and both concluded that it was not a disturbance.) Visitors would also play audio clips for each other. The fifth adult-adult pair began by using audio played through the speakers of the device, but early in the session one of the members of the pair switched to headphone use (he stated this was because the audio from his companion's electronic guidebook was distracting him). His companion continued to listen to audio through the speakers of the device.

As mentioned above, both adult-child pairs used audio played through the speakers of a single device.

Visitors stated they preferred audio because, unlike text, it allowed them to look at objects while they learned about them. They also said the shared audio environment was more social (possible reasons for this are discussed further below). Visitors did say that they used text in a limited way for specific purposes, e.g., to see the spelling of a word, or to check whether they had heard something correctly. Additional discussion of visitor choice of delivery mode appears in [27].

Audio was also preferred in some cases because it seemed to be a more effective means of getting a companion's attention than reading text aloud. One visitor (J) initially read aloud information from text descriptions to her companion (L) but then resorted to audio mode when she realized that playing audio clips was a more effective way to get her companion's attention. When J switched to audio mode, she said, "[I] have to play the audio to get your attention, huh?" A similar phenomenon occurred with an adult-child pair (W and V): on multiple occasions the child began to read a text description to his father and was interrupted by his father's playing the corresponding audio description. This same pair briefly coordinated the use of two devices to simulate a combined text/audio mode, the father instructing the son, "You get the text and I'll get the audio."

4.3   Visitor Attention

Visitors did interact heavily with the electronic guidebooks. Visitors selected an average of 37 descriptions, some selecting up to 69 (the latter indicating that visitors viewed or played some of the 42 descriptions more than once, e.g., either to listen to the content again individually, or to share it with their companion). While visitors did attend to the electronic guidebooks, they did not generally dominate visitors' attention. Visitors spent a great deal of time interacting with their companions and looking at objects in the room. More detailed discussion of visitor attention and the user interface appear in [4,27].

4.4   Visitor-Visitor Engagement

While we saw surprisingly little variation in areas such as the use of separate versus shared devices and the choice of delivery mode, we observed an extremely wide range of degree of interaction within the pairs. At one extreme, visitors stayed continuously engaged with each other throughout their visit, having a shared electronic guidebook experience, e.g., negotiating to choose a description and commenting on the descriptions once they heard them. At the other extreme, visitors rarely engaged with each other, focusing most of their attention on the electronic guidebooks and the objects in the room. Other visitors represented intermediate positions along the continuum, e.g., some visitors displayed a "rubberband" behavior in which they cycled between being engaged and disengaged. For example, J and L would look at objects and listen to descriptions independently for a while, but then one of them would share something with the other and they would become re-engaged. Further variation occurred because single pairs would often have a number of different behaviors, e.g., W and V started by using individual devices and then moved to a shared device.

The electronic guidebook helped visitors move fluidly from states of disengagement to states of re-engagement. For example, when a visitor's companion played audio through the speakers, that visitor could see/hear when their companion was listening to a description and therefore that visitor could identify or anticipate a moment when talk might be readily received by their companion. Further, audio played through the speakers created a shared information context in which each visitor knew what the other had heard.

Within a given pair, the members would often have different behaviors. For example, one visitor would often be more likely to select a description, or one visitor would be more likely to orient their guidebook physically to their companion (so that their companion might easily hear it).

Recall that we observed visitors using paper guidebooks and then using electronic guidebooks. We have not yet conducted a formal analysis of visitor interaction while using the paper guidebooks. However, our preliminary observations indicate that electronic guidebook use generally preserved many of the pair's behavioral properties as compared with the paper guidebook use. The one exception was the pair in which one of the participants used headphones; while they interacted extensively when using the paper guidebooks, they had minimal interaction when one member used headphones with their electronic guidebook. This suggests that the use of shared audio does not interfere with the visitors' social interaction in the way that other technologies such as headphones do.

5   Storytelling Model

In this section, we show that the visitors' interaction with the electronic guidebooks had a storytelling structure. Visitors followed the conversational conventions of traditional storytelling in their interactions with the electronic guidebooks, treating the descriptions as stories. By following these conventions, visitors assigned the guidebook a conversational role. Further, they used the storytelling structure as a resource to physically and contextually *align* themselves so they could participate in fulfilling sharing episodes.

We now introduce the three sequentially structured phases of traditional storytelling: preface, telling, and response. Stories in conversation traditionally adhere to the following structure [22]: first, there is a *preface* for the story. In the preface, the storyteller requests and is granted the right to take an extended speaking turn while telling the story, since ordinarily a speaker would not be allowed to hold the floor for as long as a story requires. For example, a speaker may say something like, "I have a funny story" and a listener may say, "uh huh" or "go ahead." Second, there is the *telling* of the story itself. During the telling, the listeners will often make utterances that encourage the speaker to continue, or utterances that indicate a sympathetic response. Third, listeners make some appropriate *response* at the conclusion of the story, e.g., laughing.

In the following subsections, we discuss how the three phases are paralleled in visitor practices of guidebook use. Note that each phase can be located in the examples as follows: the conversation before the electronic guidebook description is the preface, the electronic guidebook description and any concurrent comments from the visitors comprise the telling, and conversation after the electronic guidebook description is the response.

In this section and the one that follows, it will be important to keep in mind that we are using the word "storytelling" to refer to a sequential interactional structure that is well-defined in the context of conversational analysis. Storytelling often has other meanings in the HCI and cultural heritage communities; we discuss this further in Section 7.

5.1   Preface

During this phase, visitors attempted to come into alignment with each other's activities and to create a conversational place for the storytelling to occur. One of the key parts of this phase was deciding what object description[4] (story) to listen to. In this section, we begin by discussing verbal coordination around the choice of

---

[4] Recall from Section 2 that visitors actually choose an object in the interface; this choice triggers a description associated with that object.

Example 2 The story of Mrs. Roth's painting

R: I want to know about that.
                (R points to the painting on R-PDA display)

G: About the painting?

R: Yeah. (R points to the painting in the room)

G: Yeah, okay. (G points to the painting in the room)

R-PDA: *This is a portrait of Mrs. Roth painted by her friend Lloyd Sexton, a*
                well-known Hawaiian painter. In the photograph from which Sexton
                created the picture, she was holding daffodils. Sexton replaced the
                daffodils, which Mrs. Roth did not care for, with Queen Elizabeth
                roses of which she was very fond.

G: (laughs) Diju- diju get that? They had a picture with daffodils so
                they made a painting and put roses in her hand, (laughs) that's
                neat, (laughs) I personally prefer daffodils.

description. We then discuss how the displays of the devices are used as tools for
coordinating object choice.

5.1.1 Visitors Verbally Coordinated Choice of Description

Coordination relating to choice of description ranged from minimal to elaborate. In
some cases, coordination would occur before a particular description had been
listened to by either participant, or in fact even chosen. One common occurrence was
the joint choice of a description. For example, one visitor might ask another what
they would like to listen to next. Often this would lead to the selection of a
description that both visitors would listen to. Another common occurrence was one
visitor announcing that they were about to listen to a description of a given object.
Example 2 shows one such interaction, in which the grandchild (R) tells her
grandmother (G) that she is about to select a painting. Note that coordination over
choice of description often includes identifying the subject of the description in the
room, e.g., in Example 2, R and G both point to the physical painting that is about to
be described.

   In some cases, coordination of description choice would occur when one visitor
(the initiator) encouraged their companion to listen to or read a description the
initiator had just completed. Sometimes the initiator would share text snippets from
the description. Other times they would make more general statements like, "Check
out over here." Often the initiator would play the audio description for their
companion, beginning the storytelling phase.

   Example 3 shows a particularly strong effort to share a specific description.
Visitor V reads a description of false books and then makes multiple attempts to share
information from the description with his father (W). Although W is acting
independently, searching for a description for a different object, V does eventually
succeed in getting W's attention and plays the audio clip. As an aside, note that W
refers to the guidebook's description as a "story."

   In visitor interaction, the electronic guidebook did get a turn in conversation. If
visitors were speaking during the preface phase, and the description began (signaling

Example 3 The story of the false books

(V displays description of books in text mode)

W:	Wonder if there's a story on this ta- on the desk. (W switches PDA to fireplace wall)
V:	False books.
W:	Hm?
	(0.4)
V:	False books, heh heh.
	(1.2) (W selects an object on his PDA, but no information is available for that object)
W:	That's the chair. (W switches PDA to reception room wall)
V:	Oh yeah, these are false books, eh huh.
W:	Eheh, are they? (W walks around V towards bookcase on reception room wall)
V:	Yeah.
W:	Really?
	(0.4) (V switches his electronic guidebook to audio mode)
W:	Let's hear about it. (As W is speaking, V selects the description of the books)
V-PDA:	*Many of the top shelves contain false books. They are lighter than normal books, so they reduce the stress on the bookcases. Many are made of greeting cards, clothing, fabric, et cetera.*
W:	Eh hah, that's a riot. (W looks at V and smiles)
	(0.2) They're just for looks.

the start of the telling phase), visitors generally stopped speaking, effectively allowing themselves to be interrupted by the guidebook.

5.1.2 Visitors Used Electronic Guidebook Displays to Coordinate Choice of Description

The display of the device was a useful tool for coordinating the selection of descriptions, e.g., specifying the object that was about to be selected. Visitors most commonly demonstrated object selection or other activities on their own electronic guidebooks, rather than on their companion's. For example, if visitors were trying to get their companion to select an object, they would point to that object on their own electronic guidebook (or in the room) rather than on their companion's electronic guidebook. Sometimes this involved quite a bit of work.

For example, V was reading the textual description for an object. When his companion, W, wanted to get the same description on his device, V closed the window containing the textual description to bring up the object selection screen, pointed to the object, and then reinvoked the textual description. In other words, he opted to perform a series of relatively cumbersome operations on his device rather than simply pointing to the object on W's device.   This was a fairly common interaction. By contrast, pointing to, touching, or otherwise operating a companion's device was extremely uncommon.   For example, we only observed one or two instances in which a visitor touched their companion's device.

Presumably to facilitate these types of interactions, visitors would hold the electronic guidebooks and stand so that they could see each other's devices, e.g., a common pose was for one visitor to stand looking over the shoulder of another visitor. We also believe that largely differing heights may impact certain visitors, e.g., the child in the parent-child pair was apparently rarely able to see the screen on his father's device.

5.2   Telling

Often, an explicit preface for the story did not occur, or did not result in the participants being fully aligned at the beginning of the electronic guidebook's storytelling. This is entirely natural, since full coordination can be inefficient and perhaps uncomfortable in that it may preclude independent activity.   Therefore, preface-related activities sometimes occurred during the telling. In this subsection, we first discuss how alignment attempts fail and discuss repairs that are done (or not done) to bring visitors into alignment. We then discuss other behaviors that occur during the telling, specifically focusing on physical behaviors for sharing audio and visitor comments that are interleaved with the guidebook's telling of the stories.

5.2.1 Launched Stories Prompted Visitors to Align

In many cases, visitors were fully aligned when the telling began. However, as mentioned above, sometimes visitors would choose a description and start to play it without full agreement from their companion. In some cases, the companions would stay nearby and listen to this description, and in other cases, they would continue with independent activity.

In another type of phenomenon, visitors would often observe their companion listening to or reading a description and attempt to participate. For example, visitors might walk across the room to examine an object while listening to a description. In this case, their companion would sometimes follow them to listen to the description and comment. Visitors would also eavesdrop on each other's devices. Sometimes when visitors heard an object described by their companion's guidebook, they would select that description on their own device. Visitors would also explicitly ask other visitors what they were doing, e.g., J approached L (who was listening to a description) and said, "Okay, what'd you find?" J then chose the description of the same object on her electronic guidebook. Visitors generally seemed open to all these types of approaches or mimicry of their behavior. We did not observe any behaviors or verbal exchanges that suggested privacy issues.

Additionally, once an object had been selected for description, we often saw further attempts to establish a shared understanding of which object was being described, e.g., the person who selected the description would often point at the corresponding object in the room during the description.

5.2.2 Visitors Physically Shared Electronic Guidebooks during the Telling

The desire to hear the audio on a companion's electronic guidebook (or to have a companion hear the audio on one's own electronic guidebook) affected visitor behavior in several ways. (Recall that visitors had a choice of reading text descriptions or listening to them through headphones or through speakers on the device at a low volume, and that in the study most descriptions were played through speakers on the device at a low volume.) To share descriptions, visitors generally stood close together.

If either visitor attempted to move away while the description was playing, visitors had to coordinate their positions to maintain a shared audio context. In some cases, one visitor would attempt to move away while the description was still playing, e.g., to investigate the object being described. If the visitor who moved away was not the one holding the guidebook playing the audio, they would often quickly return to the side of the visitor playing the description. If the visitor who moved away was the one playing the description, the other visitor would employ one of a number of behaviors to stay involved in the activity. For example, we saw adults put their hands on children's shoulders to prevent them from moving away. One parent (W) gave a general instruction to his child: "If you're gonna play it, [then] stay near so I can hear it." (This was rare – almost all communication around this topic was non-verbal.) As mentioned above, people also frequently followed their companions who were playing audio descriptions. Some visitors also showed an awareness of their companion's needs while playing audio descriptions. For example, while a description was playing, a parent walked from one side of his child to the other so that he could more clearly see the object being described; while he was moving, the parent held his electronic guidebook to his child's ear so that his child's listening would not be interrupted. See Figure 4. Similarly, on one occasion V moved away from W to approach an object. As V walked away, he switched the electronic guidebook from his left hand to his right hand, which brought it closer to W (who was on his right side).

5.2.3 Visitors Interleaved Comments with the Story

While the audio was playing, visitors would respond to the electronic guidebook as they might to a storyteller, e.g., they would utter affirmatives such as "uh huh" or brief responses such as "interesting." Such interleaved comments were made at "appropriate" points in the electronic guidebook's utterances, e.g., pauses between sentences. Visitors did not generally make lengthy comments while the guidebook was delivering a description, i.e., they did not generally interrupt it. Visitor tolerance may have been improved by the fact that the descriptions are quite short (the longest being 23 seconds).

In Example 4, A and S listen to a description of the stain pattern on the floor. Notice how they interject brief comments while the description is playing. Also note that these comments are neatly aligned with sentence boundaries, as they would be for a human speaker.

Fig. 4 W moves from one side of V to the other to get a better view of the object being described. As W moves, he brings the guidebook near V's ear so V's listening will not be interrupted

5.3   Response

The crucial moment in the story is the moment of response. Visitors went to a great deal of effort during the preface and telling phases to make sure they were positioned to share a response to the story. At the conclusion of a description, visitors very frequently shared reactions. For example, listeners made comments like "wow" or offered an opinion or made a joke. In the examples in this paper, we see some of the possible behaviors. In Example 1, A and S discuss the extravagance of the wedding gift. In Example 2, G retells the story, presumably because R does not laugh. This type of retelling or elaboration in the absence of an appropriate response is another common phenomenon in storytelling. In Example 3, W laughs and comments that the information conveyed is "a riot." In Example 4, A and S study and discuss features of the object described.

The guidebook descriptions also prompted visitors to tell their own stories. For example, a discussion of how the family spent Christmas at Filoli led J to remark on an upcoming Thanksgiving celebration of her own. When studying charcoal sketches of previous owners of Filoli, a child (R) volunteered that her own sketch had been done by an artist at the mall.

Regarding physical space, after the description was completed, one of the visitors would often step away from the other, sometimes to go investigate the object which was being described (this investigation would sometimes be followed by a reaction), or sometimes apparently simply to create slightly more space between the two visitors (while listening to a description, visitors often stood very close together).

6   Discussion

Having described the fit between the observed behavior and the storytelling model, we now summarize the key points resulting from the application of the model to the

Example 4 The story of the floor

S:	(0.4) There, floor again, that's floor again.
S-PDA:	*The floor is made of oak wood carved with gouging planes. [After the gouges were made, stain was*
A:	[yeah
S:	[that's, that's interesting,
S-PDA:	*applied and puddled in the holes.*
A:	Wow.
S:	Hm, [that's interesting.
S-PDA:	[*This technique was popular in the early nineteen hundreds when Filoli was built. The effect wears away with use, as can be seen in the floor by the door to the room.*
S:	Ehm uh huh, see here it's darker there, kind of interesting.
A:	(Points towards corner) By you.
S:	Heh.

data. First, we discuss how visitors became aligned so they could share the storytelling experience. We then discuss how the electronic guidebook functioned in a conversational role. We next talk about ways in which visitors benefited from the shared storytelling experience. Finally, we discuss the implications of the visitors' desire to share.

6.1   Alignment

In many cases, visitors went to a great of effort to become aligned so they could hear the same content at the same time:

- Visitors chose a delivery mode that facilitated a shared audio experience (audio through speakers). This delivery mode also facilitated re-engagement by revealing conversation availability and by making it easy to eavesdrop.
- Visitors negotiated the choice of descriptions. Some of these negotiations were fairly mutual. Others were *push* behaviors in which one visitor would encourage their companion to join them in an activity (e.g., "Check out over here."). Still other behaviors were *pull* behaviors in which one visitor would try to join another visitor (e.g., "What did you find?"). Push and pull behaviors could be verbal or non-verbal, e.g., pointing to an object in the room was a frequently observed push behavior.
- Visitors oriented their electronic guidebooks to their companions and oriented themselves to their companion's devices, e.g., they held their guidebooks so their companions could see/hear them, and they stood so they could see/hear their companion's devices.

Note that visitors did not want to be fully aligned at all times. Visitors often disengaged and conducted activities independently. Visitors were also very articulate about wanting to use separate electronic guidebooks. Visitors' desire for control over their experience is discussed further in [27].

6.2   The Conversational Role of the Electronic Guidebook

By analyzing the structure of the storytelling interactions, we see that the electronic guidebook was allocated a role in the conversation, e.g., the electronic guidebook was granted turns in the conversation, it was allowed to introduce topics of conversation, and visitors verbally responded to it. This affordance of the electronic guidebook (that it may be treated as a conversational interactant) allowed visitors to integrate the electronic guidebook in their naturally occurring conversations. By including the electronic guidebook in their existing interaction, visitors were able to incorporate it without fundamentally changing the way that they interacted with each other, e.g., the degree to which they engaged with each other was similar whether they were using a paper guidebook or an electronic guidebook. This preservation of fundamental interaction did not occur when headphones were used.

6.3   Shared Response

By integrating the electronic guidebook in their conversation, visitors became aligned so they could have shared responses to electronic guidebook content. The shared response was particularly enabled by the conversational structure of the storytelling; this structure by definition includes a place for a response, a participatory moment for the visitors. Visitors used this moment to share their reactions to information, and they also used the content of the stories as a branching-off point for their own stories. These are gratifying social interactions that are not possible with all designs, e.g., headphones preclude them. Further, the shared responses positioned the visitors to launch new storytelling sequences with the electronic guidebooks, thereby leading to more social interaction.

6.4   Drive to Share

As seen in this study, visitors found ways to incorporate an electronic device in their social interaction. This gave them a more fulfilling experience. Perhaps designing devices that simulate properties of conversational interaction (e.g., real human voices, short turns to promote opportunities for humans to turn-take) can help users of mobile devices integrate these devices into their existing interactions with other people.

Further, visitors manipulated themselves and their devices so they could see and hear the contents of each other's devices, e.g., they held them in unnatural positions and positioned themselves so they could more easily see their companion's devices and vice versa. This suggests that device design should facilitate sharing of audio and visual content.

7   Related Work

Our goal in this project has been to improve visitor experience as measured against essentially self-perceived motivations. This is along the lines of those who assess the quality of learning-oriented leisure activity [8,12]; our evaluation did not focus on, e.g., the learning environment [10] or the aesthetic experience [11] per se. (Of course, one of our design goals was to minimize the amount of work the visitors needed to do to gather information in order to maximize their opportunity to both learn about and appreciate the objects.)

With that in mind, our work can be compared to specific previous efforts in the engineering domain, the museum studies domain, and their intersection. We discuss each in turn. We then (briefly) relate our work to more general discussions of the social aspects of technological artifacts.

7.1   Electronic Guidebook Design

Electronic guidebook products include a wide variety of systems from industry leaders Acoustiguide and Antenna Audio, as well as from other vendors such as Ameritech (smARTour), JVC (Audio Guidance System), Organic (eDocent), Visible Interactive (iGo), and Vulcan Northwest (Museum Exhibit Guide). Many research systems have also been built (see, e.g., [6-7,13,16-19,21]).

Our system differs from previous systems in its reliance on a lightweight visual interface based on photographic images [4]. It also differs in its use of independent navigation mechanisms for different stages of the object selection task [3]. Finally, it provides the option of either text or audio presentation (through headphones or speakers) of identical content.

7.2   Museum Studies

Some of the relative advantages of audio and text presentation are well understood in the cultural heritage community. For example, Serrell notes that audio allows simultaneous use of eyes and ears but tends to isolate the listener [25]. Acoustiguide's marketing literature states that research "based on a series of surveys at client sites... proves that visitors who access Acoustiguide interpretations learn more about exhibitions – and enjoy them more" [1], and some of this is borne out in the academic literature (e.g., [24]). However, we believe that our observations about short, conversationally compatible audio clips are novel and are not obviously predictable from studies of, e.g., short text labels [25]. Our results on visitor usage of individually controlled, sharable audio are new as well.

In a study of exhibit label reading, McManus observed high rates of "text echo," the inclusion of label text in conversation [14]. The widespread uses of audio sharing in our study (both deliberate and eavesdropped) demonstrate that technology can be used to help visitors introduce label content into conversation directly. McManus also suggested that visitors process – and are inclined to treat – exhibit labels *as conversation*. Again, our findings indicate that technology can bring visitor experience even more in line with this inclination, particularly if the audio descriptions are short enough to easily integrate in existing conversations with companions.

Vom Lehn *et al.* have examined visitor interaction in museums using a qualitative methodology similar to the one used in this paper [26].   While they are studying interactional patterns, their work does not have a personal technology component analogous to an electronic guidebook.

7.3   Electronic Guidebook Studies

A variety of research systems have been designed, built, and deployed but few have resulted in in-depth studies.   For example, HyperAudio [16] was deployed but only results of pre-design studies have been reported [19].   Similarly, Hippie [17] was deployed and received initial feedback, but the results of user evaluations are not available [18]; the same is true of Plantations Pathfinder [21]. We are aware of only two electronic guidebook studies resembling ours.   In both cases, the methodology was, like ours, based on a combination of interviews, observation, and device activity log analysis.   A University of Salford team evaluated the design of a tablet computer guidebook prototype at the Museum of Science & Industry in Manchester [7], and a Lancaster University team evaluated the design of another tablet computer guidebook prototype in historic Lancaster [6].

Unlike previous work, our study takes an applied conversation analytic approach to examining how visitors interact with electronic guidebooks, and how visitor-visitor interaction is impacted by electronic guidebook design.

7.4   Social Properties of Technological Artifacts

Reeves and Nass argue that individuals' interactions with computers, television, and new media are fundamentally social [20].   Our focus is somewhat different, since we argue that integration of the electronic guidebook into conversation facilitates interaction among participants.   Further, we are studying the process by which this interaction becomes social.   Finally, where Reeves and Nass conducted their studies in laboratory conditions, we are studying natural behaviors in largely unrestricted environments.

The Campiello project designed and evaluated a community information service for the use of both tourists and local residents in Venice [9].   In a month-long deployment study, careful design around social use aspects (e.g., support for group use of kiosks) proved to be a critical factor in system acceptance [2].

Depending on the context, "storytelling" can mean many things. For example, it is widely accepted in the museum studies community that visitors retain more information if the information is related as a cohesive story [8], which is why so many exhibits are structured in this way.   As another example, much of the work on children and computing has focused on mechanisms for the creation and effective social use of stories.   Our emphasis here is on storytelling as a framework of conversational roles and sequentially organized acts, on the ways that our visitors found to work an artifact (the guidebook) into this framework, and on the aspects of the artifact that facilitated this act.

8   Conclusions and Future Work

Our electronic guidebook prototype had a substantive impact on visitors' ability to interact with each other.   Visitors predominantly chose audio played through speakers, which allowed them to include the electronic guidebook in their conversation with their companions.   We found that these interactions followed the structure of storytelling.   As a result, visitors were positioned to share moments in which they responded to stories told by the electronic guidebooks.   These interactions led to experiences that were significantly more social than those that occur with traditional headphone audio tours.

Our current work includes further analysis of the data collected in the course of this study as well as application of our findings.   For example, we are studying what drives a visitor's inquiry into a particular object (e.g., independent observation of the object in the room, a companion's interest in the object, or the presence of a description in the guidebook).   We are also applying the iterative design approach [15], using the lessons learned about sharing to design our next prototype.

Acknowledgments

We are deeply indebted to Tom Rogers and Anne Taylor of Filoli for their generous assistance with this project.   We also thank Tom for his perceptive comments on the design of the prototype, Maribeth Back for assistance in recording the audio clips, and Beki Grinter, Bob Moore, Morgan Price, Peter Putz, Terkel Skaarup, Michaele Smith, Erik Vinkhuyzen, and Marilyn Whalen for their helpful insights.

References

1.   "Why an Audio Tour?" Acoustiguide Corp., New York, Dec. 2000. http://www.acoustiguide.com/why/
2.   Agostini, A., G. De Michelis and M. Divitini, "Ubiquitous Access to Community Knowledge Via Multiple Interfaces: Design and Experiences," in *Universal Access in HCI* (Proc. 1st Conf., New Orleans, LA, Aug. 2001), C. Stephanidis (ed.), Lawrence Erlbaum & Assoc., 2001, to appear.
3.   Aoki, P. M. and A. Woodruff, "Improving Electronic Guidebook Interfaces Using a Task-Oriented Design Approach," *Proc. 3rd ACM Conf. on Designing Interactive Sys.*, New York, Aug. 2000, 319-325.
4.   Aoki, P. M., A. Hurst and A. Woodruff, "Tap Tips: Lightweight Discovery of Touchscreen Targets," *ACM SIGCHI Conf. on Human Factors in Comp. Sys. Extended Abstracts*, Seattle, WA, Mar. 2001, 237-238.
5.   Beard, G.W., *Attingham: The First Forty Years*, Attingham Trust, London, 1991.
6.   Cheverst, K., N. Davies, K. Mitchell, A. Friday and C. Efstratiou, "Developing a Context-Aware Electronic Tourist Guide: Some Issues and Experiences," *Proc. ACM SIGCHI Conf. on Human Factors in Comp. Sys.*, den Haag, the Netherlands, Apr. 2000, 17-24.

7. Evans, J. A. and P. Sterry, "Portable Computers & Interactive Museums: A New Paradigm for Interpreting Museum Collections," *Proc. 5th Int'l Cultural Heritage Informatics Mtg.*, Washington, DC, Sep.1999, 93-101.
8. Falk, J. H. and L. D. Dierking, *Learning From Museums*, Altamira Press, Walnut Creek, CA, 2000.
9. Grasso, A., D. Snowdon and M. Koch, "Extending the Services and the Accessibility of Community Networks," in *Digital Cities* (Proc. Kyoto Meeting, Kyoto, Japan, Sep. 1999), T. Ishida and K. Isbister (eds.), Springer Verlag, Berlin, 2000, 401-415.
10. Hein, G. E., "The Constructivist Museum," *J. Educ. in Museums 16* (1995), 21-23.
11. Hein, H. S., *The Museum in Transition*, Smithsonian Institution Press, Washington, DC, 2000.
12. Hood, M. G., "Staying Away: Why People Choose Not to Visit Museums," *Museum News 61*, 4 (Apr. 1983), 50-57.
13. S. Long, D. Aust, G. D. Abowd and C. Atkeson, "Cyberguide: Prototyping Context-Aware Mobile Applications," *ACM SIGCHI '96 Conference Companion*, Vancouver, BC, Canada, April 1996, pp. 293-294.
14. McManus, P. M., "Oh, Yes They Do: How Museum Visitors Read Labels and Interact with Exhibit Texts," *Curator 32*, 3 (1989), 174-189.
15. Newman, W. M. and M. G. Lamming, *Interactive System Design*, Addison Wesley, Reading, MA, 1995.
16. Not, E., D. Petrelli, O. Stock, C. Strapparava and M. Zancanaro, "Person-Oriented Guided Visits in a Physical Museum," *Proc. 4th Int'l Cultural Heritage Informatics Mtg.*, Paris, France, Sep. 1997, 69-79.
17. Oppermann, R. and M. Specht, "A Nomadic Information System for Adaptive Exhibition Guidance," *Proc. 5th Int'l Cultural Heritage Informatics Mtg.*, Washington, DC, Sep. 1999, 103-109.
18. Oppermann, R. and M. Specht, "A Context-Sensitive Nomadic Exhibition Guide," in *Handheld and Ubiquitous Computing* (Proc. 2nd Int'l Symp., Bristol, UK, Sep. 2000), P. Thomas and H. W. Gellersen (eds.), Springer Verlag, Berlin, 2000, 127-142.
19. Petrelli, D., A. De Angeli and G. Convertino, "A User-Centered Approach to User Modeling," in *User Modeling* (Proc. 7th Int'l Conf., Banff, Alberta, June 1999), J. Kay (ed.), Springer Verlag, Berlin, 1999, 255-264.
20. Reeves, B. and C. Nass, The Media Equation: How People Treat Computers, Television, and New Media Like Real People and Places, CSLI Publications, Stanford, California, 1996.
21. Rieger, R. and G. Gay, "Using Mobile Computing to Enhance Field Study," in *Computer Supported Collaborative Learning* (Proc. 2nd Conf., Toronto, Ontario, Dec. 1997), R. Hall, N. Miyake and N. Enyedy (eds.), L. Erlbaum & Assoc., Mahwah, NJ, 1997, 215-223.
22. Sacks, H., "An Analysis of the Course of a Joke's Telling in Conversation," in *Explorations in the Ethnography of Speaking*, R. Bauman and J. Sherzer (eds.), Cambridge University Press, Cambridge, 1974, 337-353.

23. Sacks, H., "Notes on Methodology," in *Structures of Social Action: Studies in Conversation Analysis*, J.M. Atkinson and J. Heritage (eds.), Cambridge University Press, Cambridge, 1984, 21-27.
24. Screven, C. G., "The Effectiveness of Guidance Devices on Visitor Learning," *Curator 18*, 3 (1975), 219-243.
25. Serrell, B., *Exhibit Labels*, Altamira Press, Walnut Creek, CA, 1996.
26. vom Lehn, D., C. Heath and J. Hindmarsh, "Exhibiting Interaction: Conduct and Collaboration in Museums and Galleries," *Symbolic Interaction 24* (2001), to appear.
27. Woodruff, A., P. M. Aoki, A. Hurst, and M. H. Szymanski, "Visitor Attention and Electronic Guidebooks," *Proc. 6th Int'l Cultural Heritage Informatics Mtg.*, Milan, Italy, Sep. 2001, to appear.

Who, What, When, Where, How:
Design Issues of Capture & Access Applications

Khai N. Truong, Gregory D. Abowd, and Jason A. Brotherton

College of Computing & GVU Center, Georgia Institute of Technology
Atlanta, Georgia 30332-0280, USA
{khai,abowd,brothert}@cc.gatech.edu

Abstract. One of the general themes in ubiquitous computing is the construction of devices and applications to support the automated capture of live experiences and the future access of those records. Over the past five years, our research group has developed many different capture and access applications. In this paper, we present an overview of six of these applications. We discuss the different design issues encountered while creating each of these applications and share our approaches to solving these issues (in comparison and in contrast with other work found in the literature). From these issues we define the large design space for automated capture and access. This design space may then serve as a point of reference for designers to extract the requirements for systems to be developed in the future.

1   Introduction

In his seminal 1991 Scientific American article, Mark Weiser describes a vision of ubiquitous computing in which technology is seamlessly integrated into the environment and provides useful services to humans in their everyday activities [34]. Over the years, one of the services envisioned is the automated capture of everyday experiences made available for future access. Automated capture and access applications leverage what computers do best – record information. In return, humans are free to fully engage in the activity and to synthesize the experience, without having to worry about tediously exerting effort to preserve specific details for later perusal.

This research theme is not unique to ubiquitous computing. Vannevar Bush was perhaps the first to write about the benefits of a generalized capture and access systems when he introduced the concept of the memex [8]. The memex was intended to store the artifacts that we come in contact with in our everyday lives and the associations that we create between them. Over the years, many researchers have worked towards this vision. As a result, many systems have been built to capture and access experiences in classrooms [2, 3, 20], meetings [4, 9, 10, 12, 13, 19], and other generalized experiences [23, 29, 32]. In our research group, we have also looked at how the capture and access of experiences can assist people in a variety of situations

G. D. Abowd, B. Brumitt, S. A. N. Shafer (Eds.): Ubicomp 2001, LNCS 2201, pp. 209-224, 2001.
© Springer-Verlag Berlin Heidelberg 2001

including college lectures [1, 31], software engineering design meetings [26], impromptu meetings [6], military strategic planning sessions, academic conferences [11], distributed meetings [25], and inside the home.

We define *capture and access* as the task of preserving a record of some live experience that is then reviewed at some point in the future. Capture occurs when a tool generates an artifact that documents the history of what happened. The artifacts, or *captured data*, are recorded as *streams of information* that flow through time [7]. The tools that record experiences are the *capture devices*; and the tools used to review captured experiences are the *access devices*. A *capture and access application* can exist in the simplest form through a single capture and access device or in a more complex form as a collection of capture and access devices [18]. Under our definition, some tools are already inherent capture and access devices; e.g. pen and paper, cameras and camcorders. However, some of these tools only support a single user during the capture of the information. Others limit access to occur at only a single location at a time. More compelling applications are often built to support a larger community with more universal access.

In this paper, we present a design space for capture and access applications. We map out five dimensions in this design space and discuss the key attributes of each dimension. Six different case studies (in the form of overviews of work we have created in the past) are used to formulate this design space. As we describe each application, we compare and contrast our approach for building each application with other work found in the literature. In doing so, we show that these issues we present are ones other researchers have faced too. By discussing multiple approaches we are able to discuss tradeoffs between these approaches. Collectively, this design space and these six case studies can act as a point of reference for future capture and access application designs.

2   Review of Capture and Access Applications

Over the past five years, we have explored the use of capture and access in a variety of situations. Different applications have been built for different environments. In this section we will overview and discuss the approaches taken to build these applications. We begin with the human-centered motivation for each capture and access application, then describe briefly some details of the system we have built and relate our application to others reported in the literature. All of these applications motivate our desire to provide a more general description of the design space of capture and access applications.

2.1   Classroom 2000

2.1.1   Motivation

As technology has been introduced into classrooms, instructors are given the ability to present more information during each lecture, with the goal of providing a richer learning experience. As a result, students are often drowned with information and forced into a "heads down" approach to learning. While students are busy copying down everything presented in class, they are potentially distracted from paying attention to the lecture itself. An instructor produces a lot of artifacts while teaching (lecture slides, handwritten annotations, and spoken words), which students attempt to preserve in their notes. The Classroom 2000 project aimed to alleviate some of the student's burden by recording much of the public lecture experience [1, 7].

2.1.2 How It Works

To capture what the instructor writes, we used electronic whiteboards (e.g., the LiveBoard [12] or a SmartBoard [27]). For instructors who teach with a prepared presentation, we converted the presentation into slides displayed on the electronic whiteboard that can be written on; otherwise, it acts as a simple whiteboard. To capture what the instructor says and does, the classroom contains microphones used to record the audio and a single camera to capture a fixed view of the classroom. Finally, to capture other web accessible media the instructor may want to present, a web proxy was used to monitor and record the web pages visited during each class.

Immediately after each class, all the different captured streams of information are processed to create an on-line multimedia-augmented set of lecture notes in a form that supports student review. In order to build the appropriate access interface, we considered when and where most studying would occur. While classes are regularly scheduled activities that occur in specific rooms (thereby, specifying when and where capture occurs), when and where students review the notes will largely vary. Because the notes are multimedia enhanced, we require an electronic format. We decided that it would make sense that the notes are available in a web-accessible format. This infrastructure would also allow students to review the notes at their own convenience.

2.1.3 Related Work

Rather than instrumenting the classroom with augmented capture devices (such as the LiveBoard as an augmented whiteboard and PCs that pull web pages from a logging web proxy), the Lecture Browser application [20] and other whiteboard applications such as the ZombieBoard [5] and BrightBoard [28] rely on cameras and vision techniques to capture the materials written and presented on the boards, as well as to detect changes. The tradeoff between these two approaches lies in the granularity of capture as well as the level of intelligence built in to the capture systems. By instrumenting the physical objects the user interacts with, we are able to obtain a finer level of granularity in the interaction history without needing to apply much intelligence into the system. For example, when the instructor writes on the electronic whiteboard, we can easily access information at the stroke level. Capture devices that rely on machine vision face a greater challenge to extract this level of information. For example, occlusion by the lecturer can prevent the system from seeing all of the writing as it is being written. As a result, the change detected is not a stroke level, but at a cluster level (or a coarser level of granularity).

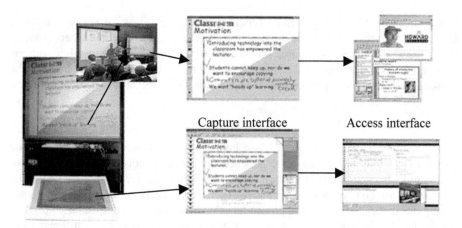

Fig 1. Classroom 2000 & StuPad. At the top of the figure is shown the public capture of Classroom 2000. The bottom portrays the personalized augmentation of the public capture provided by StuPad

2.2   StuPad (<u>Stu</u>dent Note<u>Pad</u>)

2.2.1   Motivation

The goal of Classroom 2000 was to help relieve students from needing to tediously copy down all the notes presented during class. However, because Classroom 2000 lecture notes are captured through actions performed strictly by the instructor(s), it excludes students from being able to make the notes personally meaningful. As a result, some students still take a small amount of private notes with pen and paper. When students study, they are forced to manually integrate the electronically automatically captured lecture notes (provided by Classroom 2000) with their own private notes on paper – a nontrivial task. To better support the integration of each student's notes with the Classroom 2000 notes, student notes needed to also be in an electronic format that could be synchronized with the other captured streams of information. We wanted to create a system that integrates the public streams of information captured by Classroom 2000 into each student's electronic notebook during the lecture, giving students the ability to personalize the material as it being captured.

2.2.2   How It Works

To support the personalization of the captured experience, we built the Student Notepad (or StuPad) system to provide students with an interface that is capable of integrating the prepared presentation, digital ink annotations and Web pages browsed from the public classroom notes into each student's private notebook (during the capture phase). Relatively affordable video tablet technology allowed us to instrument the students' desks with a note-taking environment that is networked and at least as powerful as the electronic whiteboard at the front of the class.

During class, the act of writing is more natural for students to perform and less distracting than typing. Outside of class, it is hard to predict when and where students will review the notes; therefore, the access application was designed to run on networked computers with the more traditional keyboard/mouse interface. The personalized notes are reviewed over the web to facilitate students to be able to review the notes anywhere anytime.

2.2.3   Related Work

Other systems, such as the Audio Notebook [29] and Dynomite [36] are private systems used only to capture an experience for just that individual. NotePals [10] allows users to each privately capture their notes during the live experience. After the experience, all the users notes are gathered to form a collective view of the experience during the access phase. This approach takes into consideration that some points may be missing in different people's notes, or that the users' views may be different. The NoteLook system [9] also supports the integration of both public and private content. The NoteLook system provides users with an array of camera views that can be used to take snapshots of the public presentation when a seminar participant requests. Once the snapshot is integrated into the user's private notebook, private annotations can be placed on top of it. The subtle difference between NoteLook and StuPad lies in NoteLook's reliance on the participants to devote effort and awareness (as well as a little anticipation) on when to request the public information to be added into their personal notebook.

2.3   SAAMPad (Software Architecture Analysis Method Pad)

2.3.1   Motivation

Software evolution is a difficult and time-consuming software development activity that can be enhanced when designers have a more complete understanding of the rationale underlying the current architecture for an existing system and the implication of any changes resulting from the evolution. To understand why a system is built a certain way, the rationale behind the design must be preserved for future designers and developers. However, it is sometimes difficult to record all the rationale into a document. Often, this rationale is not discussed anywhere outside of the design meetings. The Software Architecture Analysis Method (SAAM) was developed at the Software Engineering Institute in the mid to late 1990's to support the organized discussion of architectural rationale [16]. SAAM is a people-oriented process and centers around group meetings where people produce scenarios to help extract how changing requirements impact an already existing system. A typical SAAM session is a live event involving discussions by 3-10 of the stakeholders involved in the system including users, designers, managers and facilitators that is centered around drawings of the architecture on a public display.

2.3.2   How It Works

We prototyped a capture and access system to support the capture of SAAM sessions (see Figure 2). Both the architectural diagrams and the discussions around these diagrams provide the rationale behind the architecture of a system. The diagrams and discussions are, therefore, important aspects of the meetings that we want to capture and relate later on. By converting the public display to an electronic whiteboard surface and recording the discussion with digital streaming media technology, we were able to capture the SAAM sessions and then provide the ability to salvage summary information afterwards.

The primary capture application was designed to capture the architectural drawings generated during these meetings. As the participants discussed the specifics details about a component, the application stored that part of the discussion under the appropriate architectural block. When each scenario is presented, both the architectural diagrams and discussions that come about are captured. After all the scenarios are captured, they can be reviewed to assess the implications and the rationale of changes to system to determine how to evolve the system properly.

 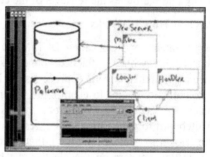

Fig. 2 Software Architecture Analysis Method Pad. The left shows stakeholders participating in the capture of a software design meeting. The right shows the access of a SAAM session

2.3.3   Related Work

Some capture and access systems used in meetings, such as the Marquee [33] and the Filochat [35] are private note-taking systems and do not capture a shared group perspective of the discussion – rather, they capture the individual note-taker's view. However, in some meetings, particularly in design meetings, it is more important to have the shared understanding of how a system is designed (or how it is agreed to be designed) be preserved for posterity. SAAMPad captures the evolution scenarios presented by a stakeholder.

Tivoli [24] draws the most similarity to the SAAMPad system. It introduces the notion of "domain objects" to represent very specific kinds of artifacts that are captured. In order to capture very specific kinds of artifacts (such as software architecture diagrams in SAAMPad, or Intellectual Property (IP) documents in Tivoli), these applications rely on knowledge of the well-defined formal aspects of the live experience.

2.4   DUMMBO (Dynamic, Ubiquitous, Mobile Meeting Board)

2.4.1   Motivation

Not all meetings can be scheduled ahead of time, resulting only from serendipitous encounters. The subject of what people talk about during these opportunistic meetings is not known ahead time, nor is it known in advance who is involved, or even how long the meeting will last. Public whiteboards are the site of where a lot of these types of informal meetings take place. These boards are often placed in locations where there is a reasonable flow of traffic to encourage anyone who passes to discuss ideas and to brainstorm with one another. However, it is difficult to know when someone is involved in an informal discussion at the whiteboard versus just doodling on it. This presents a challenge for how to support the unintrusive capture of informal meetings in a way that facilitates the retrieval of the conversation and writings on the whiteboard.

2.4.2   How It Works

We created a system called DUMMBO [6] (see Figure 3), using a non-projecting SmartBoard with an attached sound system, to capture informal and opportunistic meetings. When anyone approaches the board and picks up a pen to write, the board automatically begins to capture the writing and discussion. After a certain period of inactivity, recording will stop. Sensing technology is instrumented near the whiteboard to detect the people present during each meeting. If two or more people are known to be near the board, then recording of the conversation will occur even if no writing appears on the electronic whiteboard. A Web interface is provided to support the access of this collection of unstructured meetings. The context of an informal meeting (who was there, when and where it occurred) is used to help an individual find a meeting of interest. Users may browse through a timeline displaying periods of activity at the board and may apply filters (who, where, when) to pinpoint a meeting of interest. Once an appropriate time period has been selected, and the correct meeting has been retrieved, the access interface allows the user to replay the whiteboard activity, synchronized with the audio.

2.4.3   Related Work

Xerox PARC's Flatland project [22] has also looked at the capture and access of informal activities, but it uses time as the only mechanism used to retrieve historical information. Flatland was designed to support informal activities within a private office. DUMMBO is intended to support the capture of informal activities on a public whiteboard where many people can interact with it at any given time. For the situation that DUMMBO is intended to support, time alone is not good enough to help users forage through a potentially large set of information to find just their discussion.

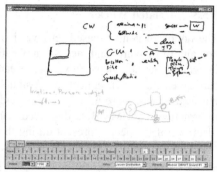

Fig 3 DUMMBO. The left shows the instrumented electronic whiteboard that sits in a public space. The right shows the context-based access interface

2.5   The Conference Assistant

2.5.1   Motivation

Large academic conferences often have multiple tracks of concurrent activities. Paper presentations, demonstrations, special interest group meetings, etc., can all occur simultaneously. During any given time period, conference attendees can move about and listen to any of the presentations of relevant interest. To help remember what was seen, attendees can take notes to document the sessions they attended. The abundance of potentially novel and interesting information presents the attendees with a conflict between taking notes and synthesizing the sessions. Furthermore, the large amount of information, ranging over many different topics makes it difficult to organize the notes.

2.5.2   How It Works

The Conference Assistant [11] is a mobile capture and access application that allows users to take notes at distributed presentations. As attendees arrive at a conference, they are a given a handheld PDA for use during the conference. Rather than needing to take detailed notes, presentations are captured by the rooms. As a result, conference attendees can take summary notes on the personal and mobile devices. After the conference concludes, each attendee's notes can be integrated with the presentations.

When attendees move about between presentations, their mobility presents a challenge for integrating each user's private notes with the appropriate presentation they had seen. The Conference Assistant is not only a capture and access application but is also a context-aware application, logging the physical location of the user at all time (through use of RF ID positioning technology). As presentations are given, they are captured and tagged as given in certain locations. After the conference ends, when an attendee reviews a talk she attended, the location information is used to integrate the personal notes with the actual presentation information.

2.5.3   Related Work

The notion of context-based retrieval is not novel, but rather is seldom used in the domain of capture and access applications. Most applications use time as the integrating variable between various streams of information. However, when multiple capture-enabled environments are available and users can move between any of these physical spaces, more information beyond time is needed to integrate the appropriate information.   DUMMBO, described earlier, uses time, location, as well as the identities of the people present during the live experience to retrieve the appropriate set of information. Systems such as StuPad, described earlier, and NoteLook [9] allow the personalization of captured information in settings such as classrooms or seminars but assume fixed location. NotePals (which also has been used at conferences as well as classrooms), like the Conference Assistance, integrates the notes based on matches in context, such as location, etc.

2.6   TeamSpace

2.6.1   Motivation

Project group meetings are used to discuss various aspects of the group project. Meetings can be devoted to understanding the team's progress; specifics on how important parts of the projects are implemented (or will be implemented) are sometimes presented, agendas are drawn out, and schedules and responsibilities are defined. Traditionally, these meetings involve multiple people who come together at a mutual location. As companies look to grow world wide, the nature of the work place is now a distributed environment with multiple people at different geographical locations collaborating in a large project. The distributed work environment means that these meetings now occur through a virtual connection while people remain scattered in multiple (and often remote) locations.

2.6.2   How It Works

The TeamSpace project supports the capture of these meetings as multimedia meeting notes as part of a larger set of shared artifacts created and maintained for each project [25]. Meetings are typically held in a number of meeting rooms and/or offices. A capture application was built to capture and share streams of information between the different instances of it (running at the different sites involved in the meeting).   The different streams of information the application supports include presentation slides, annotations, agenda items, action items, and video frames. Telephone connections are used to provide an audio connection between these physical spaces. Thus audio is captured through the phone line, although potentially a voice over IP solution could be instrumented as well.

2.6.3   Related Work

In comparison to other meeting capture and access applications, TeamSpace can be used to capture a single collocated collaborative meeting (such as Tivoli, etc.). However, TeamSpace allows for multiple people to collaborate in the capture of the streams of information (similar to DOLPHIN [30]). Furthermore, it goes beyond just allowing multiple devices to control a single meeting surface (such as Pebbles [21]). More compellingly, TeamSpace provides multiple people and multiple locations with the chance to participate in the capture of information. The key difference is everyone can capture information and it must be shared across all location.

3   Design Space of Capture & Access Applications

The designs of the six applications presented above, as well as those applications found in the literature, face a variety of issues. The minimal set of issues that need to be addressed can be extracted when five design dimensions across two phases relevant to all capture and access applications are taken into consideration in the design. For each of these applications, the *capture* phase is typically the live experience duration to be preserved, while the *access* phase happens when these records are reviewed. For each of these phases, designers must determine:

- *Who* are the users during capture and access?
- *What* is captured and accessed?
- *When* does capture and access occur?
- *Where* does capture and access occur?
- *How* is capture and access performed?

3.1   The Who Dimension

Building a capture and access application is like building any kind of application: it is extremely important to identify *who* the users are. The *who* component of a capture and access application deals with the scale of users and the users' roles. For different kinds of situations, there may be a different number of users participating in that experience. Furthermore, the people involved during the capture of an experience do not necessarily have to be those who will be accessing the information. In some situations, even though the people present during the live experience are the same set of people who will access the captured information, they may not all directly participate in the capture of the experience. Each person present during the capture or the access of the experience may have a part in the experience. In understanding each person's part, designers can design systems to support specific roles in the capture and access of the experience. As Grudin points out, much of the success of groupware systems depend on who amongst the participants are actually doing the work and who can directly benefit from the work [14]. There is much similarity between groupware and capture and access applications. Beyond recognizing who are the users, designers should also design applications to take advantage of people's roles in the experience. When a single user who plays a major role in an experience (such as an instructor during class) can capture information on behalf of all those present (the students) to review in the future, there is clear benefit for the students to have an automated capture system developed around the activities of the instructor.

3.2   The What Dimension

There are many everyday activities that can be aided by the services provided by capture and access applications. However, each live experience may vary in the amount of pre-defined structure. Identifying the formal characteristics of the experience helps identify the parts of the experience that can be captured and how to design an application to record this set of information. Once data has been captured, users can review the live experience. However, the live experience can never be fully recorded. While the actual experience sets the ceiling for what is captured, the amount of information actually captured sets the ceiling for the access of the experience. To increase the fidelity of the access experience, more streams can be captured and integrated; collectively, they can give a more accurate the account of the experience. The *what* dimension is defined by the number of streams of information captured for later access. One approach is to set the scale as high as possible by capturing as much information as possible. Information can always be processed and filtered; however, when uncaptured information is lost to the past, there is no way to recreate it. On the other hand, information is captured so that it can be accessed in the future – capture is meaningless without access. Whereas it is important to make the live capture as complete as possible, there is also no value in doing the capture if there is no reasonable and useful access to the captured record. Hence, the needs of access should not be ignored. If a low fidelity of access is all that is ever going to be required, then there is no need to capture more information than what is needed. The tradeoff between the two approaches is the effort used to design a system to capture as much as possible versus the effort used to understand the access needs for that system.

3.3   The When Dimension

The *when* dimension deals with issues related to when capture occurs, when access occurs, and the time difference between the capture and access activity. Knowing when capture occurs means devices and applications can be designed to take advantage of this known piece of context to infer others – predicting and customizing the right kinds of capture services to initiate automatically for unique situations. Some experiences occur periodically or with some frequency. However, when experiences occur unplanned or on irregular intervals, applications must be ready for capture at any point and flexible enough to adapt to the changing requirements of the situational context. Using knowledge of when access occurs can also inform the design of the access devices and applications. Knowledge of when access occurs can be used to provide the users with the right applications for the right available resources. Not knowing this information means "anytime" access support must be provided, where the context of the access experience is unknown and applications must be built to support impoverish resources.

The time difference between the capture and access activity can also be used to inform the design of the applications. Short-term capture and access applications are typically used as reminder systems. Xcapture [15] and Where-Were-We [17] are examples of near-term capture and access applications, capturing either audio or video of an activity and allowing the users to index into the captured streams when they need to be reminded of certain pieces of information during an activity. When the access of information occurs only immediately after it has been captured (or within a day or two), persistent storage of the information may not be necessary. Medium-term applications typically have data accessed in the weeks to months range of time after it has been captured. These applications will need to physically store the information and furthermore can process and transduce the information into friendlier formats than the raw data that is captured. Finally, long-term applications store information as records for posterity. Information needs to persist for much longer periods of time than other types of applications and it may make sense to provide users with a synthesized summary of the experience with an interface that supports being able to drill down to the exact point that the user(s) want to review.

3.4   The Where Dimension

The *where* dimension addresses the physical locations involved in a capture and access phases. Most capture and access applications handle experiences that occur in a single location. However, it is becoming more commonplace for people in many different places to collaborate and essentially share an experience remotely. Furthermore, capture and access applications must also take user mobility into consideration.

Knowing where capture occurs means being able to instrument the physical space involved with capture devices and applications ahead of time. Identifying where access occurs can help inform the design of the access applications. Knowledge of where people will want to access information will provide understanding to the resources they have available – what kind of machines the users have available to them, the kind of input and output capabilities they have, etc. If access occurs in the same environment as the live experience (i.e. there is an overlap between where capture and access occurs) specialized devices can be instrumented to be both capture as well as access tools.

3.5   The How Dimension

The tools and methods for capturing and accessing information as well as the scale of devices form the last dimension: *how*. Capture and access applications are typically built as a confederation of tools. The number of devices that are used in a system defines the scale of devices for capture and access applications. At one end of the scale, only a single device is used in the application. A key question in the building of capture and access devices is whether the device that is doing the capture can also be used to provide the access. In some instances, personal and portable devices play dual roles as both the capture and the access devices. When a device does not support the access of its captured content, or is not the best tool to use when accessing the captured experience, there is a need to identify what are the other devices that support access to the information. In most cases, capture is often done using a number of devices and so a certain amount of effort must be devoted to coordinating these devices to work together. If the tools users work with can be identified ahead of time, designers can augment these devices with capture or access capabilities. Devices and applications can be instrumented to support the explicit interaction of the users to capture information or they can be fully automated to support capture. Explicit capture of experiences is more common, but requires effort on the part of the users. We can ease the explicit production method by automating the capture of materials – making the capture implicit. Fully implicit capture applications can make capture completely transparent to the user and can be done in the background. However, from the designer's point of view, these systems will require some level of intelligence. For example, systems that rely solely on cameras to capture will also need vision techniques to detect changes in the material that is being captured. Systems that rely on explicit interactions can be instrumented to capture at a higher level of granularity. The tradeoff between these two approaches lies in the granularity of capture as well as the level of intelligence built in to the capture systems. By instrumenting the physical objects the user interacts with, we are able to obtain a finer level of granularity in the interaction history without needing to apply much intelligence into the system.

4 Conclusion

The five dimensions we have outlined, as well as the list of key attributes for each dimensions, are not exhaustive. Clearly, privacy and security are among the list of those issues not mentioned here. These issues are certainly not lesser in importance; in fact, these issues may be the more challenging ones to explore. Instead the issues we have outlined here are what we believe to be common ones that need to be considered when building *any* capture and access application. As a result, these five dimensions should always be addressed at the start of the design of a capture and access application. By identifying the *who*, *what*, *when*, *where*, and *how* components of a capture and access application, it is possible to extract the functional requirements in the development of a system.

In generalizing a design space for capture and access applications, we examined the issues involved in the design of not only the capture and access applications we have created but those of related work found in the literature. When we assess both our own work and other's with respect to the design space, we can see the parts of this space that existing applications populate, as well as the holes in this space that remain to be explored. Few projects have explored the following issues:

- Long-term access of captured data
- Capture of informal experiences
- Capture of distributed and remote experiences
- Capture mobility
- The personalization of capture
- Context base (context rich) capture and access
- Instrumentation of dual role devices
- More variety in the types of devices that are augmented with capture and access capabilities

In future work, we will present a prototype for an infrastructure to capture and access (known as InCA – Infrastructure for Capture and Access) which will look at how the task of building a capture and access system can be facilitated through lower level support that includes reusable components that form building blocks for the capture, storage, and subsequent access of the experiences.   We identify five dimensions for capture and access in this paper. InCA aims to support developers in the development of any application ranging anywhere on these dimensions.   By making it easier to build systems that exists in this design space, application developers will be able to build more compelling capture and access applications in the future. Furthermore, they will be able to explore issues that have been previously unvisited, such as those listed above.

Acknowledgements

The authors are members of the Future Computing Environments (FCE) group at Georgia Tech. We would like to thank all the visiting researchers and other members of the FCE group who have helped to shape this paper.   We would like to acknowledge Heather Richter and Anind Dey for their contributions to some of the projects discussed in this paper.   The TeamSpace project discussed in this paper is joint research performed between Georgia Tech, IBM Research and Boeing.   Other research projects discussed are funded through various organizations (including the National Science Foundation, DARPA, and the Army Research Lab) and a number of industrial sponsors, including the members of the Aware Home Research Initiative, Sun Microsystems and Hewlett-Packard.

References

1.   Abowd, G. D., Classroom 2000: An experiment with the instrumentation of a living educational environment. IBM Systems Journal. 38(4) (1999) 508-530
2.   Bacher, C., et al. Authoring on the Fly.   A New Way of Integrating Telepresentation and Courseware Production. In *Proceedings of ICCE 1997.* Kuching, Sarawak, Malaysia (1997)
3.   Berque, D. Using a Variation of the WYSIWIS Shared Drawing Surface Paradigm to Support Electronic Classrooms. In *Proceedings of HCI International 1999.* Munich, Germany (1999)
4.   Bianchi, M. AutoAuditorium: A Fully Automatic, Multi-Camera System to Televise Auditorium Presentations. In *Proceedings of DARPA/NIST Smart Spaces Technology Workshop.* (1998)
5.   Black, M. J., et al. The Digital Office: Overview. In Proceedings of 1998 AAAI Spring Symposium on Intelligent Environments. (1998)
6.   Brotherton, J. A., Abowd, G. D., and Truong, K. N. Supporting Capture and Access Interfaces for Informal and Opportunistic Meetings. Georgia Institute of Technology Technical Report GIT-GVU-99-06 (1998)
7.   Brotherton, J. A., Bhalodia, J. R., and Abowd, G. D. Automated Capture, Integration, and Visualization of Multiple Media Streams. In *Proceedings of IEEE Multimedia and Computing Systems.* Austin, TX (1998)
8.   Bush, V.: As We May Think, in *Atlantic Monthly.* (1945)

9.   Chiu, P., et al. NoteLook: Taking Notes in Meetings with Digital Video and Ink. In *Proceedings of ACM Multimedia 1999*. Orlando, FL (1999) 149-158

10. Davis, R. C., et al. NotePals: Lightweight Note Sharing by the Group, for the Group. In *Proceedings of CHI 1999*. Pittsburgh, PA (1999) 338-345

11. Dey, A. K., et al. The Conference Assistant: Combining Context-Awareness with Wearable Computing. In *Proceedings of ISWC 1999*. San Francisco, CA (1999) 21-28

12. Elrod, S., et al. Liveboard: A large interactive display supporting group meetings, presentations and remote collaboration. In *Proceedings of CHI 1992*. Monterey, CA (1992) 599-607

13. Ginsberg, A. and Ahuja, S. Automating envisionment of virtual meeting room histories. In *Proceedings of ACM Multimedia 1995*. San Francisco, CA (1995) 65-76

14. Grudin, J.: Groupware and Social Dynamics: Eight Challenges for Developers, in *Communications of the ACM*. (1994). p. 92-105

15. Hindus, D. and Schmandt, C. Ubiquitous Audio: Capturing Spontaneous Collaboration. In *Proceedings of Computer Supported Collaborative Work 1992*. Toronto, Canada (1992) 210-217

16. Kazman, R., et al. SAAM: A Method for Analyzing the Properties of Software Architectures. In *Proceedings of International Conference on Software Engineering (ICSE 16)*. (1994) 81-90

17. Minneman, S. and Harrison, S. Where were we: Making and using near-synchronous, pre-narrative video. In *Proceedings of ACM Multimedia 1993*. (1993) 1-6

18. Minneman, S., et al. A confederation of tools for capturing and acessing collaborative activity. In *Proceedings of ACM Multimedia 1995*. San Francisco, CA (1995) 523-534

19. Moran, T. P., et al. "I'll Get That off the Audio": A Case Study of Salvaging Multimedia Meeting Records. In *Proceedings of CHI 1997*. Atlanta, GA (1997) 202-209

20. Mukhopadhyay, S. and Smith, B. Passive Capture and Structuring of Lectures. In *Proceedings of ACM Multimedia 1999*. Orlando, FL (1999) 477-487

21. Myers, B. A., Stiel, H., and Gargiulo, R. Collaboration Using Multiple PDAs Connected to a PC. In *Proceedings of Computer Supported Cooperative Work 1998*. Seattle, WA (1998) 285-294

22. Mynatt, E. D., et al. Flatland: New Dimensions in Office Whiteboards. In *Proceedings of CHI 1999*. Pittsburgh, PA (1999) 346-353

23. Newman, W. and Wellner, P. A Desk Supporting Computer-based Interaction with Paper Documents. In *Proceedings of CHI 1992*. Monterey, CA (1992) 587-592

24. Pedersen, E. R., et al. Tivoli: An Electronic Whiteboard for Informal Workgroup Meetings. In *Proceedings of ACM INTERCHI 1993*. Amsterdam, The Netherlands (1993) 391-398

25. Richter, H., et al. Integrating Meeting Capture within a Collaborative Team Environment. In *Proceedings of UbiComp 2001*. Atlanta, GA (2001)

26. Richter, H., Schuchhard, P., and Abowd, G. D. Automated capture and retrieval of architectural rationale. Georgia Institute of Technology Technical Report GIT-GVU-98-37 (1999)
27. Smart Technologies, Inc. SmartBoard. http://www.smarttech.com.
28. Stafford-Fraser, Q., et al. BrightBoard: A Video-Augmented Environment. In *Proceedings of CHI 1996*. Vancouver, Canada (1996) 134-141
29. Stifelman, L. J. The Audio Notebook.Ph.D. Thesis, Media Laboratory, MIT (1997)
30. Streitz, N. A., et al. DOLPHIN: Integrated Meeting Support across Liveboards, Local and Remote Desktop Environments. In *Proceedings of Computer Supported Collaborative Work 1994*. Chapel Hill, NC (1994) 345-357
31. Truong, K. N., Abowd, G. D., and Brotherton, J. A. Personalizing the Capture of Public Experiences. In *Proceedings of UIST 1999*. Asheville, NC (1999) 121-130
32. Wactlar, H., et al. Informedia Experience-on-Demand, Capturing, Integrating and Communication Experience across People, Time and Space. http://www.informedia.cs.cmu.edu/eod.
33. Weber, K. and Poon, A. Marquee: A tool for real-time video logging. In *Proceedings of CHI 1994*. Boston, MA (1994) 58-64
34. Weiser, M., The computing for the 21st century. Scientific American. 265(3) (1991) 94-104
35. Whittaker, S., Hyland, P., and Wiley, M. Filochat: Handwritten notes provide access to recorded conversations. In *Proceedings of CHI 1994*. Boston, MA (1994) 271-277
36. Wilcox, L., Schilit, B. N., and Sawhney, N. Dynomite: A Dynamically Organized Ink and Audio Notebook. In *Proceedings of CHI 1997*. Atlanta, GA (1997) 186-193

Unearthing Virtual History: Using Diverse Interfaces to Reveal Hidden Virtual Worlds

Steve Benford[1], John Bowers[2], Paul Chandler[1], Luigina Ciolfi[3], Martin Flintham[1], Mike Fraser[1], Chris Greenhalgh[1], Tony Hall[3], Sten Olof Hellström[2], Shahram Izadi[1], Tom Rodden[1], Holger Schnädelbach[1], and Ian Taylor[1]

[1] The Mixed Reality Laboratory, University of Nottingham, UK
{sdb,pdc,mdf,mcf,cmg,sxi,tar,hms,imt}@cs.nott.ac.uk
[2] Centre for User-Oriented IT-Design (CID), Royal Institute of Technology (KTH), Stockholm, Sweden
{bowers,soh}@nada.kth.se
[3] Interaction Design Centre, University of Limerick, Ireland
{Luigina.Ciolfi,Tony.Hall}@ul.ie

Abstract. We describe an application in which museum visitors hunt for virtual history outdoors, capture it, and bring it back indoors for detailed inspection. This application provides visitors with ubiquitous access to a parallel virtual world as they move through an extended physical space. Diverse devices, including mobile wireless interfaces for locating hotspots of virtual activity outdoors, provide radically different experiences of the virtual depending upon location, task, and available equipment. Initial reflections suggest that the physical design of such devices needs careful attention so as to encourage an appropriate style of use. We also consider the extension of our experience to support enacted scenes. Finally, we discuss potential benefits of using diverse devices to make a shared underlying virtual world ubiquitously available throughout physical space.

1   Introduction

Museums, galleries, cultural heritage and tourism are promising application domains for ubiquitous technologies. Personal and handheld devices coupled with embedded and projected displays can enrich experience inside a traditional museum or gallery [1, 4, 11]. Mobile technologies can enhance cultural experiences when exploring a surrounding city [5]. We are interested in how a combination of the two might provide visitors with rich and engaging cultural experiences that connect a conventional museum or gallery to a surrounding city or site of special interest. Our approach involves providing participants with diverse interfaces for detecting, revealing and experiencing events that are taking place in a parallel 3D virtual world; that is a virtual world that is hidden behind, but potentially ubiquitously available from, everyday physical space in both indoors and outdoors locations.

G. D. Abowd, B. Brumitt, S. A. N. Shafer (Eds.): Ubicomp 2001, LNCS 2201, pp. 225-231, 2001.

2   A First Demonstration – Unearthing Virtual Artifacts on the Nottingham Campus

We have created a museum experience where participants explore an outdoors location, hunting for buried virtual artifacts that they then bring back to a museum for more detailed study. Inspired by the results of previous museum projects, our intention is that the process of actively searching for history will be engaging for visitors and will also lead them to critically reflect on the information that they discover [12]. At the beginning of the experience participants are told the following (fictional) back-story:

During the construction of our campus in 1999 builders unearthed four ancient artifacts: a samurai sword, a maiolica dish, an ivory box of dominoes, and a bell (objects from the collection at the nearby Nottingham Castle museum). Scientists have since discovered that physical artifacts radiate traces of their history. When they are buried for long periods of time these traces can leak into the surrounding earth, and can subsequently be detected and captured using specialized sensing instruments. Unfortunately, our builders failed to note the locations where the objects were unearthed.

Part 1: outdoors – locating the target objects and capturing their history

Groups of participants head outside and search an island on our campus using a "virtual history meter", a device that informs them of their proximity to various virtual objects that actually exist in a 3D virtual model of the campus. This device consists of a laptop and a Compaq iPAQ that communicate with one another and also with computers in the nearby laboratory over a WaveLAN network. The global position of the laptop as given by an attached GPS device is transmitted back to computers in the laboratory, enabling them update the position of an avatar in the virtual world that represents the search party. In turn, the computers running the virtual world update the mobile laptop with measures of this avatars' proximity to different fragments of the virtual objects. For brevity, our initial demonstration is limited to three fragments from one object, the maiolica dish.

It can be difficult to create a satisfactory and reliable visual overlay of a virtual world on an outdoors scene due to a combination of limited tracking accuracy and variable lighting conditions [3]. We have therefore opted for an alternative approach that is primarily based upon audio information. The proximities of the search party to the three fragments are sent to a computer in the laboratory that is running an application that sonifies the party's location in relation to the fragments. Each fragment has a different pulsing synthesised tone associated with it that increases in amplitude and pulse rate as the search party get closer to it. The mix of the three tones is transmitted to the wireless laptop. When our participants are within a (configurable) distance of a fragment, they are deemed to have acquired it. They now hear a different tone and the iPAQ device displays an appropriate image and some accompanying text.

Figure 1 shows two participants searching our campus next to the corresponding image of their avatar in the virtual world as it encounters one of the fragments.

Fig. 1 Hunting for fragments of virtual objects outdoors

Part 2: inside the museum – viewing the captured history

The search party brings the captured virtual history back to the museum in order to view it in detail. Each captured fragment is loaded onto a periscope, a rotating ceiling-mounted screen that allows a user to view and hear a virtual world by turning about a fixed virtual location. Grasping and rotating the periscope rotates one's viewpoint in the virtual world and controls the mix and spatialisation of associated audio (both ambient sounds and commentary) that is heard through wireless headphones. A small projector mounted on the base of the periscope projects an additional view onto surrounding screens that is supplemented with four external audio speakers. This public display is intended to allow the experience to be shared by groups of visitors (e.g., families) and to attract other visitors to the exhibit.

The periscope user finds that they have been transported back to the island, but this time as a 3D model, and that a historical scene from the object's past has now appeared at the location where they found the fragment. By rotating the periscope, they can explore the scene, trigger spoken information and mix related sounds. Inspired by the presentation of the actual dish at the Castle Museum, one scene depicts the event that is painted onto the dish, a second tells of how and where the dish was made, and a third tells so of how it came to be in Nottingham. Figure 2 shows the periscope and an example scene.

2.1   Implementation

Our demonstration has been implemented through the coordinated use of the MASSIVE-3 and EQUIP software platforms and applications authored in the MAX/msp audio programming environment [15]. MASSIVE-3 is a platform for distributed virtual worlds. It can support between ten and twenty mutually aware avatars in a shared virtual world communicating using real-time audio and has previously been used to create a variety of on-line storytelling events [6]. EQUIP is a dynamically extensible framework for integrating C++/Java based applications with a variety of interfaces and devices, ranging from wireless portable devices through to fully immersive systems. EQUIP provides applications and devices with one or more shared tuple-like data spaces through which they can publish and subscribe to each others' data. For example, our virtual history meter publishes its GPS updates to an EQUIP data space so that they can then be read into a MASSIVE-3 virtual world. In return, MASSIVE-3 publishes the positions of fragments in the world that can then be read by the meter. An EQUIP module was also developed which (in part 1) published the GPS data as MIDI continuous controllers to communicate with the sonification and (in part 2) sent periscope angle to a panoramic mixing application which triggered commentary sound files, generated ambient textures algorithmically, and controlled the overall mix and spatialisation. The operation of EQUIP, its integration with MASSIVE-3 and its role in supporting this demonstration are not covered here (but see [8]).

Fig. 2 Viewing the captured fragments indoors

2.2   Immediate Reflections

Our initial demonstration was given to a small audience of invited participants, including a curator from Nottingham's Castle Museum and sociologists who have been studying visitor behaviour in museums. A round-table discussion suggested a number of possible refinements. For this paper we focus on those comments that relate to the design of the virtual history meter.

- It was possible, but quite slow and sometimes difficult to locate the target fragments outdoors. The island presents a featureless landscape and the virtual fragments were not sited at obvious locations. Users probably needed to be more systematic and painstaking about searching than they were.
- Several participants commented that they expected the handheld devices – the iPAQ and GPS – to be sensitive to orientation. In other words, that the sonification would change according to the direction in which these devices were being pointed.

Of course, we might directly address these comments by changing the locations, spacing and target sizes of the fragments and adding a directional compass to the wireless device. However, it is also interesting to speculate whether a different physical design for the wireless device would have encouraged a more appropriate style of use to suit the original set-up. What if the GPS sensor had been embedded into something resembling a metal meter? Would this have encouraged more systematic searching over the ground? Would participants expect a larger ground-hugging device such as a metal meter to be as sensitive to orientation as a hand held pointing device? In future experiences we should pay greater attention to the physical design of devices in order to ensure that they communicate their intended style of use rather than just relying on off-the-shelf devices.

3   Extending with Enacted Scenes

In order to be able to create richer historical experiences we have extended our system to support enacted scenes. Users, represented as avatars enter the virtual world, move around, manipulate objects and talk to one another. MASSIVE-3 allows such scenes to be enacted live or to be saved as 3D recordings that can subsequently be replayed in a live virtual world [7]. In this way, actors can stage scenes from the past and tour guides, curators and teachers can quickly create customized virtual tours that to be played out into physical space.

Two further technical innovations support these ideas. First, we have created a version of the virtual history meter that tracks avatars as they move around the virtual world (showing their positions on a radar style display on the iPAQ) and that allows users to listen in to their dialogues (via the laptop). Second, we have experimented with a technique for projecting "shadow avatars" into physical environments so as to give fleeting impressions of ghostlike figures from a parallel world. When an avatar passes by a specific location in the virtual world, its shadowy image (with associated sound) is projected onto the wall or floor of the equivalent physical location. This shadow technique demonstrates a further class of device for revealing the virtual world, one in which users do not have to carry any specialised equipment at all or even have any intention to experience the world. Such techniques could be used to attract the attention of bystanders so as to draw them into virtual events.

4   Diverse Interfaces onto a Ubiquitous Virtual World

We finish with some general reflections on the approach of using diverse devices to access a shared virtual world. Conventional augmented reality employs physical or video see-through displays to overlay a virtual world on the physical [2]. Recent projects have begun to move augmented reality outdoors, for example exploiting handheld displays and wearable computers with see-through head-mounted displays [3,9]. Other researchers have also explored the use of hand-held devices to interact with immersive virtual environments [10, 14].

Our approach focuses on how very diverse devices can provide radically different experiences of a virtual world at different times and in different places. Some devices will offer high fidelity and accurately registered views of the virtual along the lines described above. However, others will offer more impressionistic views of the virtual, for example audio sonifications as demonstrated by our virtual history meter or projected shadow avatars. We propose that our approach offers a number of benefits.

Variable engagement – heterogenous interfaces can allow participants to vary their engagement with the virtual world. An unfolding story may gradually introduce participants to a virtual world. Bystanders have only a fleeting awareness of virtual events, whereas committed players may be fully involved. Participants in a long-term event may vary their level of engagement over time.

Variable tracking – the display of the virtual can be configured to match the accuracy of tracking in different locations. Where accurate tracking is available the user may be offered a fully 3D view of the virtual. Where it is not, they may be offered more impressionistic views.

Variable physical environments – sound-based representations of the virtual may be able to accommodate bright and variable lighting conditions where it might be problematic to project detailed graphical views.

Orchestration – staff in the virtual world can monitor and dynamically shape participants' experiences from behind-the-scenes, for example moving virtual objects to make them easier or harder to find. In fact, our demonstration supported an additional interface, a table-top projection of the virtual world as an interactive map, for this purpose.

Finally, connecting multiple wireless physical devices to a common underlying virtual world brings advantages from a systems perspective. VR research has developed a repertoire of techniques that use virtual space to manage information flows among large numbers of communicating users [13]. These techniques can be directly applied to mobile devices that are tracked and represented in a virtual world. For example, a group of PDAs that are proximate in the virtual world (i.e., whose virtual "auras" have collided or who are in a common virtual "locale") would automatically join the same server or multicast group and so communicate with one another.

Acknowledgements

This work has been carried out within the SHAPE project under the European V Framework Disappearing Computer Initiative and the EQUATOR Interdisciplinary Research Collaboration funded by EPSRC in the UK. Please note that the authors are listed purely in alphabetic order.

References

1. Aoki, M. and Woodruff, A., Improving Electronic Guidebook Interfaces Using a Task-Oriented Design Approach, Proc. DIS 2000, Aug 2000, 319-325.
2. Azuma, R. T., "A Survey of Augmented Reality", Presence: Teleoperators and Virtual Environments, 6(4): 355-385, Aug. 1997.
3. Azuma, R., The Challenge of Making Augmented Reality Work Outdoors, In Mixed Reality: Merging Real and Virtual Worlds (Yuichi Ohta and Hideyuki Tamura, eds), 1999, Springer-Verlag.

4. Benelli, G., Bianchi, A., Marti, P., Not, E., Sennati, D. (1999a). "HIPS: Hyper-Interaction within Physical Space", in Proceedings of IEEE ICMCS99, Florence, June 1999.
5. Cheverst, K., Davies, N., Mitchell, K., Friday, A. and Efstratiou, Developing a Context-Aware Electronic Tourist Guide: Some Issues and Experiences, Proc. CHI'2000, 17-24, The Hague, Netherlands, ACM Press.
6. Craven, M., Taylor, I., Drozd, A., Purbrick, J., Greenhalgh, C., Benford, S., Fraser, M., Bowers, J., Jää-Åro, K., Lintermann, B, Hoch, M., Exploiting Interactivity, Influence, Space and Time to Explore Non-linear Drama in Virtual Worlds, *Proc. CHI'2001*, Seattle, US, April 2-6, 2001, ACM Press.
7. Greenhalgh, C., Purbrick, J., Benford, S., Craven, M., Drozd, A. and Taylor, I., Temporal links: recording and replaying virtual environments, *Proc. ACM Multimedia 2000*, L.A. October 2000.
8. Greenhalgh, C., Izadi, S., Rodden, T. and Benford, S., The EQUIP platform: bringing together physical and virtual worlds (forthcoming).
9. Höllerer, T., Feiner, S., Terauchi, T., Rashid, G., Hallaway, D., Exploring MARS: Developing Indoor and Outdoor User Interfaces to a Mobile Augmented Reality System , In: Computers and Graphics, 23(6), Elsevier Publishers, Dec. 1999, pp. 779-785.
10. Krebs, A., Dorohonceanu, B. and Marsic, I., Collaboration using Heterogeneous Devices – from 3D Workstations to PDAs, In Proceedings of the IASTED International Conference on Internet and Multimedia Systems and Applications (IMSA'2000), pages 309-313, Las Vegas, NV, November 20-23, 2000.
11. Oppermann, R. and Specht, M., Adaptive Support for a Mobile Museum Guide, Proc. Workshop on Interactive Applications of Mobile Computing (IMC'98).
12. Rayward, W. B. & Twidale, M. B. (1999) "From Docent to Cyberdocent: Education and Guidance in the Virtual Museum", Archives and Museum Informatics, 13, 23-53, 1999.
13. Singhal, Sandeep and Zyda, Michael "Networked Virtual Environments – Design and Implementation," (chapter 7) ACM Press Books, SIGGRAPH Series, 23 July 1999, ISBN 0-201-32557-8, 315 pages.
14. Watsen, K., Darken, R., and Capps, M., "A Handheld Computer as an Interaction Device to a Virtual Environment," 3rd International Immersive Projection Technology Workshop (IPTW'99), Stuttgart, Germany, 1999.
15. MAX/msp. www.cycling74.com. Link visited 18/07/01.

KISS the Tram:
Exploring the PDA as
Support for Everyday Activities

Thorstein Lunde and Arve Larsen

Norwegian Computing Center (NR), Oslo, Norway
{thorstein.lunde,arve.larsen}@nr.no

Abstract. Most of today's common PDA applications do not leverage the prospects of the PDA. We want to explore PDAs and other mobile devices as new media, focusing on their unique qualities, not as limited PCs. Moreover, we focus on support for everyday life. We present a user test of an application for catching the tram based on this approach, as well as guidance from the ever relevant principle *"Keep it simple, stupid!"*

1 Introduction

A real personal assistant is there to assist you in your everyday life. He does so by managing your schedule, contacts, correspondence, etc. A Personal Digital Assistant (PDA) can be seen as having the same purpose. Most current PDA applications focus on tasks inherited from other technologies such as the Filofax and your favourite email application. In this context the physical characteristics of the PDA, for instance its limited screen size, may be a limitation for the design and development and applications.

Support for everyday activities should be provided beyond the notion of a memory-prosthesis; that is the calendar, the todo-list, the contact database etc. One should free oneself from the restricted thinking based on models from traditional, stationary systems. We want to explore the PDA and other mobile devices as new media in themselves. This exploration is aimed at providing input for future research on mobile devices, each according to their unique qualities.

We want to consider the characteristics of the PDA as providing an advantage and focus on its unique capabilities. To help us see the PDA in a new way, our focus is on supporting people in their efforts to catch the tram home. Our purpose is to explore the use of the PDA for supporting everyday activities.

We have developed a highly focused application and given it to users to explore how they perceived the application and the support it provided. In section 2 we present works of others relevant to our own. Section 3 gives a brief description of our application. Section 4 describes our user test and our findings. In section 5 we give some concluding remarks.

G. D. Abowd, B. Brumitt, S. A. N. Shafer (Eds.): Ubicomp 2001, LNCS 2201, pp. 232–239, 2001.
© Springer-Verlag Berlin Heidelberg 2001

2   Related Work

Past and current research in mobile computing tend to focus on the fundamental challenges of the restricted resources commonly available in mobile devices [10,4]. Kristoffersen and Ljungberg have argued that most applications for mobile devices are so strongly influenced by traditions from the stationary world that they might just as well be stationary [5,6]. They suggest focusing on the mobility of users and their devices, describing different modalities of mobile work. This is discussed in relation to alternative paradigms for user interface. Others have proposed focusing on the mobility of tasks [9], identifying dynamic user configuration, limited attention capacity, high-speed interaction and context dependency as important characteristics of mobile work. Although these results from mobile work help avoid the influence of a traditional, stationary approach, we feel that one should free oneself even more. In our case, we have sought inspiration from everyday appliances, for instance the watch and traffic lights.

Support for catching the tram can be described as *everyday computing*, that is *"to support informal and unstructured activities typical of much of our everyday lives"* [1, page 42]. In particular, one must consider that these kinds of activities may not have a clear beginning or end, and that multiple activities may operate concurrently. Any interface should be continuously present at the periphery of the user's attention.[1]

Deciding when to leave work for home is often done when working on something else. In a typical office work setting, one's attention is usually directed to the computer screen. Our application should be in the periphery of this attention field.

One way of minimising the attention required could be to give some sort of reminder saying *"Go home!"*, perhaps in a slightly more polite tone. Others have worked on making such reminders context sensitive and able to adapt according to the changing context. These approaches place a focus on two different aspects of the required support:

1. identifying and providing programmatic access to and processing of context information (see for instance [2] and [3]), and
2. developing algorithms that learn from the user's changing context, for instance in relation to time and location, and using that information to improve context sensitivity (see for instance [7]).

We feel that even if we could make our reminders as smart as we want them, this kind of mechanism represent a type of solution to a group of problems fundamentally different from that of catching the tram. Support for unstructured and informal tasks should be given as information and suggestions, not reminders or decisions.

3   KISS the Tram

Since our goal is to support catching trams that run all day, we want a user interface that is continuously present at the periphery of the user's attention. A quick glance should be enough the get the information one needs.

A guiding principle behind the design itself was *"Keep it simple, stupid!"*, hence the name of the application. For this initial test we wanted no interaction beyond one's personal settings.

Our test application is implemented on a PocketPC. The screen is divided into three vertical sections. A basic assumption is that for any given test subject, three stations for public provide a good starting point for leaving the workplace. The test site has five possible stations, two subway stations, one tram station and two bus stops. Subjects chose three stations that suited them. The application itself was mapped to one of the device's application buttons, making it easy to review it when needed.

Figure 1 shows some typical screen shots of our application. The three stations are presented in separate panels. A station is always presented in the same panel. Each panel includes three types of information. The name of the station is written on the top. The departure time for the next tram you are likely to catch is written at the bottom of the panel.

The main functionality of the application is to present the urgency of your decision. If it is too early to leave for the tram, the panel itself is black with the text *"Too early"* in the middle. If it is time to pack the panel turns green, showing the text *"Time to pack"*. The next two levels are based on your walking and running speed. When it is time to start walking at your normal pace, the panel turns yellow showing the text *"Walk"*. Once your fastest walking speed is insufficient to catch the tram, the panel turns reed showing *"RUN"*. Once your fastest running speed is insufficient, the panel turns black again.

Fig. 1. Screen shots

For this prototype, we provide the user with the option of specifying the information related to himself, that is the time needed to pack, his ordinary walking speed, his fastest walking speed and his fastest running speed.

The schedule of each station varies in complexity. One of the subway stations is served by only one line in 15-minute intervals during the day and 30-minute intervals in the evening. The bus stops are similar, with the 30-minute intervals starting earlier in the evening. Two lines service the other subway station, with changes in the interval between departures sometime in the evening. Three different lines service the tram station. One of the lines only runs in the early morning and early evening. The interval between departures from this station varies several times during the day.

4   Our User Test

We chose a quantitative approach as the basis for our exploration. Six IT students and seven IT researchers tested the application for approximately one week each. All of the subjects worked in the same geographic area and used public transport as their main means of transportation.

All subjects were shown how to start the application and how to work around known bugs. They were told little or nothing about how the application actually worked. After one week of testing all but one of the subjects were engaged for a semi-structured interview. The last one gave us written feedback before we got around to scheduling an interview.

Our analysis of these interviews has given four major findings relevant to our exploration:

1. *The support provided by the application was perceived as useful.*
2. *This type of application could make people see PDAs in a new way.*
3. *While in the cradle the PDA can be used as a complement to the PC.*
4. *The right type of support can make people feel borne by technology.*

1: Usefulness of Support for Everyday Activities

When analysing the interviews, we discovered that the different users used four different models to describe how the application actually worked. These four models can be described as

- *a chronological list of departures (misleading),*
- *a list showing trams in two directions relative to a station (wrong),*
- *an advanced watch (orthogonal), and*
- *departures from three different stations (correct).*

Given that the application was not explained to the subjects, this is not surprising. Still, even though some of these are actually wrong, most of the subjects indicated that the application gave them more control. More importantly, they felt that they caught more trams and all of them considered the application useful.

Different reasons for the perceived usefulness were given. Some described themselves as unstructured or whimsical. These people had a common strategy for catching the tram. They would work normally and at some time decide to head home. They would then leave the office, walk to a station and wait for the next tram. These users indicated that the application changed their strategy and that they felt that they had to wait less for the tram where they did not know the schedule. One of them even used to run, because if he just missed a tram he would at least know that he did his best.

Other subjects had a working knowledge of the time schedule for their normal tram. For their normal travel, these users just indicated that the application could be useful. However, since the application showed three different alternatives, some of these users indicated that the application was very useful when they had to catch one of the other lines.

2: Seeing the PDA in a New Way

When analysing how the different users related *KISS the Tram* to other PDA applications they had knowledge of, we made an interesting observation. One user had had a PDA for some time without using it. He commented that this application made him see his PDA in a new way. He also commented that this kind of application could actually make him start to use it.

One user compared our application to Trafikanten [11], a web-based travel planner for public transportation in Oslo. He commented that *KISS the Tram* was simple and felt that it was *"more immediate"*, making it more suitable for his use.

Another aspect of seeing the PDA in a new way is taken from the answers we got on how this application may be extended or the concept applied in other areas. Some suggestions tried to connect our application to known applications, such as reminders and travel-planners. Others expressed that the application inspired them to envision new applications they had never thought about before.

3: Use of the PDA in the Cradle

Putting the PDA in its cradle is usually associated with synchronising with a computer and charging the PDA's batteries. *KISS the Tram* is designed for use even when the PDA is in its cradle. One user commented that he liked being able to detect the changes in colour in the corner of his eye. He also commented that since the colours keep changing over and over again, this was somewhat distracting during the day when he wasn't going anywhere.

Another user said he liked the idea of having the display present next to his screen. His problem was that he already used the PDA's screen for displaying the Today list, a list showing his appointments for the day and his todo items.

Both these users discussed the possibility of having *KISS the Tram* appear only when needed. The first wanted to reduce the distraction caused by the colour changes, the other to enable him to continue using the Today screen.

Another wanted the application on the task bar during the day, and then "zoom" in to cover the whole screen sometime during the evening. This zoom could be triggered in several ways. The user could manually zoom in or out. The application could also allow the user to specify a time span for when he was planning to leave that day. Another possibility discussed was to have the application automatically adapt to the users normal work rhythm, zooming in sometime before the user usually leaves. All these three varieties could of course be available together or independent of each other.

4: Borne By Technology

One user described an actual situation where he was on the phone with a friend he was going to meet. He used a travel planner on the web to find out how to get to his friend's place. By coincidence the first leg of his journey was using bus 23 east, one of the lines shown on his version of *KISS the Tram*. When he discovered that he expressed that he *"felt in a way borne by technology ... [laughter] ... yes, it was really like that ... a very particular feeling - now you really have support ... so this [KISS the Tram] was for me very useful then and there"*.

This event has two interesting aspects. The first is a direct experience resulting in a concrete feeling of being borne by technology. He did not have an explicit goal that he wanted to achieve using the PDA. Furthermore, he did not do anything through an interface. We believe that the application's simplicity is vital in providing this feeling. Support is given without any explicit interaction.

5 Concluding Remarks and Future Work

The user test of our application provided useful information about support for everyday activities. We feel that the following aspects should be explored further.

Our first observations are that the users found the application useful in their everyday lives. Secondly, this type of application may give people inspiration to see their PDAs in a new way. When exploring the PDA or other mobile devices as new media this inspirational effect should be taken account. More importantly, our future exploratory projects should in turn be inspired by this feedback.

Our test users found it natural to use the PDA in its cradle. Few applications seem to consider this type of use. The effects of the users' feeling of support should be considered. We believe that this is related to the simplicity and directness of the application.

What surprised us is the wealth of opinions our test subjects expressed about our simple application and the mundane task of catching the tram. Catching the tram is seldom considered a major problem, but it still seems to engage people in a significant way.

We want to continue these types of experiments, focusing on everyday activities. It is our goal to free ourselves even more from the paradigm of the PDA as a small computer. To quote Henry Mintzberg:

> *"It is discovery that attracts me to this business, not the checking out of what we think we already know."* [*8, page 584*]

Acknowledgements

The work described herein was in its entirety financed by NR. We would like to thank Dalip Dewan for making it possible.

We would also like to thank all of our test subjects for volunteering to test our application for an entire week.

Thanks to Michael Gritzman for invaluable discussion on the user interface in particular and design in general. Thanks also to Anders Kluge for providing the initial inspiration for this work.

References

1. Gregory D. Abowd and Elizabeth D. Mynatt. Charting past, present and future research in ubiquitous computing. *ACM Transactions on Computer-Human Interaction*, 7(1):29–58, March 2000. 233
2. Anind K. Dey and Gregory D. Abowd. CybreMinder: A context-aware system for supporting reminders. In *Proceedings from the Second International Symposium on Handheld and Ubiquitous Computing 2000*, Lecture Notes in Computer Science 1927, pages 172–186, 2000. 233
3. Alan Dix, Tom Rodden, Nigel Davies, Jonathan Trevor, Adrian Friday, and Kevin Palfreyman. Exploiting space and location as a design framework for interactive mobile systems. *ACM Transactions on Computer-Human Interaction*, 7(3):285–321, September 2000. 233
4. Jin Jing, Abdelsalam (Sumi) Helal, and Ahmed Elmagarmid. Client-server computing in mobile environments. *ACM Computing Surveys*, 31(2), June 1999. 233
5. Steinar Kristoffersen and Fredrik Ljungberg. Your mobile computer is a stationary computer. Presented at the workshop on Handheld CSCW during CSCW'98. http://www.nr.no/~steinar/workingpapers/cscw98.pdf. 233
6. Steinar Kristoffersen and Fredrik Ljungberg. "Making place" to make it work: Empirical explorations of HCI for mobile CSCW. In *Proceedings of the International Conference on Supporting Group Work (GROUP'99, Phoenix, AZ)*, New York, 1999. ACM Press. 233
7. Natalia Marmasse and Chris Schmandt. Location-aware information delivery with ComMotion. In *Proceedings from the Second International Symposium on Handheld and Ubiquitous Computing 2000*, Lecture Notes in Computer Science 1927, pages 172–186, 2000. 233
8. Henry Mintzberg. An emerging strategy of "direct" research. *Administrative Science Quarterly*, 24:582–589, December 1979. 238
9. Jason Pascoe, Nick Ryan, and David Morse. Using while moving: HCI issues in fieldwork environments. *ACM Transactions on Computer-Human Interaction*, 7(3):417–436, September 2000. 233

10. M. Satyanarayanan. Fundamental challenges in mobile computing. In *Proceedings of the fifteenth annual ACM symposium on Principles of distributed computing*, pages 1–7, Philadelphia, PA, 1996. 233
11. Trafikanten. Web site for public transport travel planning in Oslo. http://www.trafikanten.no/. 236

Subtle and Public Notification Cues for Mobile Devices

Rebecca Hansson, Peter Ljungstrand, and Johan Redström

PLAY research studio, The Interactive Institute
Box 620, 405 30 Göteborg, Sweden
rebecca.hansson@interactiveinstitute.se
http://www.playresearch.com/

Abstract. Mobile information technology increasingly influences everyday life. When used in social contexts several problems regarding how mobile devices convey notifications arise. Auditory notification cues, such as those generally used by mobile phones, can be intrusive and attention demanding. Tactile cues, such as vibrations, are very private and subtle. However, since it is hard for other people nearby to perceive such cues, it can be awkward to understand the actions which a notification cue can give rise to, i.e., tactile cues are not public. We discuss the design space of notification cues for mobile devices and propose an exploration of the space which combines the two dimensions of subtlety and publicity. We conclude with a description of current and future work.

1   Introduction

Mobile information technology such as mobile phones and PDAs (Personal Digital Assistants) can provide users with services that make it easier for them to keep themselves available to and contact others, to organize their time and to become notified of important events. There is a great interest in such devices among both professionals and consumers. One consequence of the proliferation of mobile information technology is that its use influences almost all social situations including situations outside the typical work setting, since the device is on at all times and follows its user rather than being bound to a specific location (e.g. work or home).

One of the prime functionalities of mobile devices is to notify their users of certain events. For instance, mobile phones notify users of incoming calls, and PDAs convey notifications regarding events scheduled in the users' digital calendars. Notification cues emanating from these devices are in many situations perceived as inappropriate, both by the owner of a device and to the people nearby. Problems regarding how notifications are conveyed from mobile devices, in particular in social settings, need to be addressed.

In this paper, we explore complementary ways of conveying notifications from mobile devices. The ambition has been to explore various notification cues which might be more socially acceptable. First we discuss some of the problems with notifications, and then sketch the design space of notification cues for mobile devices. We conclude with a description of current and future work.

G. D. Abowd, B. Brumitt, S. A. N. Shafer (Eds.): Ubicomp 2001, LNCS 2201, pp. 240-246, 2001.
© Springer-Verlag Berlin Heidelberg 2001

2   Background

Presently, notifications from mobile devices are conveyed mainly by sounds and beeps, and to a lesser extent by tactile cues such as vibrations. Below we will present problems specific to the use of auditory and tactile notification cues in social settings, and also introduce a few terms which can be helpful when trying to understand the issues involved.

2.1 Auditory Notification Cues

Current auditory notificiation cues can be attention demanding, distinct and intrusive and therefore be perceived as inappropriate in many social situations. Ling writes: "The beeping and ringing is by nature an intrusive sound not unlike the sound of an alarm clock" [1], referring to the different auditory cues used by mobile phones. The individual user often address such problems by disabling the notification cue in certain social contexts, such as at business meetings or at the cinema [1, 2]. It is questionable, though, whether this is a satisfactory solution, since the notification cue might convey information which is both important and valuable to the user.

This question is related to the problem of communication deficiency as defined by Ljungberg and Sørensen: „Communication deficiency characterizes situations where people are subjected to communication which they are interested in, but where the mode of communication is undesired" [3]. Auditory cues for mobile devices are typically designed to attract maximum attention and to be able to penetrate even a very noisy sound environment. The notification in itself requires the recipient to, more or less instantly, direct her attention towards it.

We use the term *attention overload* to describe the phenomenon which arises when people are overwhelmed and interrupted by intrusive and attention demanding external events, such as loud auditory cues or flashing bright lights. Attention overload concerns not only the owner or holder of a mobile device, but also other people nearby. They might not have an interest in an auditory notification cue conveyed by someone else's device, but their attention is still very much drawn to it.

We use the term *subtlety* to describe how well a notification cue conveys information in a non-intrusive and gentle manner. Vibration, for instance, has the advantage of being very subtle. An intrusive notification cue might, however, contribute to the creation of attention overload since it, in social contexts, often demands the attention of the user as well as of other people nearby.

2.2 Tactile Notification Cues

Tactile notification cues are sometimes problematic in social environments. A vibration is an example of a tactile notification cue, and a device which conveys notifications using such a cue is typically carried close to the body to enable the user to perceive the notification. Thus, the device is typically not very visible to other people in the user's surroundings, and it can be difficult for them to comprehend the user's reaction to a 'hidden' and personal cue, i.e. the device's notification cue is not *public*. However, a traditional wrist-watch is public to the extent that it is often worn visible to others and when the user looks at it and walks away, it is a situation which people usually interpret in terms of causality. But, consider the following scenario:

> *Sharon is standing in the corridor with Reynolds and Mark, telling them about the latest board meeting. Suddenly Sharon's mobile phone, placed in her pocket, starts to vibrate. Sharon feels it, stops talking, and picks up the phone to say -Hello.*

To Sharon it was perfectly natural to pick up the phone and answer, because she had felt the vibration cue and had understood that someone wanted to reach her. To Reynolds and Mark, on the other hand, their ongoing conversation was abruptly interrupted since they had received no forewarning of what was about to happen. They could not, as Sharon, interpret the situation at hand, because the notification cue was hidden to them. Due to this, Sharon stopped taking part in the conversation. This could have happened even if the notification cue had been public, but now the social interaction between them was further disturbed. Handsfree headsets for mobile phones have introduced a similar issue, where people can appear to be talking to themselves, because their headsets are hardly noticeable to others [4].

A *public* notification cue initializes a course of events which is transparent to people near the person receiving it. An auditory cue from a mobile phone is public and people in the user's surrounding can easily understand the relation between hearing an auditory cue from a mobile phone and seeing someone pick up a mobile phone to answer. A non-public, i.e. private, notification cue initializes a course of events which is hidden, more or less, to people nearby the user of the device. It might increase the risk for misinterpretations of a user's actions in social environments.

3   Combining Subtle and Public Qualities

By creating a model spanning these two dimensions and characterizing related research in relation to the model, we hope to better understand the complex relationships between subtleness and publicity with regard to notification cues. Figure 1 illustrates two dimensions of modes of notifications; subtle vs. intrusive, and private vs. public, represented as a two-by-two matrix.

To avoid social misinterpretations as well as the problem of attention overload, it is desirable to design notification cues which combine the qualities of being subtle and public. Today very few mobile devices convey notifications in both a subtle and public manner. Thus, we suggest an exploration of the area which is indicated in the first quadrant in figure 1. Such notification cues would function as a complement to already existing notification cues.

Depending on what context the user of the mobile device is in and on the nature of the information conveyed, different kinds of notifications cues need to be used. The kind of notification cues investigated here are especially intended for use in social contexts where there is a need for immediate response from the user. The cue would ideally be subtle enough to avoid being intrusive and public enough to make the transition between the user receiving a notification cue and instantly responding to it comprehensible to people nearby. However, when the user is not in a social context or when the user receives notifications which do not need to be responded to at once, a tactile cue could be quite sufficent. An auditory cue can be the best choice in other situations; it can for instance convey more complex notificiations, such as verbal messages. It is a challenge to successfully combine various modalitites and notification designs with different contexts of use. Several context-aware mobile systems that change their manner of notification depending on what environment its user is in [5, 6] and on what information is to be conveyed [2] have been developed. We will not elaborate more on technical issues here since it is beyond the scope of this paper.

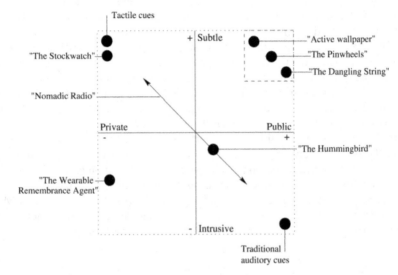

Fig. 1. A model for visualizing subtleness vs. publicity with regard to notification cues

3.1 Related Work

The concepts of *calm technology* [7] and *ambient displays* [8] have inspired this research as they are non-intrusive in character and mostly convey information publicly. A number of systems have been characterized: public as well as private and subtle as well as intrusive systems (see fig. 1). *The Stockwatch* is a personal and mobile ambient display which uses temperature to convey information about changes in stock rates [9]. The back of a watch becomes a display which changes its temperature depending on fluctuations in the user's stock. *The Hummingbird* is a small portable device which supports social awareness between people who frequent the same physical location [10]. If two people, carrying Hummingbirds, are in each other's vicinity the Hummingbirds starts to vibrate and „hum", making the users aware of each other's presence. *The Wearable Remembrance Agent* uses a headworn see-through display and acts as an *augmented memory* for its user by displaying timely text messages [11]. *Nomadic Radio* is a wearable notification tool which uses audio messaging to convey scalable and contextual notifications. It conveys notifications differently depending on message priority, usage level, and environmental context [2]. *Active Wallpaper* is an ambient display which makes its spectators aware of the human activity at the workplace by projecting light on a wall

[8]. *The Pinwheels* is an ambient fixture which visualizes an artificial airflow and uses it as a medium to convey different sorts of information [12]. Finally, *the Dangling String* is a piece of art by Natalie Jeremijenko, often used as an example of calm technology [7]. It is an eight foot long ethernet cable, connected to a small motor mounted in the ceiling. It vibrates at different speeds depending on the activity on the adjacent computer network.

Four of these systems are not situated within the first quadrant, i.e. they do not combine subtle and public properties. The Stockwatch is very private and the notifications which it conveys are not perceivable to anyone but its user. It is also very subtle since it conveys the information using gradual temperature changes. Due to this, it is situated at the upper left corner of the second quadrant. The Hummingbird is the only device that lies within the fourth quadrant; it is public to the extent that it emits a soft sound when it detects another Hummingbird, but since it uses an auditory cue it can be perceived as somewhat intrusive. The Wearable Remembrance Agent is placed in the third quadrant; it is very private, but it is also intrusive to a certain extent since its user needs to explicitly focus on the display in order to receive the information conveyed. The headworn display can also cause disturbance in social settings. People can, for instance, find it difficult to have a conversation with someone wearing such a display. When trying to place the Nomadic Radio system in the model, we found that since it changes its notification cue depending on what context its user resides in, it cannot be placed at a fixed point in the model. Rather, it continuously moves between different places in the model, from being subtle and private to being louder and more public. Its movements is illustrated by the diagonal line in the figure. The Dangling String, on the other hand, is public and calm and therefore situated within the indicated area in the first quadrant. Active wallpaper and the Pinwheels, being public and subtle ambient displays, are also located within this area.

Two of the described systems are very private, one is public and intrusive, one moves between different states while three of them are situated within the specified area. The Stockwatch, for instance, is very subtle and private, which is well suited for its application - personal stock information should probably not be very public. Since it conveys a very *slow* notification cue which the user does not have to respond to directly there is no need for such changes. It could be discussed though, whether the Hummingbird could convey its notifications in a more subtle manner or not. Most importantly this illustration indicates that we can learn from calm technology and ambient displays when attempting to combine subtle and public qualities.

4   Current and Future Work

The Reminder Bracelet was our first effort to create a design example within the indicated area [13]. It is a bracelet which is connected to a PDA and it conveys visual notifications regarding events scheduled in the PDA's calendar. It is an attempt to combine the properties of subtlety and publicity when designing notification cues, and also to draw on the properties of calm technology and ambient displays. Informal formative studies have been conducted and even though the prototype's technical implementation could be improved, the underlying concept was clearly understood by the users and they all responded positively to it. They commended the ambition to design notification cues with a low demand for the user's attention as well as a high level of acceptance in social contexts.

However, it was also clear that the users felt that the concept of subtle and public notification could be further improved. Thus, the design space of subtle and public notification has to be explored using more design examples based on other approaches to these problems as well. Another issue of importance in future work, concerns the reactions by people in the user's vicinity. We need to perform studies of people in social contexts in order to learn more about the impact of different forms of public notification.

4.1 Personalization

We are exploring the design space of notifications on several different levels and besides continuing the work on subtle and public notifications we are looking at notification cues from a less functionality focused point of view. Besides the apparent functional use, mobile notification cues are increasingly used to express symbolic and personal attributes related to lifestyle, personal image, etc.

Given the importance of the "personalization" [14] of technology as it enters our everyday life, the design of notification cues might have to be approached from a different perspective. When designing for personal expression, we will explore emotional and expressive values. For instance, we can use approaches such as the one used in [15], where experimental design of information appliances were used to explore its possible emotional and aesthetical role.

In the case of mobile phones, people have found their way to personal expression by means of re-programmable melodies. A powerful possibility would be to enable people to combine several different kinds of notification cues. This would open up for a richer variety of ways for a person to find her own expression. The future challenge would then be not so much to support reprogramming of existing notification tools, but to come up with entirely new ways for devices to notify their users that also enable people to express themselves in various ways.

Obviously, exploring the design space of notification cues from this perspective is very different from exploring it from a functional point of view, and we strongly believe that it is valuable to combine these perspectives.

5   Conclusion

In this paper we presented several issues regarding the use of notification cues in social contexts. We suggested to combine the properties of subtlety and publicity when designing notification cues in order to make them fit more smoothly into social settings. The Reminder Bracelet was a first design example, but the design space of subtle and public notifications has to be further explored. More design examples should be developed and several user studies need to be conducted. It is also important to consider personal expressions in relation to notification cues.

References

1. Ling, R. (1998). „One can talk about common manners!": The use of Mobile Telephones in Inappropriate Situations. In: *Telektronikk (Telenor R&D Journal)* 2, 1998, pp. 65-76.
2. Sawhney, N. and Schmandt, C. (1999). Nomadic Radio: Scaleable and Contextual Notification for Wearable Audio Messaging. In: *Proceedings of CHI'99*, ACM Press, pp. 96-103.
3. Ljungberg, F. and Sørensen, C. (1998). Are You „Pulling the Plug" or „Pushing Up the Daisies"?. In: *Proceedings of the Thirty-First Hawaii International Conference on System Sciences*, IEEE Computer Society Press, Vol. 1, pp. 370-379.
4. Fukumoto, M. and Tonomura, Y. (1999). Whisper: a Wristwatch Style Wearable Handset. In: *Proceedings of CHI'99*, ACM Press, pp. 112-119.
5. Marmasse, N. and Schmandt, C. (2000). Location-Aware Information Delivery with ComMotion. In: *Proceedings of HUC'00*, Springer-Verlag, pp. 157-171.
6. Schmidt, A., Asante Aidoo, K., Takaluoma, A., Tuomela, U., Van Laerhoven, K. and Van de Velde, W. (1999). Advanced Interaction in Context. In: *Proceedings of HUC'99*, Springer-Verlag, pp. 89-101.
7. Weiser, M. and Brown, J. (1995). Designing Calm Technology. In: *PowerGrid Journal, v 1.01,* [http://www.ubiq.com/hypertext/weiser/calmtech/calmtech.htm], Last visited July 4, 2001.
8. Wisneski, C., Ishii, H., Dahley, A., Gorbet, M., Brave, S., Ullmer, B. and Yarin, P. (1998). Ambient Displays: Turning Architectural Space into an Interface between People and Digital Information. In: *Proceedings of the International Workshop on Cooperative Buildings (CoBuild'98)*, Springer-Verlag, pp. 22-32.
9. Wisneski, C. (1999) The Design of Personal Ambient Displays, M.Sc. Thesis, May 1999, MIT Media Laboratory, Mass. MA.
10. Holmquist, L.E., Falk J. and Wigström, J. (1999) Supporting Group Collaboration with Inter-Personal Awareness Devices. In: *Personal Technologies*, Springer, Vol. 3, No. 1-2, pp. 13-21.
11. Rhodes, B. (1997). The wearable remembrance agent: a system for augmented memory. In: *Personal Technologies, Special Issue on Wearable Computing*, Springer, Vol. 1, No. 4, pp. 218-224.
12. Dahley, A., Wisneski, C. and Ishii, H. (1998). Water Lamp and Pinwheels: Ambient Projection of Digital Information into Architectural Space. In: *Extended Abstracts of CHI'98,* ACM Press, pp. 269-270.
13. Hansson, R. and Ljungstrand, P. (2000). The Reminder Bracelet: Subtle Notification Cues for Mobile Devices. In: *Extended Abstracts of CHI 2000 (Student Poster),* ACM Press, pp. 323-325.
14. Väänänen-Vaino-Mattila, K. and Ruuska, S. (2000). Designing Mobile Phones and Communicators for Consumers' Needs at Nokia. In: *Bergman, E. (ed.): Information Appliances and Beyond; Interaction Design for Consumer Products*, Morgan Kaufmann, pp. 169-204.
15. Gaver, B. and Martin, H. (2000). Alternatives; Exploring Information Appliances through Conceptual Design Proposals. In: *Proceedings of CHI 2000*, ACM Press, pp. 209-216.

InfoScope: Link from Real World to Digital Information Space

Ismail Haritaoglu

IBM Almaden Research, San Jose, CA 95120
ismailh@almaden.ibm.com

Abstract. We describe an information augmentation system (infoS-
cope) and applications integrating handheld device with a color camera
to provide enhanced information perception services to users. InfoScope
uses a color camera as an input device to capture scene images from the
real world and utilize computer vision techniques to extract information
from real world, convert them into digital world as text information and
augment them back to the original scene location. The user can see both
the real world and information together on display of the handheld device. We have implemented two applications: First one is an automatic
sign/text translation for foreign travelers where a user may use infoScope
whenever they want to see texts or signs in their own language where
they are originally written in foreign language in the scene and extracted
from scene images automatically by using computer vision techniques.
The second application is "Information Augmentation in the City" where
a user can see information associated with building, or a place, overlaid
onto real scene images on their PDA's display.

1 Introduction

The real physical world and digital information space are coming closer and
closer as wireless communication, mobile display and camera technologies and
continue to advance. That introduces new research areas, such as, augmented
reality, location-aware pervasive computing. An exiting array of new opportunities and applications emerge as small and inexpensive wearable computers and
pervasive devices are becoming widely available and acceptable. These devices
introduces new concepts on how user interact with objects in the real world.
At IBM research, we are conducting exploratory research to provides enhance
information perception services which is becoming desirable and profitable way
to interact with information in the real world as those wearable and handheld
devices are becoming as a part of daily life. In this paper, we describe an information augmentation system (InfoScope) for handheld devices to augment
2D text information onto real scene images. The system does not requires very
precise registration between real world and virtual world. We implemented two
prototype applications to demonstrate capabilities of infoScope:

First prototype application is an automatic sign/text translation for foreign
travelers where people use infoScope to translate the text and signs in the scene

G. D. Abowd, B. Brumitt, S. A. N. Shafer (Eds.): Ubicomp 2001, LNCS 2201, pp. 247–255, 2001.
© Springer-Verlag Berlin Heidelberg 2001

Fig. 1. Examples of information augmentations: foreign text translation (top-row) and building recognition and navigation (bottom-row)

in their own language where they are originally written in a foreign language in the scene, and they can see the translated text in the scene image as shown in Figure 1 (top row). Second application is Information Augmentation in the City that provide functionality that user can use infoScope as a visual input device to interact with objects in the real world, e.g., buildings, historical places when they need enhanced information about them, as shown in Figure 1 (bottom row).

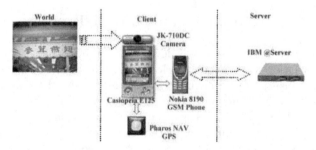

Fig. 2. Device architecture of infoScope: Camera attached PDA, GSM Phone and GPS device combined together in client side

1.1   System Architecture

As commercial available PDA devices have memory and processing power limitation, we preferred current implementation of InfoScope system on client/server type architecture. Client side consists of a color camera (Casio JK-710DC Color

Digital Camera) attached personal digital organizer(Cassiopeia E125) which has 32M memory and 150Mz Mimp Processor, runs under Windows Pocket 3.0 OS, wireless connection through GSM modem (Nokia 8190 GSM Phone) that allows client send partial image and other information to server, and a Global Positioning system (Pharos Nav-180 GPS) that provide accurate location information. Server side consist of an IBM eServer gives the system processing power and internet connectivity as shown in Figure2. In the following sections, we describe scene text translation application in Section 2 and information augmentation system in City in Section 3. Section 4 will explained discussion and future work about infoScope.

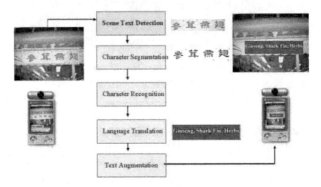

Fig. 3. System diagram of text translation application

2   Scene Text Translation for Foreign Travelers

The first application that we have developed for infoScope is an automatic sign/text translation for foreign travelers. The language is a big problem for people who are visiting foreign countries especially where the characters in this foreign language is very different than the one their own language, e.g., Japanese versus English. Even typing of these characters to language translator devices using keyboard would be a problem as the characters in foreign language is not familiar to them. We developed a prototype that people can see the scene text as they see them in their own language. InfoScope can extracting the scene text information automatically where text is a part of real world, such as, warning or information signs, price tags, advertisements on billboards, and translate it to desired language and replace the portion of the scene image with the translated text.

Color camera capture the snapshot of the real world the real world and brings it to digital world. The system integrates computer vision techniques to extract text and characters from the captured scene image, recognize the characters and words written in foreign language and convert them to ASCII text, and translate

Fig. 4. Examples of text translation and augmentation: left images shows what user sees, middle one is extracted text, right images shows final version of image that user sees on their PDA's

them in to desired language. After that, the translated text are overlaid back to location where the original foreign text are on the scene image. Therefore user can see the translated text in the same place in the image where the original one was. We implemented the system as a prototype for translating Chinese text/sign to English. In Figure 3, the system diagram of automatic text/sign translation are shown. There are five main modules which will be briefly explained following subsections: Scene text selection, character detection and segmentation, character recognition, translation and augmentation. Currently, scene text selection and augmentation is working on client side (PDA) and other module are computed at server site. Camera is used for input device, where user select sub image of scene where the text are visible, and send the selected images and information to server via wireless communication. Server does the compute-intensive image processing (segmentation, and recognition) and translating, and send the translated text back to client. Then clients augments the translated text on the image and user can see it on the same place where the original was written. Three example of text-extraction, translation and augmentation are shown in Figure 4.

Text in video appears as either *scene text* [6] or *superimpose text*. Most of the previous content based image retrieval systems has been designed to extract superimpose images which is relatively easier to detect , such as, captions, commercials, tickers in news segments, where they can be used to index in to video for searching [4,5,10]. As infoScope system is an interactive system and amount of response and processing power is very limited on PDA, user will select bounding box of the text region, then characters are extracted automatically using image enhancements and segmentation methods. Also each selected regions is going to be verified whether it contains text using edge densities.

Fig. 5. text character extraction steps: original image(a), foreground character region in different colors (b), final extracted characters with their bounding boxes and computed text lines (c)

2.1   Character Segmentation

Scene images have significant variability in color. Noise, illumination changes can cause a gradient of color levels in pixels across the same region in the characters. That makes the character segmentation difficult. Therefore, we first enhance the scene images using a stable filter, the Symmetric Neighborhood Filter (SNF) [14], which is an edge-preserving smoothing filter which performs well for both edge-sharpening and region smoothing.

After the image enhancement, we applied a hierarchical connected components(HCC) analysis on the SNF-enhanced images to segment the images in to regions where the pixel level connectivity are considered in first level of segmentation and region-level connectivity are considered in other levels. We compare the color similarities of border pixels of each adjacent regions in region-level segmentation. After hierarchical connected components, we convert the segmented images to binary black/white images where the background regions will be colored white and regions which may contain text will be colored black so that we can use that binary segmentation in character recognitions. Background regions has low edge density values and most of time they are bigger than text regions and encapsulate other regions, whereas text regions has high contrast with its background, sharp horizontal or vertical edges and shapes, close proximity with other characters in the word. Those properties of the scene texts can be easily observed in discrete wavelet transformed images. Recently, discrete wavelet transform (DWT) based techniques have become popular for indexing and image retrievals as edges and shapes of the objects can be easily estimated in DWT domain. We defined a text-similarity measure for each pixel location in scene image based on discrete wavelet coefficients. In Figure 5 (c) final background regions segmentation are shown, each character region is colored different color and background regions are colored with white.

After the character segmentations, text-line boundaries are computed in order to group the regions into text-lines so that we can send each text-line to character recognition engine. Pixels on each character regions are projected on the y-axis and histogram of the projection of each horizontal value y are computed. Each text lines appear as a peak on the horizontal projection histograms. The locations of the peaks shows the text lines. Each character regions are group together as they are in same text-lines. In our prototype, we are integrating Chinese and Japanese character recognition engines and Chinese and Japanese to English translator which has been developed by IBM China and Tokyo research Lab.

3   Information Augmentation in the City

Information Augmentation in the City is an prototype application built under infoScope that provide functionality to users that they can use their PDA's as a visual input device for interaction with real world, e.g., buildings, historical places wherever they need enhance information. Information Augmentation in the City integrates a color camera, a global positioning system (GPS), a wireless modem with a PDA to help people can get necessary information about what they are seeing around them. People can point their PDA to a building or a place where they would like information (e.g., name of the place, operation times, stores in the building) and color camera captures the scene and convert the real world scene into digital world as an color image. Then user selects the place or building by drawing a bounding box around it, then infoScope processes that sub-image to recognize which building it is using color-similarity based computer vision techniques, once it is recognized, enhanced information (e.g., name of the building, address, history) can be retrieved and augmented on the original images.

The object recognition is one of the difficult problem in computer vision and there has been many research in last four decades to come up more general object recognition algorithms. There are model-based or appearance-based object recognition techniques which works pretty well for small number of objects. Once the objects in your databases are more than hundreds or thousands, generic object recognition algorithms start producing false positives. Therefore, it is difficult to solve scene recognition using only camera based solution. To be able bring to scene recognition algorithm into solvable with current techniques, we integrated the location information (GPS) into systems, such that, if we know roughly where we are in the world, we may know which building and places are in close distance to us, hence the number of building, places around us is limited,

Fig. 6. An example of information augmentation for rental house hunting. User select the bounding box (left-top) and information will be display on the the image (righ-top). Similarity values are computed between only five candidate building in the database where their physical location is close distance to current users physical location

so we can apply one of the object recognition heuristics based on color and shape similarity to recognize the building with a high accuracy.

Most of the current available global positing devices gives location information (latitude and longitude) with in a 10-20 meter accuracy. Location information can limits the number of building that user can see at that time, in other words it limits the search space for recognition. When user select a building in the image, we do not need to search and compute the similarity between the selected building image and all the image of buildings in our database, we only need to search and compute the similarity of any building that could be visible and close proximity to the user based on location of user.

We implemented two *Information Augmentation in the City* applications. First one is similar to a city guide that helps tourist to get more information about historic places and building, while they are walking at San Francisco. We created a database which contains images of buildings, parks, and places on embarcadero street (0.5 mile) in downtown San Francisco (total 48 building and places in the database), and those places associated with information. Second application is like a realtor guide where people can get information about the building, such as, whether they are rental or a open house, rental price or selling price, age, while traveling within Powel street in San Francisco (15 building). We used appearance-based building recognition techniques based on normalized RGB color similarity with edge orientations similarities [13]. We use color distributions which is computed using $m - bin$ normalized RGB color histograms to model the building. In Figure 6, an instance of building recognition is shown, user selects the building by drawing bounding box on the image, GPS provides physical location information, system computes similarities between selected region and buildings in the database which is close distance to physical location of the user (shown bottom rows), information which is associated with the building which yield maximum similarity distance score are shown to user.

4   Discussion and Future Work

We described an information augmentation systems with two example applications which combines pervasive devices with augmented reality and computer vision techniques to provide functionality to user that they can interact real world through the camera-attached PDA's.

There has been similar research on developing augmented reality and information annotation device since 1990 [1,2,3,7,8,11,12]. We concentrated on implementing infoScope prototypes using PDAs instead of wearable computers with head mounted display because of both social and technical reasons : the social reason is that PDA's is going to be more socially acceptable them see-through head mounted display (HMD) and they are going to be widely used in near future, technological reason is that see-through HMD based solutions needs more accurate calibration and registration with display and camera as it is open-loop system where you cannot use image based registration techniques. One of the crucial problem in augmented reality research is 3D registration between real and virtual world which requires precise calibration between camera world. However, registration problem was relaxed in infoScope using computer vision techniques and user interactions as the virtual world is going to overlay on to PDA's 2D scene image which can be interpreted as a close-loop AR system where image based registration can be used. Object detection and recognition is another problem that is not easy to solve using current computer vision techniques, however, as users can interactively select the text that they want to be translated, or building that they an to know more about in infoScope system, the detection problems came to the level that we can applied current computer vision techniques to solve it. Also as we can get location information using GPS devices, the general object recognition problem became a simple image comparison problem that we applied easily color and edge based similarity methods.

We encountered two major technical problem while developing the infoScope: speed of wireless communications, processor power limitation of available PDA's. Current implementation of infoScope application requires wireless communication that it can send data to server where compute intensive image processing methods are computed. We are using GSM wireless networks which provides 9600 bps speed. On the average, sending a portion of the scene images takes around 10 sec, and as we are sending only text information back to PDA, it takes less than 1sec. Image processing computations takes less than 3 sec on the server site. Therefore, the augmented text information will be available sec later after user select the region. It is still slow for an interactive application, however when the new generation PDA which will have more than two CF slots on board is available, we will replace the GSM modem with IEEE 802.11 wireless connections or when available 3G modems that provide very fast connection so user will get information less than 5 second in future prototypes.

We tested our text/sign augmentation system where we are in Chinatown at San Francisco in which many text was written handwriting in Chinese characters (Figure 4), our system successfully works inside a Chinese store where the labels about the items and their prices was translated to English. Preliminary feedback from user was very positive when they can read them easily.

5 Acknowledgement

I would like to thanks to Jim Spohrer for his useful discussion and support.

References

1. R. Azuma, Tracking Requirements for Augmented Reality, Communications of the ACM 36 No. 7, 50-51 (July 1993). 254
2. S. Feiner, B. MacIntyre, and D. Seligmann, Knowledge-Based Augmented Reality Communications of the ACM 36 No. 7, 53-62 (July 1993). 254
3. S. Feiner, B. MacIntyre, T. Hollerer, and A. Webster, A Touring Machine: Proto-typing 3D Mobile Augmented Reality Systems for Exploring Urban Environments, Personal Technologies 1 No. 4, 208-217 (1997). 254
4. A. Jain and B. Yu Automatic Text Location in Images and Video Frames in Proc. IEEE Pattern Recognition, Vol 31, 1998 251
5. R. Lienhart Automatic text recognition for video indexing In Proc. ACM Multi-media 96, pp: 11-20. Nov, 1996 251
6. J. Ohya, A. Shio, and S. Akamatsu, Recognizing Characters in Scene Images IEEE Trans. On Pattern Analysis and Machine Intelligence, Vol 16 Feb, 1994 250
7. J. Rekimoto, NaviCam: A Magnifying Glass Approach to Augmented Reality, MIT Presence (August 1997), 254
8. J. Rekimoto, Y. Ayatsuka, and K. Hayashi, Augment-able Reality: Situated Com-munication Through Physical and Digital Spaces, Wearable Computers: The Sec-ond International Symposium on Wearable Computers, Pittsburgh, PA (October 19-20, 1998), pp. 68-75. 254
9. T. Ridler and S. Calvard Picture thresholding using an interactive selection method IEEE Transactions on Systems, Man and Cybernatics 8(8), 1978
10. J. C. Shim, C. Dorai, R. Bolle, Automatic Text Extraction from Video for Content-Based Annotation and Retrieval In. Proc. Of International Conference on Pattern Recognition, pp. 1998. 251
11. J. Spohrer, Information In Places, IBM System Journal, Vol 38, No. 4 - Pervasive computing 254
12. T. Starner, B. Schiele, and A. Pentland, Visual Contextual Awareness in Wear-able Computing, Wearable Computers: The Second International Symposium on Wearable Computers, Pittsburgh, PA (October 19-20, 1998), pp. 50-57. 254
13. M. Swain and D. Ballard, Color Indexing Interotional Journal of Computer Vision, 7(1), 1991 253
14. T. Westman, D. Harwood, T. Laitinen, and M. Pietikainen. Color Segmentation By Hierarchical Connected Components Analysis with Image Enhancement by Sym-metric Neighborhood Filters. In Proceedings of the 10th International Conference on Pattern Recognition, pages 796, June 1990. 251

At Home with Ubiquitous Computing: Seven Challenges

W. Keith Edwards and Rebecca E. Grinter

Computer Science Laboratory, Xerox Palo Alto Research Center
Palo Alto, California 94304, USA
{kedwards,grinter}@parc.xerox.com

Abstract. The smart home offers a new opportunity to augment people's lives with ubiquitous computing technology that provides increased communications, awareness, and functionality. Recently, a
number of trends have increased the likelihood that the aware home
can soon become a reality. We examine a number of challenges from
the technical, social, and pragmatic domains that we feel must be overcome before the vision of the smart home, posited by ubiquitous computing research, can become a reality. Our hope in raising these issues
is to create a conversation among researchers in the varied disciplines
that make up ubiquitous computing. In particular, we hope to raise
awareness of the existing literature on the adoption, use, and history of
domestic technologies, as well as the use of situated studies, and the
benefits that these can bring to bear on the design and evaluation of
technologies for the home

Keywords. Home, ubiquitous computing, context-awareness, domestic technologies, evaluation

1   Introduction

The notion that we could eventually live in so-called "smart homes"—domestic environments in which we are surrounded by interconnected technologies that are, more
or less, responsive to our presence and actions—seems increasing plausible. Trends
such as Moore's Law, the proliferation of networkable devices, wireless technologies,
and an increasing vendor focus on technologies for the home (perhaps arising from a
belief that the office is a technology-saturated market) are driving awareness of the
smart home idea out of academia and into mainstream thinking [5, 12]. Still, however, the most advanced glimpses of the potential future of domestic technologies can
be found in settings such as the Aware Home laboratory at Georgia Tech [10].

While initiatives such as the Aware Home can teach us about what a smart home
could provide to its "occupant-users," social and technical questions remain. In this
paper we present a number of challenges that we feel must be overcome before the
smart home concept can begin to move to reality. These challenges are based on field
studies, research in progress, and analysis of the adoption of other domestic technologies. These challenges concern not just technical direction, but also the social and

G. D. Abowd, B. Brumitt, S. A. N. Shafer (Eds.): Ubicomp 2001, LNCS 2201, pp. 256-272, 2001.
© Springer-Verlag Berlin Heidelberg 2001

ethical directions of ubiquitous computing in the home. Our purpose in this paper is two-fold. First, we hope to illuminate some implications of technical change that must be understood in order to produce domestic computing technology that is not simply ubiquitous, but also calm [28, 29]. Second, we hope to show that field studies and the existing literature on the adoption, use, and history of domestic technologies can support and influence the design and evaluation of technologies for the smart home.

2   The Seven Challenges

In this section we present the seven challenges; these challenges are based in the technical, social, and pragmatic domains. They cover problems that arise from the ways in which we expect smart homes to be deployed and inhabited; technical questions of interoperability, manageability, and reliability; social concerns about the adoption of domestic technologies and the implications of such technologies; and design issues that arise from considering just how smart the smart home must be.

2.1   Challenge One: The "Accidentally" Smart Home

Current research into domestic technologies has, for obvious reasons, taken an intentional approach to designing and building the smart home. That is, the environment has been designed from the ground up to support and evaluate technologies deployed there. Since pervasive infrastructure for ubiquitous computing does not exist in today's homes, houses must be explicitly outfitted for these sorts of technologies, and new applications must be created that are specifically written to serve as a test bed for smart home research.

However, while new homes may eventually be purpose-built for such smart applications, existing homes were not designed as such. Perhaps homeowners may decide to "upgrade" their homes to support these new technologies. But it seems more likely that new technologies will be brought piecemeal into the home; unlike the "lab houses" that serve as experiments in domestic technology today, these homes will not be custom designed from the start to accommodate and integrate these technologies. We call this phenomenon the "accidentally" smart home—a home that contains an accretion of technological components embedded in an environment that has not benefited from a holistic, ground-up approach to design and integration.

Ignoring for a moment the implications when disparate (and potentially conflicting) technology is meant to interpret and act on the behavior of its occupants[1], we can envision plausible problems with even the most mundane smart home technologies. Imagine, for example, that homeowners wake one weekend, and come downstairs looking forward to their first cup of coffee and Cartalk on NPR.[2] To their surprise, no sound emerges from their speakers. The reason is that their neighbors have purchased new Bluetooth-enabled speakers which, when first installed, associate themselves

---

[1] See challenge seven.

[2] Cartalk did not sponsor this research, it's just a very good show.

with the nearest sound source; in this case, the original homeowners' Bluetooth-enabled stereo. Meanwhile, the neighbors are abruptly awakened to tales of car repair.

This is one scenario made likely by the accidentally smart home. The general question that this scenario raises is how will the occupant-users adapt to the idea that their home has suddenly reached a level of complexity at which it becomes unpredictable. A specific question this scenario raises is how will they begin the process of making sense of what has happened. How will they begin the process of "debugging" their home to determine what has happened to their speakers?

In this simple scenario, it is precisely the wirelessness of the speakers that makes them compelling to the homeowners—the speakers can be untethered and placed exactly where they want to hear music. But it is also this same wirelessness that does away with the traditional affordances for understanding the connectivity between the speakers and the stereo (or indeed that the speakers can and should be connected to the stereo in the first place).

In particular, the homeowners may not realize that their wireless speakers can actually connect themselves to sound sources in another house as easily as to sound sources within the home. Models of connectivity are explicit when physical wires are present: the "range" of connectivity is apparent, connections are observable, and connections don't change on their own. The intangible models of connectivity that wireless technologies bring must be learned.

The general question, then, is how will occupant-users build up a model of how to control, use, and debug technologies that will interact with one another in the environment? What will the experience of the home as a whole be when these technologies are brought in gradually, and without the benefit of a top-to-bottom design? Will the occupant-users be prepared to manage their smart home when the time comes? Particularly when these complex technologies offer fewer physical affordances than we are used to?[3]

Technology positivists may say that this is "simply a design problem," and they are correct in the sense that the underlying technology itself does not dictate the behavior described here. Perhaps future models of connection will require that homeowners set a security key for all of their devices, or the vendor of the neighbors' speakers will develop a UI so intuitive and reliable that the neighbors would never make this mistake.

While this may be true, such a sidestep doesn't remove the fact that the situation described above *does* present a complex design challenge. The design challenge is to provide affordances to help users understand the technology. Consider, for example, the recent publicity given to IEEE802.11b wireless networking security failures. This technology—with industry backing and emphasis on ease of use and security—has famously provided impromptu connections to law firms, corporate offices, and development houses from passers-by in cars an on park benches [3, 18]. Here is an exam-

---

[3] While the focus in this section has been on intelligibility problems that arise when there is an accretion of interoperable technology, we believe that these problems are inherent in many of the visions of ubiquitous computing, in which technological artifacts, computational processing, and environmental sensing are made—to some degree—invisible and inaccessible to their users.

ple of a real world "design problem" much like the one described above, and which has clearly not yet been solved. Concisely, the problem is one of intelligibility in the face of radical—and perhaps unexpected—connectivity.

If we take as a given that few homes in the "real world" will ever be designed, top to bottom, as a holistic system of well-meshed, interoperable components, then a number of questions become important.

- What kinds of affordances do we need to provide to occupant-users to make the system intelligible? (e.g., Is the device recording, displaying, manipulating information about me)
- How can I tell how my devices are interacting? (e.g., What are my devices interacting with, and how do they choose?)
- What are the boundaries of my smart home? (e.g., What are the walls? How much privacy do I have?)
- What are the potential configurations of my devices? (e.g., What connects with what, what won't connect, and why?)
- How can users be made aware of the affordances of the entire home itself? (e.g., what are the possible and impossible configurations of this home?)
- Where will the locus of interaction be in a system that exists in no one place, but rather represents the sum of many interoperable (and changing) parts? (e.g., where does the UI *live*?)
- How do I control these devices, and the whole system? (e.g., Where are the controls, what visualizations of the whole system do I have?)

Current domestic technologies—with their only limited ability to connect with one another, and strong affordances of connection—do not provide good models for the smart home. Such a home will need to present its occupants with an intuitive sense of the possibilities it affords, the current state of the systems within the home, interfaces for controlling the systems in the home as a whole, and a means by which "accidents" (such as a neighbor hijacking their speakers) can be repaired or—even better—prevented in the first place. And these abilities must be provided and maintained in an environment in which new devices are added, old devices are removed, devices from different manufacturers may coexist, and wireless connectivity may extend beyond the walls of the home itself.

The challenge for homeowners with these devices will be to understand when their houses make the transition from dumb to smart and manage that transformation. The challenge for ubiquitous computing is to help homeowners understand their accidentally smart homes by providing insights into what these devices can do, what they have done, and how we control it.

2.2   Challenge Two: Impromptu Interoperability

The previous section discussed the challenge of ensuring that an environment will be intelligible when it comprises a number of components, each of which may have been acquired at different times, from different vendors, and which were created under different design constraints and considerations. And yet while this is clearly a crucially important challenge, it is predicated on the notion that such disparate components will be able to interoperate *at all*.

We believe that impromptu interoperability—not just the simple ability to interconnect, but the ability to do so with little or no advance planning or implementation—is implicit in much of the current literature of ubiquitous computing in the home. With fluid, impromptu interoperability, individual technologies have the potential to create a fabric of complementary functionality. Without it, the smart home of the future is likely to be characterized by islands of functionality, as the sets of devices that were explicitly built to recognize each other can interoperate, but other sets of devices cannot. (Such a world is likely to be one of software upgrades, version mismatches, and driver installations, which leads to our third challenge in the next section.) Such interoperability, while a challenge in its own right, increases the challenges of intelligibility as discussed in the previous section.

The chief obstacle limiting such impromptu interoperability now is that, in general, every device or software service must be explicitly written to understand *every other type* of device or software that it may encounter. If the applications on my PDA are to be able to print, then those applications (and the operating system on which it is built) must be explicitly written to understand and use the notion of a "printer"—what such a thing is, how to communicate with it, and why one would talk to it in the first place.

Without this *a priori* agreement on both syntax and semantics, interoperability is difficult if not impossible. And yet the smart home (as well as other visions of ubiquitous computing outside the home) posits the existence of a rich fabric of devices and software, somehow all seamlessly interconnecting with one another.

Must we agree on a complete set of standards for how these entities will be defined and used, known to all parties before any implementation can begin? Will we have to restrict our environments to only using devices and software that "fit" with the protocols already in place?

This challenge goes beyond mere standards. While standards for particular domains—printing, image capture, data storage—allow an entity to communicate with an entire *class* of devices or services using a standard protocol, they do not alleviate the core problem: that it is implausible to expect that all classes of devices or services will be known to all others, and that we can thus define standards for every type of device or service *a priori*. Instead, new models of connectivity are needed.

Research has begun to explore such models. Most of these models work by standardizing communication at the syntactical level (protocols and interfaces) and leaving to it a human to impose semantics. The event heap work at Stanford [9], for example, establishes a common tuple space protocol that all parties agree to implement. Particular tuples in the space may have meaning to certain parties, however, and that semantic agreement is implemented by the developer ("this tuple represents a request to scan an image," for example). The CoolTown project [16] leverages existing protocols (HTTP) and content encodings (HTML) to allow arbitrary entities that "understand" the language of the web to interact. The Speakeasy project at Xerox PARC [7] defines a set of interfaces that leverage mobile code to extend the behavior of entities in the environment; the end user provides the semantic knowledge to decide when and whether to use a particular entity.

These projects represent steps toward new models of interconnectivity, but the problem space is large and novel. Our challenge is to ensure that the future of the smart home is not one of incompatibility and isolated islands of functionality, but rather one in which occupant-users can expect the systems in their home to work together fluidly. We believe that this challenge requires radical new models of connectivity and interoperability that reach beyond simple prior agreement on standard protocols and interfaces.

2.3   Challenge Three: No Systems Administrator

As computers enter the home in greater numbers, individuals find themselves becoming systems administrators. Indeed, the average home computer user now has to concern herself with chores that would seem familiar to a mainframe systems operator from the days of the high priesthood: upgrading hardware, performing software installation and removal, and so on. The advent of always-on broadband connections and in-house networks have finally brought to our homes the few systems administration tasks that had so far eluded us: network and security administration. These are chores that are overwhelmingly complex and understood by few, even among "early adopters."[4] What will the situation be when our homes are filled by complex technological artifacts that are meant to interoperate with each other and with the outside world?

As designers of technology, we cannot plausibly expect such advanced knowledge of potential occupant-users of the smart home, if we expect anyone to actually wish to inhabit such homes. Indeed, if the lack of ability or interest in home "administration" chores as mundane as plumbing, electrical wiring, or appliance repair is any indication, there will effectively be *no* systems administrator in the smart home.

How, then, will we design technologies for the smart home that require no on-site expert? Fortunately, there are models for administration-free use of complex technologies other than general-purpose computing systems.

Traditional appliances, for example, are single-function devices that provide simple controls, straightforward affordances, and generally good ease of use (most people can use the office microwave oven without reading the instruction manual, for instance). When such a device breaks (which happens rarely), users are not expected to fix it themselves. Instead, an expert is called who comes to the house to make the repair.

There has been a move, recently, toward "appliance-centric" computing in which digital devices embody some single function [19]; we consider it an open question, however, as to how well this approach will scale, especially when such appliances are asked to interact with other sorts of devices in fluid ways (see Challenge Two).

Perhaps a more fitting model for administration in the smart home can be found in existing utilities, such as the telephone and cable television networks. In the utility model, most of the "intelligence" in the system resides in the network itself. The

---

[4] Note, for example, the recent publicity given to home computers being systematically hacked via their persistent broadband connections, a problem once confined to large companies, governments, and universities [13]. Consequently, sales of home firewalls are surging [23].

home contains only the most simple and minimal "front end" functionality needed to access the network. The telephone system is, of course, the most well-known example of this model: a simple, rotary telephone can be used to access any other telephone in the world, including cellular telephones that didn't exist at the time the rotary phone was built. This expanding functionality is available because the sophistication of the back-end network is increasing. The cable TV network, with its set-top boxes, is another example of the utility model, as are ISPs such as AOL and MSN, who bundle and preconfigure their networking software to create turnkey internet access points.

Generalizations of this model have been proposed by others as a solution for "outsourced" home administration, by organizations such as the Open Services Gateway Initiative [21].

Either of these approaches—the appliance model, or the utility model—brings with it a number of attendant technical and design challenges. In the appliance model, the challenges are largely in the design domain: how can these small devices deliver rich interactions with an ever-expanding coterie of technology in the home, without losing the simplicity that its their raison d'etre? In the utility model, how can we design technical solutions for remote diagnosis, administration, and software upgrades (in particular, with the security to prevent the kid next door from performing his own, unwarranted, remote diagnosis, administration, and upgrades)?

Regardless of the overall model chosen, occupant-users will still have some administration that they will have to do, simply because not all of the dynamics of the home can be known by the developer of the appliance, or the owner of the utility. The particular ways in which individual devices are used by members of the home, for example, may need to be reflected in configurations, security parameters, and device interactions that can only be implemented by the owners of those devices—not some external third party.

These issues of domestic technology usage form our fourth challenge.

2.4   Challenge Four: Designing for Domestic Use

The last decade has seen many studies showing how users adopt technology in surprising and unpredictable ways. Most of these have focused on office technologies, which are notably different than technologies for the home [15]. We agree with Abowd and Mynatt [2] that there is a need for studies of domestic settings to inform design. In this section we argue that studies of how the telephone and electricity were adopted in the home provide compelling evidence for further studies, and show what studies of the modern home reveal about design of technologies.

The telephone must be among the most ubiquitous technologies in the home. The study of its adoption reveals that while its inventors foresaw a social role for the phone, its initial vendors did not [8]. The telephone company did not believe that sociability was an important or appropriate use of their technology. It was not for several decades, and after the telephone was broadly adopted, that the Bell System promoted the device as a mechanism for having conversations with distant friends and family.

The adoption of the landline telephone could be viewed as a triumph of user persistence over vendor beliefs. Recently, phone adoption has received new attention because of wireless devices. Palen et al. [22] observed that individuals tend to purchase wireless phones for emergency and coordination reasons, and do not consider sociability to be important. However, within weeks of purchasing the phone these same owners used it for social calls.

The adoption of landline and wireless phones suggests that vendors and even users find it hard to foresee how they will use a technology. Electricity, another pervasive domestic technology, shows that new uses sometimes do not last. At the turn of the century, the homes of the wealthy were often outfitted with electrically-conducting rails in the floors; "electricity girls," equipped with metal shoes and wearable light fixtures, would entertain party guests by moving from room to room, carrying their own illumination [20]. Findings from these analyses reinforce the need for conducting studies of domestic settings and relying on analysis of the stable and compelling routines of the home, rather than supposition, company dictate, fad, or marketing.

Recent studies of domestic settings have taken this approach. They highlight a variety of findings, many of which stem from the fact that domestic technologies are not "owned" by an individual. Many are governed by household rules that determine: who uses what device, when, where, whether they pay, how old they are, and for what purposes.

For example, in their study of set-top box use in various homes, Hughes et al. [14] describe a relationship between technology use and space "ownership" within the home. They observed that occupants used technologies such as the television to indicate that they controlled behavior in that part of the home. They found that others knew and respected these routines. When occupants had conflicts over television use, they settled disputes by buying another television or making the current one more mobile. Finally, they observed that the television accommodates multiple usage requirements by making it possible for different occupants to watch their own programs [14]. Video and TiVo technologies make the television even more accommodating. Television and its associated technologies fit into the home by being portable and flexible to occupants' requirements.

Our study of wireless text messaging in the home shows how devices are used and shared. We found that the teenagers used text messages to arrange times to talk on the landline phone or use the computer to Instant Message [11]. Since both the phone and the computer were shared devices in their own homes and their friends' houses, teens used a technology that they individually owned to coordinate times when they all had access to those shared devices.

We also found that teenagers used "quiet" technologies such as text messaging to avoid disturbing the routines of other people. Quiet technologies do not ring or require voice interactions. Text messaging was quiet, and consequently allowed the teenagers to communicate without other household members being aware of or disturbed by the interaction. In this case text messaging meets the requirements of its users as well as those who are not using it but are sharing the same space.

In summary, smart technologies—indeed *any* technologies—will be disruptive to the home environment. Predicting these disruptions is difficult, as illustrated by the cases at the opening of this section. The challenge for designers, then, is to pay heed to the stable and compelling routines of the home, rather than external factors, including the abilities of the technology itself. These routines are subtle, complex, and ill-articulated, if they are articulated at all; thus, there is a great need for further studies of how home occupants appropriate and adapt new technologies. Only by grounding our designs in such realities of the home will we have a better chance to minimize, or at least predict, the effects of our technologies.

2.5   Challenge Five: Social Implications of Aware Home Technologies

Understanding how technologies fit into daily routines is one aspect of designing the smart home. However, technologies have other social implications that also bear examination. In this section, we describe some social implications of aware home technologies that merit discussion within this community, as well as presenting opportunities to engage other research disciplines in discourse about the future we are designing.

Abowd and Mynatt [2] have addressed the social implications of ubiquitous computing, privacy in particular. We believe this focus is very appropriate, since privacy is important. However, we believe that there are other broad social implications of domestic technologies which are not as widely explored by members of the ubiquitous computing community. Studies illustrate other potential consequences of domestic technologies, and we focus on two of these: "labor saving" and good parenting.

Some historical studies have challenged the belief of technologies as being labor saving devices. The washing machine is one of those technologies. The washing machine was pitched as a labor saving device, and even though initial models did not go through a cycle automatically or spin-dry, they did reduce the labor of wash day.

However, washing machines arrived around the same time as a host of other devices, including hot water heaters, irons, and indoor bathrooms. All of these technologies in concert changed users' expectations of "acceptable" hygiene and washing: with so many conveniences, why limit yourself to washing yourself and your clothes once a week?

While individually these devices did save labor, the combination of all of them changed the nature of work in the home. Over time, these devices changed society's expectations about what things would be done, how often, and by whom. Indeed studies of domestic technologies do not show conclusively that work was reduced; more significantly, some suggest that the amount of unpaid work in the home done by women rose dramatically [26].

The washing machine encourages us to take a critical perspective on whether smart home technologies are "labor saving" or whether they, like other devices already at home, merely shift the burden of work. Who will do that work and why?

Other studies show how technologies do not just affect occupant-users, but can become part of broader national debates. Studies of the television and mobile phone show that these devices have influenced how many parents think about "good parenting" [14, 24]. With television, good parenting discussions focus on how much and what kind of programming children may watch. This has, in the United States, led to a broader national debate about the content of television programming. Results of this discussion include a rating scheme for programs, and technologies such as the V-chip.

The mobile phone appears to be taking a similar role in Europe, particularly in countries that have high rates of mobile phone adoption among teenagers and pre-teens [24]. There, "good parenting" emphasizes two values of mobile phones. First, giving children mobiles helps them learn how to manage bills and money. Second, mobiles allow parents to safely give children increased independence.

As others have noted, smart homes have privacy implications. However, privacy is just one of several social implications of domestic technologies. In this section, we examined two other social aspects of automation in the home: how apparently labor saving devices can actually be labor changing devices, and how technologies influence societal beliefs about good parenting. There are undoubtedly others.

To summarize, there are social consequences that can arise unforeseeably when technology is placed into the home setting. These consequences cannot be reliably predicted from studies of domestic routine, since they alter these routines—and indeed the basic expectations about home life—so drastically. The classic social aspect of computing, privacy, has been explored and addressed by much prior research, from computer-supported cooperative work to ubiquitous computing. But there are other social aspects of domestic computing, as noted here, and their implications can be far reaching. The challenge for us as designers is to be aware of the broader effects of our work, and to realize that even technologies as simple as the washing machine can have broad changes on the dynamics of the home and society itself.

2.6   Challenge Six: Reliability

We can expect that a paramount concern of occupants (if not developers) of smart home technologies is reliability. The range of domestic technologies present in the home today—televisions, telephones, washing machines, microwave ovens—are, by and large, exceedingly reliable, even though these are devices of great complexity. A modern digital television set-top box, for example, contains a number of specialized microprocessors devoted to high-bandwidth decompression, cryptography, rendering, and network communications back to the service provider. And yet, these devices virtually never crash, unlike our desktop computer systems.

Achieving expected levels of reliability, especially when coupled with the ad hoc accretion of devices that may be expected in smart homes, is a great challenge. Dealing with that challenge depends on understanding the reasons that these devices are so much more reliable than "traditional" desktop software systems. Some of these reasons include:

- Differences in development culture
- Differences in technological approaches
- Differences in expectations of the market
- Differences in regulations

First, the development cultures of domestic technologies differ widely from those of desktop, general-purpose computing systems. Embedded systems developers have tended to be much more wary of systems crashes, since it is unwieldy to patch or upgrade a device in the field. A washing machine vendor, for example, would likely fold if it had to recall its products for upgrades as often as traditional software vendors issue patches.

Of course, reliable software systems do exist. These kinds of systems give us insight into how much work it may take to make reliable ubiquitous technologies for the home. Telephone switches illustrate this well; for example, Lucent Technologies

5ESS maintains its reliability goal of 99.9999% (less than 10 seconds of downtime a year) [17]. Meeting this reliability goal means that regular upgrades, such as the ones that provide occupant-users with new services, must be performed while the switch is processing other calls. In other words, this reliability requirement manifests itself within the system architecture. Other parts of the system work on monitoring events that could lead to downtime and either fixing them or reporting them as appropriate [17]. Designing for reliability requires devoting substantial time and resources that will affect the system architecture. Practices such as these must be integrated into the development cultures that will build smart home technology.

The second difference is in the technological approaches taken by domestic technology developers and those in the desktop market. In current connected domestic technologies, the bulk of functionality is placed in the *network*, not in the device itself. In the telephone system, for example, the telephone itself is the least complicated part of the system. And yet it provides access to new functionality available through the network without an upgrade or patch. Digital television systems, likewise, place the bulk of functionality in the network, rather than the client-side device. This is a "utility" approach, in which the client technologies are shielded from upgrades and enhancements in the network, and yet can take advantage of new functionality when available. It is significant to note that embedding intelligence in the network is precisely counter to many of the approaches taken by developers of Internet-based technologies, in which most intelligence resides at the edges of the network. For ubiquitous computing applications, one design challenge will be determining what kind of balance of intelligence to maintain between the edges and the center of the network.

Additionally, the technological approaches taken by designers should account for the need to degrade gracefully. By this we mean that if a component in a richly interconnected system fails it should not bring down the rest of the system. Traditionally, systems have achieved the ability to degrade gracefully through redundancy—data and services are replicated and available on multiple machines. Such an approach may, however, trade off against the goals of simplicity, intelligibility, and ease of administration, which are all requirements for domestic technologies. How to address this tension is a challenge for system designers.

A third difference is simply in the expectations of the various marketplaces. Consumers expect that their appliances will not crash (they have, unfortunately, developed a tolerance for crashes in general purpose computing systems). It is the reliability of so many technologies that has allowed the consumer to actually forget about them as complex technical entities. One hardly thinks of administering the phone or configuring the television. Instead, in large part these technologies blend into the home and become part of the fabric of the home. Crashing phones or televisions would be unwelcome in this setting.

These expectations have been vigorously reinforced by publications and organizations that exist to identify reliable technologies and uncover lemons.[5] Magazines such as *Consumer Reports* in the USA and *Which* in the UK provide information

---

[5] In the United States cars that do not provide reliably and consequently need repairs early on in their lives are known as lemons. Lemon laws exist to protect the consumer from being sold a "lemon."

about a wide variety of domestic appliances often assessing the reliability as part of their reviews. Organizations such as the Underwriters Laboratories in the USA exist to thoroughly test such technologies before they enter the home.

Fourth, and finally, there are differences in regulation. While the home, as Kidd et al [15] say, is a "free choice environment" for its occupant-users, it is a highly regulated environment for those who provide services into that space. In many Western countries the various utilities that service your home are obligated to deliver a certain level of service, or face regulatory punishments. Insurance companies may demand to see certain levels of safety (such as building upgrades, seismic retrofitting, electrical system changes, and so forth) before they will insure a home. In addition to these *de jure* regulations are *de facto* standards for the home.

All these differences have contributed to services being reliably delivered into the home. Bringing the benefits of ubiquitous computing into such environments may involve creating a development culture that can produce reliable devices consistently, making design choices about how to handle intelligence at the edges of the network robustly, meeting expectations set by other devices, and working toward regulations and standards set by a multitude of agencies. This challenge extends beyond the research community to those who develop, deliver, regulate, and consume these new services.

2.7   Challenge Seven: Inference in the Presence of Ambiguity

Systems in which machine processing is used to control or assist human behavior have a long and less-than-storied track record in the history of computer science. Examples of such systems come from domains as disparate as workflow tools that force users into formal patterns of work [27], and—more recently—Clippit, the Microsoft Office Assistant, which attempts to intuit the actions of a user and offer help.

And yet, much of the literature of ubiquitous computing depicts machine inference of human state and intent as being a crucial factor in the benefits such environments will bring. For example, the literature posits smart meeting rooms that share the notes of the participants [1], and telephone calls that follow their intended recipients throughout a building [25].

Clearly, some of these examples are dependent only on simply detecting and acting on some knowledge of the state of the world from sensor inputs, while other examples are based on a presumption that the system can correctly infer what the user would do him- or herself, if left to his or her own devices.

This begs the question: just how smart does the smart home have to be? How much inference is required for these environments to be successful? What benefits can be achieved with limited inference, or with no inference at all? In the absence of oracular artificial intelligence, how will we design such environments so that their occupants have models about what they can expect their homes to do for them, and how to fix the results of interpretations gone bad?

One constant in published visions of ubiquitous computing is that computing is employed in a physical space to bring functions to users in their everyday work, and that these systems are, to some degree at least, aware of their surroundings, and of their users [25]. The physical world is, of course, what might be termed a "highly analog" environment, presenting a great deal of ambiguity and uncertainty of input—much greater than even the domain of Clippit.

Intelligence in such a world can take a number of forms, some of which make greater assumptions than others. Some of the more obvious of these include:

- The environment can interpret the meaning of sensor data to reflect some state of the world. For example, the system might assume that I am in a room because my active badge is in a room.
- The environment can infer that some state exists by aggregating a number of other factors. For example, if a number of people are gathered together in a meeting room, the system might assume that a meeting is taking place.
- The environment may attempt to infer my intent from its view of the state of the world. For example, the system might assume that because I am in a meeting, I might want to share my meeting notes with others in the meeting.
- Finally, the system may preemptively act on assumptions of intent. For example, if the system assumes I may want to share my meeting notes, it may go ahead and make those available to other meeting participants (or ask me if it should do so).

All of these modes of intelligence can be found represented in the literature of ubiquitous computing (see [6], for a similar categorization). And all are subject to error, of varying degrees and types.

For example, the simple sensing case may report that I am present in a room when, instead, I have simply left my active badge on the desk. These are what might be called "phenomenological" problems—do sensors reflect reality or merely the state of the sensors—and can, in all likelihood, be largely overcome by more and better sensor technology (although perhaps at a cost of privacy and user control). And—perhaps more importantly—the cost of incorrect inferences is low if the system does little with the inferred information.

More dramatic problems become apparent as uncertain inferences and decisions are compounded. Most troubling is the attempt at inferring some internal human intent and then, perhaps, taking action on it, especially when such an inference is based on layers of ambiguous interpretation and input, or requires a level of intelligence that even humans would find difficult.

Our challenge, then, is to discern what functions of the smart home are possible with limited inference, which are possible only through inference, and which require an oracle. The first category comprises good candidates for implementation, since limited machine interpretation means that there is limited possibility of error. The third category, systems that require omniscient understanding of human intent in order to function well, are perhaps better abandoned.

The middle category, we feel, is the most interesting, and presents important problems in design and technology. Systems that rely on inference will never be right all of the time, and thus users will necessarily have to have models of how the system arrives at its conclusions. These models must not only concern themselves with the actual rules of inference ("when people gather in the living room, display the television schedule"), but also the capabilities of the system's sensors ("how does the system know I'm in the living room in the first place?").

Users must know what to expect from their homes in the same way that, say, a user knows that dropping temperature outside will cause the thermostat to turn on the heating [4]. Such predictability depends on:

- The system's expected behavior in the face of this condition is known.
- The system's facilities for detecting or inferring this condition are known.
- Provision is made for the user to override the system's behavior.

Achieving these three conditions is more complicated when the inferences made by the system are more complex, and when even basic sensing is unreliable or open to interpretation.

The challenge for smart home designers is to create systems that ensure that users understand the pragmatics of sensors, interpretation, and machine action as well as they understand the pragmatics of devices in their homes now. From a technical perspective, the challenge of developers is to ensure that ambiguity is not hidden from the parts of the system (or the users) that need access to it, and to ensure that inference—when performed at all—is done in a way that is predictable, intelligible, and recoverable.

3   Discussion

In this paper, we have presented seven challenges for ubiquitous computing research in the home setting. Although we have divided these challenges for the purposes of discussion, there are clearly interesting connections and overlap among them.

First, there are a number of problems that arise that are unique to the smart home setting itself. Existing houses were not designed to be smart, and office technologies are often intended to be just that—technologies for the office rather than the home. The realities of the home setting, coupled with the fact that adoption of home technologies is likely to be incremental and disjoint for the foreseeable future, give rise to our first and fourth challenges.

Second, we believe that there are a host of technical, implementation, and systems design issues that are often underestimated. Further (and perhaps more importantly) the *tradeoffs* among these issues are not well understood in the home setting. The stringent requirements for reliability, the fact that there will be no formal systems administrator (nor will most homeowners be likely to want to undertake such a role), and the desire for interoperability all trade off against each other. For example, it is relatively easy to make an easily administered and reliable device if that device never needs to communicate with or use any other services in the home. We believe that finding the right balance between these requirements is crucial.

Third, and as always, the social impact of new technologies is hard to predict. The home setting is not novel in this respect, although the social dynamics and relationships within the home make it perhaps a more volatile setting than the office or other public spaces.

Finally, we believe that an overarching philosophical question that should be addressed by designers of smart home technology is, simply, how smart does the smart home have to be to provide utility to its occupant-owners? To some degree, this question permeates all of the others we have raised, since it is precisely the "smartness" of the smart home that makes it disruptive to the domestic order, gives rise to the architectural and implementation tradeoffs mentioned above, and makes the social adoption of this technology so unpredictable.

We believe that the chief challenge that will be faced by the designers (and, potentially, the occupants) of the smart home is balancing the desire for innovative technological capabilities with the desire for a domestic lifestyle that is easy, calming, and—at lease in terms of technology—predictable.

4   Conclusions

This paper has presented seven challenges that we believe must be successfully addressed for the smart home to be a viable place to live. These challenges span across technical, social, and pragmatic domains.

Our hope in raising these issues is to create a conversation among researchers in the varied disciplines that make up ubiquitous computing. In particular, we hope to raise awareness of the existing literature on the adoption, use, and history of domestic technologies, as well as the use of situated studies, and the benefits that these can bring to bear on the design and evaluation of technologies for the home.

Acknowledgements

We would like to thank our PARC colleagues who challenge us to think more clearly about the challenges confronting ubiquitous computing. Special thanks to Diana Smetters for the wireless speakers example.

References

1. Abowd, G.D.: Classroom 2000: An Experiment with the Instrumentation of a Living Educational Environment. IBM Systems Journal, 38 (4). (1999) 508-530
2. Abowd, G.D.,Mynatt, E.D.: Charting Past, Present, and Future Research in Ubiquitous Computing. ACM Transactions on Computer-Human Interaction, 7 (1). (2000) 29-58
3. Arbaugh, W.A., Shankar, N.,Wan, Y.C.J.: Your 802.11b Wireless Network has No Clothes. University of Maryland, Department of Computer Science (Technical Report). (2001)
4. Bellotti, V.,Edwards, W.K.: Intelligibility and Accountability: Human Considerations in Context Aware Systems. to appear in Human Computer Interaction, 16. (2001)
5. Buderi, R.: Computing Goes Everywhere. Technology Review, Jan/Feb. (2001) 53-59
6. Dey, A.K.: Understanding and Using Context. to appear in Personal and Ubiquitous Computing, 5 (1). (2001)
7. Edwards, W.K., Newman, M.,Sedivy, J.Z.: The Case for Recombinant Networking. Xerox PARC Technical Report (2001)

8. Fischer, C.S.: America Calling: A Social History of the Telephone to 1940. University of California Press, Berkeley, CA (1992)
9. Fox, A., Johanson, B., Hanrahan, P.,Winograd, T.: Integrating Information Appliances into an Interactive Workspace. IEEE Computer Graphics & Applications, 20 (3). (2000) 54-65
10. Georgia Institute of Technology.: Aware Home Research Initiative. http://www.cc.gatech.edu/fce/ahri/.
11. Grinter, R.E.,Eldridge, M.: y do tngrs luv 2 txt msg? In Proceedings of the Ninth European Conference on Computer-Supported Cooperative Work ECSCW '01. Bonn, Germany, Dordrecht, Netherlands: Kluwer Academic Publishers, (2001)
12. Hales, L.: Blobs, Pods and People. The Wall Street Journal, Sunday March 25. (2001) W34
13. Harvey, D.: Broadband Security: Who's Responsible? Home Office Computing Magazine, August. (2000)
14. Hughes, J., O'Brien, J.,Rodden, T.: Understanding Technology in Domestic Environments: Lessons for Cooperative Buildings. In Proceedings of the First International Workshop on Cooperative Buildings (CoBuild'98). Darmstadt, Germany, Heidelberg, Germany: Springer-Verlag, (1998), 248-261
15. Kidd, C., Orr, R.J., Abowd, G.D., Atkeson, C.G., Essa, I.A., MacIntyre, B., Mynatt, E.D., Starner, T.E.,Newstetter, W.: The Aware Home: A Living Laboratory for Ubiquitous Computing Research. In Proceedings of the Second International Workshop on Cooperative Buildings (CoBuild'99). Pittsburgh, PA, Heidelberg, Germany: Springer-Verlag, (1999)
16. Kindberg, T.,Barton, J.: A Web-Based Nomadic Computing System. HP Labs Technical Report HPL-2000-110, http://cooltown.hp.com/papers/nomadic/nomadic.htm. (2000)
17. Lucent Technologies.: Press Announcement: 5ESS Reliability. http://www.lucent.com/press/0699/990602.nsb.html.
18. Markoff, J.: Flaw in Popular Wireless Standard. New York TImes, http://www.nytimes.com/2001/04/03/business/03FLAW.html.
19. Norman, D.A.: Invisible Computer: Why Good Products Can Fail, the Personal Computer is so Complex and Information Appliances are the Solution. MIT Press, Cambridge, MA (1999)
20. Nye, D.E.: Electrifying America: Social Meanings of a New Technology. MIT Press, Cambridge, MA (1990)
21. OSGi: Open Services Gateway Initiative. http://www.osgi.org/.
22. Palen, L., Salzman, M.,Youngs, E.: Going Wireless: Behavior and Practice of New Mobile Phone Users. In Proceedings of the ACM Conference on Computer Supported Cooperative Work (CSCW 2000). Philadelphia, PA, New York, N.Y.: ACM Press, (2000), 201-210
23. Race, T.: Adding Firewalls to Home PCs. The New York Times, March (12). (2001)
24. Rautiainen, P.,Kasesniemi, E.-L.: Mobile communication of children and teenagers: case Finland 1997-2000. In Proceedings of the Workahop on "The social consequences of mobile telephony: the proceedings from a seminar about society, mobile telephony and children". Oslo, Norway, (2000)

25. Schilit, B.N., Adams, N.I.,Want, R.: Context-Aware Computing Applications. In Proceedings of the Workshop on Mobile Computing Systems and Applications. Santa Cruz, CA, IEEE Computer Society, (1994), 85-90
26. Schwartz Cowan, R.: More Work for Mother: The Ironies of Household Technology from the Open Hearth to the Microwave. Basic Books, Inc., New York, NY (1983)
27. Suchman, L.: Speech Acts and Voices: A Response to Winograd et al. Computer Supported Cooperative Work: An International Journal, 3 (1). (1995) 85-95
28. Weiser, M.: The Computer for the Twenty-First Century. Scientific American. (1991) 94-104
29. Weiser, M.,Brown, J.S.: Designing Calm Technology. PowerGrid Journal, 1 (1). (1996) http://powergrid.electriciti.com/1.01

Privacy by Design – Principles of Privacy-Aware Ubiquitous Systems

Marc Langheinrich

Distributed Systems Group, Institute of Information Systems, IFW
Swiss Federal Institute of Technology, ETH Zurich
8092 Zurich, Switzerland
www.inf.ethz.ch/~langhein/

Abstract. This paper tries to serve as an introductory reading to privacy issues in the field of ubiquitous computing. It develops six principles for guiding system design, based on a set of fair information practices common in most privacy legislation in use today: notice, choice and consent, proximity and locality, anonymity and pseudonymity, security, and access and recourse. A brief look at the history of privacy protection, its legal status, and its expected utility is provided as a background.

1 Introduction

Privacy has been a hot-button topic for some time now. But so far its impact on a field where its relevancy is obviously high - ubiquitous computing - has been rather minimal. An increasing number of research projects are under way in the field of Internet privacy [6,16,18], some work has already been done in the field of Computer Supported Collaborative Work [5,21], but only a small amount of work has so far been accomplished in the area of ubiquitous or pervasive computing.

While some ubiquitous computing research projects explicitly address privacy [2,12], so far solutions in the field have been ad-hoc and specific to the systems at hand. One reason is surely the fact that ubiquitous computing is still in its infancy, with only a few dozen research groups around the world developing comprehensive systems. But it is also the privacy topic itself that is elusive: typically situated in the realms of legal studies, computer scientist have a hard time approaching a subject that is more often a social, even ethical issue.

This article tries to serve as an introductory reading for the interested computer science researcher, especially in the field of ubiquitous computing. It gives a brief background on privacy - its history and the issues surrounding it, touches on various legal implications, and tries to develop a comprehensive set of guidelines for designing privacy-aware ubiquitous systems.

2 Privacy

Instead of trying to give yet another definition for something for which "no definition ... is possible, because [those] issues are fundamentally matters of

G. D. Abowd, B. Brumitt, S. A. N. Shafer (Eds.): Ubicomp 2001, LNCS 2201, pp. 273–291, 2001.

values, interests, and power" [15], the following tries to look at privacy from three angles: its history, its legal status, and its utility.

Discussions about privacy have a long history, and various historical changes have brought about a change in perspective of our privacy needs. Consequently, much of this discussion has been incorporated into various regulatory and legal frameworks around the world, each with various effects. Last but not least, recent developments in technology have sparked a discussion about the necessity of strict privacy protection, which might not only be infeasible to administer, but also inconvenient to live with.

2.1 A Brief History

Privacy has been on people's mind as early as the 19th century, when Samuel Warren and Louis Brandeis wrote the influential paper "The Right to Privacy" [25], motivated largely by the advent of modern photography and the printing press. While Brandeis defined privacy as "the right to be let alone" (arguing against nosy reporters who would take pictures of people without permission – previously one had to sit still for a substantial amount of time, otherwise the picture would be all blurred), most people nowadays think of it more as "the right to select what personal information about me is known to what people" [26].

Privacy became a hot issue once again in the 1960s when governments discovered automated data processing as an effective means to catalog its citizens. Remembering the Nazi exploitation of detailed public records in World War II (allowing them to easily find the Jewish population of any city they raided), many European nations passed various "data-protection" laws in order to prevent any misuse of such centrally stored information. Lately, the increased use of credit cards, and last not least the dawn of the Internet, have made privacy protection a hot-button topic once again.

Over the course of time, the primary focus of privacy has shifted according to technological developments. Privacy issues can be traced as far back as 1361, when the Justices of the Peace Act in England provided for the arrest of peeping toms and eavesdroppers, establishing the first notion of behavioral, or *media privacy* [20]. In the 18th century, English parliamentarian William Pitt wrote, "The poorest man may in his cottage bid defiance to all the force of the Crown. It may be frail; its roof may shake; the wind may blow though it; the storms may enter; the rain may enter – but the King of England cannot enter; all his forces dare not cross the threshold of the ruined tenement" [27]. This form of privacy is often referred to as *territorial privacy*. With the increased use of the telephone system in the 1930s, *communication privacy* received much attention with the case of Olmstead vs. United States in 1928, which questioned the legality of wiretapping by the United States government. The privacy of the person, often called *bodily privacy*, was seriously violated only a few years later, when Nazi leadership decided to conduct compulsory sterilization, as well as gruesome medical experiments, on parts of the non-Aryan population. The increased use of governmental electronic data processing in the 1960s and 1970s finally created the issue of *information privacy*.

While the first four aspects of privacy have by now been very well established in most legal frameworks around the world, often directly defined as constitutional rights, it is information privacy that creates most of the troubles today. Even though laws covering information privacy have been around for more than 30 years, the rapid progress in technology, most recently the commercial success of the World Wide Web, continuously challenges legislation that has been initially devised in a time of room-sized mainframes and punch cards. The next section looks at two of the more influential pieces of privacy legislation – the US Privacy Act of 1974 and the EU Directive 95/46/EC of 1995 – and how they can influence the design of data processing systems such as ubiquitous devices and their infrastructure.

2.2   Legal Issues

While it was the small German state of Hesse that actually passed the world's first data protection law in 1970, one of the most influential pieces of early privacy legislation was the US Privacy Act of 1974. In defining the principles, the appointed governmental advisory committee created the notion of *fair information practices*, a significant policy development that influenced privacy policies worldwide. The principles of fair information practices, which in turn are based on work by Columbia University political economist Alan Westin, are basically as follows:

1. **Openness and transparency:** There should be no secret record keeping. This includes both the publication of the existence of such collections, as well as their contents.
2. **Individual participation:** The subject of a record should be able to see and correct the record.
3. **Collection limitation:** Data collection should be proportional and not excessive compared to the purpose of the collection.
4. **Data quality:** Data should be relevant to the purposes for which they are collected and should be kept up to date.
5. **Use limitation:** Data should only be used for their specific purpose by authorized personnel.
6. **Reasonable security:** Adequate security safeguards should be put in place, according to the sensitivity of the data collected.
7. **Accountability:** Record keepers must be accountable for compliance with the other principles.

Even though its principles of fair information practices were incorporated into all major pieces of privacy legislation worldwide, the Privacy Act of 1974 was no success at home [15]. In 1980, the Organization for Economic Co-operation and Development (OECD) codified the fair information practices in the OECD Guidelines [22] in order to prevent a proliferation of varied privacy protection laws that might harm economic growth by creating accidental trade-barriers.

While European countries continued to develop and refine omnibus protection acts covering both governmental and private data collection, US legislation followed up with a patchwork of sectorial laws that only addressed very specific needs as they arose (e.g., the Fair Credit Reporting Act of 1970, Video Privacy Protection Act of 1988, Family Education Rights and Privacy Act of 1994).

It took until 1995 before a similar influential piece of legislation would be passed again, this time in Europe. The European Union's *Directive 95/46/EC on the protection of individuals with regard to the processing of personal data and on the free movement of such data* [14], often called "The Directive" for short, is for privacy legislation of the ending 20th century what the Privacy Act of 1974 was for the early privacy laws.

The Directive's main impact is two-fold. Firstly, its article 24/1 limits data transfers to non-EU countries only to those with "an adequate level of privacy protection." The lingering threat of being cut off from European data flows has prompted more than a dozen countries worldwide to revise their privacy legislation in order to comply with the provisions of the directive (in case of the US this resulted in a much debated self-certification framework called the Safe Harbor Principles [24] – more on this below).

Secondly, the Directive not only subsumes and refines the fair information practices described above, but its article 7 adds the notion of *explicit consent*: Personal data may only be processed if the user has unambiguously given his or her consent (exceptions are made for legal and contractual purposes). This practically disallows all types of data collection (except for when required by law) and requires a case-by-case explicit consent by the data subject.

As much as computing professionals would like to ignore legal issues when designing computer systems and only concentrate on the actual technical possibilities, the enactment of the Directive in 1998 created a milestone for privacy protection too large to ignore. While not all of the 15 EU member states have finalized their respective national legislation that will actually serve as an implementation of the Directive yet (the Directive only serves as a framework to create a common ground across legislation in all of its member states), its revised data protection requirements have long become a reality both within Europe and for countries doing business with Europe.

Already the e-commerce sector has begun pondering the implication of such legislation, and both new technology and regulation has been drawn up to support enactment of the Directive outside of Europe. The *Safe Harbor* agreement between the US and the European Commission serves as an experiment in self-regulation: in order to receive the designation "provides adequate level of privacy protection," companies willing to continue doing business with Europe need to self-certify adherence to a set of voluntary guidelines compatible with the spirit of the Directive, whose compliance will be overseen by the the Department of Commerce.

The effectiveness of this approach remains to be seen. US privacy advocates resent the Safe Harbor agreement in favor of a comprehensive, European-style privacy legislation for the private sector, while US companies itself are only slow to sign up for it: As of April 2001, only 30 companies have self-certified themselves to be in compliance with the agreement, the only major one being Hewlett-Packard [24].

No matter how well or quickly transnational agreements like Safe Harbor will get adopted: the Directive represents a new turn in the history of privacy legislation, both stressing the relevance of privacy protection in the age of digital data processing, and the importance of international cooperation in order to achieve it.

2.3   Does Privacy Matter?

"You already have zero-privacy anyway, get over it." This citation from Sun CEO Scott McNealy summarizes an increasingly common attitude toward privacy, as technology more and more allows comprehensive digital dossiers about every single person to be compiled and queried in real time. While never before in history the average citizen has been more concerned with his or her personal privacy (as many public polls worldwide [8,11,17] repeatedly indicate), critics such as Amitai Etzioni, University professor at George Washington University, and Peter Cochrane, former head of Advanced Research and Technology at British Telecom Laboratories, argue that – more often than not – life is actually better without privacy.

Cochran [9] argues both from a technological and from an utilitarian point of view: "We have never enjoyed total anonymity in the past world of paper, so why should we expect it to be remotely possible in a world of bits?" Not only might it be infeasible to put into effect most of the well intended privacy legislation, it might actually do more harm than good: "Should I be knocked unconscious in a road traffic accident in New York – please let the ambulance have my medical record."

Etzioni [13] extends this argument for the better of society: If the FBI is able to decipher secret email messages, it can better prevent terrorists from planning their operations. If newborns are tested for HIV, immediate treatment can significantly increase their life expectancy while revealing information about their parents that those would rather avoid. With this approach, Etzioni is more in line with a traditional European perspective, one that puts much more trust in its governments than the US-American culture: Given sufficient democratic safeguards, governmental control benefits all citizens, as their representatives know what is good for society and will not abuse their powers.

Brin [7] has much of the same intent as Etzioni, but approaches it from a different, more traditional US perspective which distrusts government agencies, law enforcement, and big corporations per default. Brin argues that we can choose to make the increased surveillance of public places and buildings a setting for greater freedom. If not only a few powerful entities control such information, but if it is shared among all of us, everyone will be watching each other and thus have nothing to fear. He, too, suggests that surveillance technology could become a public resource to assure our safety and that of our children.

The issues raised by the authors above and their colleagues are as follows:

- **Feasibility:** what can technology achieve (or better: prevent)? All laws and legislation require enforceability. If privacy violations are not traceable, the much stressed point of accountability (as developed in the fair information practices) becomes moot.
- **Convenience:** the advantages of free flow of information outweighs the personal risks in most cases. Only highly sensitive information, like sexual orientation, religion, etc might be worth protecting. Semi-public information like shopping habits, preferences, contact information, even health information, might better be publicly known so that I can enjoy the best service and protection possible.
- **Communitarian:** personal privacy needs to be curbed for the greater good of society (trusting the government). Democratic societies may choose to appoint trusted entities to oversee certain private matters in order to improve life for the majority.
- **Egalitarian:** if everybody has access to the same information, it ceases to be a weapon in the hands of a few well-informed. Only when the watchers are being watched, all information they hold about me is equally worth the information I hold about them. Eventually, new forms of social interaction will evolve that are built upon these symmetrical information assets.

The answer probably lies, as it does so often, somewhere in the middle. Clearly it won't be possible to provide a fail-safe, comprehensive privacy protection that can't be subverted. Clearly one has to balance privacy practices and goals with the convenience or inconvenience associated with them – if people need to go to great length to protect their privacy, they won't. Clearly there have been and there will be greater communitarian goods that should allow trusted entities to selectively curb some of our privacy – if they are properly overseen by independent organizations such as data protection commissioners common in Europe and many Commonwealth nations. And clearly society will and has to change, given the large changes that technology brings about – new forms of social interactions and ethics will evolve that will make things socially acceptable that haven't been so in the past.

What is important is to realize that all this still leaves much to be done in the field of privacy protection: Just where are the borders of technical feasibility when it comes to protecting our personal information? Just how much of our personal data should we be allowed to give up for the sake of convenience before society (or government, in most cases) steps in and prevents us from selling our soul? How are we to weight the greater good of society against our personal protection, and whom are we trusting with such sensitive issues? And last not least: how can we influence what will and what will not constitute acceptable social behavior in the future by designing our systems in a certain way that supports such behavior?

We will touch upon some of these critique in the Guidelines and Principles section further below, when we explore the design space for privacy-respecting ubiquitous systems. But first it might be in order to revisit the field of ubiquitous computing itself and examine it more closely in the light of the above-mentioned privacy issues: Why does work in the field of ubiquitous computing command a heightened awareness for privacy issues? What differences in our lives will an ubiquitous environment make, and how can we extrapolate from these changes on how future privacy codes must be implemented and used, given the existing ones?

3   Social Implications of Ubiquitous Computing

What is it that makes ubiquitous computing any different from other computer science domains with respect to privacy? Why should computer scientists in this particular domain be any more concerned with such vague notions of liberty, freedom, and privacy? Four properties come to mind:

- **Ubiquity:** Ubiquitous computing is everywhere – this is its essence, its explicit goal. Consequently, decisions made in ubiquitous system and artifact design will affect large, if not every part of our lives, from crossing a street to sitting in the living room to entering an office building.
- **Invisibility:** Not only should computers be everywhere, we want them to actually disappear from our views. With the ever shrinking form factor of computing and communication devices, this goal seems far from being science fiction. Naturally, we will going to have a hard time in the future deciding at what times we are interacting with (or are under surveillance by) a computing or communication device.
- **Sensing:** As computing technology shrinks and processing power increases, so does the abilities of sensors to accurately perceive certain aspects of the environment. Simple temperature, light, or noise sensors have been around for quite some time, but next generation sensors will allow high quality audio and video feeds from cameras and microphones smaller than buttons. Even emotional aspects of our lives, such as stress, fear, or excitement, could then be sensed with high accuracy by sensors embedded in our clothings or in our environment.
- **Memory amplification:** Advancements in speech and video processing, combined with the enhanced sensory equipment available soon, make it actually feasible to perceive memory prosthesis, or amplifiers, which can continuously and unobtrusively record every action, utterance and movement of ourselves and our surroundings, feeding them into a sophisticated back-end system that uses video and speech processing to allow us browsing and searching through our past.

Database technology and (much later) the Internet already gave both researchers and implementers a taste of the social responsibility these systems entail. Lessig argues in [19] that technical decisions made during the design of any computer system, for example the TCP protocol, in effect constitute legal implications of what is and what is not possible to enforce or conduct in such a system. With the tremendous growth and ubiquity of the World Wide Web, computer technology affects far more than the rather small elite of techno-savvy academics, but reaches out to senior citizens and entire families as well.

Ubiquitous computing, with its far reaching implications described above, will take this entanglement of computer technology and society at large one step further (probably only the last step before we begin implanting computational devices into our body our even our consciousness). With a densely populated world of smart and intelligent but invisible communication and computation devices, no single part of our lives will per default be able to seclude itself from digitization. Everything we say, do, or even feel, could be digitized, stored, and retrieved anytime later. We may not (yet) be able to tap into our thoughts, but all other recording capabilities might make more than up for that lack of data.

In a sense, this might sound very familiar to those in the field of Artificial Intelligence, who have for almost half a century not only improved learning algorithms and devised ontologies, but also pondered the philosophical and social implications of thinking machines. Ubiquitous computing, in comparison, seems to come in low and fast under the radar screen: Most of its immediate applications sound far too mundane to excite the imagination of popular fiction authors in a way artificial intelligence has done. Philosophers and sociologists are not yet aware of the seemingly endless advances that processing power, storage systems, sensors, material science and miniaturization will offer us in the not too distant future. And legal scholars are still trying to make sense of the implications that todays or even yesterdays technologies such as border less hypertext (i.e., the World Wide Web) has brought upon national legislation created 20-30 years ago.

With only few people outside of the field being aware of the tremendous changes ahead, it falls upon ourselves to contemplate the effects of our doing. We cannot rely on lawmakers and sociologists to be fully aware of the vast possibilities and implications that the technology so obviously presents to us. It is us who need to understand the potential and danger of our advancements, and develop sound conventions and guidelines according to well-established principles that will help us drive technology into a responsible and socially acceptable direction.

4   Principles and Guidelines

Before we set out drawing up our guiding principles, we must focus on what exactly we are trying to accomplish, especially given the substantial critique set forth in section 2.3.

In particular, this means that we are *not* trying to achieve total security, let alone total privacy. Undoubtedly, professional surveillance by spies and private investigators will continue to happen, just as it has happened in the past. New technologies may be found that will be able to (partially) sniff out such surveillance devices. Eventually, better surveillance methods will counter this advantage again. The fact that there have been and always will be a few rotten apples will not spoil the whole batch of technical possibilities ahead for us.

What we can and will be able to achieve is prevent unwanted accidents – data spills of highly personal information that people who have never asked for it suddenly find at their doorstep. What we can do is allow people who *want* to respect our privacy to behave in such a way, so that we will eventually be able to build a long lasting relationship based on mutual trust and respect. And what should also be within our reach is achieving a good balance of convenience and control when interacting with ubiquitous, invisible devices and infrastructures.

Following the fair information practices and their recent enhancements through the enactment of the European Directive, we can identify seven main areas of innovation and system design that future research in ubiquitous computing will need to focus on. The next sections will elaborate each of the concepts in the order of both technical feasibility and relevance, ranging from the fundamental notion of notice and consent to the more general non-technical practices such as data minimization and use limitation.

4.1 Notice

The most fundamental principle of any data collection system (and ubiquitous systems will, in some respect, play such a role) is the Principle of Openness, or simply Notice. In most legal systems today no single data collection – be it a simple id tracking activity or a full fledged audio visual recording – can go unnoticed of the subject that is being monitored (that is, as long as the subject can be personally identified).

Again, ubiquitous devices will per definition be ideally suited for covert operation and illegal surveillance, no matter how much disclosure protocols are being developed. It will always take special detection equipment to be reasonably sure that a certain room or area is not being overheard by others. But openness goes a long way when we want to prevent the mass-market "smart" coffee cup to turn *inadvertently* into a spy-tool par excellance! Imagine the casual user of a memory-amplifier-coffee-cup accidentally leaving her cup in her colleagues office – only to find in the evening that her colleague has spent most of the day gossiping about her, completely unaware of the spying coffee cup. Even though such accidental recordings for the most part cannot be upheld in courts, the damage is done and the social implications far outweigh the legal ones under such circumstances.

What would be helpful is some kind of announcement system, very much like a radio traffic announcement system, where car stereos will interrupt the playing of a CD or tape if an important traffic announcement comes up. Other analogies would be the `robots.txt` file on World Wide Web servers which allows Web robots to check for the "house rules" before excessively traversing a site, or the well-known emergency frequencies for radio communications that are reserved and constantly monitored for emergency communications. All these examples have in common the notion of a well-known mechanism, a well-known location for the publication of information. Clients interested in this particular information do not need to spend time and energy on searching for it, they can readily access it should such information be available (given that they know about the well-known location for publishing it).

Depending on the type of device, different announcement mechanisms would need to be found. Constant radio broadcasts, for example, would rapidly drain battery of small mobile devices, while it would be perfectly acceptable for rooms and buildings to ceaselessly announce such information. RFID tags could be used to passively announce data collection without using any batteries at all. The restricted storage size of such labels could be enhanced by outsourcing such information to a publicly available Web site and linking to it by merely placing its URI on the label.

As to what the format of such an announcement would be, a similar initiative for Internet Privacy has already covered a lot of ground in this area: The *Platform for Privacy Preferences* project, or P3P for short, has been developed at the World Wide Web Consortium (W3C) by a working group with representatives from industry, privacy advocate groups and universities [10]. P3P allows Web sites to describe their data collection practices in a machine readable way, which can then be read and displayed by P3P-enabled browser software. Users can configure their browsers to accept or reject certain types of policies (i.e., "reject any privacy policy that uses my home address for marketing purposes") and thus automate the nowadays tedious process of judging the acceptability of a sites practices.

Obviously, power consumption and connectivity problems in the field of ubiquitous computing will make it difficult to directly reuse results from Internet research projects. However, the main merit of this work lies in the carefully crafted privacy policy vocabulary: using XML as the encoding format, more than a dozen elements allow Web sites to accurately describe the data they collect, the purpose for doing so, the recipients of the data, their retention, and any dispute mechanisms they have in place in order to deal with customer complaints. The difficulties of coming to a consensus for a vocabulary that is acceptable to both privacy advocates and industrial marketers alike probably accounts for much of the 3 years this project has taken. It is currently in its final phase and already a number of both Web sites and software developers have begun incorporating the protocol into their systems.

Using a declaration format like P3P and announcing it via one or more well-known mechanisms would form the bottom line for any privacy-aware ubiquitous system. Depending on the actual setup of the system, a single announcement might cover a multitude of devices. For example, an office building might make such an announcement for all of the devices that are installed inside, whenever someone enters through its front doors. Rooms in the building might repeatedly reference this main declaration for all sensors or devices the room is equipped with. A wearable system, on the other hand, might be represented by single declaration from its owner's cell phone. Single, autonomous devices that can be operated independently of such central services would require their own announcement capabilities. For example, a future coffee cup with a sophisticated memo function would need to be able to announce its data collection practices even in the absence of any central unit the holder might wear (as long as the cup would actually collect any data without such a central unit).

Not every single device would need to be identified in such an announcement. The goal is to exhaustively enumerate all *types* of data collected, not the individual devices doing so. It does not really matter how many sensors record audio data in a certain room - the fact that audio recording is done at all is the important information. Collation is always possible, and overstating the actual data collection perfectly legal. An office building could collectively declare that audio recording is done in all of its room, even if not all of them actually had sensors equipped. It is up to the owner of the device or system to decide if such overstatement is in her best interest. Of course, certain practices might not be legal in most countries, which place severe restrictions on surveillance such as wiretapping or video recording (see more about that in the use limitation section below).

4.2   Choice and Consent

With the enactment of the EU Directive that refined and extended the well-known fair information practices, it is not enough anymore to simply *announce* and *declare* data collection - it also requires collectors to receive *explicit consent* from the data subject. The Directive thus effectively prohibits any collection and usage of personal information, except for certain legal procedures (law enforcement, public health, etc) or when explicitly consented by the individual.

The most common form of explicit consent nowadays is still the written contract. By showing the signature of the data subject under a corresponding piece of text, collectors can in most cases effectively demonstrate that they have received the explicit consent of the subject. In the world of electronic transactions, however, explicit consent is not that easy to come by.

Even though digital signatures based on public-key cryptography are a well established concept, the actual usage of such signatures is still in its infancy. So far, no public-key-infrastructure (PKI) has actually achieved widespread usage, which makes the actual verification of signatures, as well as their revocation, difficult.

But it is not only a question of authenticity that makes digital signatures hard to use, it is also the requirement of explicitness: A certain statement may very well be signed with the secret key of a certain individual, but had the individual actually any knowledge of signing that particular statement, or was it her personal software agent that handled the task in the background, without the user's knowledge?

In electronic commerce, such explicit consent is often achieved by requiring the press of a button to initiate data transfer. In a ubiquitous computing setting, a press of a button might not only be physically impossible (because none of the devices present support a tactile interface), it might also be unusable: With hundreds of devices from a multitude of collectors constantly querying my information as I walk down a busy street, pressing the OK button on my cell phone every time I want to authorize transfer will surely annoy even the most patient person.

Another often overlooked problem the notion of consent poses to system design is the requirement of choices: With only one option available, getting consent comes dangerously close to blackmailing. Imagine that in order to enter a public building, you must agree to completely unacceptable practices. Certainly you could always walk away from such a deal, but can you really? (Some might argue that this is no different from most supermarkets today, which already feature a comprehensive video surveillance system. In most legal systems, such surveillance is possible under very restrictive guidelines that place restrictions on purpose, use, and retention of such video feeds.)

In order to make consent a viable option, more than the "take it or leave it" dualism must be offered. Office buildings could offer me to track my position within the building in order to offer customized navigational services. If I choose to decline, it must be possible to selectively disable the tracking functionality without either shutting down the whole system for all other visitors, or me not entering the building.

Advancements in audio and video processing might make such choices available for selective recordings: Instead of requiring all participants of a meeting to consent to a comprehensive audio or video recording, the system could only track those who agree to the recording, while the voices of all others will be muted, their picture on videos anonymized. A simple solution along similar lines was used in the Classroom 2000 project at Georgia Tech, where classroom recordings would focus on the teacher and his replies, while voices and faces of students where deliberately of low quality [2].

4.3 Anonymity and Pseudonymity

Given the difficulties in asserting explicit consent in electronic communications, one viable alternative to personal data collection are the notions of anonymity and pseudonymity. Not only are they an important option when offering clients a number of choices (so that those who wish to remain anonymous can remain so), they also allow the legal collection of certain types of data without requiring user consent.

Anonymity can be defined as "the state of being not identifiable within a set of subjects." The larger the set of subjects is, the stronger is the anonymity [23]. A large number of both free and commercial anonymity services are already in widespread use on the World Wide Web. Using anonymizing proxies, for example the popular www.anonymizer.com, or more sophisticated "mixes", like the "Freedom" software product of the Canadian software company Zero-Knowledge, Internet users can already today hide their IP address from the Web site hosting the accessed page.

Even though the technology behind such services is already well established, such methods might not be feasible in a ubiquitous computing environment. Communications between small ubiquitous devices will often happen in a much more dynamic environment, where long chains of communication (like they are used in mixes) might not last long enough because devices constantly enter or leave the scene. Direct communications on the other hand often disclose my real identity, unless wireless protocols would be adapted to use one-time addresses instead of their fixed hardware (MAC) address (as it is done in the Bluetooth standard). Sensing hardware is also different from network cards: My real-world appearance, unlike my cyberspace one, cannot be disguised that easily – any video camera can get a clear enough shot of me if it's pointed at my face.

Anonymity has also disadvantages from an application point of view. Being anonymous prevents the use of any application that requires authentication or offers some form of personalization. Pseudonymity is an alternative that allows for a more fine grained control of anonymity in such circumstances: by assigning a certain ID to a certain individual, this person can be repeatedly identified until she changes to a different ID. Using the same pseudonym more than once allows the holder to personalize a service or establish a reputation, while always offering her the possibility to step out of that role whenever she wishes.

Whether anonymous or pseudonymous – if data cannot be traced back to an individual (i.e., if it is unlinkable), the collection and usage of such data poses no threat to the individuals privacy. Consequently, legal frameworks such as the EU Directive lay no restriction on the collection of anonymous (or pseudonymous) data. Determining when certain type of information can be linked back to a person, however, is more often than not subject of debate. For example, even randomly generated pseudonyms might be linkable under certain circumstances: In case a pseudonym is used in conjunction with a certain fact that is easy to identify in a sufficiently small set, linking becomes trivial. An active badge might be programmed to change its ID every five minutes, though the fact that the tracking system is able to exactly pinpoint its location would make this change obvious (and thus linkable) in the logs.

Data-Mining technology allows much more remote coincidences to be assembled into a single coherent picture, therefore greatly increasing the potential of *any* type of information to be used for linking. Although German privacy-commissioners have argued for placing severe restrictions on the use of data-mining applications [1], their call might not be realistic.

4.4   Proximity and Locality

It seems that our above observations regarding the feasibility of certain desirable aspects in a privacy-aware ubiquitous system – such as clear notices, explicit consent, and unlinkable pseudonymity – might prove too difficult for efficient and reliable implementation. One possibility to face this technological reality while still preserving some desirable state of protection, even when this means some form of sociological adjustment, are the principles of proximity and locality.

The idea of proximity is basically a practical solution to much of what makes notice and consent hard. Instead of announcing each and every data collection, taking care to get the required consent, and handle those frequent cases where various people do not give their consent, imagine the following: Future society (and with it the legal system) will accept the fact that personal gadgetry (like coffee mugs or "smart" clothing) can record conversations and behaviors *whenever its owner is present*. Just as if people would never forget a thing they witnessed. Note that this does not mean that people would suddenly be omniscient – their memory prosthesis (i.e., their coffee mugs) would only grant them the gift of indefinite recollection (currently most legal systems treat any recording without the explicit consent of all parties as surveillance, which is only allowed by law enforcement in certain, court-ordered situations). In case the owner would accidentally leave such a device so that it could witness a conversation or meeting of other people in her absence, all sensory equipment would be turned off until the owner's presence would be detected again.

Such a detection mechanism could be simple. Of course, future advanced sensors could use biometry to check if the cup's owner is actually holding it. It could also use the presence of certain IDs in the clothing of the owner as a trigger: Only if a certain predefined signal would be emitted from the owner's wearable computer, its sensors would be operational. The problem would be further simplified if the cup's data storage would be outsourced to the holder's wearable computer: In this case it would be sufficient to simply check for the presence of any type of outsourcing facility, in effect acting as a collection device for anybody holding the cup (or sitting next to it).

Although this would alleviate a number of technical problems, recording each and every conversation and behavior would be more than just chatting with friends who suddenly have very good memory. Storage also allows your friends playing this information to people unknown to you, who then effectively witness events they were no part of. While one might still be comfortable with the idea of friends having a good recollection of past discussions together, one would certainly be less comfortable with their friends playing their recordings to a group of strangers for entertainment value.

Along similar lines as the idea of proximity aims the notion of *locality*. Instead of working out complicated authentication protocols that govern the distribution of collected information, so that it is in compliance with whatever recipient information has been previously announced, information could simply be tied to places at which it is collected. Should a table in a room on a ground floor be allowed to ask the flowerpot on the hallway outside to contact the light fixtures in the staircase for the information that the soda machine on the 3rd floor is currently acquiring? Should my printer tell everybody walking by what it is printing at the moment, only to have them pass this information on to the people they meet on the subway or at the airport, until this data ends up on the other side of the world?

In essence, one would require that information is not disseminated indefinitely, even not across a larger geographic boundary, such as buildings or rooms. Information collected in a building would stay within the building's network. Anybody interested in this information would need to be actually physically present in order to query it. Once present, however, no additional authentication would be required anymore – the printer in the hallway would be happy to tell anybody passing by and stopping for a chat which documents (and by whom) were printed on it last night.

This concept resembles privacy protection (or the lack of it) in small, rural communities: Everybody knows everything about each other, and is only too happy to tell. Once someone leaves the boundaries of the village, however, access to information about its inhabitants becomes difficult, if not impossible. Though word of mouth allows information to travel far beyond the originating locality, the information value drastically decreases with increasing distance.

In such a scenario, observing anything from a larger distance becomes impractical. Even though it is not impossible to acquire certain information, it ultimately requires physical locality to its source. This wouldn't be too far from our current status quo where law enforcement or private investigators routinely interview witnesses for their version of the events – only that coffee mugs and tables cannot talk. Not yet.

4.5   Adequate Security

Not surprisingly, talking about privacy almost always leads to security considerations. In most discussions, the significance of the latter is often perceived much higher than that of the former. The idea is tempting: once we solve security, that is, once we are able to achieve authenticity and trusted communications, privacy will be a by-product that follows inevitably from a secure environment.

Secure communications and storage methods have been around for quite some time, and security experts are constantly refining the algorithms to keep up with the rapid technological development. However, ubiquitous devices will introduce a whole new set of constraints, mainly in the areas of power consumption and communication protocols: there is only so much energy to power an embedded processor in, say, a felt pen, that it will perhaps not be enough to compute the product of two 2048-bit prime numbers. And a pair of smart shoes will probably pass a store front in a few seconds, barely enough time to go through with an orderly security protocol for establishing a secure communication.

Even with GHz Desktop power, security experts question if absolute security can ever be achieved. True, 2048-bit public key encryption is probably secure for the foreseeable future. But in order to prevent misuse, keys need to be encrypted by pass-phrase, which invites the usual problem of choosing nicknames of family members or friends, or writing them down next to the keyboard. Smartcards are often hailed as the ultimate personal security device, but these, too, need to be protected from unauthorized use once they fall into the wrong hands. And even if biometrics will ever allow us to use our fingerprints or retinas to replace personal passwords, key distribution and management for tens and hundreds of small and miniature personal devices (everything from socks to umbrellas to door knobs) will almost certainly challenge the most clever user interface.

We can reduce much of this complexity by employing robust security only in situations with highly sensitive data transfer, such as financial transactions, or the transfer of medical information. In most other cases, the principle of proportionality applies: cracking a 512-bit key might be feasible given the proper hardware, but if cracking the code would mean a reward of only $10, this would hardly be worth the effort. Similarly, sending temperature data from a sensor to its base station might not need to be encrypted at all. After all - if an eaves-dropper is close enough to overhear its low-power radio communication taking place, he might as well sense the current temperature by himself.

Here the principle of locality becomes relevant again: if we start broadcasting otherwise innocuous information like temperature or noise levels from a certain local context across many hops to physically distant (or separated) places, we effectively create surveillance devices. If, however, such data is sent only locally and not transmitted further, the lack of encryption is of no concern, therefore simplifying implementations at a reasonable level of compromise.

The important aspect to realize is that security might not be the panacea it appears to be, and it might not need to be that panacea either. If we consequently apply principles like proximity, locality, and proportionality, much of our basic infrastructure could indeed function without any explicit security model at all, while still adequately respecting the privacy needs of its users.

4.6 Access and Recourse

Trusting a system, and especially a system as far reaching as a ubiquitous one, requires a set of regulations that separate acceptable from unacceptable behavior, together with a reasonable mechanism for detecting violations and enforcing the penalties set forth in the rules. Both topics belong more into the realm of legal practice, where laws and codes of conduct will need to be revised or newly established in order to address the special requirements of typical ubiquitous computing environments.

However, technology can help implementing specific legal requirements such as use limitation, access, or repudiation. Augmenting a P3P-like protocol with something like digital signatures would allow for non-repudiation mechanisms, where parties could actually prove that a certain communication took place in case of a dispute. Database technology could provide data collectors with privacy-aware storage technology that would keep data and its associated usage practices as a single unit, simplifying the process of using the collected data in full compliance with the declared privacy practices. Sophisticated XML linking technology could enable the data subject direct access to his or her recorded information in order to enable the required access rights.

The principles of Collection and Use Limitation set forth in the fair infor-mation practices can further simplify such access requirements. In essence, they require data collectors to

- only collect data for a well-defined purpose (no "in-advance" storage)
- only collect data relevant for the purpose (not more)
- only keep data as long as it is necessary for the purpose

Together with anonymization or pseudonymization, these principles might save both time and effort that would otherwise be spent in order to properly collect, protect, and manage large amounts of sensitive personal information.

5   Summary and Outlook

What lies at the intersection of privacy protection and ubiquitous computing is easy to imagine: the frightening vision of an Orwellian nightmare-come-true, where countless "smart" devices with detailed sensing and far-reaching communication capabilities will observe every single moment of our lives, so unobtrusive and invisible that we won't even notice! Ron Rivest calls this the "reversal of defaults": "What was once private is now public", "what was once hard to copy, is now trivial to duplicate" and "what was once easily forgotten, is now stored forever." Clearly, "something" needs to be done, as nearly all work in ubiquitous computing points out, yet little has so far been accomplished.

Some of the principles mentioned above seem readily implementable, given the proper protocols: limiting the number of communication hops any message can travel enforces locality; creating simple proximity behavior for personal devices prevents unwanted surveillance; and devising communication protocols that use temporary, random IDs can provide some base-line anonymity. Implementing other guidelines might require a good amount of work: finding the adequate security settings for a given scenario (there might be widely different requirements for certain parts of a system), deriving low-power transparency protocols that are both expressive and compact enough, and creating a simple mechanism for pseudonymity-based identity management. Some of this might be achieved by porting existing solutions to a low-power environment, others might need to be re-engineered from scratch. Some large research effort will probably be required to fulfill needed trust requirements (implementing digital signatures and their corresponding public-key infrastructure) and back-end systems (privacy-aware databases and access technologies).

As important as it is to take existing laws and codes of practices into account, which can and must serve as important guidelines for creating privacy-respecting infrastructures – it is equally important to remember that laws can only work *together* with the social and technological reality, not against them. If certain legal requirements are simply not enforceable, technological or procedural solutions need to be found, or the law changed.

Maybe it is indeed time that we face the new technological realities and accept the fact that personal data collection will continue to advance and erode privacy as we know today. But new paradigms will take place of old and unrealistic assumptions, and new forms of human interactions will evolve in society, just as we have learned to live with the specters (i.e., modern photography) that haunted Warren and Brandeis more than 100 years ago.

References

1. 59th Conference of Privacy-Commissioners in Germany. Data Warehouse, Data Mining und Datenschutz.   See HTML version of the resolution passed at www.datenschutz-berlin.de/doc/de/konf/59/datawa.htm, March 2000. 285

2. Gregory D. Abowd and Elizabeth D. Mynatt. Charting past, present and future research in ubiquitous computing. *ACM Transactions on Computer-Human Interaction, Special issue on HCI in the new Millenium*, 7(1):29–58, March 2000. 273, 284

3. Philip E. Agre and Marc Rotenberg, editors. *Technology and Privacy: The New Landscape*. The MIT Press, 1998. 290

4. Helmut Baeumler, editor. *E-Privacy*. Vieweg Verlag, Braunschweig, Germany, 2000. 290

5. Victoria Bellotti and A. Sellen. Design for privacy in ubiquitous computing environments. In *Proc. of the European Conference on Computer-Supported Cooperative Work*, 1993. 273

6. Oliver Berthold and Hannes Federrath. Identitaetsmanagement. In Baeumler [4], pages 189–204. 273

7. David Brin. *The Transparent Society*. Perseus Books, Reading MA, 1998. 277

8. Business Week/Harris Poll. A growing threat. *Business Week*, March 2000. 277

9. Peter Cochrane. Privacy. Sovereign, May 1999. 277

10. Lorrie Cranor, Marc Langheinrich, Massimo Marchiori, and Joseph Reagle. The platform for privacy preferences 1.0 (p3p1.0) specification. W3C Candidate Recommendation, HTML Version at www.w3.org/TR/P3P/, December 2000. 282

11. Lorrie Faith Cranor, Joseph Reagle, and Mark S. Ackerman. Beyond concern: Understanding net users' attitudes about online privacy. Technical Report TR 99.4.3, AT&T Labs-Research, April 1999. 277

12. Mike Esler, Jeffrey Hightower, Tom Anderson, and Gaetano Borriello. Next century challenges: Data-centric networking for invisible computing. In *Proceedings of MobiCom'99*, Seattle, 1999. 273

13. Amitai Etzioni. *The Limits of Privacy*. Basic Books, New York NY, 1999. 277

14. European Commission. Directive 95/46/ec of the european parliament and of the council of 24 october 1995 on the protection of individuals with regard to the processing of personal data and on the free movement of such data, November 1995. 276

15. Robert Gellman. Does privacy law work? In Agre and Rotenberg [3], chapter 7, pages 193–218. 274, 275

16. Ruediger Grimm, Nils Loehndorf, and Philip Scholz. Datenschutz in Telediensten (DASIT). *DuD - Datenschutz und Datensicherheit*, 23(5):272–276, 1999. 273

17. Harris Interactive. IBM multi-national consumer privacy survey, October 1999. 277

18. Marit Koehntopp and Andreas Pfitzmann. Datenschutz next generation. In Baeumler [4], pages 316–322. 273

19. Lawrence Lessig. *Code and other Laws of Cyberspace*. Basic Books, New York NY, 1999. 279

20. James Michael. *Privacy and Human Rights: An International and Comparative Study, With Special Reference to Developments in Information Technology*. Dartmouth Pub Co. / UNESCO, 1994. 274

21. E. Mynatt, M. Back, R. Want, M. Baer, and J. Ellis. Designing audio aura. In *Proceedings of the ACM Conference on Human Factors in Computing Systems (CHI'98)*, Los Angeles, CA, April 1998. 273

22. Organisation for Economic Co-operation and Development (OECD). Recommendation of the council concerning guidelines governing the protection of privacy and transborder flows of personal data, September 1980. 275

23. Andreas Pfitzmann and Marit Koehntopp.   Anonymity, unobservability, and pseudonymity – a proposal for terminology. In Hannes Federrath, editor, *Proceedings Workshop on Design Issues in Anonymity and Unobservability*, volume LNCS 2009. Springer Verlag, 2001.   284

24. US Department of Commerce. Safe harbor website. `www.export.gov/safeharbor/`. 276, 277

25. Samuel Warren and Louis Brandeis. The right to privacy. *Harvard Law Review*, 4:193 – 220, 1890.   274

26. Alan F. Westin. *Privacy and Freedom*. Atheneum, New York NY, 1967.   274

27. William Pitt, Earl of Chatam (1708–1778). Speech on the excise bill.   274

TrekTrack:
A Round Wristwatch Interface for SMS Authoring

Anders Kirkeby, Rasmus Zacho, Jock Mackinlay, and Polle Zellweger

University of Aarhus, Denmark
anders@kirkeby.com
rasmuz@imv.au.dk
{mackinlay,zellweger}@daimi.au.dk

Abstract. The user interface for text messaging via SMS has changed little since the technology was introduced on cell phones. Authoring text with a phone keypad is tedious and error-prone. Furthermore, the cell phone intrudes into other activities while hands hold it for authoring. In this paper we suggest a future alternative user interface for SMS messages based on a round wristwatch device. Two button-wheels are used to access a round hi-res color display. Text input is done with a round soft keyboard that maps intuitively to the button-wheels using the angular and radial movements of polar coordinates. Furthermore, a wristwatch device has an aesthetics that is less intrusive than a cell phone. Since the device is always deployed, authoring is easily interrupted to use the hands for other tasks. Informal user evaluation of a prototype implementation suggests that this novel round design provides an improved user experience for authoring SMS compared to cell phones.

Keywords: Mobile computing, round display, polar coordinate navigation, SMS, text entry, input devices, wheel interface, angular movement, radial movement.

1 Introduction

Sending short text messages using cell phones has become enormously popular among large segments of cell phone users worldwide, mainly younger people. In some markets the Short Message Service technology, SMS, has been in mainstream use for many years. Despite the popularity of SMS, the user interface has not changed significantly since it was introduced on cell phones. Entering text with a phone keypad is tedious and error-prone [7]. Many cell phones require multiple presses to enter a character. Others use dictionary-based methods such as T9, pioneered by Tegic Communications [8]. However, both multi-press and T9 have problems. Furthermore, cell phones create an intrusive user experience. At least one hand must hold the cell phone while a message is being authored. Text messaging is often done in a mobile context, in which that hand might be needed for other tasks.

G. D. Abowd, B. Brumitt, S. A. N. Shafer (Eds.): Ubicomp 2001, LNCS 2201, pp. 292-298, 2001.
© Springer-Verlag Berlin Heidelberg 2001

In this paper we examine an alternative solution to authoring text messages for SMS based on a wristwatch metaphor. Our aim is to improve the overall user experience for authoring text messages.

2   State of the Art for SMS Text Input

On current cell phones the *multi-press technique* for text input assigns each of the 12 dialing keys a unique sequence of characters. The sequence can be anywhere between 3 and 10+ characters long. Common characters are often printed on the keys. When a key is pressed its character sequence is activated. Repeatedly pressing that key cycles through the sequence. A pause or a different key causes the character to be selected. The multiple presses and the required delays to type doubled letters yield a tedious and relatively slow typing method [2].

Several improvements have been suggested to alleviate some of the shortcomings of this input scheme. The most commercially successful is T9 [8]. It uses one press per key with a dictionary to suggest valid words from the multiple possibilities for the current input key sequence. Although this anticipatory system improves input speed for experienced users, incorrect predictions can confuse users [7].

3   The Round Approach

We suggest an alternative based on a round wristwatch metaphor. Our first goal was to make the text input process simpler and more intuitive by designing a small and complete soft keyboard to be used with two analog button-wheels, wheels that can also be pressed as buttons. In addition, we wanted to integrate SMS features directly into the design without adversely affecting ease of use [5]. In current SMS implementations, accessing features such as capitalization or entering number mode may require navigating through hierarchical menus. We address this trade-off between features and ease of use by reducing the perceived complexity of the task, thus providing a better user experience [9]. By using a higher resolution display (comparable in pixel density to current computer screens) and changing the input paradigm, we make most functionality directly accessible on a single small display and eliminate deep hierarchies.

The initial idea was to use the two button-wheels to control the x- and y-coordinates of a cursor similar to the computer mouse. During informal user testing the small scale of the device combined with a freely moving cursor proved an impractical solution. Adding a snapping movement helped some, making the cursor move to characters and functions only, yet it was still impractical to move around a standard rectangular soft keyboard.

Our solution was to "think round." A round display, round input devices, and a polar coordinate mapping solved the problem. By translating the wheel rotational input to polar coordinates, one wheel moves the snapping cursor in an angular fashion and another controls radial movement. For this to be effective, the character layout was changed from a rectangular format to concentric rings.

3.1   Hardware

The hardware prototype used for testing the software user interface prototype was a rough model made from simple materials. It was not designed to test appearance issues, only to allow the users to physically use the wheels and buttons while it was strapped to their wrist. A compromise in the hardware prototype meant there were two wheels and two buttons mounted underneath the wheels. The intended design calls for just two button-wheels – combined wheels and buttons.

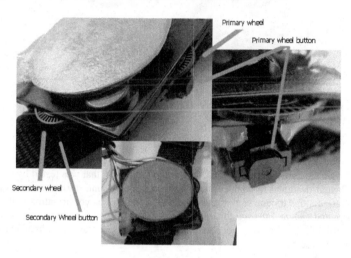

Fig. 1. Hardware prototype. The TrekTrack project focused on a wristwatch device, thus the strap, which also has the advantage of maintaining the orientation of the device. However, the input device could also be installed in other devices, such as a cell phone

Mounting the wheels on the side of the display allows for a natural mapping for the wheel controlling the angular movement. This mounting *under* the visual interface surface also has an advantage over such wheel designs as the Navi™ Roller [4] by Nokia: the wheel can have a larger diameter allowing for better control. A high level of control is paramount when using the TrekTrack text input.

Equipping the device with two dials that can be used simultaneously allows for rapid 2D positioning, an improvement over the 1D rotary navigation supported by the dial on the VuMan wearable computer [1].

The hardware prototype included a dummy display and was connected to the software prototype via a serial interface. A fully working version requires a round display with an active surface diameter of 35mm, minimum 8 colors and at least 127 pixels across (~ 0.28mm/px).

3.2   Software

We did not have access to a round display suitable for the purpose. Instead we built a prototype for a conventional laptop screen. The prototype is fully functional including the ability to send SMS messages.

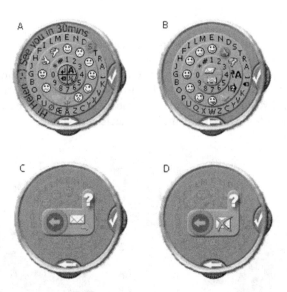

Fig. 2. Screens from software prototype. (A) is the initial design that was tested by users. (B) is the revised layout designed to compensate for shortcomings found during user testing of (A). (C) and (D) are dialogs unique to the revised model and serve as confirmation dialogs for the *Send Message* and *Delete Message* functions in the center of the revised layout (B). The initial layout (A) offered no obvious cue about how to send the message, which caused some confusion for test users

In the following, the revised input display layout, Fig. 2.B-D, will be used as the basis for explanation. The display is comprised of five concentric rings. The outer blue ring holds the text arc, where the input text appears as it is entered (see below). Inside this ring, the outermost character ring holds all of the letters of the alphabet, together with *Space* and *Backspace*. Because these reside in a single ring, they can be accessed quickly using a single button-wheel. The character layout represents an initial choice based on letter frequency and ergonomics that has not yet been tested or tuned. The third ring holds a set of emoticons and two function icons located at the right edge: *Capitalize Next Character* and *Show More Characters* (the arrow icon), which activates a secondary input screen that contains the remaining 30 characters from a standard keyboard, with room for 20 additional characters or functions as desired. The fourth ring holds the numbers, and within the inner circle the final tasks of either *Send Message* or *Delete Message* can be selected.

The *text arc* is a part of the outer ring used for displaying the message being written. The most recent input character appears near the 1 o'clock position, while preceding characters rotate counterclockwise. Characters are placed on a circular baseline to increase readability of words; the arc is limited to 180° as a compromise between length and readability. For compactness, a proportional width font is used, allowing approximately 35 characters to be displayed. Any preceding characters in the message are retained in memory, but no scrolling method is currently provided to view them.

Note that although text and icons are fairly small, SMS is generally more popular with younger people. Thus legibility is less of an issue.

To enter a text message, the user uses primarily the outer input ring, since it contains most letters, *Space* and *Backspace*. The user moves the green marker around the ring using the primary button-wheel on the right. When the desired letter is reached, pressing the primary button-wheel causes that letter to appear near the 1 o'clock position in the surrounding blue ring. To enter a character from one of the other rings, the user uses the secondary button-wheel at the bottom of the display to move the marker radially from ring to ring across the display. When the desired ring is reached, the user again uses the primary button-wheel to move around that ring to the desired character or function.

With most common characters in one ring, much of the authoring task becomes a linear snapping movement to the user, thus simplifying authoring. To further increase text entry speed, an acceleration effect is added. Good control through large diameter wheels makes it easier to exploit the acceleration. Several test users benefited from the acceleration, as they quickly learned to give the primary wheel a quick spin to reach distant characters.

4   User Response

We conducted informal user testing with 2 female and 4 male participants representing a reasonable spread in terms of age (15-29) as well as SMS and computer experience. Participants wore the prototype input device on their wrists and looked at the nearby display. Participants were introduced to the functionality of the device, but were given no instructions on how to perform any specific tasks. Completing the fixed scenarios took between 8 and 17 minutes depending largely on the individual user's SMS experience.

The users got accustomed to the interface surprisingly quickly. They quickly stopped scanning the interface before acting. Testing revealed several design flaws which resulted in some of the modifications already described: *Backspace* was placed in the innermost ring, thus slowing input, and there was no clear way to send the message once composed. However, the overall feedback was very positive. The experienced SMS user who finished the scenarios first exclaimed "This is so easy!" after having written multiple error-free messages.

5   Related Work

Other projects have made related attempts to use round text input designs. These are generally used with pen input devices and use gestures [6] or text rings [3] similar to ours to minimize the distance between characters and increase input speed. TrekTrack uses a small display area without the need for a stylus.

The VuMan wearable computer used a large dial with separate buttons to make selections in a hypertext network [1]. The VuMan designers also realized that a dial input device was well matched to a circular arrangement of items to be selected.

TrekTrack extends the idea to two button-wheels, one to control movement around a ring, and the other to control angular movement to change between rings. This permits rapid access to any one of a large number of items on the screen, making it reasonable for text entry.

6   Conclusions and Future Work

The TrekTrack round wristwatch approach to SMS messaging appears to be a promising alternative to current cell phone methods. A wristwatch aesthetics allows the device to be permanently deployed, allowing authoring to be interrupted for other activities. Two button-wheels support intuitive input with an ergonomic design. Large wheels mounted under the display support fine motor control. They also map intuitively to a round soft keyboard via polar coordinate movements.

There are several directions we would like to investigate further. Implementing a fully wearable self-contained prototype would be ideal. We would also like to do quantitative user testing on the actual effectiveness of the design. Implementing an anticipatory dictionary could be beneficial in efficiency studies. Additional editing functionality would also be valuable.

The emphasis in this paper has been on SMS authoring. However, the input method could be used as a general way to do text input in a multitude of devices. The small form factor makes it easy to fit into a compact device. With just two button-wheels mounted under the display, this input method provides a rich interface without significant demands on the device surface real-estate or the need for a stylus.

Finally, given their ubiquity and "at hand" position on the arm, wristwatches represent a fertile area for user interface design. However, wristwatches have a radically different aesthetic from most mobile computers and phones. We believe "thinking round," as we have in the design of the TrekTrack SMS interface, is the way to design effective user interfaces for wristwatch devices.

References

1. Bass, L., Kasabach, C., Martin, R., Siewiorik, D., Smailagic, A. & Stivoric, J. The design of a wearable computer. Proceedings of CHI '97 pp 139-146.
2. Goldstein, M., Book, R., Alsio, G. & Tessa, S. Ubiquitous input for wearable computing: qwerty keyboard without a board. Proceedings of the First Workshop on Human Computer Interaction with Mobile Devices, available at http://www.dcs.gla.ac.uk/~johnson/papers/mobile/HCIMD1.html
3. Mankoff, J. & Abowd, G. D. Cirrin: a word-level unistroke keyboard for pen input. In Proceedings of ACM UIST'98, pp 213-214.
4. Nokia Corp. Available at http://www.nokia.com/phones/7110/phone/new/roller.html
5. Odlyzko, Andrew. The visible problems of the invisible computer. First Monday 4(9) (September 1999), available at http://firstmonday.org/

6. Perlin, K. Quikwriting: continuous stylus-based text entry. In Proceedings of ACM UIST'98, pp 215-216.
7. Silfverberg, M., MacKenzie, I. S., & Korhonen, P. Predicting text entry speed on mobile phones. Proceedings of CHI 2000, pp 9-16.
8. Tegic Communications, available at http://www.tegic.com/
9. Thackara, John. The design challenge of pervasive computing. CHI2000 keynote, available at http://www.doorsofperception.com/projects/chi/

A Compact, Wireless, Self-Powered Pushbutton Controller

Joseph A. Paradiso and Mark Feldmeier

Responsive Environments Group, MIT Media Laboratory
20 Ames St. E15-351, Cambridge, MA 02139
{joep,geppetto}@media.mit.edu

Abstract. We describe a compact piezoelectric pushbutton and associated minimal circuitry that is able to wirelessly transmit a digital ID code to the immediate region (e.g., 50-100 foot radius) upon a single button push, without the need of batteries or other energy sources. Such devices have the potential of enabling controls and interfaces to be introduced into interactive environments without requiring any wiring, optical/acoustic lines of sight, or batteries.

1   Introduction

As copious interactive devices are built into the smart environments of tomorrow, a major issue will be how they are controlled. Although remote acoustic and optical sensing will increasingly open voice and vision channels as the requisite processing and algorithms improve, there will still be a need for deliberate tactile gesture, which is at the moment provided by hardwired interfaces or various kinds of remote controls. Both of these solutions can often have drawbacks - e.g., wiring is expensive and inflexible, while remote controls need batteries that require periodic replacement. A potential solution to some of these difficulties would be the development of a wireless controller that is able to transmit its function code without needing to be wired or powered, drawing its energy directly from the controlling gesture.

Indeed, one of the earliest remote controls worked in this way. The Zenith "Space Command"[1], introduced for televisions in 1956, housed 4 aluminum rods tuned to different ultrasonic frequencies spaced between 35 and 45 kHz. When a button was hit, it struck the corresponding rod, producing an ultrasonic pulse that was decoded at the TV, which then performed the appropriate function. Although ultrasonic communication has its share of difficulty (e.g., interference and false signals from clanking metal, annoyance to dogs, etc.), it persevered in TV remote controls for roughly 25 years before giving way to the active IR devices in common use today. Both ultrasound and infrared communication require a direct or reflected line-of-sight, however, which can limit their utility in many scenarios. Wireless RF controllers, such as automotive keyless entry buttons, avoid this problem, since radio waves in their frequency bands pass freely through people and nonmetallic objects. Although

G. D. Abowd, B. Brumitt, S. A. N. Shafer (Eds.): Ubicomp 2001, LNCS 2201, pp. 299-304, 2001.
© Springer-Verlag Berlin Heidelberg 2001

their current drain is fairly modest, they still require batteries, which occasionally (and often at inopportune times) need replacement.

Various developers and researchers have worked on harnessing the energy exerted when pushing buttons to eliminate or reduce the need for batteries in the attached devices. One example is a scheme proposed for tapping the excess energy exerted when typing on a laptop[2] by building little magnetic generators around each key. Related projects have designed self-powered transmitters that send an RF pulse when a door is opened[3] or a piezoelectric crystal is struck[4]. Another example, closer to the theme of this article, can be found in a young child's toy from Japan called the "Pipi"[5]. This is a simple batteryless remote control with one button; when pushed, it launches an impulse into a small piezoelectric element, which produces a spark that drives a Hertzian resonator, creating an RF signal that is detected by a battery-powered companion receiver (placed up to a few feet away), which then beeps like a pager. Although these projects demonstrate passively-powered RF communication, the transmissions are largely uncoded, hence don't easily allow for multiple buttons or any control complexity.

At the MIT Media Lab, we developed a pair of sneakers with flexible piezoelectric structures placed under the insole to generate power as the user walked. We first presented this system to the Wearable Computing community in 1998[6]. As the piezoelectric materials were bent and compressed, energy was innocuously extracted and stored, allowing a 12-bit digital ID code to be wirelessly transmitted from the shoe across a large room after every 3-5 steps[7]. The work presented in this paper evolved from this system. By using a rigid piezoceramic element in a spring-loaded striker instead of the flexible elements used in the shoe and introducing a transformer matched to the piezoelectric's characteristics, we have produced a device that provides ample power to transmit a robust digital ID code across the entire floor of a building with only a single push.

2   Technical Design

A piezoelectric conversion mechanism is employed in the switch due to its low weight, small size, minimal complexity, and minimal cost. To obtain the highest efficiency of mechanical-to-electrical energy conversion, the piezoelectric element must be operated at its mechanical resonance. To do this, the element is impacted for a very short duration and then released, allowing it to self-oscillate at its resonant frequency. Since piezoelectrics produce high voltages at low currents, and standard electronic circuitry requires low voltages at high currents, a step down transformer is used to couple the two and better match impedances. The inductance of the transformer [L] and the capacitance of the piezoelectric element [C] form a resonant circuit - the transformer thus must be selected appropriately for this "LC" electrical resonance to equal the element's mechanical resonance for optimum energy transfer. After passing through the transformer, the electrical energy is rectified, stored in a capacitor, and regulated down to the required voltage (3V) of the RF circuitry.

Figure 1 shows the circuit diagram. A 4.4 μF tank capacitor integrates the charge transferred from a button strike. This, in-turn, powers a MAX666 low-dropout linear regulator, which provides a stable (although very inefficient) +3 volts supply until the tank capacitor's charge is drained. When the MAX666 is activated, the HT12E digital ID encoder is enabled, producing a repeating 12-bit serial ID broadcast via the On-Off-Keyed (OOK) transmitter module.

The key components of this device are shown at left in Figure 2. The leftmost device is the piezoelectric button, the core of a Scripto "Aim 'N Flame" lighter with the spring action modified to deliver a softer strike. This button is 35mm long and 7mm in diameter, has a deflection of 3.5mm at a maximum force of 15N, and a total activation energy of 30mJ with a mechanical resonance near 50 kHz and a capacitance of 18 pf.   At right is the transformer, an amorphous-core device manufactured for electronic flash applications with a 90:1 turns ratio that transforms a peak of a few thousand volts at the piezo element to 30 volts at the tank capacitor. The piezo-transformer ensemble operates at 7% mechanical-to-electrical efficiency, delivering 2 mJ of energy per push. This translates to the order of 0.5 mJ at 3 Volts after the linear regulator.

The ID code is generated with the Holtek HT-12E encoder that produces eight bits of ID and four bits of data. The transmitter is the RFM HX1003 that runs at 418MHz, consumes 7.5 mW, and can transmit up to 50 feet. The receiving base station requires four successful receipts of the twelve-bit code before a complete transfer is registered.

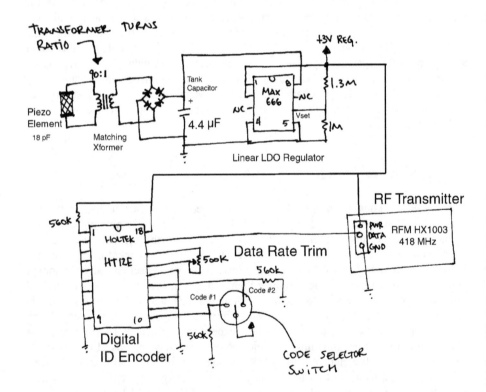

Fig. 1. Schematic diagram of self-powered pushbutton electronics

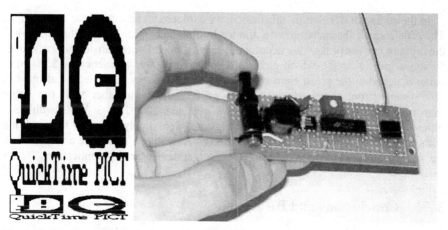

Fig. 2. Critical components (left – not including US quarter) and operational prototype board (right) for self-powered wireless ID pushbutton transmitter of Fig. 1

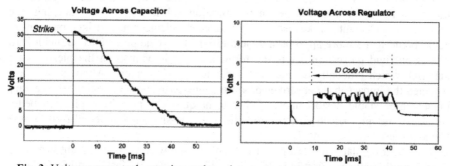

Fig. 3: Voltage across tank capacitor and regulator output voltage vs. time for a single press

The required time for successful completion of transmission is 20ms. Since the energy drain of the transmitter dominates over the remainder of the circuit, the total energy consumption is approximately 7.5mW for 20ms, totaling 150μJ. As outlined above, our button produces ample power for this application. As seen in Figure 3, at roughly 10 ms after the strike, the regulator becomes active, providing power to the transmitter and encoder circuitry for at least 30 ms (the ripple is due to the cyclic load of the OOK code, and the spike is a transient coupled in from the strike).

Our prototype circuit board for the pushbutton transmitter, containing all needed components, is shown at right in Figure 2. Note that the size of this prototype is much larger than needed, as through-hole components were used here for simple assembly. With surface-mount packages and more advanced assembly techniques, the circuit size should be very compact, dominated by the components of Figure 2 (left), which weigh about 8 grams. Production expense is likewise small, falling well under $5. per unit. The wire leading up to the top-right of the photo acts as a 1/4-wave whip antenna for the transmitter, and the trimpot is provided for adjusting the ID data rate in tests - it's not needed in practice.

In the course of developing this device, we explored variations on the components. The efficiency of the transformer is limited by flux leakage and core saturation when the primary current peaks. We accordingly tried a much larger transformer (with over 50 times greater mass), which gave us a somewhat better efficiency of 8.3% after being matched to the piezo element. We then used a larger piezoelectric element in this system (from the sparker of a gas grill igniter) - together with the larger transformer and appropriate matching, we obtained 20 mJ at 3 Volts with 13% efficiency. As the small components of Figure 2 were amply adequate for powering our system (and are much more conducive to packing onto a miniature circuit board), we were thankfully able to avoid using these larger devices in this application.

3   Conclusions and Discussion

This study has proven that a compact, wireless, self-powered, ID-transmitting pushbutton can indeed be built. The performance of our design, however, has considerable room for improvement. A prime candidate here is redesigning the transformer to reduce leakage and saturation while optimally matching the piezoelectric element. Likewise, the piezoelectric element and striker mechanism could be designed more appropriately and efficiently. One potential issue with hard strikes on rigid piezoceramics is the formation of microcracks in the piezoelectric material, which gradually degrade the generator's performance. Although we have softened the impact that our striker produces, long-term survival testing is necessary to guarantee stable performance. Other techniques can also be applied to better stimulate the piezoelectric generator, such as passive hydraulics driven at the element's resonant frequency[8].

The linear regulator used to produce 3 Volts is likewise very inefficient here with such a large voltage drop across it. A high-frequency, fast startup switching regulator, as developed in [7], would increase the efficiency of the regulation stage considerably.

In real-world applications, having one piezoelectric element and transformer per button may be inefficient. Other forms of this interface can be explored that perhaps integrate multiple passive pushbuttons or other input interfaces with a single piezoelectric striker, allowing a single piezoelectric generator to specify several degrees of freedom.

Additionally, our current device is transmit-only, hence is unable to verify the receipt of data transmission. The current prototype, however, is able to generate significantly more power than needed for simple ID transmission, especially over a shorter distance. Possibilities can then be explored for more robust operation, e.g., transmitting a more fault-tolerant digital code or first powering a low-power receiver that is able to select a band with minimal interference upon which to transmit the ID code.

Acknowledgements

The authors thank Winston Maue from the Lear Corporation for his enthusiasm and encouragement. We acknowledge the support of the Things That Think Consortium, the CC++ Consortium, and the other sponsors of the MIT Media Laboratory.

References

1. Webb, P. and Suggitt, M., **Gadgets and Necessities - An Encyclopedia of Household Innovations**," ABC-CLIO, Santa Barbara, CA., 2000, pp. 237-238.
2. Crisan, A., *Typing Power*, US Patent No. 5,911,529, June 15, 1999.
3. Johnson, P.M., MacKenzie, R.W., and Reeves, J.R., *Transmitter Circuit*, US Patent No. 3,796,958, March 12, 1974.
4. Mitchell, J.P., *Piezoelectric Pulse Amplifier*, US Patent No. 3,548,314, December 15, 1970.
5. The Pipi "Kodomo No Omocha" toy from Tomy corporation, Japan, 1998.
6. Kymisis, J., Kendall, C., Paradiso, J., Gershenfeld, N., "Parasitic Power Harvesting in Shoes," *Proc. of the Second IEEE International Conference on Wearable Computing, (ISWC)*, IEEE Computer Society Press, pp. 132-139, October 1998.
7. Shenck, N. and Paradiso, J., "Energy-Scavenging with Shoe-Mounted Piezoelectrics," *IEEE Micro*, Vol. 21, No. 3, May-June 2001, pp. 30-42.
8. J. F. Antaki et al., "A Gait Powered Autologous Battery Charging System for Artificial Organs," *Proc. of the 1995 American Society of Artificial Internal Organs Conf.*, Lippincott Williams & Wilkins, Philadelphia, 1995, pp. M588-M595.

Interacting at a Distance Using Semantic Snarfing

Brad A. Myers, Choon Hong Peck, Jeffrey Nichols, Dave Kong, and Robert Miller

Human Computer Interaction Institute, Carnegie Mellon University
Pittsburgh, PA 15213
bam@andrew.cmu.edu
http://www.cs.cmu.edu/~pebbles

Abstract. It is difficult to interact with computer displays that are across the room, which can be important in meetings and when controlling computerized devices. A popular approach is to use laser pointers tracked by a camera, but interaction techniques using laser pointers tend to be imprecise, error-prone, and slow. Therefore, we have developed a new interaction style, where the laser pointer (or other pointing technique such pointing with a finger or even eye tracking) indicates the region of interest, and then the item there is copied ("snarfed") to the user's handheld device, such as a Palm or PocketPC handheld. If the content changes on the PC, the handheld's copy will be updated as well. Interactions can be performed on the handheld using familiar direct manipulation techniques, and then the modified version is sent back to the PC. The content often must be reformatted to fit the properties of the handheld to facilitate natural interaction.

1 Introduction

As ubiquitous computing [18] becomes more common, rooms will contain devices, appliances and displays that are computer-controlled. Many research and commercial systems have investigated using laser pointers to interact with screens that are across the room [2-4, 10, 19], but these interactions are awkward and slow. This is due in part to inherent human limitations. Users do not know exactly where the beam will be when they turn it on, and it takes about one second to move it into position. Users' hands are unsteady, so the beam wiggles. And when the button on the laser pointer is released, the beam usually flies away from the target before the beam goes off.

Increasingly, people are carrying computerized devices, including Personal Digital Assistants (PDAs) such as Palm and PocketPC devices, computerized cell-phones (e.g., the Microsoft phones [16]), or even computerized watches [8]. As part of the Pebbles project, we are researching how these kinds of mobile devices will interact with other devices such as those in such a "smart room." We describe here our concept of *semantic snarfing* as a model for how mobile devices might be used to control large displays at a distance.

"Snarf" is defined by *The New Hackers Dictionary* as "to grab, especially to grab a large document or file for the purpose of using it with or without the author's permis-

G. D. Abowd, B. Brumitt, S. A. N. Shafer (Eds.): Ubicomp 2001, LNCS 2201, pp. 305-314, 2001.
© Springer-Verlag Berlin Heidelberg 2001

sion" [11]. We are using it here to refer to grabbing the contents of the PC screen onto a handheld device, usually without the knowledge of the application running on the PC.

We use the term *semantic* snarfing to emphasize that it is not always acceptable to just grab a picture or an exact copy of the interface. Instead, the meaning, or *semantics,* is often required. For example, if you want to edit some text displayed on a screen across the room, it would not be useful to copy a *picture* of the text to your mobile device. Instead, the text string itself must be snarfed, so it can be edited. Typically, the interface displayed on the mobile device must be different than on the large display, due to differences in screen size, screen properties (e.g., color or not) and available interaction techniques (e.g., stylus on the handheld vs. 2-button mouse on the PC). When editing is finished, the result must typically be transformed semantically before it is transferred back to the PC.

This research is being performed as part of the Pebbles project [7] (http://www.pebbles.hcii.cmu.edu), which is investigating the many ways that handheld and mobile devices can be used *at the same time* as other computerized devices for meetings, classrooms, military command posts, homes, and offices.

2   Related Work

A number of researchers are looking at interacting at a distance using a laser pointer. Eckert and Moore present algorithms and interaction techniques for a system with a camera looking for a laser dot [2]. One technique watches for the laser pointer to be turned off for at least one second to signify a mouse action. The specific actions are chosen using a global mode switch displayed at the bottom left corner of the screen. Kirstein and Muller describe a simple system with minimal interaction techniques for laser point tracking [4]. The Stanford iRoom project also is investigating using a laser pointer, and uses special gestures and pie menus for the interaction [19]. Recently, the XWeb system was extended with a variety of laser pointer interaction techniques, including ways to use a laser pointer for menu selection, scrolling and Graffiti-based text entry [10]. The delay times to detect the laser turning on or off and for dwelling in XWeb are at least one second each. In order to draw Graffiti accurately, the strokes have to be almost full screen, and text is entered at about 1/3 the speed for text entry on the Palm.

The snarfing concept is related to work on multi-machine user interfaces (MMUIs), where the handheld is used at the same time as a PC. Rekimoto has studied how to move information fluidly using a "pick-and-drop" metaphor among different handhelds [12] and between handhelds and a whiteboard [13]. "Hyperdragging" was introduced as a way to move data by dragging it from one device to another [14].

Closely related to the snarfing of pictures is the VNC system [15], which displays the screen from one computer on another. The user can operate the remote screen by clicking on the local picture. Implementations for handhelds running the Palm and Windows CE systems are available.

3   Motivation

In many of today's meeting rooms, there is a computer display projected on the wall, and one person controls the mouse and keyboard connected to it. SmartBoards [17] and other touch sensitive surfaces allow one or two people to interact directly with the large presentation screen, but other meeting participants must resort to manipulation by proxy—trying to describe which objects to manipulate and having the user at the controls do it. In previous work, we investigated having remote cursors controlled by handheld computers [7]. However, the most natural way for people who are distant from the screen to refer to objects is to point at them using a finger, a laser pointer, or simply a gaze. Therefore, it seems desirable to have a camera track a laser pointer dot or follow where a finger is pointing in the air, or even to use eye tracking at a distance. Cameras tracking hand or eye movements will not be able to get more than a very crude estimate of where the user is pointing. Even with a laser pointer, the shaking of the user's hand and the resolution of today's cameras results in an inability to point reliably at anything smaller than about 10 pixels. Furthermore, there is no "mouse button" on a laser pointer. Previous studies of laser pointer or gestural interaction at-a-distance have proposed a number of interaction techniques that try to overcome these problems [2] [10] [19], but they are quite awkward and slow to use. Although future computers will be able to see the laser dot at increased resolution, the amount of wiggle caused by the users' hands shaking will still be a fundamental limitation.

Given these human limitations and the awkwardness of other attempts at retrofitting today's interaction models for use by laser pointing, we decided to try a different strategy. Rather than trying to interact at a distance, we use pointing for what it is good at: referencing a broad area of interest. The objects of interest can then be snarfed onto the user's handheld mobile device so the detailed work can be performed more quickly and accurately.

Another motivation stems from the prediction that computers in future "smart environments" will be watching and listening for commands, and will be able to respond to voice and gestures. To manipulate a control that is across the room, sometimes it may be appropriate to speak a command (e.g., saying "lights on"), but other times, it may make more sense to use a control panel on a handheld mobile device (e.g., moving a continuous slider to adjust the brightness of the lights, rather than saying "darker, darker, darker, OK" or "lights to 32 percent"). Snarfing the controls onto a handheld device by pointing it at the lights would be very useful.

Other future applications of the semantic snarfing idea might include classrooms, where students might snarf interesting pieces of content from the instructor's presentation; collaborative design sessions, where people might snarf parts of an overall design for detailed analysis and editing; or military command posts, where staff members might be assigned to snarf particular items from an overall map display so they can "drill-down" into the details. This is related to the concept of using the handheld as a "magic lens" [1] for "revisualization" of data displayed on a public display. Individuals could pick which data on the public display was interesting and use their handhelds to view the data in different ways that are more meaningful and personalized.

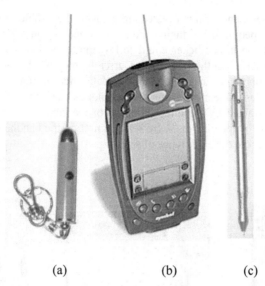

(a)	(b)	(c)

Fig. 1. A conventional, inexpensive laser pointer (a), a Symbol SPT 1700 PalmOS device with built-in laser scanner / pointer (b), and a pen with a laser pointer at one end and a stylus or ink pen at the other (c)

4   Semantic Snarfing

Given the delays and inaccuracies inherent in using a laser pointer, it is not surprising that laser pointer interaction techniques are quite awkward and slow. If a camera were trying to track where the user's finger was pointing or where a user's eyes were looking, the accuracies would be even worse. Therefore, we decided to investigate ways to make interacting at a distance more effective. Based on the success of our other Pebbles applications [6], we decided to investigate a multi-machine user interface (MMUI) that shifts part of the interaction to the user's handheld device. We implemented semantic snarfing in our new "Grabber" application that runs both on Palm and PocketPC handhelds. Like all Pebbles applications, Grabber communicates to the PC using various methods. It can communicate using a serial cable or wirelessly using IEEE 802.11 or other protocols. The Pebbles communication architecture is described elsewhere [5].

In order to make the interaction more natural, we acquired a stylus with an embedded laser pointer (Fig. 1-c). Thus, the user can hold the stylus/laser pointer with their dominant hand and use it both to point to the big screen across the room, and to tap on a Palm or PocketPC device held in the non-dominant hand. Alternatively, an integrated device like the Symbol SPT (Fig. 1-b) can be used. In either case, the laser pointer can be used to indicate the approximate area of interest on the main screen, and then the handheld's screen can be used for the detailed operations.

This mode of operation also helps support multiple users collaborating on a shared display. In real meetings, multiple people rarely seem to need to interact at exactly the same time, but turn taking is rapid and fluid. The snarfing style of interaction lets each person quickly grab what they want to work on to their private handheld, perform the necessary edits there, and then put the changes back. The Pebbles architecture already supports multiple people using their handhelds to operate on a single display at the same time [7]. If the laser tracker could follow multiple laser points, then different people could be snarfing at the same time. Currently, they would have to take turns.

Currently, Grabber can snarf three kinds of data: pictures, menus or text. The user chooses which is desired using a menu on the handheld. The area of the PC screen that is snarfed is determined by the initial position of the cursor or laser point when the user hits the "grab," "update," or 🕮 (refresh) button on the handheld. The rest of this section describes these different types of snarfing.

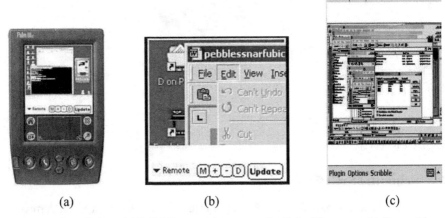

(a) (b) (c)

Fig. 2. Snarfing pictures. (a) Full PC screen shown on color Palm IIIc screen. (b) Zoomed in on Palm so pixels are 1-1, but only 3 menu items are visible. (c) PocketPC version

4.1   Snarfing Pictures

The Grabber program captures a picture of the PC's full screen and shrinks it to fit on the handheld's screen (see Fig. 2). This is related to the idea of PalmVNC [15], but we supply more features to make it easier to interact on the handheld. In Grabber, the user can control the level of zooming. When the full PC's screen in visible (Fig. 2-a and - c), it is very difficult to see any details, but the general screen layout is visible. When zoomed in all the way (Fig. 2-b), the user can easily read the text, but very little of the PC's screen can be viewed at a time (a Palm screen with 160 pixels across can only show 1/40th of a 1024x768 screen at a one-to-one pixel ratio). Intermediate levels of zooming are also available. The picture of the requested size is generated on the PC.

If the view is zoomed in, the user can pan using various buttons on the handheld. Alternatively, the Grabber can be set to automatically pan to wherever the PC's cursor is, or wherever the user's focus with the laser pointer or other coarse-grain pointing device is. This makes it seem like the picture is being snarfed back along the laser beam.

Drawing on the handheld's screen can perform various operations on the PC. In one mode, pen operations on the handheld are sent through to the PC as if they were normal mouse operations with the appropriate coordinate mappings. This makes it easy, for example, to tap on buttons, or even to draw if a drawing program is running on the PC. In the second mode, called "scribble," the user's strokes on the handheld are drawn on the PC on a transparent layer in front of what is there, so the user can draw arbitrary annotations on the screen. These scribbles can be easily erased or saved for later.

4.2   Snarfing Menus

Fig. 2 demonstrates a problem with grabbing only the picture of the PC's screen, and why we needed to implement *semantic* snarfing. In Fig. 2-b, the File menu has been popped up, but only 3 out of the 23 items in the menu fit onto the Palm screen. Scrolling down to get to the "Exit" option at the bottom, for example, would be tedious and slow.

Therefore, Grabber can instead snarf the *contents* of the menu at the focus of interest, and redisplay the menu on the handheld as a regular menu. For example, Fig. 3 shows the top-level menu and second level menus reformatted as Palm clickable lists.

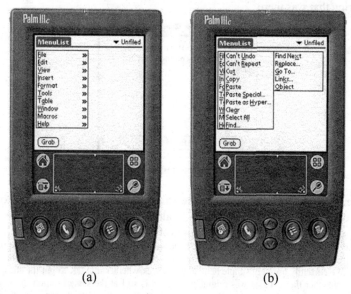

(a)   (b)

Fig. 3. Snarfing the menus onto the Palm reformats as multicolumn clickable lists. When the user taps on "Edit" in (a), all the items in the Edit sub-menu are displayed in two columns, as shown in (b)

Grabber snarfs the menus and toolbars out of unmodified, conventional PC applications using various heuristics. We can get standard Windows menubars and toolbars using various Windows calls, and menus and toolbars from Microsoft Office applications using the COM facilities. The menu or toolbar items are then sent to the handheld, where they are displayed using an appropriate set of widgets for the handheld. When the user clicks on an item with a submenu, the submenu is displayed on the handheld without involving the PC. When the user clicks on an item without a sub-menu, an appropriate message is sent to the PC to cause the selected operation to be performed.

In the future, we would like to add support for menus in other kinds of applications, in particular for menus implemented in Java Swing. We already have the capability to snarf the links out of a web page onto the handheld [6], and integrating this with the laser pointer focus mechanism might also be helpful for interacting with web pages at a distance.

4.3   Snarfing Text

Fig. 2 shows that it is impossible to read or edit text on the handheld when the full screen is showing, but when zoomed-in, you cannot see the whole line. Therefore, to enable text editing, Grabber can also snarf the text at the focus of interest. The user can choose whether to grab one line, 5 lines, or the whole text string (see **Fig. 4**). The text is then reformatted into a text string in the format of the handheld, and the user can edit it. After editing, the user can have the string put back onto the PC, to replace the old string that was there.

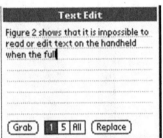

Fig. 4. Snarfing text to the Palm

In order to capture the text, various heuristics are used. We can get the text out of a standard edit control (which is used by dialog boxes, text fields, and the Notepad window), and from a Microsoft Office application using COM.

After the user is finished editing, a button on the handheld will replace the original string on the PC with the edited string. This may not work if some other user on a handheld or at the keyboard has edited the same string. We currently use very simple heuristics to check whether it is OK to put the string back, and simply check whether the text that was originally grabbed is still at the same location. In the future, we could use more sophisticated matching techniques such as those in others' multi-user text editors. We also hope to add support for snarfing the text from many other kinds of applications, including Microsoft Word and Java text widgets. We currently do not capture any text formatting information because it is much more difficult to render on the Palm, which ships with only 3 fonts.

5   Future Work

In addition to developing the above ideas further and performing user tests of seman-tic snarfing, we will be investigating how the concept of Semantic Snarfing can be applied to many other areas, and can enhance other kinds of interactions. For example, for handicapped people, the handheld might reformat the PC's screen to be much larger, or use a larger font for the text. A text-to-speech engine could read the text that is snarfed to the handheld. The text (or the labels for menu items) might even be translated into a different natural language by using a web service such as http://babelfish.altavista.com/.

As a new part of the Pebbles project, we are working on how to automatically create control panels for appliances on the handheld [9]. We call this creating a "Personal Universal Controller" (PUC) since it is customized to the one user, and the handheld will be able to control any appliance. Our preliminary studies suggest that interfaces on a handheld may be operated in 1/2 the time with 1/5 the errors as the manufacturer's interface [9]. Using the handheld in this way can be considered snarfing the user interface off of the appliance. We are using *semantic* snarfing, since a fundamental goal of the research is to automatically reformat the controls to be appropriate to the properties of the handheld, and the preferences and experience of the user. We hope to report more about this research in the future.

6   Conclusions

"Semantic snarfing" is a new interaction style, where a laser pointer, finger or eye gaze indicates the region of interest, and then the item at that point is copied ("snarfed") to the user's handheld device, where further interaction takes place. It is predicted that more and more of people's everyday devices such as cell phones and watches will become wirelessly networked to computers and appliances through technologies such as IEEE 802.11 and BlueTooth. Billboards, stores, and other information services may be able to deliver their content in different formats, so the mobile devices will then be able to snarf information from many kinds of information displays, and format it in an appropriate way for the mobile device's screen. In this ubiquitous computing world, people will want to use whatever devices they have at hand to operate or investigate screens or appliances at a distance. It will therefore be increasingly important that the information and controls be able to be semantically snarfed to any kind of mobile device.

Acknowledgements

For help with this paper, we would like to thank Al Corbett and Bernita Myers, and all the users of the Pebbles applications who have provided useful feedback.

This research is supported by grants from DARPA, Microsoft and the Pittsburgh Digital Greenhouse, and by equipment grants from Symbol Technologies, Palm, Hewlett-Packard, Lucent, IBM and SMART Technologies, Inc. This research was performed in part in connection with contract number DAAD17-99-C-0061 with the U.S. Army Research Laboratory. The views and conclusions contained in this document are those of the authors and should not be interpreted as presenting the official policies or position, either expressed or implied, of the U.S. Army Research Laboratory or the U.S. Government unless so designated by other authorized documents. Citation of manufacturer's or trade names does not constitute an official endorsement or approval of the use thereof.

References

1.   Bier, E.A., *et al.* "Toolglass and Magic Lenses: The See-Through Interface," in *Proceedings SIGGRAPH'93: Computer Graphics.* 1993. **25**. pp. 73-80.

2.   Eckert, R.R. and Moore, J.A., "The Classroom of the 21st Century: The Interactive Learning Wall." *SIGCHI Bulletin,* 2000. **23**(2): pp. 33-40.

3.   Horn, G.A.V., "Proxima's new Ovation+ projection panels do up multimedia." *Byte (on-line),* 1995. http://www.byte.com/art/9501/sec12/art9.htm.

4.   Kirstein, C. and Muller, H. "Interaction with a projection screen using a camera-tracked laser pointer," in *Multimedia Modeling; MMM '98 Proceedings.* 1998. pp. 191 -192.

5.   Myers, B.A., *An Implementation Architecture to Support Single-Display Groupware.* Carnegie Mellon University School of Computer Science Technical Report, CMU-CS-99-139 and Human Computer Interaction Institute Technical Report CMU-HCII-99-101, May, 1999. http://www.cs.cmu.edu/~pebbles/papers/pebblesarchtr.pdf.

6.   Myers, B.A., *et al.* "Extending the Windows Desktop Interface With Connected Handheld Computers," in *4th USENIX Windows Systems Symposium.* 2000. Seattle, WA: pp. 79-88.

7.   Myers, B.A., Stiel, H., and Gargiulo, R. "Collaboration Using Multiple PDAs Connected to a PC," in *Proceedings CSCW'98: ACM Conference on Computer-Supported Cooperative Work.* 1998. Seattle, WA: pp. 285-294. http://www.cs.cmu.edu/~pebbles.

8.   Narayanaswami, C. and Raghunath, M.T. "Application Design for a Smart Watch with a High Resolution Display," in *Proceedings of the Fourth International Symposium on Wearable Computers (ISWC'00).* 2000. Atlanta, Georgia: pp. 7-14. http://www.research.ibm.com/WearableComputing/factsheet.html.

9.   Nichols, J.W. "Using Handhelds as Controls for Everyday Appliances: A Paper Prototype Study," in *ACM CHI'2001 Student Posters.* 2001. Seattle, WA: pp. 443-444. http://www.cs.cmu.edu/~pebbles/papers/NicholsRemCtrlShortPaper.pdf.

10. Olsen Jr, D.R. and Nielsen, T. "Laser Pointer Interaction," in *ACM CHI'2001 Conference Proceedings: Human Factors in Computing Systems.* 2001. Seattle, WA: pp. 17-22.

11. Raymond, E.S., *The New Hacker's Dictionary.* Second Edition ed. 1994, Cambridge, MA: The MIT Press. See also: http://www.fwi.uva.nl/~mes/jargon/.

12. Rekimoto, J. "Pick-and-Drop: A Direct Manipulation Technique for Multiple Computer Environments," in *Proceedings UIST'97: ACM SIGGRAPH Symposium on User Interface Software and Technology.* 1997. Banff, Alberta, Canada: pp. 31-39.

13. Rekimoto, J. "A Multiple Device Approach for Supporting Whiteboard-based Interactions," in *Proceedings SIGCHI'98: Human Factors in Computing Systems.* 1998. Los Angeles, CA: pp. 344-351.

14. Rekimoto, J. and Saitoh, M. "Augmented Surfaces: A Spatially Continuous Work Space for Hybrid Computing Environments," in *Proceedings SIGCHI'99: Human Factors in Computing Systems.* 1999. Pittsburgh, PA: pp. 378-385.

15. Richardson, T., *et al.*, "Virtual Network Computing." *IEEE Internet Computing*, 1998. **2**(1): pp. 33-38. http://www.uk.research.att.com/vnc/.
16. Shim, R., "First look at MS 'Stinger'-based phone." *ZDNet UK Online*, 2000. http://www.zdnet.co.uk/news/2000/31/ns-17218.html.
17. SMART Technologies, "SMART Board 580," 2001. http://www.smarttech.com/.
18. Weiser, M., "Some Computer Science Issues in Ubiquitous Computing." *CACM*, 1993. **36**(7): pp. 74-83. July.
19. Winograd, T. and Guimbretiere, F. "Visual Instruments for an Interactive Mural," in *ACM SIGCHI CHI99 Extended Abstracts*. 1999. Pittsburgh, PA: pp. 234-235. http://graphics.Stanford.EDU/projects/iwork/papers/chi99/.

The Everywhere Displays Projector:
A Device to Create Ubiquitous Graphical Interfaces

Claudio Pinhanez

IBM Thomas Watson Research Center
P.O. Box 218, Yorktown Heights, NY 10598 -USA
pinhanez@us.ibm.com

Abstract. This paper introduces the Everywhere Displays projector, a device that uses a rotating mirror to steer the light from an LCD/DLP projector onto different surfaces of an environment. Issues of brightness, oblique projection distortion, focus, obstruction, and display resolution are examined. Solutions to some of these problems are described, together with a plan to use a video camera to allow device-free interaction with the projected images. The ED-projector is a practical way to create ubiquitous graphical interfaces to access computational power and networked data. In particular, it is envisioned as an alternative to the carrying of laptops and to the installation of displays in furniture, objects, and walls. In addition, the use of ED-projectors to augment reality without the use of goggles is examined and illustrated with examples.

1   Introduction

Ubiquitous computing envisions a world where it is possible to have access to computer resources anywhere and anytime to the data and services available through the Internet [1]. Since most of current software and Internet data is designed to be accessed through a high-resolution graphical interface, to truly ubiquitously compute today users need devices with reasonable graphical capabilities. This means carrying laptops everywhere, wearing computer graphics goggles, or installing monitors and displays on the surfaces of spaces and objects, such as desks, fridges, and entrance doors. Or, simply, to resign to the low-resolution displays of mobile phones or PDAs.

In this paper we explore an alternative approach to create ubiquitous graphical interfaces. Our idea is to couple an LCD/DLP projector to a motorized rotating mirror and to a computer graphics system that can correct the distortion caused by oblique projection. As the mirror moves, different surfaces become available to be used as displays. Also, we plan to employ a video camera to detect hand interaction with the projected image using computer vision techniques.

Our target is to develop a projection-based system that creates interactive displays everywhere in an environment by transforming a surface into a projected "touch screen." Such an *Everywhere Displays projector* can be installed, for example, on the ceiling of a space, to provide a generic computer interface to users in that environment (see Fig. 1).

G. D. Abowd, B. Brumitt, S. A. N. Shafer (Eds.): Ubicomp 2001, LNCS 2201, pp. 315-331, 2001.
© Springer-Verlag Berlin Heidelberg 2001

For example, an ED-projector can be installed in a meeting room and be used not only to project images on the walls but also to create individual displays for each of the participants of a meeting. Instead of today's meeting tables populated by bunkering personal laptops, a small set of ED-projectors can be shared by the participants to access their personal data, but easily reconfigured to allow teamwork. For instance, two people can be paired together to work on a sub-problem using a display projected in front of them while the other participants keep discussing the main themes using a display projected on the wall.

Moreover, ED-projectors have the ability to provide computer access in public environments without the risk of equipment being broken or stolen. Instead of carrying a computer, PDA, or phone everywhere, users can simply request a computer display, maybe by making a gesture to an overhead camera, and receive the projected image on a surface near their location. For example, an ED-projector in a store can transform pieces of white cardboard attached to shelves into interactive displays with product information. Unlike traditional kiosks, there is no need to bolt monitors and computers to the floor.

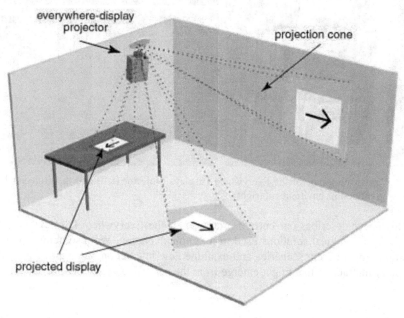

Fig. 1. Using the Everywhere Displays projector to create displays on different surfaces in an environment

In other words, we are proposing a shift in the display paradigm, which ceases to be regarded as a device to be installed in an environment, or carried along by a user and becomes a service provided by a space, like electric power or phone lines. But like any innovation, ED-projectors not only solve a problem but also create a new set of applications. For instance, if information about location and identity of objects in an environment is known, an ED-projector can be used as a device to augment reality without requiring users to wear goggles. It can lead a visitor to its destination in a building by directly projecting arrows on the floor; or project information directly onto the objects being assembled in an industrial plant. The ED-projector enables a computer system not only to augment a physical space with information but also to "act" in that environment and its users by projecting light patterns and symbols on objects and people.

Fig. 2. Current prototype of the Everywhere Displays projector (left) and the projector being used in an office-like environment (right)

This paper describes our current prototype of the Everywhere Displays projector and the technological solutions used in its implementation. We also demonstrate applications for different scenarios and examine new interaction paradigms for human-computer interaction that might emerge from the pervasive use of ED-projectors.

2   The Everywhere Displays Projector

The *Everywhere Displays projector*, or simply *ED-projector*, is composed of an LCD/DLP projector and a computer-controlled pan/tilt mirror. The projector is connected to the display output of a host computer that also controls the mirror. The left-side picture of Fig. 2 shows a prototype of an ED-projector built with an off-the-shelf rotating mirror used in theatrical/disco lighting, connected through a DMX network to the host computer.

In the configuration shown in Fig. 2-left, the projector's light can be directed in any direction within the range of approximately 60 degrees in the vertical and 230 degrees in the horizontal. When positioned in the upper corner of a room (such as shown in Fig. 1), this prototype is able to project in most part of the two facing walls, half of the two adjacent walls, and almost everywhere on the floor.

Fig. 3. Perception of contrast: global brightness (left); local brightness (middle); and a photo-montage simulating the perceived contrast (right)

Figure 2 also shows the current prototype of the ED-projector in use in an office-like environment. The top-right of Fig. 2 shows the ED-projector helping collaborative work. Notice the projector on the right upper corner of the picture and the angle of the rotating mirror used to direct the light onto the wall. The bottom-right picture of Fig. 2 shows the same surface being used to project the picture of an artwork as decoration for the room. Both photos were taken under normal office lighting conditions.

ED-projectors are feasible today due to the technical advances in two areas: video projectors and computer graphics engines. Current LCD/DLP projectors are able to create images that have enough contrast to be seen even when lights are turned on. Fast and cheap computer graphics engines are necessary to correct for the distortion caused by oblique projection. This and other implementation issues are discussed in the following sections.

2.1   Brightness and Contrast

Projecting images in a brightly lit room is possible because the human vision system perceives brightness and contrast locally. Consider a white wall in an environment with normal lighting: if no image is projected, subjects would describe the brightness of the wall as "white." However, if a white and black pattern with sufficient brightness is projected on the same wall (typically 5 to 10 times brighter than the normal lighting), viewers perceive the white projected pattern as "white" and any neighboring area receiving only the ambient light as "black" [2].

Figure 3 exemplifies this mechanism in a situation where the ED-projector is used to create projected labels on white Styrofoam cups. The left picture of Fig. 3 shows the global brightness as "collected" by a photographic camera. In this picture, ambient light illuminates all the cups although the third cup of the top shelf also receives the projection of the pattern shown in the middle picture of Fig. 3. In the left image the projected pattern is barely visible because the photographic camera, unlike the human eye, equalizes the brightness globally. The camera takes in account the large black background of the shelf and compresses the range of brightness differences of the pattern projected on the cup into a few shades of white.

However, as shown in the middle of Fig. 3, there is enough local difference in brightness on the projected pattern to allow its clear perception if only local lighting is considered. In particular, notice that the black "OK" lettering corresponds to the white surface of the cup reflecting just the ambient light. Since human vision adjusts to local contrast, the resulting perceived brightness is more like the photomontage shown in Fig. 3-right where the projected pattern is clearly discernible.

Our first prototype employs a 1200 lumens LCD projector that has proved to have enough brightness and contrast to project images on the surfaces of an office room with the lights on. Although we have not conducted experiments to determine the perceived brightness and contrast, in typical home and office conditions a white pattern projected by our prototype is approximately 10 times brighter than its surroundings and, therefore, enough to create the illusion of contrast.

The second prototype we built employs a 3000 lumens LCD projector, enabling sharper contrast for most projected surfaces. In particular, the increase in brightness improved significantly the quality of images projected on horizontal surfaces such as tables and desks. Since such surfaces tend to be orthogonal to the sources of ambient light, the specular component of their reflected light is brighter than non-horizontal surfaces such as walls. However, with a 3000-lumen projector, even the extra brightness provided by the specular light is overshadowed by the projection light.

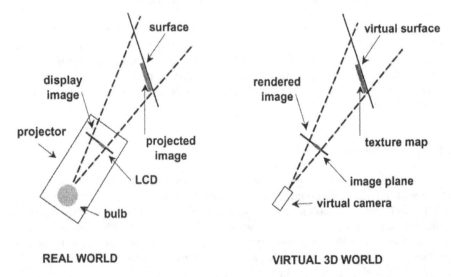

Fig. 4. Using a virtual computer graphics 3D world to correct the distortion caused by oblique projection by simulating the relationship in the real world between the projector and the projected surface

2.2   Correcting for Oblique Projection Distortion

When projection is not orthogonal to the projected surface, the projected image is distorted. In fact, as shown in Figs 1 and 2, in most cases the ED-projector is used to create displays on surfaces that are not orthogonal to the projection direction. To correct the distortions caused by oblique projection and by the shape of the projected surface (if not flat), the image to be projected must be inversely distorted prior to projection. In general, this distortion is non-linear and is computationally expensive to correct, involving the selective compression and the expansion of the original image.

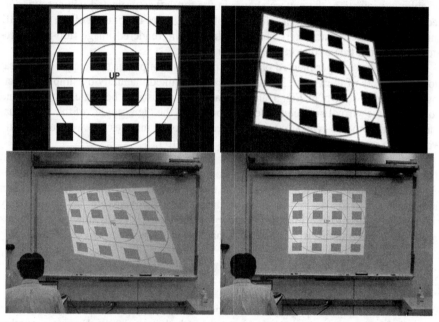

Fig. 5. Correction of oblique distortions: (left) the typical result of the oblique projection of a pattern on a surface; (right) the projection of the distorted pattern (top-right) creates a projected image free of distortion (bottom-right)

We have developed a simple scheme that uses standard computer graphics hardware (present now in most computers) to speed up this process. Our method relies on the fact that, geometrically speaking, cameras and projectors with the same focal length are identical (as observed in [3, 4]). Therefore, to project an image obliquely without distortions it is sufficient to simulate the inverse process (i.e., viewing with a camera) in a virtual 3D computer graphics world.

As show in Fig. 4, we texture-map the image to be displayed onto a virtual computer graphics 3D surface identical (minus a scale factor) to the real surface. If the position and attitude of this surface in the 3D virtual space in relation to the 3D virtual camera is identical (minus a scale factor) to the relation between the real surface and the projector, and if the virtual camera has identical focal length to the projector, then the view from the 3D virtual camera corresponds exactly to the "view" of the projector (if the projector was a camera). Since projectors do the inverse of viewing, i.e., they project light, the result is a projection free of distortions.

In practice we use a standard computer graphics board to render the virtual camera's view of the virtual surface and send the computed view to the projector. If the position and attitude of the virtual surface are correct, the projection of this view compensates the distortion caused by oblique projection or by the shape of the surface. Of course, a different calibration of the virtual 3D surface must be used for each surface where images are projected in an environment.

An example of the results of the process is depicted in Fig. 5. In a typical situation of oblique projection, the pattern shown in the top-left is projected without any correction, resulting in the bottom-left image of Fig. 5. After calibration of the virtual 3D surface and camera parameters, the projection of the rendered image (top-right) creates a projection free of distortion (bottom-right).

So far we have experimented only with projecting on planar surfaces. The calibration parameters of the virtual 3D surface are determined manually by simply projecting the pattern shown in Fig. 5 and interactively adjusting the scale, rotation, and position of the virtual surface in the 3D world, and the "lens angle" of the 3D virtual camera. This process typically takes between 10 to 20 minutes but we are currently working on its automation using techniques similar to [5].

Another simple technique to correct for distortion on planar surfaces is simply to distort the texture to be projected by a homography [6]. In this case, calibration is obtained by interactively grabbing with the mouse each corner of the projected pattern and moving it to the desired location on the surface. Alternatively, the homography can be embedded to the graphics board projection matrix [3]. Unlike the previous approach, homographies work only for planar surfaces.

2.3   Focus

We currently use a LCD projector where focus and zoom parameters can be remotely controlled by computer commands issued through the serial port. However, another problem with oblique projection is that it is not possible to put all areas of the projected image simultaneously in focus. Fortunately, current commercial projectors have a reasonable depth of focus range, enough to maintain decent focus conditions in most cases. We have succeeded in projecting on surfaces with up to 30 degrees of inclination in relation to the projection axis without significant degradation of focus. However, the problem becomes more severe as the distance between the projected surface and the projector decreases.

2.4   Display Resolution

One problem with the techniques described above to correct oblique distortion is that it creates displays with resolutions that are smaller than the projector's resolution. As can be seen in Fig. 5, the distortion correction process has to fit an irregular quadrangular into the 4:3 viewing area of typical displays. The result is that a considerable amount of display area is lost in the process.

In our prototypes we employ 1024x768 XVGA projectors. However, due to the loss of display area created by the distortion correction process, we have observed that the obtained resolution corresponds approximately to VGA, i.e., 640x480 pixels. This estimation takes in account that in the process of rendering the distorted image some pixels of the original image are compressed into single pixels of the projected image.

Other factors also influence the perceived resolution, among them the angle of projection and the texture of the projected surface. In the case of extreme angles of projection (<20 degrees), we have observed in some cases that while the center of the image is in focus, the area near the edges are somewhat blurred. This blurring is less visible if the projected image has less detail. Similarly, projecting onto textured surfaces such as carpets introduces a high frequency spatial component on the visual field, contributing to decrease the perceived resolution because of interference patterns. We are currently starting research aiming to determine how much perceived resolution is lost when projecting on surfaces of different colors, specular components, and textures.

2.5   Obstruction and Glare

Unlike LCD displays, the use of projectors as graphical displays face the problem of having the projected image being obstructed by people or moving objects in the environment. This was, in fact, one of our major concerns in the start of this project. However, our experience has shown that obstruction is far less common than we anticipated, particularly when the projector is positioned in the upper corner of a room (as shown in Fig. 1). Although we initially tried to position the projector on the center of the ceiling, the corner placement proved to be much more effective, mainly because in this situation the projection cone tends to be closer to the wall and therefore less prune to be intercepted by human beings.

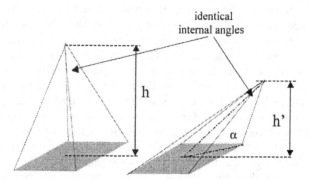

Fig. 6. Change of volume for identical internal angles

Another reason for the relative lack of obstruction is the fact that oblique projection cones are smaller than orthogonal projection cones. To see this, consider the two projection cones C and C' with identical bases and internal angle (i.e., lens configuration) and heights h and h', as shown in Fig. 6. Since the loci of all vertices of pyramids of equal base and internal angle is a sphere[1], it's easy to see that the $h' = c.h.\sin\alpha$, where c is a constant smaller than 1 that depends on the geometry of the orthogonal pyramid C.

Since the volume of the pyramid is proportional to the product of the area of the base B by the height of the pyramid, $V = 1/3\,B.h$, we obtain that the volume of the two pyramids are related by:

$$V' = V.c.\sin\alpha$$

For instance, if the angle of oblique projection α is 30 degrees, the volume of the oblique pyramid is less than half the volume of an equivalent orthogonal pyramid. Since the projection cones of oblique projections are smaller than those of orthogonal projections, we should expect a similar reduction in the likelihood of obstruction.

Similarly, the positioning of the projector on the ceiling, above human heads, contributes decisively to avoid glare and direct staring to the bulb of the projector. Again we see here a benefit of oblique projection that allows this placement of the projector on the ceiling. Although most commercial projectors today have some mechanical or electronic device to correct for keystoning (typically less than 10%), this correction does not allow the positioning of the projector sufficiently high to avoid glare. In the office-like experimental setup of our environment, however, glare happens only in very unusual situations such as when the user is sitting on the floor.

3   Making the ED-Projector Interactive

The current prototypes of the ED-projector include the functionality to project on different surfaces a 512x512 portion of the interactive desktop display of the host computer. The user can interact in real-time with this projected desktop using mouse and keyboard.

We are now starting to explore the interaction with the projected surface without the need of users having to manipulate input devices. In other words, we would like to have the projected display behaving as if it was a "touch screen," making the ED-projector a system easily usable in public spaces or in hazardous environments. The goal is to have the user interact by moving her hand over the projected surface, as if the hand was a computer mouse (see Fig. 7); and by moving the hand rapidly towards the surface, to generate a "click" event. We are currently investigating the use of a pan/tilt video camera that is controlled by the computer so it has a complete view of the projected surface (depicted in Fig. 2, installed on the top of the ED-projector).

To track the position of the hand over the surface, we are considering the development of variations of the traditional background subtraction techniques used in computer vision [7]. However, unlike those cases, we have a situation where the projected background changes significantly and abruptly over time. To overcome this problem, we are exploring two alternatives: the use of two synchronized cameras in a stereo configuration as in [8] and a method based on the estimation of the projected background of the image.

---

[1] This is the 3D equivalent of the known geometric property that for any two distinct points on a circumference, all triangles formed by the two points and one third point belonging to the arc between them have internal angles of the same size.

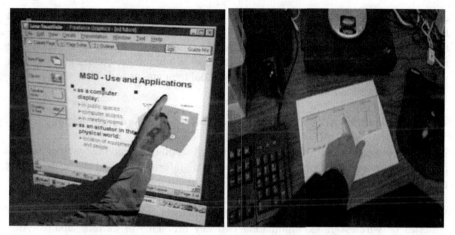

Fig. 7. Examples of interaction with the projected display by hand

The second method explores the fact that although the projected background changes, what is being projected is known to the system. Therefore, if the patterns of light reflection are known for the projected surface, it is possible to estimate how the projected image will look like when seen by the camera. In other words, we are investigating whether we can calculate the expected background based on the surface reflectance characteristics (together with the camera influence on them) and the image being projected.

The detection of "clicking" events seems to be quite more complicated. To detect a fast movement of a hand or finger towards the projected surface, we need some estimation of the distance of the hand to the surface. Although we plan to experiment with stereo vision to solve this problem, we are considering a simpler scheme based on the measurement of the width of the shadow created by the hand. As seen in Fig. 7-left, the obstruction of the projected light by the user's hand creates a black shadow, in this case to the left of the hand. As the hand gets closer to the surface the shadow decreases in width, especially in the area near the fingers. Our plan is to track the size of this shadow and use it to estimate the hand-surface distance.

A word of caution has to be made about using DLP projectors with standard video cameras. Since DLP projectors project each RGB separately, capturing the projected image with a camera normally results on images showing only one or two of the light components. The only way to overcome this problem, it is necessary to synchronize it with the projector and to increase the exposure time of the camera so it integrates all color components.

4   Using ED-Projectors in Ubiquitous Computing

The ED-projector is a generic input/output device that has been designed for use in multiple applications. These applications can be basically classified in two classes. The first class corresponds to the creation of interactive displays that provide computer access from surfaces of objects, furniture, walls, floor, etc. The second class of applications deals with typical augmented reality applications: the ED-projector can be used to point to physical objects, show connections among them, attach information to objects, and to project dynamic patterns to indicate movement or change in the real world. This section covers the applications in ubiquitous computing; the next section explores the uses of ED-projector as a tool to augment and affect reality.

4.1   Ubiquitous Access to Computational Resources and Information

The ED-projector is a tool that can create a high-resolution graphical interactive display to access computational resources, personal information, and the web. In this regard, it can be seen as a device that realizes the aspirations of ubiquitous computing [1] without the encumbering carrying of laptops or wearing of video-goggles. Since it can be installed on the ceiling of environments, it does not require the use of batteries or wireless links, eliminating two key problems of current laptops. And, unlike PDAs and phones, it does not require a change in most of today's interaction paradigms since it can provide access through a high-resolution (VGA, at least) display.

Fig. 8 depicts an example where a desktop application is moved around a room, being available in different surfaces that correspond to different uses of computer access. First, the display is laid on a desk, then moved onto a whiteboard, and finally projected on the wall besides the whiteboard. Notice that the display, in this last position, can be easily consulted while the users are scribbling on the whiteboard.

Similar applications can be created for professional environments such as hospitals where space is tightly constrained and there are restrictions on what can be carried by people. For example, a single ED-projector in an infirmary can provide on-demand computer access to nurses and doctors, freeing them from carrying laptops around. In another scenario, ED-projectors can substitute TV sets in patient rooms: although they can still be used to project TV images on the wall, they also enable computer access to data and communications from the patient's bed, without any need to move and connect equipment in the vicinity of the patient.

4.2   Collaborative Work

Video monitors, LCD screens, and PDAs are designed for individual use of computers. The only tool currently easily available for collaborative work with computer applications are LCD projectors, normally mounted on rooms to project on one of the walls, creating a "stage" effect for presentations. This configuration is awkward for collaborative work since it creates a single point of attention and distracts people from looking at each other.

There has been a significant amount of HCI and design work to provide computer access to tables (for some examples, see [9, 10]). The ED-projector is clearly a device that enables this kind of interactive work, with the advantage that the resource can be easily moved to walls, adjacent tables, etc., allowing easy reconfiguration of a meeting space for different functions and teamwork styles.

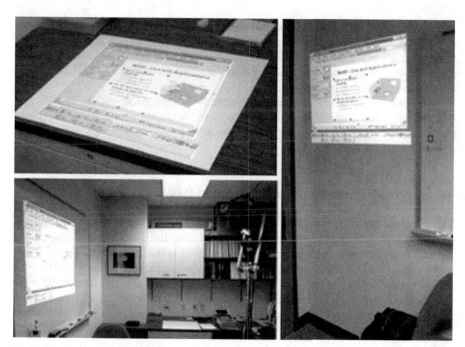

Fig. 8. The ED-projector moving a desktop application to the top of a table, to a whiteboard, and to a wall on the side of the whiteboard

Similarly, ED-projectors can be used in school classrooms. Instead of having a row of workstations with video monitors, the teacher can use ED-projectors to reconfigure the classroom for individual, group, or whole class activities. In day-care centers and kindergartens the device enables the use of walls and floors for education and entertainment, with the advantage of no infant contact with heavy or breakable objects.

There are many other similar applications in professional activities where teamwork is needed. Typical examples are surgery rooms, today crowded by arrays and arrays of bulk monitors displaying information and video imagery, and monitoring vital signs. A set of ED-projectors seems to substitute such configuration with the advantage that vital information can be easily brought in close proximity to nurses and physicians for detailed inspection or interaction.

4.3   Computer Access in Public Spaces and Hazardous Environments

The ED-projector can also be used to provide computer and information access in spaces where traditional displays can be broken or stolen, or create hazardous conditions, such as in public spaces or areas subject to harsh environmental conditions. Examples of spaces in the first category are waiting areas of transportation facilities such as subway stations and airports. The ceiling mounting of the ED-projector protects it against vandalizing, while the mirror allows easy change on where information is projected. This last feature is particularly important for this kind of environment where the cost of installing or reconfiguring equipment tends to be very high.

We also envision the use of ED-projectors in factory areas where normal electric devices are not allowed due to the potential risk of sparks, or simply because the environment itself contains hazardous elements to computers (such as water). The ED-projector can be encased in glass or other transparent material and still be able to create a useful display on such areas.

Another example of a "hazardous" environment is a home kitchen. By installing an ED-projector, and without the risk of spills, falls, or short-circuits, the kitchen user can access information, watch TV or surf the web, follow recipes, or simply set and control cooking time.

4.4   Bringing Computer Access to Disabled People

The ED-projector also permits an interactive display to be brought to the proximity of a user without requiring the user to move. In particular, the ED-projector can facilitate the access and use of computers by people with locomotive disabilities. For instance, it can project an interactive display on the sheet of a hospital bed without creating the risk of patient contact with any device. The patient, in this case, can interact with the display by simply using his hand and use it to search for information, call doctors and nurses, or to obtain access to entertainment.

5   Augmenting Reality with ED-Projectors

Ubiquitous computing research tends to focus on the issue of how computer resources can be spread through physical environments so computer and network access become seamless. However, an important consequence of embedding computers to physical environments is that it becomes easier to connect the computer to functions and knowledge that are specific of that space. A computer installed on the wall of a library is a natural candidate to manage the information about the books in that space, where they are located, and even how people are using them.

All this information about the environment can be provided to users. For instance, if the computer in the library knows where the books are located, it can help a user to find them. So far such applications have been explored in the context of augmented reality, mostly through the use of semi-transparent goggles [11, 12]. However, goggles not only are heavy and cumbersome, but they also require the fast and accurate tracking of the user's head to be effective.

We are exploring the use of the ED-projector in such environments. Unlike in previous works with static projectors [9, 10, 13], the rotating mirror expands the reach of projector to almost the entire room. It also enables the augmented reality image to follow an object around an environment (as long as there is a mechanism to track it). In the rest of this section, we examine augmented reality scenarios using the ED-projector.

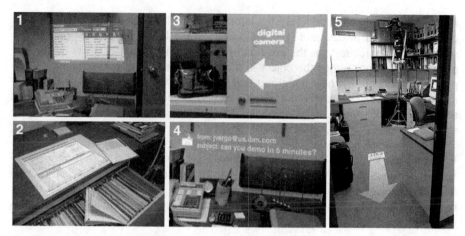

Fig. 9. Augmented reality applications of Everywhere Displays: (1) an electronic phone directory is projected close to the phone; (2) the database corresponding to a file cabinet is accessed directly from the top of the cabinet; (3) a localization system points to the position of an object; (4) a notification of the arrival of an urgent e-mail is silently projected on the wall; (5) an emergency sign projected on the floor directly points to the nearest exit

5.1   Bringing Information to a Physical Location

Most applications of augmented reality are concerned with the virtual attachment of information to places and objects in the real world. Among such applications, we have been experimenting with the ED-projector to bring information to the physical location where the information is used or needed.

Figure 9.1 shows a simple example where a phone directory is projected close to a phone device, so it becomes easy to search and inspect information about the person a user needs to call. In an ideal situation, the simple act of picking up the phone could trigger the display of the directory on that surface. Figure 9.2 exemplifies another situation where a database application accessing a list of files is projected on the top of the file cabinet that contains those files. In this situation, the user can search the computer database using any kind of complex query, obtain and refine answers, and use the results to find the corresponding files in the cabinet.

5.2   Navigation, Tagging, and Localization of Resources

ED-projectors are ideal devices to support user navigation through an environment. For instance, by installing an ED-projector in a corridor it is possible to project information on any wall, door, or area in the floor. Moreover, if the intent is to provide directions for visitors, an ED-projector-based system has the advantage that no device needs to be given or worn by the visitor. Fig. 9.5 shows an example application where the projector is used to signal the direction of an emergency exit on the floor.

In a physical environment where the position of objects or components is known to the computer, it is possible to use an ED-projector system to visually point to an object's position or to tag it with relevant information, without requiring the user to wear or carry any kind of device. Fig. 9.3 shows an example where the ED-projector responds a verbal request for the position of an object (a digital camera) by directly pointing to the location of the object in the room. The system could follow by displaying a checkout list near the object that would allow the user to update the information about the item just by touching the projected checklist. Similarly, information about the digital camera or instructions for its use could have been displayed on the same area.

Unlike systems based on goggles, it is possible to have similar applications in public spaces. As shown in Fig. 10, a ED-projector can be used in a store to provide information about specific items, help people to find products, point to special promotions and sales events, and even provide entertainment for small children. All that is required is a set of white or light-colored surfaces where the information is to be projected.

5.3   Affecting People

The ED-projector can also be used as an actuator device to affect the people occupying a physical environment. If the system has information about the position of people, it can project light patterns that indicate possibilities or constraints to their movements and actions. For example, the projector can create an "electronic doormat" that helps the control of a line of people. It can indicate, directly on the floor, that the user should not move ahead by projecting, for instance, a red line. If the user keeps moving, the red line can follow him, and maybe increase in size or blink to stress the required human response.

Another application is the delivery of notification of important events to people, anywhere, and without the disruptive use of sound. Figure 9.4 shows a simple example of an e-mail notification being displayed on a wall close to where a user is working. Of course this scenario is only feasible if the identity, position, and head attitude of the user is known.

In many ways, the ED-projector is one of the first devices that allow a computer system to seamlessly act on the physical world we inhabit. It creates a harmless "robotic arm" of light that can affect people in multiple ways. Although sound and speech have been explored in the past as computer actuators in physical spaces, the ED-projector is unique in its possibilities of creating local, pinpointed ways for a computer to act on people.

6   Conclusion and Future Work

The main purpose of this paper is to present the ED-projector, a device consisting of a rotating mirror deflecting the light of a LCD projector. Although building on the previous research on interactive projected surfaces [9, 10, 14, 15], we believe that the introduction of the rotating mirror produces a very unique device. First, it allows a single I/O device to have multiple uses in the same environment and to dynamically create new displays as needed. An ED-projector can provide computer access to a user in one moment, project a notification of e-mail arrival in the next, and, in the case of an emergency, be used to direct people to exits. Second, an ED-projector creates a simple way for a computer to act on the objects and people in a physical environment, truly integrating computer actions to the real world.

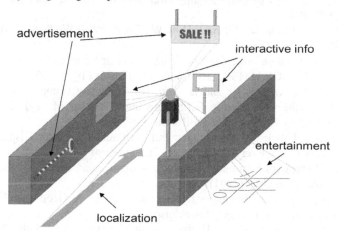

Fig. 10. Example of use of the ED-projector in a store

The basic components for building an ED-projector are easily available. We have shown in this paper that the technology for correcting for oblique projection problems is simple and easy to implement. More research is needed, however, to make the calibration of the projector a simple process and certainly a lot more on the vision-based system for hand interaction with the projected image. Those problems, however, seem to be within the scope of currently known vision techniques.

The most exciting research is, in our view, on the new paradigms of human-computer interaction afforded by the concept of everywhere displays. Here we are proposing a scenario where ubiquitous computing happens without carrying displays around or installing them on furniture and walls. Unlike most of the current thinking that looks into devices that can be carried by users, we are suggesting that graphical interactive displays can be a service provided by a space.

While initially we are expecting to support the current desktop paradigm, there is no reason to confine interaction to a rectangular frame like current monitors are forced to do. A possible avenue to explore is to consider the tangible interaction paradigm proposed by Ishii [16], but realize it without wiring or modifying the objects used for interaction. For example, a paper cup on a table can be easily transformed into a volume dial by simply projecting a scale around it with a "volume" label and responding to any rotation of the object by a user.

Finally, what kinds of collaboration can happen between human beings and computer in the moment that computers have the ability to point and affect objects and people in the real world? Kitchens and stores are particularly exciting scenarios to explore these novel concepts. We can also see situations, such as the control of a line of people mentioned above, where computers become devices able to act on people in the physical world. We are planning to explore further all these new paradigms for human-computer interaction that appear as a result of the introduction of ED-projectors in real environments.

References

1. Weiser, M.: The Computer for the Twenty-First Century. Scientific American (1991) 94-100
2. Hoffman, D.:Visual Intelligence: How We Create What We See. W. W. Norton. (1998).
3. Raskar, R.: Oblique Projector Rendering on Planar Surfaces for a Tracked User. In: Proc. of SIGGRAPH'99. Los Angeles, California (1999) 260
4. Pinhanez, C., Nielsen, F., and Binsted, K.: Projecting Computer Graphics on Moving Surfaces: A Simple Calibration and Tracking Method. In: Proc. of SIGGRAPH'99. Los Angeles, California (1999)
5. Yang, R. and Welch, G.: Automatic and Continuous Projector Display Surface Calibration Using Every-Day Imagery. In: Proc. of 9th International Conf. in Central Europe in Computer Graphics, Visualization, and Computer Vision. Plzen, Czech Republic (2001)
6. Faugeras, O.:Three-Dimensional Computer Vision: A Geometric Viewpoint. The MIT Press. Cambridge, Massachusetts. (1993).
7. Wren, C., Azarbayejani, A., Darrell, T., and Pentland, A.: Pfinder: Real-Time Tracking of the Human Body. IEEE Trans. Pattern Analysis and Machine Intelligence 19 (7) (1997) 780-785
8. Brumitt, B., Meyers, B., Krumm, J., Kern, A., and Shafer, S.: EasyLiving: Technologies for Intelligent Environments. In: Proc. of 2nd International Symposium on Handheld and Ubiquitous Computing (2000) 12-27
9. Rekimoto, J.: A Multiple Device Approach for Supporting Whiteboard-based Interactions. In: Proc. of CHI'98. Los Angeles, CA, April 18-23 (1998) 344-351
10. Underkoffler, J., Ullmer, B., and Ishii, H.: Emancipated Pixels: Real-World Graphics in the Luminous Room. In: Proc. of SIGGRAPH'99. Los Angeles, CA, August 8-13 (1999) 385-392
11. Krueger, M. W.:Artificial Reality II. Addison-Wesley. (1990).
12. Inami, M., Kawakami, N., Sekiguchi, D., Yanagida, Y., Maeda, T., Tachi, S., and Mabuchi, K.: Head-Mounted Projector for Projection of Virtual Environments on Ubiquitous Object-Oriented Retroreflective Screens in Real Environment. In: Proc. of SIGGRAPH'99. Los Angeles, California (1999) 245
13. Raskar, R., Welch, G., Cutts, M., Lake, A., and Stesin, L.: The Office of the Future: A Unified Approach to Image-Based Modeling and Spatially Immersive Displays. In: Proc. of SIGGRAPH'98. Orlando, Florida, July (1998) 179-188
14. Crowley, J. L., Coutaz, J., and Berard, F.: Things that See. Communications of the ACM 43 (3) (2000) 54-64
15. Binsted, K., Morishima, S., Nielsen, F., Pinhanez, C., and Yotsukura, T.: HyperMask: Virtual Reactive Faces for Storytelling. In: Proc. of SIGGRAPH'99. Los Angeles, California (1999) 186
16. Ishii, H. and Ullmer, B.: Tangible Bits: Towards Seamless Interfaces between People, Bits, and Atoms. In: Proc. of CHI'97. Atlanta, Georgia, March (1997) 234-241

UniCast, OutCast & GroupCast:
Three Steps Toward Ubiquitous, Peripheral Displays

Joseph F. McCarthy, Tony J. Costa, and Edy S. Liongosari

Accenture Technology Labs[1]
3773 Willow Road, Northbrook, IL 60062 USA
mccarthy@cstar.accenture.com
{tony.j.costa,edy}@cstar.accenture.com
http://www.accenture.com/cstar/

Abstract. Artifacts and surfaces that can display digital content are proliferating at a steady rate. Many of these displays will be peripheral, i.e., used for content that is not directly related to one's primary activities. However, what kinds of content would people want to see on such peripheral displays? We have begun to investigate the use of peripheral displays in three workplace contexts: within an individual office (UniCast), outside an individual office (OutCast) and in a common area (GroupCast).

1 Introduction

We often hear predictions of a technology-rich future in which our environments will be filled with artifacts that can sense and respond to us in new ways – a world filled with a multitude of cameras, microphones, visual displays and audio speakers, to name but a few. Although such a world may seem threatening or menacing in some depictions, it is possible that such developments will lead to more accommodating environments that encourage more frequent and beneficial interactions and a greater sense of awareness among the inhabitants of such spaces.

We have begun to build an environment with *ubiquitous peripheral displays* – visual displays distributed throughout the physical space of our office that supplement those used for primary work activities. Since it is impractical to distribute such displays everywhere, we are approximating, or at least moving toward, ubiquity, by focusing on the use of such displays in three contexts: inside an individual office, outside an office and in a shared space. We call the applications we have created to populate these displays with content UniCast, OutCast and GroupCast.[2]

The displays are *peripheral* in the sense that they are placed in physical locations that are outside the primary visual focus of people as they engage in their typical work

---

[1] Formerly, the Center for Strategic Technology Research (CSTaR) at Accenture.
[2] For notational convenience, we will often refer to the physical displays according to the applications running them, except where to do so would cause confusion.

G. D. Abowd, B. Brumitt, S. A. N. Shafer (Eds.): Ubicomp 2001, LNCS 2201, pp. 332-345, 2001.

activities throughout the day. UniCast displays are positioned on desktops in individual offices, to the side of the primary computer workstation; an OutCast display is embedded in a wall outside an individual office; a GroupCast display is situated off to the side in a public area with heavy traffic.

Our general goal in this work is to deploy the displays (and associated applications) as widely as possible within our group, and to investigate how – and indeed, whether – people would want to create, modify and access content on displays in a variety of contexts. We also seek to discover what kinds of differences exist in the types of content people are interested in seeing within their offices, projecting outside their offices, and encountering with other people present in public spaces.

In the sections that follow, we provide some details about the environmental context in which these applications are used, describe each of the applications in more detail, share some of our early experiences with the applications, and suggest some potential future directions for this work.

2   Environmental Context

The environmental context in which we have designed and built these applications is the physical space occupied by Accenture Technology Labs – Research, a 16,000 square foot section of the second floor of Accenture Technology Park, in Northbrook, IL, USA. There are approximately 30 members of the research group in Northbrook, including researchers, developers, technical writers and administrative staff. Over half of these people are currently using UniCast in their offices; in addition, there is currently one GroupCast display in a common area, and a single OutCast display outside of the third author's office.

The research group area has a network of over 70 ceiling-mounted nodes each housing an infrared sensor, radio frequency receiver and audio speaker, and a set of infrared badges that transmit identification signals every two seconds. Badge location information is maintained in a Microsoft SQL Server 7.0 database, with a web browser interface for accessing and administering this information. Finally, we have a collection of eleven Axis 2100 Network Cameras installed in various hallways, meeting rooms and other common areas throughout this space.

3   UniCast

UniCast is an application that allows users to specify content they would like to see on peripheral displays located within their primary workspaces. In some respects, UniCast represents an extension of the functionality provided by the PointCast system [cf. Franklin & Zdonik, 1998], which allows people to specify news topics and stock symbols about which they would like to stay informed while their desktop computer is in screensaver mode. However, UniCast is different in several key aspects: it runs continuously on a dedicated, peripheral display; it allows for a broader selection of content; it reacts to the location of its "owner" via an infrared badge system; and it is tied into and makes use of content belonging to other UniCast user profiles. Figure 1 shows an example of UniCast in one office context: the rightmost monitor is used for UniCast content (the laptop in the middle is used as the primary workstation, and the monitor on the left is running ActiveMap [McCarthy & Meidel, 1999] and EventManager [McCarthy & Anagnost, 2000]).

Fig. 1 UniCast display within one office context

Our model of interaction is primarily that of an ambient display [Weiser & Brown, 1997; Wisnewski, et al., 1998; Redström, et al., 2000] rather than the primary workstation display used for supporting a user's primary work tasks. The hypothesis is that UniCast content should be interesting, but not terribly important or urgent, since important or urgent information is (or could be) sought out directly on the primary workstation. For example, the first author uses UniCast to cycle through his favorite on-line comics (among other types of content) which help to brighten his day, but are rather peripheral to his work, and which he therefore rarely seeks out on his primary workstation.

The content for UniCast includes the usual suspects – headlines and stock information – as well as many other types of content. The current implementation includes user-configurable modules of fifteen different classes:

- *Headlines*: The top 5 headlines from any of 273 channels in 16 categories from Moreover (http://www.moreover.com/).

- *Stocks*: Any stock symbol available from Yahoo! Finance (http://finance.yahoo.com/). At most 5 stocks can be displayed per page; for modules with more than this limit, UniCast randomly selects 5.
- *Weather*: Weather information for any US zip code available from Earthlink's weather portal (http://www.earthlink.com/).
- *Traffic*: Chicagoland Expressway Congestion map provided by the Departments of Transportation of Illinois, Indiana and Wisconsin – IDOT, INDOT, and WIS-DOT – in conjunction with the AI Lab at the University of Illinois, Chicago's Electrical Engineering & Computer Science Department (http://www.ai.eecs.uic.edu/GCM/CongestionMap.html)
- *Horoscopes*: Any of the 12 signs of the zodiac available from Yahoo! Astrology (http://astrology.yahoo.com/). .
- *Web pages*: Any URL specified by the UniCast user.
- *InfoShare*: Any URL specified by *any* UniCast user; these URLs are organized by topic and/or people – either the person who posted the content or the person(s) for whom the content was posted (e.g., "I think Tony would be interested in this page") – allowing access by any of three "channels" (this is essentially used as a local "What's Cool?!" repository).
- *Announcements*: Text messages submitted through a special interface that includes a title, body and expiration date; this is mostly use for conference and workshop announcements. Subscription is "all or nothing."
- *Reminders*: Visual and aural reminders of regularly scheduled events for the entire group. Events are individually selectable.
- *WebCams*: Live content from any of 11 Axis 2100 Network Cameras positioned in public spaces throughout the research group area (the video streams from these cameras can only be viewed behind the Accenture firewall, and the URLs are not circulated outside of our group).
- *In/Out List*: A list of who is in the office today (as well as when and where they were last seen) and who is away, based on information gathered through our infrared badge system. People to track are individually selectable. This module is labeled "ActiveMap" for historical reasons (see McCarthy & Meidel [1999] for more information).
- *Factoids*: 363 different "factoids" manually collected from various sources on the web, organized into 8 categories (Culture, History, Human Body, Nature, Recycling, Science, Space and General). Subscription is by category.
- *Flashcards*: Short questions and answers; a default set of US State Capitols augmented by whatever flashcards people add.
- *Artwork*: 1000 images, organized into 10 categories, from Corel's Super Ten Royalty-Free Art Photo Pack. Subscription is by category.
- *Pictures*: Digital images uploaded to a shared directory. Images are individually selectable.

Users first select a module class to install and then add personalized selections or preferences to that instance of the module. For example: for the web page module, any number of URLs can be specified (and different instances of the web page module can have different sets of URLs); for headlines, there is a form with checkboxes for listing news categories; and for weather, the user enters one or more U.S. zip codes. Every instance of a module has a range of times for each day of the week (including an easy way to specify all day and/or every day), and a priority level from 1 (lowest) to 5 (highest).

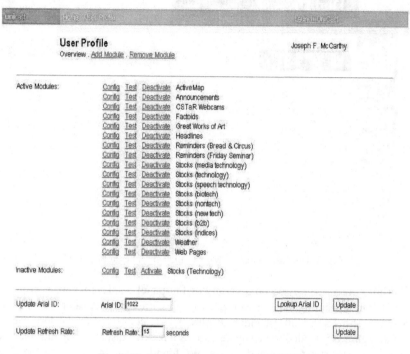

Fig. 2 UniCast profile maintenance interface

Each user's modules and preferences are stored in their UniCast profile (see Figure 2). UniCast randomly cycles through modules in the profile, generating content that is delivered to the user's UniCast display for a fixed period of time (the default is 15 seconds, but this can be modified by the user) before moving on to the next module. Priorities are implemented using a vector scheme wherein copies of module instances are placed in the vector – one copy for each level of priority (e.g., 5 copies for the highest priority items) – and then vector items are randomly selected for display.

Adding modules and editing module preferences in the UniCast Profile is done using a web browser, usually on the user's primary workstation (but optionally on the UniCast display). As the profile is modified, changes are instantly reflected in the content being delivered to the user's UniCast display. This enables UniCast content to be displayed all the time on a device other than the user's primary workstation. In addition to increasing UniCast's usage and utility (initial UniCast observations indicated that usage and utility was greatly diminished when it was used on a primary workstation), it also provides the ability to maintain the simplicity of the device (eliminate a keyboard and mouse) while providing users with a richer environment when detailed customization is desired.

Fig. 3 UniCast content ("Wine of the Day") being displayed

UniCast content is viewed on a variety of flat-panel displays we have installed in individual offices throughout our workplace (see Figure 3 for an example of a UniCast display screen). Each UniCast video display unit is connected to the local network and, although it is intended to mostly be used as a passive display, each unit includes a touch-screen and/or keyboard and mouse. We found that users wanted to be able to pause and occasionally go back to a page displayed on UniCast (especially pages that had a high density of text). The Java-based interface provides the user with minimal control of the display using a set of finger-sized button controls to *pause* or *resume* the cycling, to go *back* to the most recently displayed page. An additional *send* button to allow users to transfer content from their peripheral displays to a browser on their primary workstations for further exploration is currently under development.

The behavior of UniCast is tied into the infrared badge infrastructure in our office environment. By sensing the owner's location, the UniCast display toggles between two modes: home and away. When the user is in his or her office (*home* mode), Uni-Cast displays content as described above. When the user leaves his or her office, the UniCast display switches to an *away* mode that either displays the user's current location in the office (using the infrared badge system) or a message predetermined by the user.

4   OutCast

OutCast is a variation on the peripheral display theme. Whereas UniCast is directed toward a user within his or her own office space, OutCast is directed toward coworkers near the user's office (see Figure 4). Rather than display information that is only of interest to the owner, OutCast displays information about the owner that is intended for others to view. In many ways, OutCast reflects a behavior that is pervasive throughout the office environment – the posting of articles, cartoons, photographs, and other paraphernalia on office doors. OutCast picks up on this behavior and moves it into the electronic realm, enhancing it where possible.

Fig. 4 OutCast display outside an office

OutCast runs in a web browser, and is displayed on an NEC 2010 flat-panel monitor augmented by a MicroTouch touch-screen, embedded in a cubicle wall and connected to a Pentium II computer. Visitors to this office can access any of the following types of content (note: "owner" will refer to the occupant of the office):

- *Biography*: Information about the owner from his or her personal web page (see Figure 5).
- *Calendar*: Any entries in the owner's Microsoft Outlook Calendar that are not marked private.
- *Location Information*: Based on the owner's infrared badge.
- *Project Information*: Brief descriptions of each of the owner's projects.
- *Demonstrations*: Online demonstrations of projects (where applicable).
- *Favorites*: A list of URLs to be shared with passersby.
- *Text Message*: The ability to leave the owner a message using a touch-screen virtual keypad.

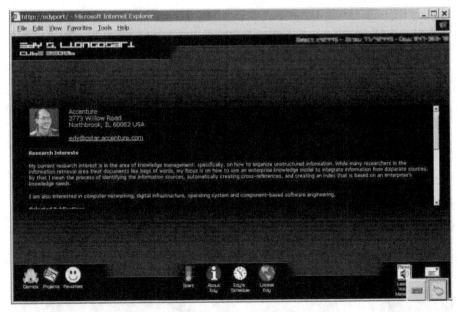

Fig. 5 OutCast displaying Biography content

One capability in OutCast that is not yet incorporated into UniCast is the ability to tie into existing enterprise applications and database resources. For example, calendar information can be pulled from the centralized calendaring system for the office, and project and biography information can be pulled from their corresponding web pages or databases.

Although we consider OutCast to be an example of a peripheral display, in that it is not used as a primary workstation, OutCast employs a distinctly different interaction paradigm form UniCast. Whereas UniCast is largely passive, offering minimal interaction, OutCast has the ability to toggle between a passive mode, where content randomly cycles much as UniCast content does, and an active mode, where a user can interact with the display to navigate through and explore each module's content or leave a text message for the OutCast display owner. We are exploring ways add a video capture capability to the display – or, rather, the wall – which would enable video messages to be left, and to adapt the displayed content to different visitors or classes of visitors, where visitors are identified via their infrared badges.

5   GroupCast

A physical space that can sense people in the vicinity, and has knowledge of their interests, can use this information to create new informal interaction opportunities for these people. For example, a shared public display in a workplace, combined with a tracking system, can display information of mutual interest to the people passing by the display. People may choose to take advantage of this information to initiate a conversation with someone about whom they may know very little, leading to an increased sense of community in the workplace [Deutsch, 1995; Naylor, et al., 1996; Putnam, 2000].

Other researchers have investigated how to create greater awareness among people who are electronically connected but not physically collocated [Zhao & Stasko, 2000; Sawhney, *et al.*, 2001; Greenberg & Rounding; 2001]. Our focus has been how to create greater awareness of each other when people are gathered together – or passing each other – in the same physical space. We also want to distinguish our work from other work using large public displays in the foreground to support the performance of primary work activities (e.g., Streitz, *et al.*, [1999]); although GroupCast uses a large public display, it is intended to be more of a background or peripheral display, and we believe that the content is more likely to spark informal conversations if it is not directly related to work activities.

As an example scenario of GroupCast in action, suppose Joe and Teresa pass each other in the hallway fairly regularly and yet know very little about each other. However, the "Wine of the Day" web site pops up as they both pass by a GroupCast display, leading to a spontaneous and serendipitous discussion about the merits of old-vine zinfandels (see Figure 6). After the discussion ends, they both go away, knowing a little more about each other, and, assuming the discussion did not deteriorate into a vicious argument, they are more likely to have conversations (on wine and other topics) in the future.

Fig. 6 GroupCast in context of use

One of the stumbling blocks we encountered in the initial design of GroupCast was how to acquire content that would be of mutual interest to people. We first considered using a large web-based form displaying content areas that people could rate with respect to their interest level (this was the approach we took with MusicFX [McCarthy & Anagnost, 1998, 2000], which adapted aural aspects of the workout place rather than visual aspects of the workplace). When people passed each other in front of the GroupCast display, content in the intersection of their interests would be displayed.

However, we soon discovered we had conflicting goals: having a profile that would be broad enough to include content of potential interest to a large number of people, and yet still be small enough so that we could reasonably expect people to specify that content, e.g., by filling out a form. By the time we had amassed enough potential content in our profile form, we were fairly confident that no one (besides those working on the project) would take the time to fill it out.

After we launched UniCast, we had an insight: instead of using the intersection of known interests of both (or all) people near the display, just display content that one of the people had already specified in their UniCast profile. Although that content might not match the profile of the other people, it is still of interest to at least one person passing by, and may still generate the desired conversation [opportunity] between the passersby. Using the UniCast profile, we can rely on people's own self-interest in customizing content that they will see regularly (in their office), rather than struggling with the somewhat less rewarding task of specifying content that only is available when they are in a public area.

6   User Experience

UniCast, GroupCast and OutCast have been in use – though also under continuous development – for several months. We have collected qualitative and quantitative data about the use of UniCast from a variety of users; however, due to the small number of installations of OutCast and GroupCast (one each), we are not yet in a position to provide much data on our other applications. The qualitative data presented in this section is based on interviews conducted with four UniCast users; the quantitative data is based on analysis of the profiles of all eighteen users.

All UniCast users run the application on a display that is peripheral to their primary workstation display. Most users have a separate computer to run the application, however one runs it on a second monitor attached to a workstation, though that workstation itself is not this user's primary workstation, providing this user with two peripheral displays (the other display is used for two purposes -- a browser window which has the MyYahoo portal and an instance of AOL's Instant Messenger).[3]

Of the fifteen classes of content modules available in UniCast, the most popular modules among the users we interviewed were the Web Pages modules, allowing

---

[3] See Grudin [2001] for a more extensive study on the use of multiple monitor ("multimon") usage. We concur with his assertion that there is generally poor software support of such use, particularly among laptop computers. Since most of our colleagues use laptops as their primary workstations, we provide [older] desktop computers & laptops to power the UniCast displays.

people to add any arbitrary web site to the stream of content that cycles through their UniCast display. Other popular modules cited include Weather, Factoids, WebCams and the infrared badge-based In/Out List ("ActiveMap"). These last two are particularly interesting, since they raise a number of privacy issues among some people. Our group appears to have a high tolerance for [perceived] privacy intrusion, since more than 90% of the group wears their badges regularly, and only one person has complained about the web cameras (and even that person appears to have grown used to them).

The least popular modules that were cited by interviewees are those for Traffic and Reminders. In the case of the former, we believe that this is due to the fact that several people have commuting patterns not covered by the Chicagoland Expressway Congestion Map. In the case of the latter, we believe this may be due to an ineffective design on the reminders (particularly with respect to the audio component of reminders, which some people find annoying).

We also have some information as to how people are customizing their UniCast profiles (see Table 1). The first column lists the module class name. The second column shows the average number of selections per module class, e.g., the average number of stocks or average number of headline channels a person is monitoring through UniCast. The third column shows the minimum number of selections per module class and the fourth column shows the maximum number of selections per module class. Note that there may be more than one module instance per class (which is why one person has 13 webcam selections when there are only 11 webcams).

Table 1 Numbers of instances and selections of UniCast modules

Module Name	# of Users who created a module instance	Average Selections / Module	Minimum Selections/ Module	Maximum Selections/ Module
Internal Webcams	18	9.1	1	13
Weather	17	2.4	1	4
Headlines	16	22.2	4	58
Stocks	15	16.4	4	74
Web Pages	13	12.5	2	42
Factoids	12	5.8	4	8
Artwork	12	6.0	2	10
ActiveMap	11	13.7	12	16
Announcements	10	3.0	3	3
Horoscopes	8	1.4	1	2
Pictures	8	9.0	3	39
Reminders	8	3.8	2	6
Flashcards	6	25.5	1	50
Traffic	6	1.0	1	1
InfoShare	5	4.4	1	9

We have also collected some informal feedback from OutCast users. Users typically use OutCast when the owner (office occupant) is away. The features that people reported liking and using most were the Location Information (to hunt down the owner in real-time, if he is in the office) and Calendar (to identify the next available opening in the owner's schedule). The least liked and used was the Text Message feature, since people were uncertain about the reliability of this function; users still tend to leave text messages using atoms – Post-It® notes – rather than bits.

7   Future Work

These three applications originated as three separate projects, but as work progresses, it is becoming increasingly apparent that there are many opportunities for sharing content and infrastructure among them. One of our near-term future goals is to come up with a common profile structure for all three applications, with an interface that allows users to easily specify which content is intended for which application (and physical setting).

In UniCast, we want to continue work on our InfoShare module; it was only recently made available, and we don't have many users who have created instances of the module. We think that increased use of this module can help create a greater sense of community among people in the group (another mechanism for learning about each other's interests, without being physically co-present). We also need to be more diligent about keeping our Announcement information fresh (and well populated – several people have commented that modules with few items get boring quickly).

With GroupCast, we'd eventually like to investigate other ways of using the profiles, such as using an intersection of the profiles (returning to the original design) or the set difference between profiles (since that would ensure novelty on at least one person's part). We also want to create multiple installations of GroupCast, and have at least one be in a space where there is something that helps attract people and keep them lingering for at least a few seconds (the badges fire every two seconds, and it sometimes takes a few seconds for new content to be displayed). Our current plan is to place a water cooler or coffee maker near one installation. We also want to design an evaluation that would help us assess whether – or how well – GroupCast is accomplishing its goal of increasing social capital in the workplace.

OutCast is truly an outcast with respect to the other two applications. At present, it shares no content or infrastructure with the other two. In addition to including UniCast and GroupCast content on OutCast displays – e.g., to provide content for the screensaver, or list of Favorites – we'd like to be able to incorporate some of the infrastructure from OutCast in the others. For example, with access to an enterprise-wide calendar system, we might identify commonalities with respect to locations people have traveled, or will be traveling, to, and use that to bring up travel-related pages when people pass by a GroupCast display ... for example, showing a map of Napa Valley vineyards when Joe and Teresa next pass each other.

8   Conclusion

We have created three applications that allow us to explore peripheral displays in three contexts: within a collection of individual offices, outside an individual office and in a group setting. Early feedback on one of the applications – UniCast – has been very positive (in fact, demand is outpacing our supply of additional monitors). We are eager to expand this application and its user base, as well as conduct further development and deployment of our other applications, GroupCast and OutCast. Although we are still far from a truly ubiquitous deployment of peripheral displays, we hope that others can learn from our experience and be more inclined to experiment with their own peripheral displays in these, and other, contexts.

Acknowledgements

The authors wish to thank Jeremy Goecks, who helped build an early version of GroupCast, Mitu Singh, who built some of the components used in OutCast, and all the members of our research group who have used these applications and provided valuable feedback on how they use – and would like to use – peripheral displays in a variety of contexts.

References

1. Deutsch, Claudia H. 1995. Commercial Property; Communication in the Workplace; Companies Using Coffee Bars to Get Ideas Brewing. *The New York Times*, 5 November 1995.
2. Franklin, Michael, and Stan Zdonik. 1998. Data in your Face: Push Technology in Perspective. In *Proceedings of the 1998 ACM Conference on Management of Data (SIGMOD '98)*, Seattle, pp. 516-519.
3. Greenberg, Saul, and Michael Rounding. 2001. The Notification Collage: Posting Information to Public and Personal Displays. In *Proceedings of the 2001 ACM Conference on Human Factors in Computer Systems (CHI 2001)*, Seattle, pp. 514-521.
4. Grudin, Jonathan. 2001. Partitioning Digital Worlds: Focal and Peripheral Awareness in Multiple Monitor Use. In *Proceedings of the 2001 ACM Conference on Human Factors in Computer Systems (CHI 2001)*, Seattle, pp. 458-465.
5. Harper, Richard H. R. 1992. Looking at Ourselves: An Examination of the Social Organisation of Two Research Laboratories. In *Proceedings of the ACM 1992 Conference on Computer Supported Cooperative Work (CSCW '92)*, pp. 330-337.
6. McCarthy, Joseph F., and Theodore D. Anagnost. 1998. MusicFX: An Arbiter of Group Preferences for Computer Supported Collaborative Workouts. In *Proceedings of the ACM 1998 Conference on Computer Supported Cooperative Work (CSCW '98)*, Seattle, pp. 363-372.

7. McCarthy, Joseph F., and Theodore D. Anagnost. 2000. MusicFX: An Arbiter of Group Preferences for Computer Supported Collaborative Workouts. In *Proceedings of the ACM 2000 Conference on Computer Supported Cooperative Work (CSCW 2000) Video Program*, Philadelphia, PA, p. 348.

8. McCarthy, Joseph F., and Theodore D. Anagnost. 2000. EventManager: Support for the Peripheral Awareness of Events. In Peter Thomas, Hans W. Gellersen (Eds.) *Handheld and Ubiquitous Computing*. Proceedings of the Second International Symposium (HUC 2000), Bristol, UK, September 2000. Lecture Notes in Computer Science, Vol. 1927, Springer – Verlag, Heidelberg, pp.227-235.

9. McCarthy, Joseph F., and Eric S. Meidel. 1999. ActiveMap: A Visualization Tool for Location Awareness to Support Informal Interactions. In Hans W. Gellersen (Ed.) *Handheld and Ubiquitous Computing*. Proceedings of the First International Symposium (HUC '99), Karlsruhe, Germany, September 1999. Lecture Notes in Computer Science, Vol. 1707, Springer – Verlag, Heidelberg, pp. 158-170.

10. Naylor, Thomas H., William H. Willimon and Rolf Österberg. 1996. The Search for Community in the Workplace. *Business and Society Review,* 97:42-47.

11. Putnam, Robert. 2000. Bowling Alone: The Collapse and Revival of American Community. Simon & Schuster.

12. Redström, Johan, Peter Ljungstrand and Patricija Jaksetic. 2000. The Chatter-Box: Using Text Manipulation in an Entertaining Information Display. In *Proceedings of Graphics Interface 2000*, Montréal, Canada.

13. Sawhney, Nitin, Sean Wheeler and Chris Schmandt. 2001. Aware Community Portals: Shared Information Appliances for Transitional Spaces. In *Journal of Personal and Ubiquitous Computing*, 5(1):66-70.

14. Streitz, Norbert A., Jörg Geißler, Torsten Holmer, Shin'ichi Konomi, Christian Müller-Tomfelde, Wolfgang Reischl, Petra Rexroth, Peter Seitz and Ralf Steinmetz. 1999. i-LAND: An Interactive Landscape for Creativitiy and Innovation . In *Proceedings of the 1999 ACM Conference on Human Factors in Computing Systems (CHI '99)*, Pittsburgh, PA, pp. 120-127.

15. Weiser, Mark, and John Seely Brown. 1997. The Coming Age of Calm Technology. In Peter J. Denning & Robert M. Metcalfe (Eds), *Beyond Calculation: The Next Fifty Years of Computing*. Springer – Verlag, pp. 75-85.

16. Wisneski, Craig, Hiroshi Ishii, Andrew Dahley, Matt Gorbet, Scott Brave, Brygg Ulmer and Paul Yarin. 1998. Ambient Displays: Turning Architectural Space into an Interface between People and Information. In Norbert A. Streitz, Shin'ichi Konomi and Heinz-Jurgen Burkhardt (Eds.) *Cooperative Buildings - Integrating Information, Organization and Architecture*. Proceedings of the First International Workshop on Cooperative Buildings (CoBuild '98), Darmstadt, Germany. Lecture Notes in Computer Science, Vol. 1370. Springer - Verlag, Heidelberg, pp. 22-32.

17. Zhao, Qiang Alex, and John T. Stasko. 2000. What's Happening? The Community Awareness Application. In *2000 ACM Conference on Human Factors in Computer Systems (CHI 2000) Extended Abstracts*, The Hague, pp. 253-254.

Multibrowsing:
Moving Web Content across Multiple Displays

Brad Johanson, Shankar Ponnekanti, Caesar Sengupta, and Armando Fox

Stanford University

Abstract. Although ubiquitous computing hardware technology is widely available today, we believe one key factor in making ubiquitous computing useful is a framework for exploiting multiple heterogeneous displays, whether fixed or on mobile computing devices, to view and browse information. To address this issue, we propose *multibrowsing*. Multibrowsing is a framework that extends the information browsing metaphor of the Web across multiple displays. It does so by providing the machinery for coordinating control among a collection of Web browsers running on separate displays in a ubiquitous computing environment. The displays may be "public" (e.g. wall-sized fixed screens) or "private" (e.g. the screens of individuals' laptops or handhelds). The resulting system extends browser functionality for existing content by allowing users to move existing pages or linked information among multiple displays, and also enables the creation of new content targeted specifically for multi-display environments. Since it uses Web standards, it accommodates any device or platform already supported by the Web and leverages the vast existing body of Web content and services. We describe the design and implementation of multibrowsing and a variety of scenarios in which we have found it useful in our test bed ubiquitous computing environment.

1 Introduction

Although the Internet has been active for over thirty years, it was the simple-yet-powerful information sharing mechanism provided by the Web, that significantly enhanced the usefulness of Internet-connected computers and led to the wide and rapid adoption and development of the Internet. In the last few years, we have seen the beginnings of a similar trend: ubiquitous computing hardware has become increasingly affordable and mainstream. However, we are still awaiting the catalyst applications that will help ubiquitous computing "take off", just as the Web did for Internet-based computing.

We believe one such application is flexible information movement. In this paper, we describe one such information movement system, *multibrowsing*, a framework for movement of web content across the displays in an ubiquitous computing environment. The presence of multiple display surfaces is a common feature of ubiquitous computing environments. For example, the iRoom is an experimental conference/workroom we have built as part of the Stanford Interactive Workspaces project [5]. As envisioned by Weiser [12], the iRoom includes

G. D. Abowd, B. Brumitt, S. A. N. Shafer (Eds.): Ubicomp 2001, LNCS 2201, pp. 346–353, 2001.
© Springer-Verlag Berlin Heidelberg 2001

three whiteboard-sized touch-sensitive screens, a bottom projected table-top display, and multiple laptops and handhelds. Multibrowsing allows web content to be freely moved across these displays. In particular:

1. A web page currently displayed in a browser on an enabled machine can be redirected to any other display in the environment without direct interaction with the target display.
2. A web page currently displayed on any display in the environment can be "pulled onto" a local browser without the need for copying the URL and typing it in the local browser.
3. Web pages can be purpose-designed for multi-display viewing by embedding links which open content on other displays in the environment.

We have found these capabilities to be useful in the iRoom, especially for meetings and presentations. Multibrowsing has also proven useful in offices with multiple PCs. Several other systems such as iLand's Passage [10], pick-and-drop [8], augmented surfaces [9], and Greenberg et al. [4] have also addressed the information movement problem. Multibrowsing is however unique in that it heavily leverages web technologies, thus resulting in simplicity and ease of deployment. In addition, the system strives for robustness and minimal configuration. Multibrowsing also provides a simple technique for easy authoring of content for multi-display viewing. This paper presents the multibrowsing system architecture and implementation, and gives some examples of its application in the iRoom, where it is in day-to-day use.

2   Architecture and Implementation

The following section describes the overall architecture of the system, and details of its use. This includes the butler service, which runs on machines that are multibrowse targets, the MB2Go browser plugin, and details of how embedded multibrowsing links function.

2.1   Framework

In the multibrowsing framework, displays can assume *one or more* of the three different roles described below:

1. Regular Client: A *regular client* can direct special links from web pages purpose-designed for multi-display viewing to other displays in the environment.
2. Enhanced Client: An *enhanced client* can direct any regular web page (or link on a web page) to any enabled display in the environment. Similarly, an enhanced client can "pull to itself" a web page from any enabled display in the environment.
3. Target: A *target* allows web pages to be directed to it from clients. Also, a target allows web pages displayed on itself to be "pulled off" by enhanced clients.

Typically, private devices such as laptops and handhelds function as clients and public devices such as wall-mounted and table-top displays function as targets. The system itself does not, however, prevent other configurations.

A regular client only needs an off-the-shelf web browser. Thus, handhelds, laptops, wall-mounted, and table-top displays can all function as regular clients with *no* custom multibrowse software installed. Enhanced clients are required to install a custom browser plug-in called *MB2Go*. Targets run a special service called the *butler service*. The overall architecture is shown in figure 1.

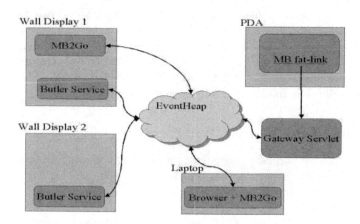

Fig. 1. Multibrowsing Architecture. Wall display 1 acts as both a target and an enhanced client. Wall display 2 acts only as a target. The laptop acts as an enhanced client while the PDA acts as a regular client. Regular clients use *multibrowse fat-links* to direct pages to other displays. The multibrowse fat-links are handled by the *gateway servlet*

2.2   Butler Service on Targets

The butler service is written using the ICrafter [7] service framework (which itself utilizes an underlying tuplespace [3] based event system called the Event Heap [5]). The service framework provides a soft-state discovery system which allows dynamic detection of available target displays. Each butler service has a unique name which remains unchanged across crashes and restarts. The butler service provides the following methods which can be invoked by sending appropriately constructed events:

- `browse(String URL)` : Causes the passed URL to be displayed on a locally running browser.
- `String getDisplayedResource()` : Returns the URL currently displayed in the top-level browser window.

Both these methods were implemented using the COM/OLE APIs exported by Internet Explorer.

2.3   MB2Go

MB2Go is a browser plug-in that consists of a Java application dynamically detects the available butler services and allows redirection of web pages. MB2Go modifies the Windows registry to add additional items to the IE context menu. When the user right-clicks on a hyperlink in IE, the context menu that appears contains an additional option called "multibrowse link". If the user selects this option, a pop-up window appears that allows the user to select the desired target from the list of discovered target displays. When the user selects a particular target, an appropriately formatted event is submitted that causes the butler service on the target to display the linked web page. The context menu that appears when a non-link area on the browser is clicked contains two additional items, "multibrowse to" and "multibrowse from", which respectively allow the user to cause the web page locally displayed to be loaded on a remote display or vice-versa. Figure 2 shows the workings of "multibrowse from". The other two cases ("multibrowse to" and "multibrowse link") are similar.

2.4   Multi-display Viewable Web Pages

Web pages can be purpose-designed for multi-display viewing using *multibrowse fat-links*. These are hyperlinks that encode a web-page display request. An example multibrowse fat-link (simplified for illustrative purposes) is shown below:

```
http://gateway/multibrowse?SvcName=Butler1&OpName=browse&param1=
www.stanford.edu
```

Clicking on this fat-link causes a form submission to the gateway servlet, which decodes the request and submits an appropriate event to the butler service instance `Butler1` to display the web page `http://www.stanford.edu`. A multibrowse fat-link can also encode multiple events thus causing several pages to be loaded on various displays with a single click. We also have a helper program that allows end-users to easily construct these fat-links.

Unlike the butler service and the plug-in, the fat-link mechanism is currently not fully portable since the fat-links hardcode the path to the local gateway servlet and the names for the target service instances. To overcome this limitation, we are currently exploring a proxy mechanism to dynamically rewrite hyperlinks for the local environment.

3   Usage Scenarios

In this section, we present typical usage scenarios of multibrowsing in iRoom. The iRoom has an 802.11b wireless network (WaveLAN) which allows appropriately-equipped laptops or handheld devices to participate in multibrowsing in addition to the large wall-mounted and table-top displays.

(a) **Modified context menu. Note the two new items "Multibrowse From" and "Multibrowse To" in the context menu**

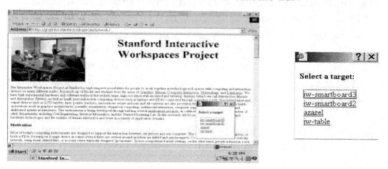

(b) **Target selection popup window. When the user selects "Multibrowse From", a window pops up that allows the user to select a target**

Fig. 2. . MB2Go Illustrated. When the user wishes to load a page displayed on a remote display on her local browser, she simply right clicks on the browser, selects "multibrowse from" (part (a)) and then chooses the desired display from the pop-up window (part (b))

3.1   Meetings

Ad-hoc meetings: We will step through the sequence of interactions in a typical iRoom research meeting to illustrate the use of multibrowsing: Susan mentions that she has heard of the new ABC wireless modem that could be useful for the handheld devices in the iRoom. Using the multibrowse plug-in from a browser on her laptop, she opens the web page of ABC modem on SmartBoard1. Meanwhile, Brad uses a search engine on his laptop and locates a site that summarizes the features of various commercially available wireless modems. Again using MB2Go, he multibrowses these webpages to the other two SmartBoards so that the group can compare the features of the modems. The ability to freely pull up information and move it to different displays is a key useful feature for such meetings.

Meeting Agenda: In iRoom meetings, meeting coordinators can prepare a "meeting-agenda" web page containing links to information relevant to the meeting. During the meeting, the coordinator opens this web page on a laptop or SmartBoard and uses MB2Go to multibrowse the linked pages to the other displays in the room. The coordinator can also pre-design the agenda web page with suitable multibrowse fat-links such that clicking on the agenda items causes them to appear on the other displays.

3.2 Presentations

One use of purpose-designed content is to enhance presentations in multi-display environments. To illustrate this, we describe a typical iRoom presentation. The "lead slide" of the presentation gives a broad overview of the project and contains several multibrowse fat-links to the other presentation slides. In a typical presentation session shown in figure 3, the lead slide is displayed on Smart-Board1. Clicking on any link on the lead slide causes detailed information about that category to be brought up on the other displays. For example, when the presenter clicks on the multibrowse fat-link "overface" on the lead slide, a web page showing the detailed block diagram of the overface system is displayed on SmartBoard2 and the primary goals of the overface system are displayed on SmartBoard3 (see figure 3). A similar chain of events occurs when "Graphical Presentation Tools" is clicked.

It is worth noting that this mechanism only needs a regular (i.e., non-enhanced) client for displaying the "controlling" slide. The presenter can also control the presentation with any other device with an off-the-shelf web browser.

4   Related Work

Multibrowsing was first discussed as an example application in [2], but details were not presented and MB2Go and dynamic discovery of targets was not operational at that time. Controlling other web browsers has been previously explored for collaborative browsing [1] [6]. The iLand project at GMD-IPSI in Darmstadt [10] has developed sophisticated groupware environments that coordinate information display using object synchronization. Pick-and-Drop [8] and augmented surfaces [9] present new metaphors for moving objects across computers. Greenberg et al. [4] present a system for moving information between PDAs and public displays. Multibrowsing is primarily distinguished by a larger reliance on off-the-shelf web technologies which results in simplicity and easier deployment. Unlike some of these projects, robustness and minimal configuration are first-class goals for multibrowsing. For example, dynamic discovery of displays in the vicinity enables the system to work transparently without any per-workspace configuration even when target displays (such as laptops) freely enter and leave the workspace. Similarly, due to soft-state service advertisement, if a butler service on a target display crashes, it is automatically removed from the list of targets. Finally, while multibrowsing is limited to web content, this

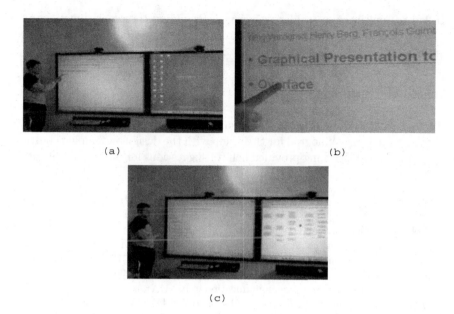

(a)   (b)

(c)

Fig. 3. Multibrowse presentation screenshots. The "lead slide" displayed on SmartBoard1 contains two multibrowse fat-links. When the user clicks on one of them ("overface"), a page describing overface automatically pops up on Smart-Board2. Note that for clarity, the figures do not show SmartBoard3

restriction is ameliorated since emerging technologies like Web Folders and Web-DAV [11] allow many types of content to be made available on the web.

5   Conclusions and Future Work

We have designed and implemented multibrowsing, a system for movement of web information across displays which leverages web technologies for simplicity. Along with robustness, and minimal configuration requirements, this simplicity makes multibrowsing easy to deploy. We are now beginning to address the following challenges:

Security: We are exploring security and access control models appropriate for both public and private targets and clients.

Increased Portability: Apart from the proxy mentioned in section 2.4 which allows construction of more portable multi-display viewable web pages, we are also exploring building a proxy that automatically replaces links on standard web pages with new versions that allow for redirection of the linked pages to displays in the current environment. Such a proxy would allow even clients without

MB2go to multibrowse regular web pages. Providing these new functions in a fully portable manner with *no* per-environment configuration is, however, challenging.

Acknowledgments

We thank Pat Hanrahan, Emre Kiciman, Brian Lee, Kathleen Liston, Susan Shepard, and Terry Winograd for their help with the design and implementation. Andy Huang and Ben Ling provided helpful suggestions for improving this draft.

References

1. CobWeb Collaborative Web Browsing
   System. http://www.cs.unc.edu/~stotts/cobweb/doc/index.html. 351
2. Fox, A., Johanson, B., Hanrahan, P., Winograd, T., "PDA's in Interactive Workspaces," *Computer Graphics and Animation*, May, 2000. 351
3. David Gelernter. Generative communication in LINDA. *ACM Transactions on Programming Languages and Systems*, 7(1), pages 80–112, January 1985. 348
4. S. Greenberg, M. Boyle and J. LaBerge. PDAs and Shared Public Displays: Making Personal Information Public, and Public Information Personal. *Personal Technologies*, Vol.3, No.1, 54-64, March. Elsevier. 347, 351
5. Interactive Workspaces Group at Stanford University.
   http://graphics.stanford.edu/projects/iwork. 346, 348
6. Netscape Conference.
   http://home.netscape.com/communicator/conference/v4.0. 351
7. Shankar Ponnekanti, Brian Lee, Armando Fox, Pat Hanrahan, and Terry Winograd. ICrafter: A service framework for ubiquitous computing environments. *Proceedings of Ubicomp '01*, October 2001. 348
8. Jun Rekimoto. Pick-and-Drop: A Direct Manipulation Interface for Multiple Computer Environments. *UIST '97*, pages 31-39, 1997. 347, 351
9. J. Rekimoto and M. Saitoh. Augmented Surfaces: A Spatially Continuous Workspace for Hybrid Computing Environments. *CHI '99*, 1999. 347, 351
10. N. A. Streitz et al. i-LAND: An interactive Landscape for Creativity and Innovation. *CHI '99*, pages 120-127, May 1999. 347, 351
11. WebDAV. http://www.webdav.org. 352
12. M Weiser. The Computer for the 21st Century. *Scientific American*, 265(30), pages 94-104, 1991. 346

On the Design of Personal & Communal Large Information Scale Appliances

Daniel M. Russell and Rich Gossweiler

IBM Almaden Research Center
650 Harry Rd, San José, CA, USA, 95120
Daniel2@us.IBM.com
Rich@RichGossweiler.com

Abstract. As large displays become less expensive and more common throughout our working environments, we believe they will become pervasive, much as telephones were the ubiquitous communication devices of the previous generation. When large displays are coupled to an authentication device (e.g., a badge reader) and put on a network, they permit very rapid personal content access. The BlueBoard project explores the design of large displays that can be used as temporary personal access points to personalized content, yet also be used as display surfaces for small groups of people who want to easily share content between themselves. We've developed several design points that make BlueBoards simple for individual and small group use – (1) p-cons to refer to a person for information access and exchange, (2) assuring users that information displayed on a BlueBoard is truly transient, (3) providing a basic set of tools for immediate walk-up use, and (4) giving the BlueBoard a sense of where it's located for contextually appropriate information display.

1 · Introduction

Displays are rapidly growing less expensive. While large displays (greater than 1m on the diagonal) are more slowly descending the price curves, it's now apparent that they too are becoming ubiquitous in many environments. [1,3,6,7,8,9,10] A recent trip (January, 2001) through the Frankfurt, Germany airport showed more than 100 large displays scattered throughout the concourses as information displays.

While kiosks have been popular items as information displays for some time, they have often suffered from an inability to act as general purpose access devices. Generally speaking, kiosks are placed in a space to sell a product or to push a particular set of information.

But when a kiosk has a simple personal authentication devices (e.g., biometric or badge readers), and is placed on a relatively high-speed network, the nature of the device changes in a fundamental way. No longer is it just a dispenser of canned in-

G. D. Abowd, B. Brumitt, S. A. N. Shafer (Eds.): Ubicomp 2001, LNCS 2201, pp. 354-361, 2001.
© Springer-Verlag Berlin Heidelberg 2001

formation, but the kiosk + personal identification device becomes a new thing – a *large information scale appliance (LISA)*.

While an information appliance is typically a small, personal device, there's no reason to not consider large devices scattered ubiquitously throughout an environment as information appliances as well. While the relatively high cost of large displays has worked against this kind of deployment, it is becoming clear that the cost is dropping quickly (and will continue), making a new kind of use possible in the near term future.

But large, shared, communal information appliances in the workplace operate under a substantially different set of assumptions than small, personal appliances. One of the chief advantages of Personal Digital Assistants (PDAs) is that they're easy and fast to use. On the other hand, they have several disadvantages: they are small and (to date) usually not on a network. As a consequence, some kinds of common work practices (e.g., looking at large, complex images, making drawings, sharing working documents) aren't practical with PDAs.

Fig. 1. The BlueBoard is a Large Scale Information Appliance offering fast access to personal information with tools for collaboration and small groups of people working side-by-side. The display has a touch screen overlay and a badge reader on the right corner for person identification. Network access is assumed

1.1   An Example: BlueBoard

We've recently built a LISA that combines a large 1.3 meter plasma display (XGA) with a touch screen and a badge reader for personal identification. In ordinary use, the BlueBoard is intended for both very fast personal use (walk up, check your calendar, walk away – all within 5 seconds), and for small group collaborative use (a small number of people stand around the BlueBoard to sketch ideas, pull up information from their personal space, compare notes, share content).

In our design, a BlueBoard has no keyboard or mouse. While this seems restrictive, our goal is not to have BlueBoards become just another personal computer – it is consciously designed to support lightweight, fast encounters and simple spontaneous collaborative meetings. We do not believe that providing full keyboard capability (and corresponding security control problems) works to the BlueBoard's advantage.

A BlueBoard is a simple device: it is a specialized display + badge reader connected to a computer running a client-side application to provide simple access to information. Again: It's not *supposed* to be a general purpose computer that runs any and all applications, but instead, a conduit to personal information that's available via HTTP connections.

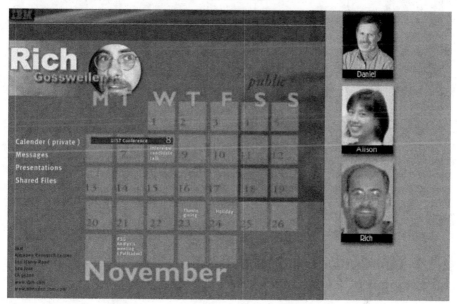

Fig. 2. A typical BlueBoard personal display. This kind of content is set up by each user as their "home content." Content displayed on the BlueBoard can be shared with another person by dragging the content (window, image, URL) to their p-con. Here, Rich is showing his home page calendar to Daniel and Alison

Swiping your badge brings up personal -- in our setup, it's an HID brand reader connected to the serial port [5]. Badge information is sent to a Badge Server database that authenticates the user, handing back a URL to that person's personal content. A "personal icon," or *p-con,* is created on the BlueBoard display off on the side in the tools area. Note that the "home page" is not immediately displayed, but becomes available only by explicilty touching one's p-con.

Clearly, such content needs to be created by the user. It's important to note that the BlueBoard system is not yet-another attempt to solve the web-site authoring problem, but rather simply presents information that is created in a separate step, linking high-value information to web content.

We are currently working towards a simplified BlueBoard content authoring tool, one that provides very simple templates to link personal content to the BlueBoard server.

Content linking is a much simpler solution than original content creation. Especially since so much content already exists, our solution of simply coalescing content into a single point of access actually simplifies many problems of data scattered everywhere over the network.

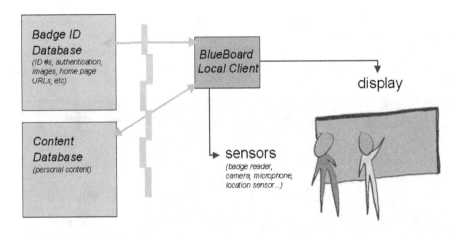

Fig. 3. A BlueBoard links backend content (on a webserver) with presentation on the large plasma display with touchscreen and badge reader. The badge ID is sent off for authentication, returning either an "unknown user" error, or an authenticated set of URLs in the Content Database. The effect is that a user "logs in" by simply swiping their badge at the display, getting rapid access to their content

2   Information Appliance Design for Personal vs. Communal Uses

There's an inherent design tension in LISAs: they are good for group work with peers standing shoulder-to-shoulder, working together. But they are also very handy for rapid personal, one-person information access. Unlike other information appliances, a LISA must support both single users and multiple users. It needs to work for a single person walking up to the BlueBoard to check their calendar, and it needs to work for small groups of people working together. Consequently, there are two very different sets of overall goals: design the LISA for individual information access, and design the LISA for multiple people using the display at the same time.

We have come to recognize that several design points need to be satisfied to balance these competing design goals.

2.1   Representing an Individual: P-cons for Fast Access & Sharing

When more than one person is using the device, the device needs to know whose content is being viewed. There also needs to be a way to easily share content among the users who are all using the board at the same time.

The *p-con* is just an image of the person representing that person's content. When a badge is swiped, a person's p-con appears in the p-con dock on the right side of the display (see Figure 2). When more than person is at the board, all of their p-cons show up on the display (currently up to six).

The p-con becomes the rapid access point for personal content. A user sets up their content ahead of time, linking items such as calendars, presentations, continually updated information (stock quotes, project status, etc.) to the home page. Then, once badged in to the BlueBoard, a finger touch on the p-con brings up the first page of their content.

The p-con is also the way to share information between simultaneous users. If one user is showing a slide from their content or an especially interesting web page, a drag-and-drop movement from the page to a p-con will deposit a copy of that content in the p-con. When the p-con's person badges out (leaves the BlueBoard session), the contents of the p-con is e-mailed to them. In this way, sharing information is extremely simple – when you see something you like, just drag it to the p-con and the content is shared.

Since all content shown on the BlueBoard is some variant of a web page, dragging an individual item (e.g., a block of text or a picture) just copies that item into the person's temporary p-con buffer. To make a copy of the entire page, the user will drag from a "whole page" handle (the title bar) to the p-con.

In essence, the p-con stores content until the user badges out. At badge out time, the contents of the p-con buffer are packed up into an email message and sent off to the p-con owner's email space.

We have consciously avoided overly complex mechanisms such as group management or automatically trying to move the p-con buffer contents into their personal content web. An important goal is that the BlueBoard be usable with a tiny amount of training. Currently, to simplify things, only people present can share content, and sharing is done by logically moving shared material into their email. In a similar vein, we've attempted complex window management schemes for doing split screens, but have not yet been able to devise a way that allows the split screen to be simple to explain and use. It's too easy to become confused between foreground and background. Since an overriding goal is simplicity, we continually return to those roots in making design choices.

2.2   Transient Information Must Be Truly Transient

When a user badges in to the BlueBoard, their content flows to that location. When they badge out, the content stored in the p-con buffer (if any) is emailed to the email address of their choice (pre-specified at BlueBoard user registration time). But equally importantly, any content that was pulled to the BlueBoard from the remote content server must be purged from the local system to avoid the possibility of compromise by later walk-up users.

To make this assurance, the BlueBoard tracks each content item as it comes into the system, tagging it with its owner's p-con ID. At badge-out time, all such content is explicitly removed (including items in the history list and any cookies that might have been created in the process).

2.3   BlueBoard Knows Its Place

A BlueBoard is a relatively static device. Weighing in at somewhat more than 68 kilograms (150 pounds), it is not an easily portable pocket-type device.

When the BlueBoard is not in use, we have found it useful to have it show a loop of content pages that are relevant to the location. In our meeting room setting, the Blue-Board puts up project web pages and other web sites of local interest (such as the IBM home page, the IBM research home page, news sites, etc.). The "attract loop" for page display is driven by a local list of pages that is tailored to the site and time. Pages are shown for a few seconds, then dissolve via an alpha-blend to the next page. When these pages are shown, the touch screen is still active. If a passerby finds the page of particular interest, just touch the screen, and the looping stops, giving full web browser capability. (We discovered that people often couldn't get to the board in time to stop the display. So we added a "back" button in the lower right corner, which works in the way you'd expect.)

We are working towards giving the BlueBoard a better sense of where it's located. Ideally, location information would be determined by a locator beacon (e.g., a in-room BlueTooth device) and then used to determine what pages would be of local interest. (Say, lab project pages would be shown on the lab BlueBoard, while corporate wide interest pages would be shown on the foyer's BlueBoard.)

Similarly, we have done initial tests allowing people in a workgroup to email mes-sages to the BlueBoard attract loop, much as was done in the Lens shared public dis-play at Apple's research lab [6] .

2.4   Tools for Short-Term, Rapid Use

Public, shared, communal devices all need to be extremely simple to use and must be intrinsically useful even without special registration. We want people to be able to simply walk up to a BlueBoard and do useful work.

To date we have built a simple toolbar that allows a passerby to gain immediate ac-cess to several functions: a whiteboard sketching tool, a calendar and a local map (showing the location of the BlueBoard in context).

These functions continue to be accessible after badging in as well. As with all other content shown on the BlueBoard, this content can be dragged to a p-con for sharing via an email connection.

3   Other Work in This Area

There are many large display projects in the research world. The DynaWall from GMD is a very large wall display with a touch surface [10] that supports people working together on a merged set of SoftBoard displays [9]. The DynaWall explores interesting issues in group work and very large scale interactions, but does not yet afford lightweight walk-up interactions or easy sharing of content.

Similarly, the Interactive Workspaces Project at Stanford [3,9] also emphasizes large, sophisticated display areas for information rich display manipulations. While they've been developing new interaction techniques for large displays, they too do not support simple walk-up, rapid use.

For lightweight information access, there are many professional providers of kiosk systems, relatively few of which offer network service access for general information (as opposed to specialized networks, such as banking networks for ATMs). Other kiosk systems [2,4] provide web services or vision-based person-tracking schemes, but none seem to actually know what users are present, or what their personal information content might be.

4   Summary

Large displays, kiosks, and information appliances are all common. Yet few have tried to be all three at once. The trend towards increasing use of large displays in public spaces creates the opportunity for a new kind of ubiquitous / pervasive device: the *large information scale appliance*; a device that delivers personal information to authenticated, identified users in a kiosk environment.

Designing large information appliances that address the needs of both the individual and the small group is a challenge: one that requires balancing the need to work across a wide variety of user populations, work for a number of simultaneous users, while operating in a variety of locations and uses.

Our goal in the BlueBoard project has been to provide very rapid access to personal content while providing the easy-to-use functions of an information appliance supporting both communal and personal use. The important difference between BlueBoard and other kiosk systems is the design of the use experience for a kiosk that knows who is using it while supporting fast access and simple sharing of content.

References

1.   Buxton, W., Fitzmaurice, G. Balakrishnan, R. & Kurtenbach, G. Large Displays in Automotive Design. IEEE Computer Graphics and applications, 20(4), (2000), 68-75
2.   Christian, A. D., Avery, B. Digital Smart Kiosk Project: About Faces. *ACM Proceedings of CHI '98.* v. 1 (1998) 155-162
3.   Fox A., Johanson B., Hanrahan P., and Winograd T., Integrating Information Appliances into an Interactive Workspace, *IEEE Computer Graphics and Applications*, 20, 3 (June, 2000), 54-65
4.   Grize, F., Aminian, M. Cybcerone: A Kiosk System Based on the WWW and Java. *interactions*, 4(6), (1997) 62-69
5.   HID Corporation, http://www.HIDCorp.com
6.   Houde, S., Bellamy, R., Leahy, L. In Search of Design Principles for Tools and Practices to Support Communication within a Learning Community. ACM SIG-CHI Bulletin, 30(2) (1998) 113-118
7.   Pedersen, E. McCall, K., Moran, T., Halasz, F., Tivoli: An Electronic Whiteboard for Informal Workgroup Meetings, *ACM Proceedings of InterCHI '93* (1993), 391-398
8.   SmartBoard. http://www.SMARTTech.com

9. Stanford Interactive Workspaces Project
    http://graphics.stanford.edu/projects/iwork/
10. Streitz, N., J. Geißler, T. Holmer, S. Konomi, C. Müller-Tomfelde, W. Reischl, P. Rexroth, P. Seitz, R. Steinmetz i-LAND: An interactive Landscape for Creativity and Innovation. In: ACM Conference on Human Factors in Computing Systems (CHI'99), Pittsburgh, Pennsylvania, USA, (1999), 120-127

Serendipity within a Ubiquitous Computing Environment: A Case for Opportunistic Browsing

Oscar de Bruijn and Robert Spence

Imperial College, Dept. of Electrical and Electronic Engineering,
Exhibition Road, London, SW7 2BT, United Kingdom
{o.debruijn,r.spence}@ic.ac.uk

Abstract. We investigate an important interaction that can take place in a ubiquitous computing environment, that of opportunistic browsing, a form of information gathering on the fly. Opportunistic browsing is characterised by being ubiquitous, unintentional and effortless. In this paper, we clarify the concept of opportunistic browsing and place it within a cognitive framework. We further discuss the nature of the interactions that can be triggered by the serendipitous discovery of information through opportunistic browsing and the importance of context-awareness, and we identify important research issues.

1   Introduction

You are having a coffee and a chat with some friends, when, suddenly, your eye catches some of the information that comes flowing by on the screen that is forms part of the table at which you are sitting (see Figure 1). It is an article about the Science Fair and you wonder if this may lead you to find information about the local astronomers club. With your finger you drag the item into the middle of the table where more detail becomes visible. After reading the text you see that the article does mention the astronomers' club, but it does not include a contact address or a hyperlink. You proceed to drag the article onto the icon representing the coffee table Agent, hoping that the information subsequently retrieved by the Agent will include the home page of the astronomers club. After some time has elapsed, during which you talked about the film you saw last night, you notice that the logo of the astronomers club comes flowing by and when you view their Web page in the middle of the table you see that it contains all the information you need to contact them. You do not want to interrupt the conversation with your friends any longer, so you simply store a link to the page on the token on your key ring so you can have a closer look at home.

This example illustrates peoples' constant need for information, even when this information is not actively pursued. The reason for not actively pursuing relevant information immediately may be that it is not clear how this information can be obtained or that the effort involved in its pursuit is perceived as being too great. Sometimes one might not even realize that the information is relevant until it is

G. D. Abowd, B. Brumitt, S. A. N. Shafer (Eds.): Ubicomp 2001, LNCS 2201, pp. 362–369, 2001.

encountered. One of the aims of this paper is to describe such serendipitous behaviour more formally and establish a framework for the development of interactive applications that support it within a ubiquitous computing environment. We argue that the realisation of ubiquitous computing environments offers unique opportunities for injecting serendipity into human-computer interactions. Especially since human beings have many interests that can be satisfied by exposure to appropriate items of information, but cannot continuously, simultaneously and consciously articulate all those interests, we should enable people to discover relevant information without requiring them to actively search for it. We now examine this kind of behaviour in more detail, place it within an appropriate cognitive model and suggest suitable interaction mechanisms.

a   b

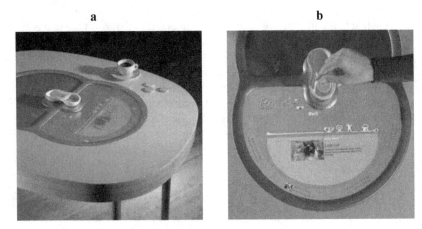

Fig. 1. (a) The coffee table supporting opportunistic browsing. (b) A close-up view of the display, showing information items that move slowly around the perimeter

2   Opportunistic Browsing

In this paper we are concerned with one particular form of browsing, one that makes opportunistic use of information we encounter as part of our everyday activities even when no conscious information seeking is intended. It is for this reason that we speak of "opportunistic browsing".

We can define opportunistic browsing (henceforth referred to as OB) as the continuous but largely unconscious monitoring and filtering of information with the potential to trigger more purposeful behaviour. The defining characteristics of OB, setting it apart from other forms of browsing, are ubiquity, being unintentional, and requiring no cognitive effort. Opportunistic browsing is ubiquitous because it is a process of information filtering that occurs all the time and everywhere, while talking to friends or driving to work. It is unintentional because people are not consciously looking for information, and it requires no cognitive effort because OB is an automatic process that is part of peoples' normal pattern of information processing.

It has often been stated that the growing amounts of information we are exposed to at every moment could increasingly lead to "information overload". However, we argue that it is not the amount of information *per se* that creates a problem. In fact, the human information processing system is uniquely equipped to cope with large amounts of information by selectively attending to potentially relevant information and ignoring irrelevant information.[1] This ability has been demonstrated repeatedly, although arguably its most well known manifestation is the "cocktail party effect" [5]. The cocktail party effect describes how a listener is able to selectively attend to the single voice that says something of interest to the listener (e.g., their name) while many different voices are audible in a room. In the next section we present a model of the kinds of cognitive activity involved in opportunistic browsing built around a theoretical construct developed by Potter [12, 13] called Conceptual Short Term Memory (CSTM).

2.1   A Cognitive Model of OB

The process of opportunistic browsing is summarised in Figure 2. It starts with the perceptual registration of content, which may be seen or heard. Each item of meaningful content (e.g., objects, phrases and scenes) results in the rapid activation of corresponding conceptual representations in CSTM.[2] These representations are, however, equally rapidly forgotten if they are not selected for retention in a more permanent form of memory (i.e., working memory). Potter [13] remarks that

"The idea is that most cognitive processing occurs on the fly, without review of material in standard short-term memory and with little or no conscious reasoning. Yet, these rapid processes are flexible, not fixed: new sentences are processed, new scenes are comprehended, important items are selected for attention even though they cannot be explicitly anticipated ..." (p. 14).

This model attributes four important characteristics to OB that result from the role of CSTM in the processing of information that we encounter in our everyday environment: (1) encountered information rapidly (within about 100ms) activates meaningful representations, (2) activation of these representations leads to the retrieval of additional relevant information from long-term memory (LTM), (3) the information retrieved from LTM may be associated with a previously unsuccessful or prematurely aborted attempt to find similar information, which may cause our attention to be drawn and an appropriate action to be initiated, and (4) the whole process up to the point where our attention is drawn to relevant information occurs with little or no conscious effort since any information that does not draw our attention is quickly forgotten.

---

[1] Information overload becomes a problem only when there is too much *relevant* information. For example, when someone has to attend to two or more sources of information and combine these in order to accomplish a task.

[2] A number of models of visual information processing assume stages in that process that serve a similar purpose to CSTM (e.g., [1], [7]).

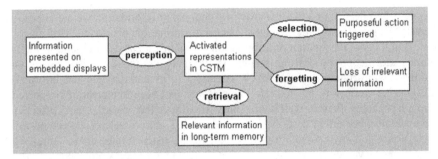

Fig. 2. A model of opportunistic browsing. Perceived information activates representations in CSTM. Association with information from long-term memory triggers a purposeful action (see text for explanation)

2.2   Browsing Typologies

Several other forms of browsing have been proposed, including forms that are similar to opportunistic browsing. Wilson [17] identifies four kinds of browsing: passive attention, passive search, active search, and ongoing search. The difference between the first two and the latter two types of browsing is the intention behind the activity. Passive attention, for example, operates while watching television or listening to the radio, where information acquisition may take place without intentional seeking. Passive search operates when search for one kind of information (or other behaviour) results in the acquisition of another kind of information that happens to be relevant. We consider both passive attention and passive search to be forms of OB in that no information seeking is intended but useful information is nevertheless acquired. In fact, we see no fundamental difference between passive attention and passive search; watching television and searching for information (other than the information acquired by OB) are just the kinds of behaviour during which OB takes place. In contrast, active search and ongoing search both involve active acquisition of information relevant to the goal of the search. Other classifications of browsing behaviour were proposed by [10] and [4], but neither of these include forms of browsing that could be considered opportunistic.

In the next section we argue that a ubiquitous computing environment can be suitably configured such that it provides an optimal environment for making serendipitous discoveries through opportunistic browsing and supports the interactions triggered by these discoveries.

3   Ubiquitous Computing

According to [15], a ubiquitous computing environment is characterised by the disappearance of the computers within it, in the sense that they have vanished into the background. Additionally, it is usefully characterised by the dictionary definition of ubiquitous ("being or seeming to be everywhere at the same time"), in the sense that the layperson need not consciously go to the computer. The computer lies behind familiar artefacts such as the coffee table, the bus stop and the information display in the shopping mall, as well as the home information terminal.

3.1   Enhancement of Serendipitous Information Retrieval

One of the most exciting opportunities created by ubiquitous computing is the possibility of enhancing serendipitous information retrieval by increasing the amount of information that is presented to a user. Relevant techniques are already appearing: the familiar scrolling news-bars (a la Times Square), the sequenced advertisement, and continuously scrolling text information such as news headlines or stock prices on the desktop display (e.g., [20], [19], [6], [8]) or television (e.g., CNN). Realisation of a ubiquitous computing environment also opens the possibility for ambient presentation of information in the periphery of people's attention [16][18]. In the context of the Living Memory project we have explored the enhancement of serendipitous information retrieval by embedding information displays in familiar artefacts such as coffee tables (Figure 1), bus stops, floors, park benches, and shopping trolleys (e.g., [9]).

Although the concept of an information fire-hose may possess worrying connotations, and must be managed with maturity, its implication of a plentiful supply of information widely available is to be preferred over some existing and developing paradigms that are either intrusive or rely on personalisation. Personalisation, for example, can severely limit the number of opportunities for serendipitous discovery. In the example of a personalised newspaper (the "Daily Me"), users would have no opportunity to read news items they might find interesting but which do not fit into the range of topics present in their personal profile.

3.2   Situated Interactions

It is reasonable to assume that the behaviour triggered by OB depends on the extent to which people can interact with the medium in which the information is presented, and hence we refer to any such behaviour as *situated interaction*. Suchman [14] introduced the term "situated action" to underscore "the view that every course of action depends in essential ways upon its material and social circumstances" (p. 50). Similarly, situated interaction depends on its material, in terms of both the information and the affordances offered by the medium in which this information is presented, and the social circumstances in terms of the location of the display and the activity the observer is engaged in. Thus, information presented on a display embedded in a coffee table triggers a different kind of interaction than information presented on a large screen display in the mall, since these represent different media and occur in different contexts. It is important that the interactions that are being triggered by the serendipitous discovery of useful information through OB do not cause too much disruption of ongoing activities. Such disruption may first of all be socially undesirable in certain situations, and it could also lead to an unacceptable increase in users' short-term memory load if they have to keep track of several ongoing activities in parallel.

3.3   Content Selection

It may appear contradictory that in order to increase the opportunities for serendipitous discovery through opportunistic browsing, some sort of selection of information is probably required. As we pointed out in section 3.1, content selection based on personal interest profiles could seriously diminish the potential for serendipitous discovery. However, we suggest that content is selected according to the context in which an information artefact is situated instead. The need for context-awareness has often been argued in relation to mobile handheld and wearable computing devices (e.g., [11]), but context-awareness may be an equally important characteristic of stationary devices that are part of a ubiquitous computing environment. For example, content could be selected according to its relevance to the location of the display. For the same reasons that apply to mobile applications, certain information may become more or less important depending upon where the user is located [5]. Selection by location could lead to the same restricted information exposure as personalisation but for the fact that users' movement through the environment is likely to take them through many different locations, ensuring their exposure to a wide variety of information. Ultimately, artefacts might be made aware of what is going on in the local community, allowing them to respond to local events and occasions [2].

4   Conclusions

One thing technology has failed to give us more of is time, and it would therefore be advantageous if we could use our time more efficiently by combining everyday activities with the search for information? This can be achieved when the environment is infused with information that can be retrieved through opportunistic browsing. In this paper we have defined a model for opportunistic browsing and argued that the human information processing system is uniquely equipped to make opportunistic use of information. We have also described some of the characteristics of the interactions that can be triggered by the serendipitous discovery of information through opportunistic browsing and discussed some important issues that need to be considered when developing new artefacts to support OB in a ubiquitous computing environment.

Many issues remain, however, opening many avenues for further research. Considerable effort will be devoted to innovation leading to new artefacts supporting opportunistic browsing, new information presentation techniques, new interaction modes and new information scenarios. To assess and guide advances in opportunistic browsing, an extensive programme of research is required that combines laboratory studies and the evaluation of both prototypes and *in-situ* applications. Finally, much will be gained through ethnographic studies of new artefacts and systems as they are developed, additionally feeding back into the innovation and development process.

Acknowledgements

The research reported in this paper was funded by the European Community (Living Memory / ESPRIT / I3 / 25621). We would like to thank the members of the Living Memory team for useful discussions and Philips Design for supplying the pictures of the coffee table.

References

1. Anderson, J.R.: Rules of the Mind. LEA, Hillsdale (1993)
2. de Bruijn, O., Purcell, P.A., Spence, R., Stathis, K.: Agent-Based Interaction Design for Connected Communities. Manuscript in preparation (2001)
3. Cherry, E.C.: Some Experiments on the Recognition of Speech, with One and Two Ears. J. of the Ac. Soc. of Am. 25 (1953) 975-979
4. Choo, C.W., Detlor, B., Turnbull, D.: Information Seeking in the Web: An Integrated Model of Browsing and Searching. FirstMonday 5 (2000) http://firstmonday.org/issues/issue5_2/choo/index.html
5. Davenport, E., Whyte, A., Barr, K., Buckner, K.: LiMe Deliverable 2.3 Taxonomies of Tools, Community Content and Narratives (1998)
6. Desktop News: http://www.desktopnews.com/
7. Ericsson, K.A., Kintsch, W.: Long-term Working Memory. Psych. Rev. 102 (1995) 211-245
8. Jotter 2000: http://www.jotter.com/
9. Living Memory: http://www.living-memory.org/
10. Marchionini, G.M.: Information Seeking in Electronic Environments. Cambridge University Press, Cambridge, UK (1995)
11. Pascoe, J., Ryan, N., Morse, D.: Issues in Developing Context-Aware Computing. In: Gellersen, H-W. (ed.): Proc. of the First Int. Symp. HUC'99. Lecture Notes in Computer Science, Vol. 1707. Springer-Verlag, Berlin Heidelberg New York (1999) 208-221
12. Potter, M.C.: Very Short-term Conceptual Memory. Mem. & Cog. 21 (1993) 156-161
13. Potter, M.C.: Understanding Sentences and Scenes: The Role of Conceptual Short-Term Memory. In: Coltheart, V. (ed.): Fleeting Memories: Cognition of Brief Visual Stimuli. The MIT Press, Cambridge, MA. (1999)
14. Suchman, L.A.: Plans and Situated Actions. The Problem of Human Machine Interaction. Cambridge University Press, Cambridge (1987)
15. Weiser, M.: The Computer for the Twenty-First Century. Scientific American, September (1991)
16. Weiser, M., Brown, J.S.: The Coming of Age of Calm Technology. http://nano.xerox.com/hypertext/weiser/acmfuture2endnote.htm
17. Wilson, T. D.: Information behaviour: An interdisciplinary perspective. Info. Process. & Manage. 33 (1997) 551-572
18. Wisneski, C., Ishii, H., Dahley, A., Gorbet, M., Brave, S., Ullmer, B., Yarin, P.: Ambient Displays: Turning Architectural Space into an Interface between People

and Digital Information. In: Norbert A. Strietz, Shin'ichi Konomi, Heinz-Jürgen Burkhardt (eds.): Cooperative Buildings, Proc. of the First Int. Workshop, CoBuild'98. Lecture Notes in Computer Science, Vol. 1370. Springer-Verlag, Berlin Heidelberg New York (1998) 22-32

19. WorldFlash, http://www.worldflash.com/
20. Yahoo, http://sg.news.yahoo.com/

Author Index